FORTY STUDIES THAT CHANGED PSYCHOLOGY

Explorations into the History of Psychological Research

Fifth Edition

Roger R. Hock, Ph.D.

Mendocino College

PEARSON

Prentice
Hall

Upper Saddle River, New Jersey 07458

Library of Congress Cataloging-in-Publication Data

Hock, Roger R.
 Forty studies that changed psychology : explorations into the history of psychological research/Roger R. Hock.—5th ed.
  p. cm.
 Includes bibliographical references and index.
 ISBN 0-13-114729-3
 1. Psychology—Experiments—History—20th century—Textbooks.
BF198.7.H63 2005
 150—dc22

2004007022

Acquisitions Editor: *Jayme Heffler*
Assistant Editor: *Kerri Scott*
Director of Marketing: *Beth Majia*
Assistant Managing Editor: *Maureen Richardson*
Production Liaison: *Fran Russello*
Manufacturing Buyer: *Tricia Kenny*
Cover Design: *Bruce Kenselaar*
Cover Illustration/Photo: *Corbis*
Composition/Full-Service Project Management: *Patty Donovan/Pine Tree Composition*
Printer/Binder: *Courier Companies*
Cover Printer: *Phoenix Color Corp.*

For Diane Perin Hock, and Caroline Mei Perin Hock

Pearson Education, Ltd., London
Pearson Education Singapore, Pte. Ltd.
Pearson Education Canada, Ltd.
Pearson Education—Japan
Pearson Education Australia PTY, Limited
Pearson Education North Asia Ltd.

Pearson Educación de Mexico,
 S.A. de C.V.
Pearson Education Malaysia, Pte. Ltd.
Pearson Education, Upper Saddle River,
 New Jersey

10 9 8 7 6 5 4 3 2 1
ISBN 0-13-114729-3

CONTENTS

PREFACE

Science moves through history along many routes and at many speeds. Slow times occur when the pace of scientific discovery seems to stagnate, making little or no progress. Then those exciting, dynamic periods suddenly burst upon the scieitific scene; new breakthroughs spark waves of dialogue, attention, research, and progress. These discoveries quite literally change what we know about how the world works. The history of psychology is no different from any other science. Many studies of human behavior have made remarkable and lasting impacts on the various disciplines that comprise the science of psychology. The findings generated from these studies have changed our knowledge of human behavior, and they have set the stage for countless subsequent projects and research programs. Even when the results of some of these pivotal studies have later been drawn into controversy and question, their effect and influence in a historical context never diminishes. They continue to be cited in new articles; they continue to be the topic of academic discussion; they continue to form the foundation for textbook chapters; and they continue to hold a special place in the minds of psychologists.

The concept for this book grew out of my many years of teaching psychology. Psychology textbooks are based on those key studies that have shaped the science of psychology over its relatively brief history. Textbooks, however, seldom give the original studies the attention they richly deserve. Usually the research processes are summarized and diluted to the point that little of the life and excitement of the discoveries remains. Sometimes, methods and findings are reported in way that can even mislead the reader about the study's true impact and influence. This is in no way a criticism of the textbook writers who work under length constraints and must make many difficult choices about what gets included and in how much detail. The situation is, however, unfortunate, because the foundation of all of psychology is research, and through a century of ingenious and elegant studies, our knowledge and understanding of human behavior have been expanded and refined to the level of sophistication that exists today.

This book is an attempt to fill the gap between the psychology textbooks and the research that made them possible. It is a journey through the *headline history* of psychology. My hope is that the way the 40 chosen studies are presented will bring them back to life, so that you can experience them for yourself. This book is intended for anyone who wishes a greater understanding of the true roots of psychology.

CHOOSING THE STUDIES

The studies included in this book were carefully chosen from those found in psychology texts and journals and from those suggested by leading authorities in psychology's many subfields. The number wasn't planned, but as the studies were selected, 40 seemed to be about right both from a historical point of view and in terms of length. The studies chosen are arguably the most famous, the most important, or the most influential in the history of psychology. I use the word *arguably*, because many who read this book may wish to dispute some of the choices. One thing is sure: No *single* list of 40 studies would satisfy *everyone*. However, the studies included here are the ones that continue to be cited most frequently, stirred up the most controversy when they were published, sparked the most subsequent related research, opened new fields of psychological exploration, or changed most dramatically our knowledge of human behavior. These studies are organized according to the major psychology branch into which they best fit, including *Biology and Human Behavior; Consciousness; Learning and Conditioning; Intelligence, Cognition, and Memory; Human Development; Emotion and Motivation; Personality; Psychopathology; Psychotherapy;* and *Social Psychology.*

PRESENTING THE STUDIES

You will find that a basic format is used consistently throughout the book to promote a clear understanding of each study presented. Each reading contains:

1. An exact, readily available reference for where the original study can be found.
2. A brief introduction summarizing the background in the field leading up to the study and the reasons the researcher carried out the project.
3. The theoretical propositions or hypotheses on which the research rests.
4. A detailed account of the experimental design and methods used to carry out the research, including, where appropriate, who the subjects were and how they were recruited; descriptions of any apparatus and materials used; and the actual procedures followed in carrying out the research.
5. A summary of the results of the study in clear, understandable, nontechnical, nonstatistical, no-jargon language.
6. An interpretation of the meaning of the findings based on the author's own discussion in the original article.
7. The significance of the study to the field of psychology.
8. A brief discussion of supportive or contradictory follow-up research findings and subsequent questioning or criticism from others in the field.
9. A sampling of recent applications and citations of the study in others' articles to demonstrate its continuing influence.
10. References for additional and updated reading relating to the study.

Often, scientists speak in languages that are not easily understood (even by other scientists!). The primary goal of this book is to make these discoveries meaningful and accessible to the reader and to allow you to experience the excitement and drama of these remarkable and important discoveries. Where possible and appropriate, I have edited and simplified some of the studies presented here for ease of reading and understanding. However, this has been done carefully, so that the meaning and elegance of the work is preserved and the impact of the research is distilled and clarified.

NEW TO THE FIFTH EDITION

This fifth edition of *Forty Studies* contains many significant and substantive changes and additions. You will find two important new studies about intelligence and gender. In addition, all the *Recent Applications* sections near the end of each reading have been updated to reflect the numerous citations of each of the 40 studies during the three years since the completion of the fourth edition (2000–2003). In that brief, three-year time span, the 40 studies discussed in this edition have been cited nearly 3,000 times! A small sampling of those articles are briefly summarized throughout this edition to allow you to experience the *ongoing* influence of these 40 studies that changed psychology. All newly cited studies are fully referenced at the end of each reading along with other relevant sources. As you read through them, you will be able to appreciate the breadth and richness of the contributions still being made by the 40 studies that comprise this book.

Over the three years since completing the fourth edition, I have continued to enjoy numerous conversations with, and helpful suggestions and counsel from, colleagues in many branches of psychological research about potential changes in the selection of studies for this new edition. Two highly influential studies I have been considering for some time have been mentioned frequently by fellow researchers, so I have included them in this edition. Although they have replaced other studies in previous editions, those studies are still available in their entirety on the Prentice Hall Web site at www.prenhall.com/psychology. Each of these two newly incorporated studies, in their own significant ways, expanded our perceptions of two very basic aspects of human nature, and added to our knowledge of the complexity and diversity of the human experience.

One of the new articles represented a major shift in how we view a basic component of who we are as humans: our gender. Most of you today are familiar with the term *androgyny* and have at least some sense that it refers to individuals who display both masculine and feminine characteristics, attitudes, and behaviors. What you may not know is that the concept of androgyny was proposed in the early 1970s by Stanford psychologist Sandra Bem. Bem challenged the traditional view of gender that placed male and female at opposite ends of a single scale, thereby creating an "either-or" conceptualization of "healthy" gender identity based on the assumption, "If you are male you *should* be masculine and if you are female you *should* be feminine." Bem, however, saw this model as lacking in its ability to describe those people who possess more of a balance of *both* masculine and feminine traits. She referred to these individuals as *androgynous* (from "andro" meaning male, and "gyn" referring to female). Moreover, she argued that androgynous people may experience certain psychological advantages due to an enhanced ability to adapt to a greater range of life's situations than those who are either strongly masculine or strongly feminine. Bem's 1974 article, included in this edition, discusses her revolutionary theory and her development of a scale to measure gender on a two-dimensional scale, capable of tapping into masculinity, femininity, *and* androgyny.

The second new study incorporated into this edition represents a body of work that has transformed how we perceive another fundamental human attribute: our intelligence. Throughout the history of psychology, most social scientists and society in general saw intelligence as a single, general ability of which each of us possesses a different amount. This conceptualization of intelligence has led us to think of some people as "smarter" than others and nurtured the concept of IQ. In the early 1980s, however, Howard Gardner, of Harvard University, proposed that human intelligence is not such a unitary phenomenon, but rather consists of an amalgam of many different, specific sets of abilities, each of which may be interpreted as a "free standing" intelligence in and of itself. In his 1983 book that forms the basis of this new reading, Gardner articulated his eight criteria for defining a specific set of skills as an intelligence and proposed that humans possess at least seven distinct intelligences. This perspective on intelligence has become known as "multiple intelligences" or *MI theory*. Today, Gardner's MI theory (now containing eight intelligences), exerts a powerful influence in virtually all educational settings. It has broadened our understanding of human intelligence in ways that serve to enhance our ability to maximize our strengths, overcome our weaknesses, and celebrate an additional quality in the rich fabric of human diversity.

Finally, to accommodate the addition of these new studies within their appropriate psychological subfield, the discussion of Kohlberg's studies of moral development has been moved from the *personality* section to *human development*. Although an argument may be made for placing Kohlberg's work under either rubric, it probably fits better in development, next to the contributions of Piaget.

THE ETHICS OF RESEARCH INVOLVING HUMAN OR ANIMAL SUBJECTS

Without subjects, scientific research is virtually impossible. In physics, the subjects are subatomic particles; in botany, they are plants; in chemistry, they are the elements of the periodic table; and in psychology, the subjects are *people*. At times, certain research procedures or behaviors under study do not permit the use of human subjects, so animal subjects are substituted. However, the overall goal of animal research is to better understand humans, not just the animals themselves. In the following pages, you will be reading about research involving both human and animal subjects. Some of the studies may cause you to question the ethics of the researchers in regard to the procedures used with the subjects. Usually, when painful or stressful procedures are part of a study being discussed, the question of ethics is noted in the chapter. However, since this is such a volatile and topical issue, a brief discussion of the ethical guidelines followed by present-day psychologists is included here in preparation for some of the studies described in this book.

Research with Human Subjects

The American Psychological Association (APA) has issued strict and clear guidelines that researchers must follow when carrying out experiments involving human participants. A portion of the introduction to those guidelines reads as follows:

> Psychologists strive to benefit those with whom they work and take care to do no harm. In their professional actions, psychologists seek to safeguard the welfare and rights of those with whom they interact . . . When conflicts occur among psychologists' obligations or concerns, they attempt to resolve these conflicts in a responsible fashion that avoids or minimizes harm . . . Psychologists uphold professional standards of conduct, clarify their professional roles and obligations, accept appropriate responsibility for their behavior, and seek to manage conflicts of interest that could lead to exploitation or harm . . . Psychologists respect the dignity and worth of all people, and the rights of individuals to privacy, confidentiality, and self-determination (excerpted from *Ethical Principles of Psychologists and Code of Conduct*, 2003; see www.apa.org/ethics/).

To adhere to those principles, researchers follow certain basic principles in carrying out all studies involving human subjects:

1. *Informed consent.* A researcher must explain to potential subjects what the experiment is about and what procedures will be used so that the individual is able to make an informed decision whether to participate. If the person then agrees to participate, this is called *informed consent*. As you will see in this book, there are times when the true purposes of an experiment cannot be revealed because this would alter the behavior of the subjects and contaminate the results. In such cases, when deception is used, a subject still must be given adequate information for informed consent, and the portions of the experiment that are hidden must be justifiable based on the importance of the potential findings.
2. *Freedom to withdraw at any time.* All human subjects in all research projects must know that they may withdraw freely from the study at any time. This may appear to be an unnecessary rule, because it would seem obvious that any subject who is too uncomfortable with the procedures can simply leave. However, this is not always so straightforward. For example, undergraduate students are often given course credit for participating as

subjects in psychological experiments. If they feel that withdrawing will influence the credit they need, they may not feel free to do so. When subjects are paid to participate, if they are made to feel that their completion of the experiment is a requirement for payment, this could produce an unethical inducement to avoid withdrawing if they wish to do so. To avoid this problem, subjects should be given credit or paid at the beginning of the procedure *just for showing up.*

3. *Debriefing and protection from harm.* Experimenters have the responsibility to protect their subjects from all physical and psychological harm that might be produced by the research procedures. Most psychological research involves methods that are completely harmless, both during and after the study. However, even seemingly harmless procedures can sometimes produce negative effects such as frustration, embarrassment, or concern. One common safeguard against those effects is the ethical requirement of debriefing. After subjects have completed an experiment, especially one involving any form of deception, they should be debriefed. During debriefing, the true purpose and goals of the experiment are explained to them, and they are given the opportunity to ask any questions about their experiences. If there is any possibility of lingering aftereffects from the experiment, the researchers should provide subjects with contact information for further discussion if necessary.

4. *Confidentiality.* All results from subjects in experiments should be kept in complete confidence unless specific agreements have been made with the subjects. This does not mean that results cannot be reported and published, but this is done in such a way that individual data cannot be identified. Often, no identifying information is even acquired from subjects, and all data are combined to arrive at *average* differences among groups.

In research involving children, parental consent is required and the same ethical guidelines apply.

As you read through the studies included in this book, you may find a few studies that appear to have violated some of these ethical principles. These studies were carried out long before formal ethical guidelines existed and could not be replicated today. The lack of guidelines, however, does not excuse past researchers for abuses. Judgment of those investigators must now be made by each of us individually, and we must learn, as psychologists have, from past mistakes.

Research with Animal Subjects

One of the hottest topics of discussion in and outside of the scientific community is the question of the ethics of animal research. Animal-rights groups are growing in number and are becoming increasingly vocal and militant. More controversy exists today over animal subjects than human subjects, probably because animals cannot be protected, as humans can, with informed consent, freedom to withdraw, or debriefing. Additionally, the most radical animal rights activists take the view that all living things are ordered in value by their ability to sense pain. In this conceptualization, animals are equal in value to humans and, therefore, any use of animals by humans is seen as unethical. This use includes eating a chicken, wearing leather, and owning pets (which, according to some animal-rights activists, is a form of slavery).

At one end of the spectrum, many people believe that research with animals is inhumane and unethical, and should be prohibited. However, nearly all scientists and most Americans believe that the limited and humane use of animals in scientific research is necessary and beneficial. Many lifesaving drugs and medical techniques have been developed through the use of animal experimental subjects. Animals have also often been subjects in psychological research to study issues such as depression, brain development, overcrowding, and learning processes. The primary reason animals are used in research is that to carry out similar research on humans clearly would be unethical. For example, suppose you wanted to study the effect on brain development and intelligence of raising infants in an enriched environment with many activities and toys, versus an impoverished environment with little to do. To assign human infants to these different conditions would simply not be possible. However, most people would agree that rats could be studied without major ethical concerns to reveal findings potentially important to humans (see the reading in this book on research such as this by Rosenzweig and Bennett).

The American Psychological Association, in addition to its guidelines on human subjects, has strict rules governing research with animal subjects designed to ensure humane treatment. These rules require that research animals receive proper housing, feeding, cleanliness, and health care. All unnecessary pain to the animal is prohibited. A portion of the APA's *Guidelines for the Ethical Conduct in the Care and Use of Animals* (2004) reads as follows:

> Animals are to be provided with humane care and healthful conditions during their stay in the facility. . . . Psychologists are encouraged to consider enriching the environments of their laboratory animals and should keep abreast of literature on well-being and enrichment for the species with which they work. . . . When alternative behavioral procedures are available, those that minimize discomfort to the animal should be used. When using aversive conditions, psychologists should adjust the parameters of stimulation to levels that appear minimal, though compatible with the aims of the research. Psychologists are encouraged to test painful stimuli on themselves, whenever reasonable (see //www.apa .org/science/anguide.html).

In this book, several studies involve animal subjects. In addition to the ethical considerations of such research, there are also difficulties in generalizing from animal findings to humans. These issues are discussed within each chapter that includes animal research. Each individual, whether a researcher or a student of psychology, must make his or her own decisions about animal research in general and the justifiability of using animal subjects in any specific instance. If you allow for the idea that animal research is acceptable under *some* circumstances, then, for each study involving animals in this book, you must decide if the value of the study's findings supports the methods used.

One final note related to this issue involves a development in animal research that is a response to public concerns about potential mistreatment. The city of Cambridge, Massachusetts, one of the major research centers of the world with institutions such as Harvard University and MIT, created the position of Commissioner of Laboratory Animals within the Department of Health and Hospitals. This was the first such governmental position and is currently held by a veterinarian, Dr. Julie Medley. Cambridge is home to 22 research laboratories that house approximately 60,000 animals. The commissioner's charge is to ensure humane and proper treatment of all animal subjects in all aspects of the research process, from the animals' living quarters to the methods used in administering the research protocols. If a lab is found to be in violation of Cambridge's strict laws concerning the humane care of lab animals, the commissioner is authorized to impose fines of up to $300 per day. However, Dr. Medley says she has never had to impose the fine, because any facility that has been found in violation, willingly and quickly corrects the problem (personal communication, September 2003)

The studies you are about to experience in this book have benefited all of humankind in many ways and to varying degrees. The history of psychological research is a relatively short one, but it is brimming with the richness and excitement of discovering human nature.

ACKNOWLEDGMENTS

I would like to express my sincere gratitude to Charlyce Jones Owen, Editorial Director of the Humanities Division at Prentice Hall, for her commitment to and support of this project from the beginning, four editions ago. I am also deeply grateful to Jayme Heffler, Psychology Acquisitions Editor at Prentice Hall for her valued support, assistance, and friendship over the past 5 years. I extend my personal appreciation to Bruce Kenselaar for continuing to lend his considerable talents in designing the cover of this and past editions. My genuine gratitude goes out to my psychology colleagues in the field who have taken the time, interest, and effort to communicate to me their comments, suggestions, and wisdom relating to past editions of this book. I have attempted at every opportunity to incorporate their valued insights into the manuscript. Thanks also to the following reviewers whose thoughtful input helped guide my changes and additions in the fourth edition: Barbara Ann Cabral, Malinde Althaus, Susan Sprecher, Robert D. Boroff, Sherman Sowby, Debra L. Golden, Paul D. Young, Kathleen M. Greaves, Bailey Drechsler, Travis Langley, Tara Lynn Torchia, M. Betsy Bergen, Lynne Kemen, Shirley Ogletree, Sandra Caron, and Jennifer L. O'Loughlin-Brooks.

Finally, to my students, friends, and colleagues at many colleges and universities who have participated in the history of this book in many tangible and intangible ways over the past 12 years (you know who you are), I extend my continuing best wishes and heartfelt thanks.

ROGER R. HOCK

1 BIOLOGY AND HUMAN BEHAVIOR

Nearly all general psychology texts begin with chapters relating to the biology of human behavior. This is not simply due to convention, but rather it is because biological processes form the basis of *all* behavior. Each of the other subfields of psychology rests on this biological foundation. The branch of psychological research that studies these processes is called *physiological* or *biological psychology*, and focuses on the interaction of your brain and nervous system, the processes of receiving stimulation and information from the environment through your senses, and the ways in which your brain organizes all this information to create your perceptions of the world.

The studies chosen to represent this basic component of psychological research include a wide range of research and are among the most influential and most often cited. The first study discusses a famous research program on right-brain/left-brain specialization that shaped much of our present knowledge of how the brain functions. Next is a study that surprised the scientific community by demonstrating how a stimulating "childhood" might produce a more highly developed brain. The third study represents a fundamental change in the thinking of many psychologists about the basic causes of human behavior, personality, and social interaction, namely, a new appreciation for the significance of your *genes*. Fourth is the invention of the famous "visual cliff" method of studying infants' abilities to perceive depth. All these studies, the latter two in particular, also address an issue that underlies and connects nearly all areas of psychology and provides for an ongoing and fascinating debate: the nature-nurture controversy.

ONE BRAIN OR TWO?
Gazzaniga, M. S. (1967). The split brain in man. *Scientific American, 217* (2), 24–29.

You are probably aware that the two halves of your brain are not the same and that they perform different functions. For one thing, the left side of your brain is responsible for movement in the right side of your body, and vice versa. Even beyond this, though, the two brain hemispheres appear to have even greater specialized abilities.

1

It has come to be rather common knowledge that, for most of us, the left brain controls the ability to use language while the right is involved more in spatial relationships, such as those needed for artistic activities. It is well known that stroke or accident victims who suffer damage to the left side of the brain will usually lose their ability to speak (often this skill returns with practice and training). Many people believe that each half, or "hemisphere," of your brain may actually be a completely separate mental system with its own individual abilities for learning, remembering, perceiving the world, and even feeling emotions. The concepts underlying this popular awareness are the result of many years of rigorous scientific research on the effects of splitting the brain into two separate hemispheres.

Research in this area was pioneered by Roger W. Sperry (1913–1994), beginning about 15 years prior to the article examined in this chapter. In his early work with animal subjects, Sperry made many remarkable discoveries. For example, consider a cat that has had surgery to cut the connection between the two halves of its brain and to alter its optic nerves so that its left eye only transmitted information to the left hemisphere and the right eye only to the right hemisphere. Following surgery, the cat appeared to behave normally and exhibited virtually no ill effects. Then the cat's right eye was covered, and the cat learned a new behavior, such as walking through a short maze to find food. After the cat became skilled at maneuvering through the maze, the eye cover was shifted to its left eye. Now when the cat was placed in the maze, its left brain had no idea where to turn and the animal had to relearn the entire maze from the beginning.

Sperry conducted many related studies over the next 30 years and in 1981 received the Nobel Prize for his work on the specialized abilities of the two halves of the brain. When his research endeavors turned to human subjects in the early 1960s, he was joined in his work by Michael Gazzaniga. Although Sperry is considered the founder of split-brain research, Gazzaniga's article has been chosen because it is a clear, concise summary of their early collaborative work with human subjects and is cited consistently in many general psychology texts. Its selection is in no way intended to overlook or overshadow either Sperry's leadership in this field or his great contributions. Gazzaniga, in large part, owes his early research, and his ongoing leadership in the area of hemispheric specialization, to Roger W. Sperry (see Sperry, 1968; Puente, 1995).

To understand split-brain research, some knowledge of human physiology is required. The two hemispheres of your brain are in constant communication with one another via the *corpus callosum,* a structure made up of about 200 million nerve fibers. If your corpus callosum is cut, this major line of communication is disrupted, and the two halves of your brain must then function independently. So, if we want to study each half of your brain separately, all we need to do is surgically sever your corpus callosum.

But can scientists divide the brains of humans? This sounds like psychology by Dr. Frankenstein! Obviously, research ethics would never allow such drastic methods simply for the purpose of studying the specialized abilities of the brain's two hemispheres. However, in the late 1950s, the field of medicine provided psychologists with a golden opportunity. In some people with very rare and very extreme cases of uncontrollable epilepsy, seizures could be virtually eliminated by surgically severing the corpus callosum. This operation was (and is) extremely successful, as a last resort, for those patients who cannot be helped by any other means. When this article was written in 1966, 10 such operations had been undertaken, and four of the patients consented to participate in examination and testing by Sperry and Gazzaniga to determine how their perceptual and intellectual skills were affected as a result of this surgical treatment.

THEORETICAL PROPOSITIONS

The researchers wanted to explore the extent to which the two halves of the human brain are able to function independently, and whether they have separate and unique abilities. If the information traveling between the two halves of your brain is interrupted, would the right side of your body suddenly be unable to coordinate with the left? If language is controlled by the left side of the brain, how would your ability to speak and understand words be affected by this surgery? Would thinking and reasoning processes exist in both halves separately? If the brain is really two separate brains, would a person be capable of functioning normally when these two brains are no longer able to communicate? Since we receive sensory input from both the right and the left, how would the senses of vision, hearing, and touch be affected? Sperry and Gazzaniga attempted to answer these and many other questions in their studies of split-brain individuals.

METHOD

The researchers developed three types of tests to explore a wide range of mental (cognitive) capabilities of the patients. One was designed to examine visual abilities. They devised a technique to allow a picture of an object, a word, or parts of words to be transmitted only to the visual area (called a "field") in *either* the right- or left-brain hemisphere, but not to both. Normally, both of your eyes send information to both sides of your brain. However, with exact placement of items or words in front of you, and with your eyes fixed on a specific point, images can be fed to only the right or the left visual field of your brain.

Another testing situation was designed for tactile (touch) stimulation. Here, participants could feel, but not see an object, a block letter, or even a word in cutout block letters. The apparatus consisted of a screen with a space under it for the subject to reach through and touch the items without being able to see them. The visual and the tactile devices could be used simultaneously so that, for example, a picture of a pen could be projected to one side of the brain and the same object could be searched for by either hand among various objects behind the screen (see Figure 1).

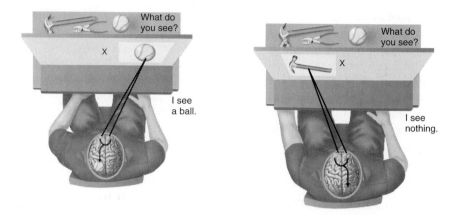

FIGURE 1   A typical visual testing device for split-brain subjects.

Finally, testing auditory abilities was somewhat more tricky. When sound enters either of your ears, sensations are sent to both sides of your brain. Therefore, it is not possible to limit auditory input to only one side of the brain even in split-brain patients. However, it is possible to limit the *response* to such input to one brain hemisphere. Here is how this was done. Imagine that several common objects (a spoon, a pen, a marble) are placed into a cloth bag, and you are then asked, verbally, to find certain items by touch. You would probably have no trouble doing so. If you place your left hand in the bag, it is being controlled by the right side of your brain, and vice versa. Do you think either side of your brain could do this task alone? As you will see in a moment, both halves of the brain are not equally capable of responding to this auditory task. What if you are not asked for specific objects, but are simply requested to reach into the bag and identify objects by touch? Again, this would not be difficult for you, but it would be quite difficult for a split-brain patient.

Gazzaniga combined all of these testing techniques to reveal some fascinating findings about how the brain functions.

RESULTS

First of all, you should know that following this radical brain surgery, the patients' intelligence level, personality, typical emotional reactions, and so on were relatively unchanged. They were very happy and relieved that they were now free of seizures. Gassaniga reported that one patient, while still groggy from surgery, joked that he had "a splitting headache." When testing began, however, these subjects demonstrated many unusual mental abilities.

Visual Abilities

One of the first tests involved a board with a horizontal row of lights. When a patient sat in front of this board and stared at a point in the middle of the lights, the bulbs would flash across both the right and left visual fields. However, when the patients were asked to explain what they saw, they said that only the lights on the right side of the board had flashed. Next when the researchers flashed only the lights on the left side of the visual field, the patients claimed to have seen nothing. A logical conclusion from these findings was that the right side of the brain is blind. Then an amazing thing happened. The lights were flashed again, only this time the patients were asked to point to the lights that had flashed. Although they had said they only saw the lights on the right, they pointed to all the lights in both visual fields. Using this method of pointing, it was found that both halves of the brain had seen the lights and were equally skilled in visual perception. The important point here is that when the patients failed to *say* that they had seen all the lights, it was not because they didn't see them, but because the center for speech is located in the brain's left hemisphere. In other words, in order for you to say you saw something, the object has to have been seen by the left side of your brain.

Tactile Abilities

You can try this test yourself. Put your hands behind your back. Then have someone place familiar objects (a spoon, a pen, a book, a watch) in either your right or your left hand and see if you can identify the object. You would not find this task to be very difficult, would you? This is basically what Sperry and Gazzaniga did with the split-brain patients. When an object was placed in the right hand in such a way that the patient could not see or hear it, messages about the object would travel to the left hemisphere and the patient was able to name the object and describe it and its uses. However, when the same objects were placed in the left hand (connected to the right hemisphere), the patients could not name them or describe them in any way. But did the patients *know* what the object was? In order for the researchers to find out, they asked the subjects to match the object in their left hand (without seeing it, remember) to a group of various objects presented to them. This they could do as easily as you or I. Again, this places verbal ability in the left hemisphere of the brain. Keep in mind that the reason you are able to name unseen objects in your left hand is that the information from the right side of your brain is transmitted via the corpus callosum to the left side, where your center for language says "that's a spoon!"

Visual Plus Tactile Tests

Combining these two types of tests provided support for the findings above and also offered additional interesting results. If subjects were shown a picture of an object to the right hemisphere only, they were unable to name it or describe it. In fact, there might be no verbal response at all or even a denial that anything had been presented. But if the patients were allowed to reach under the screen with their left hand and touch a selection of objects, they were always able to find the one that had been presented visually.

The right hemisphere was found to be able to think about and analyze objects as well. Gazzaniga reported that when the right hemisphere was shown a picture of an item such as a cigarette, the subjects could touch 10 objects behind the screen that did not include a cigarette, and select an object that was most closely related to the item pictured—in this case an ashtray. He went on to explain:

> Oddly enough, however, even after their correct response, and while they were holding the ashtray in their left hand, they were unable to name or describe the object or the picture of the cigarette. Evidently, the left hemisphere was completely divorced, in perception and knowledge, from the right. (p. 26)

Other tests were conducted to shed additional light on the language-processing abilities of the right hemisphere. One very famous, ingenious, and revealing use of the visual apparatus came when the word HEART was projected to the patients so that HE was sent to the right visual field and ART was sent to the left. Now, keeping in mind (your connected mind) the functions of the two hemispheres, what do you think the patients verbally reported seeing? If you said ART, you were correct. However, and here is the revealing part, when the subjects were presented with two cards with the words HE and ART printed on them and asked to point with the left hand to the word they had seen, they all pointed to HE! This demonstrated that the right hemisphere is able to comprehend language, although it does so in a different way from the left: in a nonverbal way.

The auditory tests conducted with the patients produced similar results. When patients were asked to reach with their left hand into a grab bag hidden from view and pull out certain specific objects (a watch, a marble, a comb, a coin) they had no trouble. This demonstrated that the right hemisphere was comprehending language. It was even possible to describe a related aspect of an item with the same accurate results. An example given by Gazzaniga was when the patients were asked to find in a grab bag full of plastic fruit "the fruit monkeys like best," they retrieved a banana. Or when told "Sunkist sells a lot of them," they pulled out an orange. However, if these same pieces of fruit were placed out of view in the patients' left hand, they were unable to say what they were. In other words, when a verbal response was required, the right hemisphere was unable to speak.

One last example of this amazing difference between the two hemispheres involved plastic block letters on the table behind the screen. When patients were asked to spell various words by feel with the left hand they had an easy time doing so. Even if three or four letters that spelled specific words were placed behind the screen, they were able, left-handed, to arrange them correctly into words. However, immediately after completing this task, the subjects could not name the word they had just spelled. Clearly, the left hemisphere of the brain is superior to the right for speech (in some left-handed people, this is reversed). But in what skills, if any, does the right hemisphere excel? Sperry and Gazzaniga found in this early work that visual tasks involving spatial relationships and shapes were performed with greater proficiency by the left hand (even though these patients were all right-handed). As can be seen in Figure 2, copying three-dimensional drawings (using the pencil behind the screen) was much more successful with the left hand.

Finally, the researchers wanted to explore emotional reactions of split-brain patients. While performing visual experiments, Sperry and Gazzaniga suddenly flashed a picture of a nude woman to either the left or right hemisphere. In one instance, when this picture was shown to the left hemisphere of a female patient:

> She laughed and verbally identified the picture of a nude. When it was later presented to the right hemisphere, she said . . . she saw nothing, but almost immediately a sly smile spread over her face and she began to chuckle. Asked what she was laughing at, she said: "I don't know . . . nothing . . . oh—that funny machine." Although the right hemisphere could not describe what it had seen, the

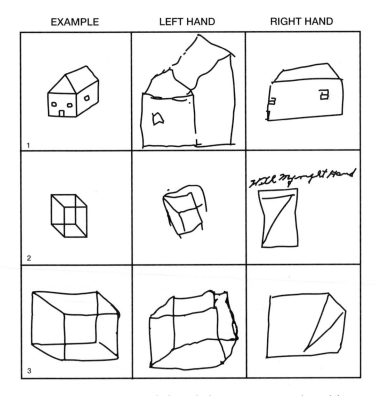

FIGURE 2   Drawings made by split-brain patients. (Adapted from "The Split Brain in Man," by Michael S. Gazzaniga.)

sight nevertheless elicited an emotional response like the one evoked in the left hemisphere. (p. 29)

DISCUSSION

The overall conclusion drawn from the research reported in this article was that there are two different brains within each person's cranium, each with complex abilities. Gazzaniga notes the possibility that if our brain is really two brains, then perhaps we have the potential to process twice as much information if the two halves are divided. Indeed, there is some research evidence to suggest that split-brain patients have the ability to perform two cognitive tasks as fast as a normal person can carry out one.

SIGNIFICANCE OF FINDINGS

These findings and the subsequent research carried out by Sperry and Gazzaniga and others are extremely significant and far-reaching. We now know that the two halves of your brain have many specialized skills and functions. Your left brain is "better" at speaking, writing, mathematical calculation, and reading and is the primary center for language. Your right hemisphere, however, possesses superior capabilities for recognizing faces, solving problems involving spatial relationships, symbolic reasoning, and artistic activities.

Our increased knowledge of the specialized functioning of the brain allows us to treat victims of stroke or head injury more effectively. By knowing the location of the damage, we can predict what deficits are likely to exist as the patient recovers. Through this knowledge, therapists can employ appropriate relearning and rehabilitation strategies to help patients recover as fully and quickly as possible.

Gazzaniga and Sperry, after years of continuous work in this area, concluded that each hemisphere of your brain really is a mind of its own. In a later study, split-brain patients were tested on much more complex problems than have been discussed here. One question asked was, "What profession would you choose?" A male patient verbally (left hemisphere) responded that he would choose to be a draftsman, but his left hand (right hemisphere) spelled by touch in block letters *automobile race* (Gazzaniga & LeDoux, 1978). In fact, Gazzaniga has taken this theory a step further. He now maintains that even in people whose brains are normal and intact, there may not be complete communication between the two hemispheres (Gazzaniga, 1985). For example, if certain bits of information, such as those forming an emotion, are not stored in a language format, the left hemisphere may not have access to it. The result of this is that you may feel sad and not be able to say why. Since this is an uncomfortable cognitive situation, the left hemisphere may try to find a verbal reason to explain the sadness (after all, language is its main job). However, since your left hemisphere does not have all the necessary data, its explanation may actually be wrong!

CRITICISMS

The findings from the split-brain studies carried out over the years by Sperry, Gazzaniga, and others have rarely been disputed. The main body of criticism about this research has focused instead on the way the idea of right- and left-brain specialization has filtered down to popular culture and the media.

There is now a widely believed myth that some people are more *right-brained* or more *left-brained,* or that one side of your brain needs to be developed in order for you to improve certain skills. Jarre Levy, a psychobiologist at the University of Chicago, has been in the forefront of scientists who are trying to dispel the notion that we have two separately functioning brains. She claims that it is precisely because each hemisphere has separate functions that they must integrate their abilities instead of separating them, as is commonly believed. Through such integration, your brain is able to perform in ways that are greater than and different from the abilities of either side alone.

When you read a story, for example, your right hemisphere is specializing in emotional content (humor, pathos), picturing visual descriptions, keeping track of the story structure as a whole, and appreciating artistic writing style (such as the use of metaphors). While all this is happening, your left hemisphere is understanding the written words, deriving meaning from the complex relationships among words and sentences, and translating words into their phonetic sounds so that they can be understood as language. The reason you are able to read, understand, and appreciate a story is that your brain functions as a single, integrated structure (Levy, 1985).

In fact, Levy explains that no human activity uses only one side of the brain. "The popular myths are interpretations and wishes, not the observations of scientists. Normal people have not half a brain, nor two brains, but one gloriously differentiated brain, with each hemisphere contributing its specialized abilities" (Levy, 1985, p. 44).

RECENT APPLICATIONS

The continuing influence of Sperry's and Gazzaniga's split-brain research echoes the quote from Levy. A review of recent medical and psychological literature reveals numerous articles in various fields referring to the early work and methodology of Roger Sperry as well as to more recent findings by Gazzaniga and his associates. For example, a study from 1998 conducted in France (Hommet & Billard, 1998) has questioned the very foundations of Sperry's and Gazzaniga's studies, namely, that severing the corpus callosum actually divides the hemispheres of the brain. The French study found that children who were born without a corpus callosum (a rare brain malformation) demonstrated that information was being transmitted between their brain hemispheres. The researchers concluded that significant connections other than the corpus callosum must exist in these children. Whether such subcortical connections are indeed present in split-brain individuals remains unclear.

Later that same year, a study was published by a team of neuropsychologists that included Gazzaniga, from several prestigious research institutions in the United States (University of Texas, Stanford, Yale, and Dartmouth). The study demonstrated that split brain patients may routinely perceive the world differently from the rest of us (Parsons, Gabrieli, Phelps, & Gazzaniga, 1998). The researchers found that when subjects were asked to identify whether drawings presented to only one brain hemisphere were drawn by right- or left-handed people, the split-brain patients were only able to do so correctly when the handedness of the artist was the *opposite* of the hemisphere to which the picture was projected. Normal control subjects were correct regardless of which hemisphere "saw" the drawings. This implies that communication between your brain hemispheres is necessary for imagining or simulating in your mind the movements of others, that is, "putting yourself in their place" in order to perceive their actions correctly.

Finally, researchers continue to explore the idea that our two brain hemispheres have separate, yet distinct consciousnesses. One such study (Morin, 2001), focused on the idea of inner speech (internal dialogue with and about yourself) as a signpost for self-awareness and consciousness. Morin proposed that your self-awareness may be quite different in your right and left cerebral hemispheres due to the greater ability of the left brain for language. However, the right brain may have the ability to perceive "the self" in a physical or bodily way, rather than through an awareness of mental processes. Therefore, Morin suggested an alternative interpretation of commissurotomy [surgical separation of the corpus callosum] according to which split-brain patients exhibit two uneven streams of self-awareness: a "complete" one in the left hemisphere and a "primitive" one in the right hemisphere" (p. 594).

Some have carried this idea a step further and applied it to some psychological disorders, such as dissociative, multiple personality disorder (e.g., Schiffer, 1996). The idea behind this notion is that in some people with intact, "nonsplit" brains, the right hemisphere may be able to function at a greater-than-normal level of independence from the left, and may even take control of a person's consciousness for periods of time. Is it possible that multiple personality disorder might be the expression of hidden personalities contained in our right hemispheres? It's something to think about . . . with *both* of your hemispheres.

Gazzaniga, M. S. (1985). *The social brain.* New York: Basic Books.

Gazzaniga, M. S., & Ledoux, J. E. (1978). *The integrated mind.* New York: Plenum Press.

Hommet, C., & Billard, C. (1998). Corpus callosum syndrome in children. *Neurochirurgie,* 44(1), 110–112.

Levy, J. (1985, May). Right brain, left brain: Fact and fiction. *Psychology Today,* 42–44.

Morin, A. (2001). The split brain debate revisited: On the importance of language and self recognition for right hemispheric consciousness. *Journal of Mind and Behavior, 22,* 107–118.

Parsons, L., Gabrieli, J., Phelps, E., & Gazzaniga, M. (1998). Cerebrally lateralized mental representations of hand shape and movement. *Neuroscience, 18*(16), 6539–6548.

Puente, A. E. (1995). Roger Wolcott Sperry (1913–1994). *American Psychologist, 50*(11), 940–941.

Schiffer, F. (1996). Cognitive ability of the right-hemisphere: Possible contributions to psychological function. *Harvard Review of Psychiatry, 4*(3), 126–138.

Sperry, R. W. (1968). Hemisphere disconnection and unity in conscious awareness. *American Psychologist, 23,* 723–733.

MORE EXPERIENCE = BIGGER BRAIN?
Rosenzweig, M. R., Bennett, E. L., & Diamond, M. C. (1972). Brain changes in response to experience. *Scientific American, 226* (2), 22–29.

If you were to enter the baby's room in a typical American middle-class home today, you would probably see a crib full of stuffed animals and various colorful toys dangling directly over and within reach of the infant. Some of these toys may light up, move, play music, or do all three. What do you suppose is the reasoning behind supplying infants with so much to see and do? Well, aside from the fact that babies seem to enjoy and respond positively to these things, it is most parents' belief, acknowledged or not, that children need a stimulating environment for optimal intellectual development and proper development of the brain.

The question of whether certain experiences produce physical changes in the brain has been a topic of conjecture and research among philosophers and scientists for centuries. In 1785, Malacarne, an Italian anatomist, studied pairs of dogs from the same litter and pairs of birds from the same batches of eggs. For each pair, he would train one subject extensively over a long period of time while the other would be equally well cared for, but not trained. He discovered later, in autopsies of the animals, that the brains of the trained animals appeared more complex, with a greater number of folds and fissures. However, this line of research was, for unknown reasons, discontinued. In the late nineteenth century, there were attempts to relate the circumference of the human head with the amount of learning a person had experienced. While some early findings claimed such a relationship, later research determined that this was not a valid measure of brain development.

By the 1960s, new technologies had been developed that gave scientists the ability to measure brain changes with great precision using high magnification techniques and assessment of levels of various brain enzymes and neurotransmitter chemicals. Mark Rosenzweig and his colleagues Edward Bennett and Marian Diamond, at the University of California at Berkeley, incorporated those technologies in an ambitious series of 16 experiments over a period of 10 years to try to address the issue of the effect of experience on the brain. Their findings were reported in the article discussed in this chapter. For reasons that will become obvious, they did not use humans in their studies, but rather, as in many classic psychological experiments, their subjects were rats.

THEORETICAL PROPOSITIONS

Since psychologists are ultimately interested in humans, not rats, the use of nonhuman subjects must be justified. In these studies, part of the theoretical foundation concerned why rats had been chosen as subjects. The authors explained that for several reasons, it is more convenient to use rodents than to use higher mammals such as carnivores or primates. The part of the brain that is the main focus of this research is smooth in the rat, not folded and complex as it is in higher animals. Therefore, it can be examined and measured more easily. In addition, rats are small and inexpensive, which is an important consideration in the world of research laboratories (usually underfunded and lacking in space). Rats bear large litters, and this allows for members from the same litters to be assigned to different experimental conditions. Finally, the authors point out, various strains of inbred rats have been produced, and this allows researchers to include the effects of genetics in their studies if desired.

Implicit in Rosenzweig's research was the belief that animals raised in highly stimulating environments will demonstrate differences in brain growth and chemistry when compared with animals reared in plain or dull circumstances. In each of the experiments reported in this article, 12 sets of three male rats, each set from the same litter, were studied.

METHOD

Three male rats were chosen from each litter. They were then randomly assigned to one of three conditions. One rat remained in the laboratory cage with the rest of the colony; another was assigned to what Rosenzweig termed the "enriched" environment cage; and the third was assigned to the "impoverished" cage. Remember that there were 12 rats in each of these conditions for each of the 16 experiments.

The three different environments (Figure 1) were described as follows:

1. The standard laboratory colony cage contained several rats in an adequate space with food and water always available.
2. The impoverished environment was a slightly smaller cage isolated in a separate room in which the rat was placed alone with adequate food and water.
3. The enriched environment was virtually a rat's Disneyland (no offense intended to Mickey!). Six to eight rats lived in a "large cage furnished with a variety of objects with which they could play. A new set of playthings, drawn out of a pool of 25 objects, was placed in the cage every day" (p. 22).

The rats were allowed to live in these different environments for various periods of time, ranging from four to 10 weeks. Following this differential treatment period, the experimental rodents were humanely sacrificed so that autopsies could be carried out on their brains to determine if any differences had developed. In order to be sure that no experimenter bias would occur, the examinations were done in random order by code number so that the person doing the autopsy would not know in which condition the rat was raised. The researchers' primary focus was on the differences in the brains of the enriched rats versus the impoverished rats.

The rats' brains were dissected and the various sections were measured, weighed, and analyzed to determine amount of cell growth and levels of neu-

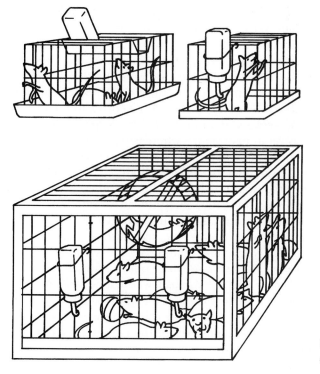

FIGURE 1 The three cage environments.

rotransmitter activity. In this latter measurement, there was one brain enzyme of particular interest called *acetylcholinesterase*. This chemical is important because it allows for faster and more efficient transmission of impulses among brain cells.

Did Rosenzweig and his associates find differences in the brains of rats raised in enriched versus impoverished environments? Here are their results.

RESULTS

Results indicated that the brains of the enriched rats were different from the impoverished rats in many ways. The cerebral cortex of the enriched rats was significantly heavier and thicker. The cortex is the part of the brain that responds to experience and is responsible for movement, memory, learning, and all sensory input (vision, hearing, touch, taste, smell). Also, greater activity of the nervous system enzyme acetylcholinesterase, mentioned previously, was found in the brain tissue of the rats with the enriched experience.

While there were no significant differences found between the two groups of rats in the number of brain cells (called neurons), the enriched environment produced larger neurons. Related to this was the finding that the ratio of RNA to DNA, the two most important brain chemicals for cell growth, was greater for the enriched rats. This implied that there had been a higher level of chemical activity in the enriched rats' brains.

Rosenzweig and his colleagues stated that "although the brain differences induced by environment are not large, we are confident that they are genuine. When the experiments are replicated, the same pattern of differences is found repeatedly. . . . The most consistent effect of experience on the brain that we found was the ratio of the weight of the cortex to the weight of the rest of the brain: the sub-cortex. It appears that the cortex increases in weight quite readily in response to experience whereas the rest of the brain changes little" (p. 25). This measurement of the ratio of the cortex to the rest of the brain was the most accurate measurement of brain changes. This was because the overall weight of the brain varies with the overall weight of each individual animal. By considering this ratio, such individual differences are canceled out. Figure 2 illustrates this finding for all of the 16 studies. As you can see, in only one experiment was the difference *not* statistically significant.

Finally, there was a finding reported relating to the synapses of the brains of the two groups of rats. The synapse is the point at which two neurons meet. Most brain activity occurs at the synapse, where a nerve impulse is either passed from one neuron to the next so that it continues on, or it is inhibited and stopped. Under great magnification using the electron microscope, it was found that the synapses themselves of the enriched rats' brains were 50% larger than those of the impoverished rats.

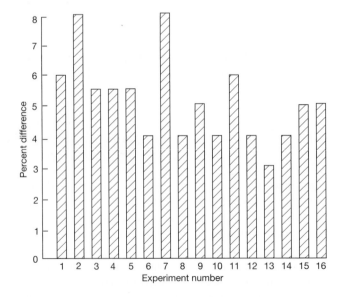

FIGURE 2   Ratio of cortex to rest of brain: Enriched compared with impoverished environment. (Results in experiments 2 through 16 were statistically significant.) (Adapted from p. 26.)

DISCUSSION AND CRITICISMS

After nearly 10 years of research, Rosenzweig, Bennett, and Diamond were willing to state with confidence, "There can now be no doubt that many aspects of brain anatomy and brain chemistry are changed by experience" (p. 27). However, they were also quick to acknowledge that when they first reported their findings many other scientists were skeptical, since such effects had not been so clearly demonstrated in past research. There were criticisms contending that perhaps it was not the enriched environment that produced the brain changes, but other differences in the treatment of the rats such as mere handling or stress.

The criticism of differential handling was a valid one in that the enriched rats were handled twice each day when they were removed from the cage as the toys were being changed, while the impoverished rats were not handled. It was possible, therefore, that the handling might have caused the results and not the enriched environment. To respond to this potential confounding factor, the researchers handled one group of rats every day and did not handle another group of their litter mates (all were raised in the same environment). No differences in the brains of these two groups were found. Additionally, in their later studies, both the enriched and impoverished rats were handled equally and, still, the same pattern of results was found.

As for the criticisms relating to stress, the argument was that the isolation experienced by the impoverished rats was stressful, and this was the reason for their less developed brains. Rosenzweig et al. cited other research that had exposed rats to a daily routine of stress (cage rotation or mild electric shock) and had found no evidence of changes in brain development due to stress alone.

One of the problems of any research carried out in a laboratory is that it is necessarily artificial. Rosenzweig and his colleagues were curious about how various levels of stimulation might affect the brain development of animals in their natural environments. They pointed out that laboratory rats and mice often have been raised in artificial environments for as many as 100 generations and bear little resemblance genetically to rats in the wild. To explore this intriguing possibility, they began studying wild deer mice. After the mice were trapped, they were randomly placed in either natural outdoor conditions or the enriched laboratory cages. After four weeks, the outdoor mice showed greater brain development than did those in the enriched laboratory environment. "This indicates that even the enriched laboratory environment is indeed impoverished in comparison with a natural environment" (p. 27).

Finally, the most important criticism of any research involving animal subjects is the question of its relationship, if any, to humans. There is no doubt that this line of research could never be performed on humans, but it is nevertheless the responsibility of the researchers to address this issue, and these scientists did so.

The authors explained that it is difficult to generalize from the findings of one set of rats to another set of rats, and consequently much more difficult to try to apply rat findings to monkeys or humans. And, although they report similar findings with several species of rodents, they admit that more research would be necessary before any assumptions could be made responsibly about the effects of experience on the human brain. They proposed, however, that the value of this kind of research on animals is that "it allows us to test concepts and techniques, some of which may later prove useful in research with human subjects."

Several potential benefits of this research were suggested by the authors in their article. One possible application was in the study of memory. Changes in the brain due to experience might lead to a better understanding of how memories are stored in the brain. This could, in turn, lead to new techniques for improving memory and preventing memory loss due to aging. Another area in which this research might prove helpful was in explaining the relationship between malnutrition and intelligence. The concept proposed by the authors in this regard was that malnutrition may make a person unresponsive to the stimulation available in the environment and consequently may limit brain development. And, the authors noted, some concurrent research suggested that the effects of malnutrition on brain growth may be either reduced by environmental enrichment or enhanced by deprivation.

RELATED RESEARCH AND RECENT APPLICATIONS

This work by Rosenzweig, Bennett, and Diamond served as a catalyst for continued research in this area. Over the more than 25 years since the publication of their article, these scientists and many others have continued to confirm, refine, and expand their findings.

For example, it has been found that learning itself is enhanced by enriched environmental experiences and that even the brains of adult animals raised in impoverished conditions can improve when placed in an enriched environment (see Bennett, 1976, for a complete review).

Some evidence exists to indicate that experience does indeed alter brain development in humans. Through careful autopsies of humans who have died naturally, it appears that as a person develops a greater number of skills and abilities, the brain actually becomes more complex and heavier. Other findings come from examinations during autopsies of the brains of people who were unable to have certain experiences. For example, in a blind person's brain, the portion of the cortex used for vision is significantly less developed, less convoluted, and thinner than in the brain of a person with normal sight.

Marian Diamond, one of the authors of the original article, has applied the results of work in this area to the process of human intellectual development throughout life. She says, "For people's lives, I think we can take a more optimistic view of the aging brain. . . . The main factor is stimulation. The nerve cells are designed for stimulation. And I think curiosity is a key factor. If one maintains curiosity for a lifetime, that will surely stimulate neural tissue and the cortex may in turn respond. . . . I looked for people who were extremely active after 88 years of age. I found that the people who use their brains don't lose them. It was that simple" (Hopson, 1984, p. 70).

Finally, two recent studies have elaborated on Rosenzweig, Diamond, and Bennett's notions of environmental influences on brain development in very diverse applications, and on two very diverse species. Addressing the issue discussed earlier relating to the problem of applying research on rats to other animals, one study examined the effects of early enrichment on an animal clearly more complex and more intelligent than rats: pigs (Sneddon et al., 2002). In this study, 84 piglets were raised in either impoverished or enriched environments from birth to 14 weeks old. In this case, rather than toys, the enriched pig environment contained extra space with peat and straw for play and comfort. At 15 to 17 weeks of age, the pigs from both groups were tested on an operant learning task in which they learned to push on a panel to receive a food reward, and a maze-learning test (see the reading on B. F. Skinner in the learning and conditioning chapter in this book for more about operant conditioning). As you might predict from Rosenzweig's research, the "pigs from enriched environments learned both the operant task and the maze task more rapidly than their counterparts from barren environments" (Sneddon et al, p. 373). Although the cognitive development of pigs may not be terribly important to humans, this study allows us to apply Rosenzweig's rat study to other animals, including humans, with greater confidence that such a generalization may, indeed, be valid.

Another recent study cites Rosenzweig's 1972 study in critiquing some recent attempts to oversimplify enrichment strategies for enhancing children's brain development (Jones & Zigler, 2002). As you can imagine, when the public learns about research such as Rosenzweig's, a popular movement may be born that sounds attractive, but has little basis in scientific fact. One of these from the 1990s, which you may have heard about, has become known as the "Mozart Effect." This fad began with some preliminary research showing that when children listen to Mozart (but not other classical composers) they become better learners. This idea has grown to the point that entire Web sites are devoted to the benefits of the "Mozart Effect" for children and adults alike, involving claims that certain music can enhance overall health, improve memory, treat attention deficit disorder, reduce depression, and speed healing from physical injuries. Jones and Zigler (2002) maintain that such popular applications of the research are ineffective and even dangerous. They contend, "brain research is being misappropriated to the service of misguided 'quick fix' solutions to more complicated, systemic issues" (p. 355). They further suggest that when scientific brain and learning research is applied carefully and correctly, it can make a "substantive contribution of high quality, intensive, multidomain interventions to early cognitive and social development" (p. 355).

Bennett, E. L. (1976). Cerebral effects of differential experience and training. In M. R. Rosenzweig & E. L. Bennett (Eds.), *Neural mechanisms of learning and memory.* Cambridge, MA: MIT Press.

Hopson, J. (1984). A love affair with the brain: A PT conversation with Marian Diamond. *Psychology Today, 11,* 62–75.

Jones, S. & Zigler, E. (2002). The Mozart Effect: Not learning from history. *Journal of Applied Developmental Psychology, 23,* 355–372.

Sneddon, I., Beattie, V., Dunne, L. & Neil, W. (2002). The effect of environmental enrichment in pigs. *Animal Welfare, 9,* 373–383.

ARE YOU A "NATURAL"?

Bouchard, T., Lykken, D., McGue, M., Segal, N., & Tellegen, A. (1990). Sources of human psychological differences: The Minnesota study of twins reared apart. *Science, 250,* 223–229.

This study represents a relatively recent and ongoing fundamental change in the way many psychologists view human behavior in its broadest sense. You can relate to this change in a personal way by first taking a moment to answer in your mind the following question: "Who are you?" Think for a moment about some of your individual characteristics: your "personality traits." Are you high strung or "laid back"? Are you shy or outgoing? Are you adventurous or do you seek out comfort and safety? Are you easy to get along with or do you tend toward the disagreeable? Are you usually optimistic or more pessimistic about the outcome of future events? Think about yourself in terms of these or any other questions you feel are relevant. Take your time. . . . Finished? Now, answer this next, and, for this reading, more important question: "*Why* are you who you are?" In other words, what factors contributed to "creating" this person you are today?

If you are like most people, you will point to the child-rearing practices of your parents and the values, goals, and priorities they instilled in you. You might also credit the influences of brothers, sisters, grandparents, aunts, uncles, and peers, teachers, and other mentors who played key roles in molding you. Still others of you will focus on key life-changing events such as an illness, the loss of a loved one, or the decision to attend a specific college, choose a major, or take a particular life course that seemed to lead you toward becoming your current self. All of these influences share one characteristic: they are all *environmental* phenomena. Hardly anyone ever replies to the question "Why are you who you are?" with, "I was born to be who I am; it's all in my genes."

Everyone acknowledges that physical attributes, such as height, hair color, eye color, and body type are genetic. More and more people are realizing that tendencies toward many illnesses such as cancer, heart disease, and high blood pressure have significant genetic components. But almost no one thinks of genes as the main force behind who they are *psychologically*. This may strike you as odd when you stop to think about it, but in reality there are very understandable reasons for our "environmental bias."

First of all, psychology during the second half of the twentieth century was dominated by a theory of human nature called *behaviorism*. Basically, the theory of behaviorism states that all human behavior is controlled by environmental factors, including the stimuli that provoke behaviors and the consequences that follow response choices. Strict behaviorists believed that the internal psychological workings of the human mind were not only impossible to study scientifically, but also that such study was unnecessary and irrelevant to a complete explanation for human behavior. Whether the wider culture accepted or even understood formal theories of behaviorism is not as important as the reality of their influence on today's firmly entrenched popular belief that *experience* is the primary or exclusive architect of human nature.

Another understandable reason for the pervasive acceptance of environmental explanations of behavior is that genetic and biological factors do not provide visible evidence of their influence. It's easy for someone to say, "I became a writer because I was deeply inspired and encouraged by my seventh grade composition teacher." You remember those sorts of influences; you see them; they are part of your past and present conscious experiences. You would find it much more difficult to recognize biological influences and say, "I became a writer because my DNA contains a gene that has been expressed in me that predisposes me to write well." You can't see, touch, or remember the influence of your genes, and you don't even know where in our body they might be located!

Finally, many people are uncomfortable with the idea that they might be the product of their genes rather than the choices they have made in their lives. Such ideas smack of determinism and a lack of "free will." Most people have a strong dislike for any theory that might in some way limit their conscious ability to determine the outcomes in their lives. Consequently, genetic causes of behavior and personality tend to be avoided or rejected. In reality, genetic influences interact with experience to mold a complete human, and the only question is, which is more dominant? Or to phrase the question as it frequently appears in the media: "*Is it nature or nurture?*"

This article by Thomas Bouchard, David Lykken, and their associates at the University of Minnesota in Minneapolis, is a review of research began in 1979 to examine the question of how much influence your genes have in determining your personal psychological qualities. This research grew out of a need for a scientific method to separate genetic influences (nature) from environmental forces (nurture) on people's behavior and personality. This is no simple task when you consider that nearly every one of you, assuming you were not adopted, grew and developed under the direct environmental influence of your genetic donors (your parents). You might, for example, have the same sense of humor as your father (no offense!) because you learned it from him (nurture) or because you inherited his "sense-of-humor" gene (nature). It appears that there is no systematic way to tease those two influences apart, right?

Well, Bouchard and Lykken would say "wrong." They have found a way to determine with a reasonable degree of confidence which psychological characteristics appear to be determined primarily by genetic factors and which are molded more by your environment.

THEORETICAL PROPOSITIONS

It's simple really. All you have to do is take two humans who have exactly the same genes, separate them at birth, and raise them in significantly different environments. Then, you can assume that those behavioral and personality characteristics they have in common as adults must be genetic. But how on earth can researchers possibly find pairs of *identical people* (don't say "cloning"; we're not there yet!)? And even if they could, it would be unethical to force them into diverse environments, wouldn't it? Well, as you've already guessed, the researchers didn't have to do that. Society had already done it for them. Identical twins have virtually the same genetic structure. They are called *monozygotic twins* because they start as one fertilized egg, called a *zygote*, and then split into two identical embryos. Fraternal twins are the result of two separate eggs fertilized by two separate sperm cells and are referred to as *dizygotic twins*. Fraternal twins are only as genetically similar as any two non-twin siblings. As unfortunate as it sounds, twin infants are sometimes given up for adoption and placed in separate homes. Adoption agencies will try to keep siblings, especially twins, together, but the more important goal is to find good homes for them even if it means separation. So, over time, thousands of identical and fraternal twins have been adopted into separate homes and raised, frequently without the knowledge that they were a twin, in different and often contrasting environmental settings.

Bouchard and Lykken began in 1983 to identify, locate, and bring together pairs of these twins. This 1990 article reports on results from 56 pairs of monozygotic reared-apart (MZA) twins from the United States and seven other countries who agreed to participate in weeklong sessions of intensive psychological and physiological tests and measurements (that this research is located in Minneapolis, one half of "the Twin Cities" is an irony that has not, by any means, gone unnoticed). These twins were compared with monozygotic twins reared together (MZT). The surprising findings continue to reverberate throughout the biological and behavioral sciences.

METHOD

Participants

The first challenge for this project was to *find* sets of monozygotic twins who were separated early in life, reared apart for all of most of their lives, and reunited as adults. Most of the participants were found through word-of-mouth as news of the study began to spread. The twins themselves or their friends or family members would contact the research institute, the Minnesota Center for Twin and Adoption Research (MICTAR), various social-services professionals in the adoption arena would serve as contacts, or, in some cases one member of a twin-pair would contact the center for assistance in locating and reuniting with his or her sibling. All twins were tested to assure that they were indeed monozygotic before beginning their participation in the study.

Procedure

The researchers wanted to be sure they obtained as much data as possible during the twins' one-week visit. Each twin completed approximately 50 hours of testing on nearly every human dimension you might imagine. They completed four personality trait scales, three aptitude and occupational interest inventories, and two intelligence tests. In addition the participants filled in checklists of household belongings (such as power tools, telescope, original artwork, unabridged dictionary) to assess the similarity of their family resources, and a family environment scale that measured how they felt about the parenting they received from their adoptive parents. They were also administered a life history interview, a psychiatric interview, and a sexual history interview. All of these assessments were carried out individually so that there was no possibility that one twin might inadvertently influence the answers and responses of the other.

As you might imagine, the hours of testing created a huge database of information. The most important and surprising results are discussed here.

RESULTS

Table 1 summarizes the similarities for some of the characteristics measured in the monozygotic twins reared apart (MZA) and includes the same data for monozygotic twins reared together (MZT). The degree of similarity is expressed in the table as correlations or "R" values. The larger the correlation, the greater the similarity. The logic here is that if environment is responsible for individual differences, the MZT twins who shared the same environment as they grew up *should* be significantly more similar than the MZA twins. As you can see, this is not what the researchers found.

The last column in Table 1 expresses the difference in similarity by dividing the MZA correlation on each characteristic by the MZT correlation. If both correlations were the same, the result would be 1.00; if they were entirely dissimilar, the result could be as slow as 0.00. Examining column 4 in the table carefully, you'll find that the correlations for characteristics were remarkably similar, that is, close to 1.00, and no lower than .700 for MZA and MZT twin pairs.

DISCUSSION AND IMPLICATIONS OF FINDINGS

These findings indicate that genetic factors (or "the genome") appear to account for most of the variation in a remarkable variety of human characteristics. This finding was demonstrated by the data in two important ways. One is that genetically identical humans (monozygotic twins), who were raised in separate and often very different settings, grew into adults who were extraordinarily similar, not only in appearance but also in basic psychology and per-

TABLE 1   Comparison of Correlations (*r*) of Selected Characteristics for Identical Twins Reared Apart (MZA) and Identical Twins Reared Together (MZT)*

CHARACTERISTIC	r (MZA)	r (MZT)	SIMILARITY r (MZA) ÷ r (MZT)**
Physiological	—	—	—
Brain wave activity	.80	.81	.987
Blood pressure	.64	.70	.914
Heart rate	.49	.54	.907
Intelligence	—	—	—
WAIS IQ	.69	.88	.784
Raven intelligence test	.78	.76	1.03
Personality	—	—	—
Multidimensional personality questionnaire (MPQ)	.50	.49	1.02
California personality inventory	.48	.49	.979
Psychological interests	—	—	—
Strong Campbell interest inventory	.39	.48	.813
Minnesota occupational interest scale	.40	.49	.816
Social attitudes	—	—	—
Religiosity	.49	.51	.961
Nonreligious social attitudes	.34	.28	1.21

*Adapted from Table 4, p. 226.
**1.00 would imply that MZA twin pairs were found to be exactly as similar as MZT twin pairs.

sonality. The second demonstration in this study of the dominance of genes is the fact that there appeared to be so *little* effect of the environment on identical twins who *were* raised in the same setting. Here's Bouchard and Lykken's take on these discoveries:

> For almost every behavioral trait so far investigated, from reaction time to religiosity, an important fraction of the variation among people turns out to be associated with genetic variation. This fact need no longer be subject to debate; rather, it is time to consider its implications.

There are, of course, those who will argue with Bouchard and Lykken's notion that the time to debate these issues is over. Some varying views are discussed in the next section. However, a discussion of the implications of this and other similar studies by these same researchers is clearly warranted. In what ways do the genetic findings reported in this study change psychologists' and, for that matter, all of our views of human nature? As mentioned earlier, psychology and Western culture have been dominated for over 50 years by environmental thinking. Many of our basic beliefs about parenting, education, crime and punishment, psychotherapy, skills and abilities, interests, occupational goals, and social behavior, just to name a few, have been interpreted from the perspective that people's experience molds their personalities, not their genes. Very few of us look at someone's behavior and think, "That person was *born* to behave like that!" We *want* to believe that people *learned* their behavior patterns because that allows us to feel some measure of confidence that parenting makes a difference, that positive life experiences can win out over negative ones, and unhealthy, ineffective behaviors can be *unlearned*. The notion that personality is a done deal the moment we are born leaves us with the temptation to say, "Why bother?" Why bother working hard to be good parents? Why bother trying to help those who are down and out? Why bother trying to offer quality education? And so on. Well, Bouchard and Lykken want to be the first to disagree with such an interpretation of their findings. In this article, they offer three of their own implications of their provocative conclusions:

1. Clearly, intelligence is primarily determined by genetic factors (70% of the variation in intelligence appears to be due to genetic influence). However, as the authors state very clearly,

   > [T]hese findings do not imply that traits like IQ cannot be enhanced. . . . A survey covering 14 countries, has shown that the average IQ test score has increased in recent years. The present findings, therefore, do not define or limit what might be conceivably achieved in an optimal environment. (p. 227)

   Basically, what he is saying is that while 70% of the variation in IQ is due to naturally occurring genetic variation, 30% of the variation remains subject to increases or decreases due to environmental influences. These influences include many that are well known, such as education, family setting, toxic substances, and socioeconomic status.

2. The basic underlying assumption in Bouchard and Lykken's research is that human characteristics are determined by some combination of genetic and environmental influences. So, when the environment exerts less influence, differences must be attributed more to genes. The converse is also true: as environmental forces create a stronger influence on differences in a particular characteristic, genetic influences will be weaker. For example, most children in the United States have the opportunity to learn to ride a bicycle. This implies that the environment's effect on bicycle riding is somewhat similar for all children, so differences in riding ability will be more affected by genetic forces. On the other hand, variation in, say, food preferences in the United States are more likely to be explained by environmental factors because food and taste experiences in childhood and throughout life are very diverse and will, therefore, leave less room for genetic forces to function. Here's the interesting part of the researchers' point: They maintain that personality is more like bicycle riding than food preferences.

   The authors are saying, in essence, that family environments exert *less* influence over who the kids grow up to be than do the genes they inherit from birth. Understandably, most parents do not want to hear or believe this. They are working hard to be good parents and to raise their children to be happy individuals and good citizens. The only parents who might take some comfort from these findings are those who are nearing their wit's end with out-of-control or incorrigible sons or daughters and would appreciate being able to take less of the blame! However, Bouchard and Lykken are quick to point out that genes are not necessarily destiny and devoted parents can still influence their children in positive ways, even if they are only working on a small percentage of the total variation.

3. The most intriguing implication that Bouchard and Lykken suggest is that it's not the environment influencing people's characteristics, but vice versa. That is, people's genetic tendencies actually mold their environments! Here's an example of the idea behind this theory: The fact that some people are more affectionate than others is usually seen as evidence that some parents were more affectionate with their children than were other parents. In other words, affectionate kids come from affectionate environments. When this kind of assumption has been studied, it is usually found to be true. Affectionate people have, indeed, received more affection from their parents. Bouchard and Lykken are proposing, however, that variation in "affectionateness" may be, in reality, genetically determined so that some children are just born more affectionate than others. Their in-born tendency toward affectionate behavior causes them to *respond* to affection from their parents in ways that reinforce the parents' behavior much more than nongenetically affectionate children. This, in turn *produces* the affectionate behavior in the parents, not the other way around. The researchers contend that genes function in this way for many if not most human characteristics. They state it this way:

> The proximal [immediate] cause of most psychological variance probably involves learning through experience, just as radical environmentalists have always believed. The effective experiences, however, to an important extent are self-selected, and that selection is guided by the steady pressure of the genome. (p. 228)

CRITICISMS AND RELATED RESEARCH

As you might imagine, a great deal of related studies have been carried out using the database of twins developed by Bouchard and Lykken. In general, the findings continue to indicate that many human personality characteristics and behaviors are strongly influenced by genes. Many attributes that have been seen as stemming largely or completely from environmental sources are being reevaluated as twin studies reveal that heredity contributes either the majority of the variation or a significantly larger proportion that was previously contemplated.

For example, studies from the University of Minnesota team found that not only is the vocation you choose largely determined by your genes, but also about 30% of the variation in your overall job satisfaction and work ethic appears due to genetic factors (Arvey et al., 1989; Arvey et al., 1994) even when the physical requirements of various professions were held constant. Other studies comparing identical (monozygotic) twins with fraternal (dizygotic) twins, both reared together and reared apart, have focused more directly on specific personality traits that are thought to be influential and stable in humans (Bouchard, 1994; Loehlin, 1992). These and other studies' findings determined that the people's variation on the characteristics of extraversion-introversion (outgoing versus shy), neuroticism (tendency to suffer from high anxiety and extreme emotional reactions), and conscientiousness (degree to which a person is competent, responsible and thorough) is explained more (65%) by genetic differences than by environmental factors.

Of course, not everyone in the scientific community is willing to accept these findings at face value. The criticisms of Bouchard and Lykken's work take several directions (see Billings et al., 1992). Some studies claim that the researchers are not publishing their data as fully and completely as they should, and, therefore, their findings cannot be independently evaluated. These same critics also claim that there are many articles reporting on case studies demonstrating strong environmental influences on twins that Bouchard and Lykken fail to consider.

In addition, some researchers have voiced a major criticism of one aspect of twin research in general, referred to as the "equal environment assumption" (i.e., Joseph, 2002). This argument maintains that many of the conclusions drawn by Bouchard and Lykken about genetic influence assume that MZ and DZ twins raised together develop in identical environments. These critics maintain that such an assumption is not valid and that fraternal twins are treated far more differently than are identical twins. This, they contend, draws the entire method of twin research as a determinate of genetic influences into question. However, several other articles have refuted this criticism and supported the "equal environment assumption" (i.e., Kendler et al., 1993).

Recent Applications

In 1999, Bouchard reviewed the nature-nurture evidence from the Minnesota twin registries (Bouchard, 1999). He concluded that, overall, 40% of the variability in personality and 50% of variation in intelligence appears to be genetically based. He also reiterated his position discussed earlier that your genes drive your selection of environments and your selection or avoidance of specific personality-molding environments and behaviors.

Research at the Minnesota twin centers continues to be very active. Some fascinating research has examined very complex human characteristics and behaviors that few would have even guessed to be genetically driven, such as love, divorce, and even death (see http://www.psych.umn.edu/psylabs/mtfs/special.htm, 2004). They have studied people's selection of a mate to see if "falling in love" with Mr. or Ms. Right is genetically predisposed. It turns out that it is not! However, the researchers have found a genetic link to the likelihood of divorce and to people's age at their time of their death.

Finally, Bouchard and Lykken's research has been applied to the larger philosophical discussion of human cloning (see Agar, 2003). If a human being is ever successfully cloned, the question is, as you are probably thinking, to what extent will a person's essence, an individual's *personality*, be transferred to his or her clone? The fear that human identity might be changed, degraded, or lost has been a common argument of those opposed to cloning. On the other hand, results of twin studies such as those of Bouchard and Lykken suggest that "the cloned person may, under certain circumstances, be seen as surviving, to some degree, in the clone. . . . However . . . rather than warranting concern, the potential for survival by cloning ought to help protect against the misuse of the technology" (Agar, 2003, p. 9). This is much more a philosophical than genetic discussion, but it makes very interesting food for thought.

Agar, N. (2003). Cloning and identity. *Journal of Medicine and Philosophy, 28,* 9–26.

Arvey, R., Bouchard, T., Segal, N., & Abraham, L. (1989). Job satisfaction: Environmental and genetic components. *Journal of Applied Psychology, 74*(2), 187–195.

Arvey, R., McCall, B., Bouchard, T., & Taubman, P. (1994). Genetic influences on job satisfaction and work value. *Personality and Individual Differences, 17*(1), 21–33.

Billings, P., Beckwith, J., & Alper, J. (1992). The genetic analysis of human behavior: A new era? *Social Science and Medicine, 35*(3), 227–238.

Bouchard, T. (1994). Genes, environment and personality. *Science, 264*(5166), 1700–1702.

Bouchard, T. (1999). Genes, environment, and personality. In S. Ceci et al. (Eds.), *The nature-nurture debate: The essential readings,* pp. 97–103. Malden, MA: Blackwell.

Joseph, J. (2002). Twin studies in psychiatry and psychology: Science or pseudoscience? *Psychiatric Quarterly, 73,* 71–82.

Kendler K., Neale M., Kessler R., Heath A., Eaves L. (1993). A test of the equal environment assumption in twin studies of psychiatric illness. *Behavioral Genetics, 23,* 21–27.

Loehlin, J. (1992). *Genes and environment in personality development.* Newbury Park, CA: Sage Publications.

WATCH OUT FOR THE VISUAL CLIFF!
Gibson, E. J., & Walk, R. D. (1960). The "visual cliff." *Scientific American,* 202 (4), 67–71.

One of the most often told anecdotes in psychology concerns a man called S. B. (initials used to protect his privacy). S. B. had been blind his entire life until the age of 52, when a newly developed operation (the now-common corneal transplant) was performed on him and his sight was restored. However, S. B.'s new ability to see did not mean that he automatically perceived what he saw the way the rest of us do. One important example of this became evident soon after the operation, before his vision had cleared completely. S. B. looked out his hospital window and was curious about the small objects he could see moving on the ground below. He began to crawl out on his window ledge, thinking he would lower himself down by his hands and have a look. Fortunately, the hospital staff prevented him from trying this. He was on the fourth floor, and those small moving things were cars! Even though S. B. could now see, he was not able to perceive depth.

Our visual ability to sense and interpret the world around us is an area of interest to experimental psychologists. And within this lies the central question of whether such abilities are inborn or learned: the nature-nurture issue once again. Many psychologists believe that our most important visual skill is depth perception. You can imagine how difficult, and probably impossible, survival would be if you could not perceive depth. You would run into things, be unable to judge how far away a predator was, or step right off cliffs. Therefore, it might be logical to assume that depth perception is an inborn survival mechanism that does not require experience to develop. However, as Eleanor Gibson and Richard Walk point out in their article, "Human infants at the creeping and toddling stage are notoriously prone to falls from more or less high places. They must be kept from going over the brink by side panels on their cribs, gates on stairways, and the vigilance of adults. As their muscular coordination matures, they begin to avoid such accidents on their own. Common sense might suggest that the child learns to recognize falling-off places by experience—that is, by falling and hurting himself" (p. 64).

These researchers wanted to study this visual ability of depth perception scientifically in the laboratory. To do this, they conceived of and developed an experimental device they called the "visual cliff."

THEORETICAL PROPOSITIONS

If you wanted to find out at what point in the developmental process animals or people are able to perceive depth, one way to do this would be to put them on the edge of a cliff and see if they are able to avoid falling off. This is a ridiculous suggestion because of the ethical considerations of the potential injury to subjects who were unable to perceive depth (or more specifically, height). The "visual cliff" avoids this problem because it presents the subject with what appears to be a drop-off, when no drop-off actually exists. Exactly how this is done will be explained in a moment, but the importance of this apparatus lies in the fact that human or animal infants can be placed on the visual cliff to see if they are able to perceive the drop-off and avoid it. If they are unable to do this and step off the "cliff," there is no danger of falling.

Gibson and Walk took a "nativist" position on this topic, which means that they believed that depth perception and the avoidance of a drop-off appear automatically as part of our original biological equipment and are not, therefore, products of experience. The opposing view, held by empiricists, contends that such abilities are learned. Gibson and Walk's visual cliff allowed them to ask these questions: At what stage in development can a person or animal respond effectively to the stimuli of depth and height? And do these responses appear at different times with animals of different species and habitats?

METHOD

The visual cliff consisted of a table about four feet high with a top made from a piece of thick, clear glass (Figures 1 and 2). Directly under half of the table (the shallow side) is a solid surface with a red-and-white checkered pattern. Under the other half is the same pattern, but it is down at the level of the floor underneath the table (the deep side). At the edge of the shallow side, then, is the appearance of a sudden drop-off to the floor although, in reality, the glass extends all the way across. Between the shallow and the deep side is a center board about a foot wide. The process of testing infants using this device was extremely simple.

The subjects for this study were 36 infants between the ages of 6 months and 14 months. The mothers of the infants also participated. Each infant was placed on the center board of the visual cliff and was then called by the mother first from the deep side and then from the shallow side.

In order to compare the development of depth perception in humans with that in other baby animals, the visual cliff allowed for similar tests with other species (without a mother's beckoning, however). These animals were placed on the center board and observed to see if they could discriminate between the shallow and deep sides and avoid stepping off "the cliff." You can imagine the rather unique situation in the psychology labs at Cornell Univer-

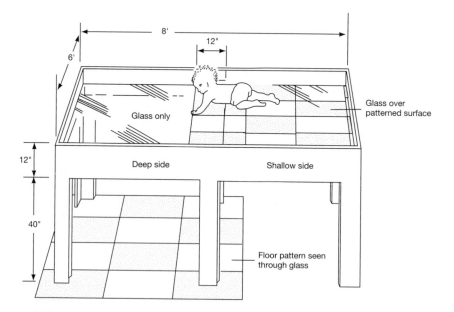

FIGURE 1   Gibson and Walk's visual cliff. From *Introduction to Child Development,* (5th ed.) by J. Dworetzky © 1993. Reprinted with permission of Wadsworth, an imprint of the Wadsworth Group, a division of Thomson Learning. Fax (800) 730–2215.

FIGURE 2　The visual cliff in testing situation. (From Mark Richards/Photo Edit/Courtesy of Joe Campos & Rosanne Kermoian.)

sity when the various baby animals were brought in for testing. They included chicks, turtles, rats, lambs, kids (baby goats, that is), pigs, kittens, and puppies. One has to wonder if they were all tested on the same day!

Remember, the goal of this research was to examine whether depth perception is learned or innate. What makes this method so ingenious is that it allowed that question to at least begin to be answered. After all, infants, whether human or animal, cannot be asked if they perceive depth, and, as mentioned earlier, they cannot be tested on real cliffs. In psychology, many answers are found through the development of new methods for studying the questions. And the results of Gibson and Walk's early study provide an excellent example of this.

RESULTS AND DISCUSSION

Nine children in the study refused to move off the center board. This was not explained by the researchers, but perhaps it was just infant stubbornness. When the mothers of the other 27 called to them from the shallow side, all the infants crawled off the board and crossed the glass. Only three of them, however, crept, with great hesitation, off the brink of the visual cliff when called by their mothers from the deep side. When called from the cliff side, most of the children either crawled away from the mother on the shallow side or cried in frustration at being unable to reach the mother without moving over the cliff. There was little question that the children were perceiving the depth of the cliff. "Often they would peer down through the glass of the deep side and then back away. Others would pat the glass with their hands, yet despite this tactile assurance of solidity would refuse to cross" (p. 64).

Do these results prove that humans' ability to perceive depth is innate rather than learned? Well, obviously it does not, since all the children in this study had at least six months of life experience in which to learn about depth through trial and error. However, human infants cannot be tested prior to six months of age because they do not have adequate locomotor abilities. It was for this reason that Gibson and Walk decided to test various other animals as a comparison. As you know, most nonhuman animals gain the ability to move about much sooner than humans. The results of the animal tests were extremely interesting, in that the ability of the various animals to perceive depth developed in relation to when the species needed such a skill for survival.

For example, baby chickens must begin to scratch for their own food soon after hatching. When they were tested on the visual cliff at less than 24 hours of age they never made the mistake of stepping off onto the deep side.

Kids and lambs are able to stand and walk very soon after birth. From the moment they first stood up, their response on the visual cliff was as accurate and predictable as that of the chicks. Not one error was made. When one of the researchers placed a one-day-old baby goat down on the deep side of the glass, it became frightened and froze in a defensive posture. If it was then pushed over the shallow side, it would relax and jump forward onto the seemingly solid surface. This indicated that the visual sense was in complete control and that the animals' ability to feel the solidity of the glass on the deep side had no effect on the response.

For the rats, it was a different story. They did not appear to show any significant preference for the shallow side of the table. Why do you suppose this difference was found? Before you conclude that rats are just stupid, consider Gibson and Walk's much more likely explanation: A rat does not depend very much on vision to survive. Because it is nocturnal, a rat locates food by smell and moves around in the dark using cues from the stiff whiskers on its nose. So when a rat was placed on the center board, it was not fooled by the visual cliff because it was not using vision to decide which way to go. To the rat's whiskers, the glass on the deep side felt the same as the glass on the shallow side and, thus, the rat was just as likely to move off the center board to the deep side as to the shallow side.

You might expect the same results from kittens. They are basically nocturnal and have sensitive whiskers. However, cats are predators, not scavengers like rats. Therefore, they depend more on vision. And, accordingly, kittens were found to have excellent depth perception as soon as they were able to move on their own: at about four weeks.

Although at times this research article (and this discussion) risks sounding like a children's animal story, it has to be reported that the species with the worst performance on the visual cliff was the turtle. The baby turtles chosen to be tested were of the aquatic variety, because the researchers expected that since the turtles' natural environment was water, they might prefer the deep side of the cliff. However, it appeared that the turtles were "smart" enough to know that they were not in water, and 76% of them crawled off onto the shallow side. But 24% went "over the edge." "The relatively large minority that chose the deep side suggests either that this turtle has poorer depth perception than other animals, or its natural habitat gives it less occasion to 'fear' a fall" (p. 67). Clearly, if you live your life in water, the survival value of depth perception, in terms of avoiding falls, would be diminished.

Gibson and Walk pointed out that all of their observations were consistent with evolutionary theory. That is, all species of animals, if they are to survive, need to develop the ability to perceive depth by the time they achieve independent movement. For humans, this does not occur until around six months of age; but for chickens and goats, it is nearly immediate (by one day); and for rats, cats, and dogs, about four weeks of age. The authors conclude, therefore, that this capacity is inborn, because to learn it through trial and error would cause too many potentially fatal accidents.

So, if we are so well prepared biologically, why do children take so many falls? Gibson and Walk explained that the human infants' perception of depth had matured sooner than had their skill in movement. During testing, many of the infants supported themselves on the deep side of the glass as they turned on the center board, and some even backed up onto the deep side as they began to crawl toward the mother across the shallow side. If the glass had not been there, some of the children would have fallen off the cliff!

CRITICISMS AND SUBSEQUENT RESEARCH

The most common criticism of the researchers' conclusions revolves around the question of whether they really proved that depth perception is innate in humans. As mentioned earlier, by the time infants were tested on the visual cliff, they had already learned to avoid such situations. A later study placed younger infants, ages two to five months, on the glass over the deep side of the visual cliff. When this happened, all of the babies showed a decrease in heart rate. Such a decrease is thought to be a sign of interest, not fear, which is accompanied by heart rate increases (Campos et al., 1978). This indicates that these younger infants had not yet learned to fear the drop-off and would learn the avoidance behavior somewhat later. These findings argued against Gibson and Walk's position.

It is important to notice, however, that while there was and still is controversy over just when we are able to perceive depth (the nativists vs. the empiricists), much of the research that is done to find the answer incorporates the visual cliff apparatus developed by Gibson and Walk. Additionally, other related research using the visual cliff has turned up some fascinating findings.

One example is the work of Sorce et al. (1985). They put one-year-old infants on a visual cliff for which the drop-off was neither shallow nor deep but in between (about 30 inches). As a baby crawled toward the cliff, it would stop and look down. On the other side, as in the Gibson and Walk study, the mother was waiting. Sometimes the mother had been instructed to maintain an expression of fear on her face while other times the mother looked happy and interested. When infants saw the expression of fear, they refused to crawl any farther. However, most of the infants who saw their mother looking happy checked the cliff again and crawled across. When the drop-off was made flat, the infants did not check with the mother before crawling across. This method of nonverbal communication used by infants in determining their behavior is called *social referencing*.

RECENT APPLICATIONS

Gibson and Walk's ground-breaking invention of the visual cliff still exerts a major influence on current studies of human development, perception, emotion, and even mental health. Here is a brief sample.

A recent study by Berger and Adolph cited Gibson and Walk's early study in their research on how toddlers analyze the characteristics of tasks involving heights, specifically crossing over a bridge (Berger & Adolph, 2003). The researchers coaxed very young toddlers (16 months) to cross bridges of various widths. Some of the bridges had handrails while others did not. They found that the babies were significantly more likely to cross wider bridges than narrower ones (pretty smart for 16 months!). More interesting, however, was the finding that they were more likely to attempt the narrow bridge if it had handrails. "Infants who explored the bridge and handrail before stepping onto the bridge and devised alternative bridge-crossing strategies were more likely to cross successfully. [These] results challenge traditional conceptualizations of tools: babies used the handrail as a means for augmenting balance and for carrying out an otherwise impossible goal-directed task" (p. 594).

Another practical application of the visual cliff study looked at the possibilities for using virtual reality to help developmentally disabled children learn to deal safely with the physical environment around them. Strickland (1996) developed a system that incorporates virtual reality to help autistic children safely explore and interact with the world around them. Often these children pose a danger to themselves because their perceptions are either distorted or not fully developed. So, for example, an autistic child might not perceive drop-offs such as those represented by the visual cliff and, therefore, be prone to dangerous falls. According to Strickland, however, virtual reality allows us to design custom programs so each individual child may gain valuable motor experience without danger of physical injury.

CONCLUSION

Through the inventiveness of Gibson and Walk, behavioral scientists have been able to study depth perception in a clear and systematic way. Behavioral scientists continue to debate the question of whether this and other perceptual abilities are innate or learned. The truth may lie in a compromise that proposes an interaction between nature and nurture. Perhaps, as various studies have indicated, depth perception is present at birth, but fear of falling and avoidance of danger is learned through experience, after the infant is old enough to crawl around enough to "get into trouble."

But whatever the questions are, elegant methodological advances such as the visual cliff allow us to continue to find the answers.

Berger, S., & Adolph, K. (2003). Infants use handrails as tools in a locomotor task. *Developmental Psychology, 39,* 594–605.

Campos, J., Hiatt, S., Ramsay, D., Henderson, C., & Svejda, M. (1978). The emergence of fear on the visual cliff. In M. Lewis & L. A. Rosenblum (Eds.), *The development of affect.* New York: Plenum Press.

Sorce, J., Emde, R., Campos, J., & Klinnert, M. (1985). Maternal emotion signaling: Its effect on the visual cliff behavior of 1-year-olds. *Developmental Psychology, 21,* 195–200.

Strickland, D. (1996). A virtual-reality application with autistic children. *Presence Teleoperators and Virtual Environments, 5*(3), 319–329.

2 PERCEPTION AND CONSCIOUSNESS

The study of perception and consciousness is of great interest to psychologists because these activities define and reveal your psychological interaction with your environment. Think for a moment about how your senses are bombarded constantly by millions of pieces of information from the combined stimuli that surround you at any given moment. It is impossible for your brain to process all of it. So, your brain organizes this barrage of sensory data into units that yield form and meaning. That's what psychologists refer to as *perception.*

Clearly, your level of *consciousness,* also commonly referred to as your *state of awareness,* governs to a large extent what you perceive and how your brain organizes it. As you go through your day, your night, your week, your year, and your life, you experience many and varied states of awareness: You concentrate (or not), you daydream, you fantasize, you sleep, you dream, maybe you've been hypnotized at some point, maybe you've used psychoactive drugs (even caffeine and nicotine count!). These conditions are all altered states of consciousness that produce various changes in your perceptions of the world and that, in turn, influence your behavior.

Within the research areas of perception and consciousness, some of the most influential and interesting studies have focused on vision, sleep, dreams, and hypnosis. This section begins with a famous and influential study that takes us to a faraway culture to reveal how our perceptions of the world around us are shaped by a lifetime of specific sensory input. The article was published in a psychology journal, but written by an anthropologist, who discovered an amazing phenomenon in his research in the Ituri Forest in what is now the nation of Congo, about how our brains learn to see and interpret the world around us. The second reading in this section contains two articles that changed psychology because they (1) discovered REM (rapid eye movement) sleep and (2) revealed the relationship between REM and dreaming. Third is an influential and controversial study proposing that dreams are not mysterious messages from your unconscious, as Freud and others would have it, but that they consist of purely physical and random electrical impulses in your brain while you sleep. And fourth is one of many studies that has influenced traditional psychological thinking by arguing *against* the widespread belief that hypnosis is a unique and powerful state of consciousness. This last study offers evidence suggesting that hypnotized people are no different from awake people; they are just a bit more motivated.

WHAT YOU SEE IS WHAT YOU'VE LEARNED

Turnbull, C. M. (1961). Some observations regarding the experiences and behavior of the BaMbuti Pygmies. *American Journal of Psychology, 74,* 304–308.

This study is a somewhat unusual one to appear in this book. Colin Turnbull (1924–1994) did not have any specific theoretical propositions, there was no clear scientific method used, and the author is not a psychologist. Nevertheless, this short article has been frequently and widely cited to demonstrate some important psychological concepts relating to your ability to perceive the world around you. Before reaching the point where Turnbull's observations can be placed in the proper context, a considerable amount of conceptual explanation is necessary. Keep in mind that we will get to the study itself, even though we may seem to be taking the long way around. Let's begin by filling in the theory behind Turnbull's discoveries, which the brevity of his article did not allow him to do.

THEORETICAL PROPOSITIONS

Two large and important fields of study within psychology are those of sensation and perception. These are fundamentally separate areas, but they are highly related. Sensation refers to the information you are constantly receiving from your environment through your senses. You are bombarded with a huge amount of sensory data every minute of every day. If you just stop and think about it for a minute, frequencies of light are reflecting off all the objects around you wherever you look, near or far. There are probably a multitude of sounds entering your ears at any moment, parts of your body are in contact with various objects, and several tastes and smells are often present. If you take your attention off this book for a moment (I know this is difficult!) and focus on each sense, one at a time, you'll begin to get some idea of the amount of "sensory input" that was beneath your level of awareness. In fact, if I do this right now I become aware of the hum from my computer, a car going by outside, a door slamming somewhere, a painting on the wall, a partly cloudy sky, the light from my desk lamp, the feel of my elbows resting on the arms of the chair, the taste of the apple I just finished eating, and so on. However, just a few seconds ago, I was not aware of any of these sensations. We are continuously filtering all this available input and using only a small percentage of it. If your sensory filtering mechanisms were suddenly to fail, the world would become so intensely confusing that you would be overwhelmed, and probably you would not be able to survive it.

The fact that the sensory world (what you see, hear, touch, taste, and smell) usually appears to you in an organized way is due to your abilities of perception. Sensations are the raw materials for perception. Your brain's perceptual processes are involved in three general activities: (1) selecting the sensations to pay attention to as discussed in the previous paragraph; (2) organizing these into recognizable patterns and shapes; and (3) interpreting this organization to explain and make judgments about the world. In other words, perception refers to how we take this jumble of sensations and create meaning. Your visual sensations of the page you are reading are nothing more than random black shapes on a white background. This is what is projected onto the retinas of your eyes and sent to the visual fields of your brain. However, you pay attention to them, organize them, and interpret them so that they become words and sentences that contain meaning.

Your brain has many tricks or strategies available to assist in organizing sensations in meaningful and understandable ways. To put Turnbull's study in proper perspective, let's take a look at several of these. The perceptual strategy you probably use the most is called *figure-ground*. A well-known example of the figure-ground relationship is pictured in Figure 1. When you look at the drawing, what do you see immediately? Some of you will see a white vase, while others will see two profiles facing one another. As you study this drawing, you will be able to see either one, and you will be able to switch back and forth between seeing the vase and seeing the profiles. You'll notice that if you look at the vase (figure), the profiles (ground) seem to fade into the background. But focus on the profiles (figure) and the vase (ground) becomes the background. We appear to have a natural tendency to divide sensations into figure and ground relationships. If you think about it, this makes the world a much more organized place. Imagine trying to spot someone in a crowd of people. Without your figure-ground abilities, this task would be impossible. When soldiers wear camouflaged clothing, the distinction between figure and ground is blurred so that it becomes difficult to distinguish the figure (the soldier) from the ground (the vegetation).

Other organizational strategies we use routinely to create order and meaning out of those chaotic sensations are called *perceptual constancies*. These

FIGURE 1 Figure-ground relationship—a reversible figure. From Charles G. Morris, *Understanding Psychology,* 7th ed., p. 101. Copyright 1990. Reprinted by permission of Prentice Hall.

refer to our ability to know that the characteristics of objects stay the same even though our sensations of them may change drastically. One of these, for example, is shape constancy. If you stand up and walk around a chair, the image of that chair projecting onto your retina (the sensation) changes with every step you take. However, you perceive the shape of the chair to be unchanged. Imagine how impossibly confusing your world would be if all objects were perceived differently each time your angle of vision changed.

Another one of these techniques is size constancy. This is the perceptual facility that is most related to Turnbull's article. Size constancy enables you to perceive a familiar object as being the same size, regardless of its distance from you. If you see a school bus two blocks away, the image projected onto your retina is the same as that of a small toy bus seen close up. Nevertheless, you perceive the distant bus to be its large, normal size. Likewise, if you are looking at two people standing in a field, one 10 feet from you and the other 100 feet in the distance, your sensation of the more distant person is of someone three feet tall. The reason you perceive that person to be of normal size is due to your ability of size constancy.

Your perceptions using any of these strategies can be tricked. This is how visual (optical) illusions work. A film director can shoot a scene in which a ship is being tossed about in a terrible storm. Even though the camera is filming a two-foot-long model ship in a special effects tank, we perceive the ship as full size because of size constancy and the lack of any comparison objects to offer cues as to its true size. In the 1980 film spoof *Airplane,* we see a room shot from a low angle directly behind a telephone on a desk (therefore, we know this phone is about to ring with important information). The phone is so close to the camera lens that it appears huge on the screen, but we see it as a normal-size phone due to our ability of size constancy. The perceptual surprise comes when the phone rings and the actor crosses the room to answer. The phone he picks up turns out to really be as huge as it looked: about three feet across!

The last important point that must be made before turning to this chapter's study concerns whether these perceptual abilities are learned or inborn. Research with individuals who were blind at birth and who later gain their sight has suggested that our ability to perceive figure-ground relationships is, at least in part, innate, that is, present from birth. Perceptual constancies, on the other hand, are a product of experience. When young children (age five and under) see cars or trains in the distance, they perceive them as toys and sometimes will ask quite adamantly to have one. By the time children reach age seven or eight, size constancy has developed, and they are able to judge sizes correctly over varying distances.

Psychologists have asked the question: What kinds of experiences allow us to acquire these abilities? And could a situation exist in which a person might grow to adulthood and not possess some of these perceptual talents? Well, Turnbull's brief report published 30 years ago shed a great deal of light on these questions.

METHOD

As mentioned at the beginning of this chapter, Turnbull is not a psychologist, but rather an anthropologist. In the late 1950s and early 1960s, he was in the dense Ituri Forest in Zaire (now Congo) studying the life and culture of the BaMbuti Pygmies. Because he was an anthropologist, Turnbull's primary method of research was naturalistic observation, that is, observing behavior as it occurs in its natural setting. This is an important method of research for psychologists as well. For example, differences in aggressive behavior between young boys and girls during play could be studied through observational techniques. Examining the social behavior of nonhuman primates, such as chimpanzees, would also require a method involving naturalistic observation. Such research is often expensive and time consuming, yet some behavioral phenomena cannot be properly researched in any other way.

Turnbull, on one excursion, was traveling through the forest from one group of Pygmies to another. He was accompanied by a young man (about 22 years old) named Kenge, who was from one of the local Pygmy villages. Kenge always assisted Turnbull in his research as a guide and introduced Turnbull to groups of BaMbuti who did not know him. Turnbull's observations that constitute this published report began when he and Kenge reached the eastern edge of a hill that had been cleared of trees for a missionary station. Because of this clearing, there was a distant view over the forest to the high Ruwenzori Mountains. Since the Ituri Forest is extremely thick, it was highly unusual to see views such as this.

RESULTS

Kenge had never in his life seen a view over great distances. He pointed to the mountains and asked if they were hills or clouds. Turnbull told him that they were hills, but they were larger than any Kenge had seen before in his forest. Turnbull asked Kenge if he would like to take a drive over to the mountains and see them more closely. After some hesitation—Kenge had never left the forest before—he agreed. As they began driving, a violent thunderstorm began and did not clear until they had reached their destination. This reduced visibility to about 100 yards, which prevented Kenge from watching the approaching mountains. Finally, they reached the Ishango National Park, which is on the edge of Lake Edward at the foot of the mountains. Turnbull writes:

> As we drove through the park the rain stopped and the sky cleared, and that rare moment came when the Ruwenzori Mountains were completely free of cloud and stood up in the late afternoon sky, their snow-capped peaks shining in the afternoon sun. I stopped the car and Kenge very unwillingly got out. (p. 304)

Kenge glanced around and declared that this was bad country because there were no trees. Then he looked up at the mountains and was literally speechless. The life and culture of the BaMbuti were limited to the dense jungle and, therefore, their language did not contain words to describe such a sight.

Kenge was fascinated by the distant snow caps and interpreted them to be a type of rock formation. As they prepared to leave, the plain stretching out in front of them also came clearly into view. The next observation makes up the central point of this article and this chapter.

Looking out across the plain, Kenge saw a herd of buffalo grazing several miles away. Remember that at such a distance, the image (the sensation) of the buffalo cast onto the retinas of Kenge's eyes was very small. Kenge turned to Turnbull and asked what kind of insect they were! Turnbull replied that they were buffalo even bigger than the forest buffalo Kenge had seen before. Kenge just laughed at what he considered to be a stupid story and asked again what those insects were. "Then he talked to himself, for want of more intelligent company, and tried to liken the distant buffalo to the various beetles and ants with which he was familiar" (p. 305).

Turnbull did precisely what you or I would do in the same situation. He got back into the car and drove with Kenge to the grazing buffalo. Kenge was a very courageous young man, but as he watched the animals steadily increase in size, he moved over next to Turnbull and whispered that this was witchcraft. Finally, as they approached the buffalo and he could see them for the size they truly were he was no longer afraid, but he was still unsure as to why they had been so small before, and wondered if they had grown larger or if there was some form of trickery going on.

A similar event occurred when the two men continued driving and came to the edge of Lake Edward. This is quite a large lake, and there was a fishing boat two or three miles out. Kenge refused to believe that the distant boat was something large enough to hold several people. He claimed that it was just a piece of wood, until Turnbull reminded him of the experience with the buffalo. At this, Kenge just nodded in amazement.

During the rest of the day spent outside the jungle, Kenge watched for animals in the distance and tried to guess what they were. It was apparent to Turnbull that Kenge was no longer afraid or skeptical, but was working on adapting his perceptions to these entirely new sensations. And he was learning fast. The next day, however, he asked to be returned to his home in the jungle and again remarked that this was bad country: no trees.

DISCUSSION

This brief research report dramatically illustrates how we acquire our *perceptual constancies*. Not only are they learned as a result of experience, but these experiences are influenced by the culture and environment in which we live. In the jungle where Kenge had spent his entire life, there were no long-range views. In fact, vision was usually limited to about a hundred feet. Therefore, there was no opportunity for the BaMbuti to develop size constancy, and, if you stop to think about it, there was no need for them to do so. Although it has not been directly tested, it is possible that these same groups of Pygmies may have a more highly developed ability for figure-ground relationships. The logic here is that it is extremely important for the BaMbuti to distinguish those animals (especially the potentially dangerous ones) that are able to blend into the surrounding background vegetation. This perceptual skill would seem less necessary for people living in a modern industrialized culture.

In regard to size constancy, Turnbull's observational study may offer us an explanation for why this ability is learned rather than innate. Certain perceptual skills may be necessary for our survival, but we do not all develop and grow in the same situation. Therefore, to maximize our survival potential, some of our skills are allowed to unfold over time in ways that are best suited to our physical environment.

SIGNIFICANCE OF FINDINGS AND RECENT APPLICATIONS

Turnbull's work fueled the fire of behavioral scientists who address the question of the relative influence of biology versus environment (learning) on our behavior: the "nature-nurture" controversy. Turnbull's observations of Kenge's perceptions points strongly to the nurture or environmental side of the issue. In a fascinating series of studies by Blakemore and Cooper (1970), kittens were raised in darkness except for exposure to either vertical or horizontal stripes. Later, when the cats were taken out of the dark environment, the ones who had been exposed to vertical lines responded to the vertical lines on objects in the environment, but ignored horizontal lines. Conversely, the cats exposed to horizontal lines during development later appeared to recognize only the presence of horizontal figures. The cats' ability to see was not damaged, but some specific perceptual abilities had not developed. These particular deficits appeared to be permanent.

Other research, however, has suggested that some of our perceptual abilities may be present at birth, that is, given to us by nature without any learning needed. For example, one study (Adams, 1987) exposed newborn infants (only three days old) to squares of various colors of light (red, blue, green) and to squares of gray light at the exact same brightness. All these very young infants spent significantly more time looking at the colorful squares than at the gray ones. It is unlikely that infants had the opportunity to learn that preference in three days, so these findings provide evidence that some of our perceptual abilities are innate.

The overall conclusion from research in this area is that there is not a single definitive answer regarding the source of our perceptual abilities. Turnbull and Kenge clearly demonstrated that some are learned, but others may be innate or part of our "factory-installed standard equipment." The one sure point here is that this area of research is bound to be pursued far into the future.

It should be noted that this article by Turnbull, even though it appeared in a psychology journal, has made lasting contributions to Turnbull's own field of anthropology and has helped to illustrate important crossovers between the two fields. Psychologists have continually been informed about the underlying causes of human behavior by studying it across cultural borders and ethnic boundaries. Conversely, anthropologists have broadened their scope of study through an awareness of the psychological underpinnings of human behavior in societal and cultural settings (e.g., see Fisher & Strickland, 1989; GalaniMoutafi, 2000).

Finally, what is perhaps most indicative of Turnbull's ongoing influence in the field of psychology is the observation that his 1961 article and his related book (Turnbull, 1962), continue to be cited and quoted in most general psychology texts as demonstrations of environmental influences on human perceptual development (e.g., Morris, 2003; Kalat, 2002). Colin Turnbull died in 1994 at the age of 70. He was one of the most famous and most unconventional anthropologists in the history of the field. If you are interested in learning more about the details of his life, an excellent, well-reviewed biography has been published recently, titled *In the Arms of Africa: The Life of Colin M. Turnbull* (Grinker, 2000), or a briefer summary of his life by Bower (2000).

Adams, R. J. (1987). An evaluation of color preference in early infancy. *Infant Behavior and Development, 10,* 143–150.

Bower, B. (2000). The forager king. *Science News, 158,* 170–171

Blakemore, C., & Cooper, G. F. (1970). Development of the brain depends on physical environment. *Nature, 228,* 227–229.

Fisher, J., & Strickland, H. (1989). Ethnoarchaeology among the Efe Pygmies, Zaire: Spacial organization of campsites. *American Journal of Physical Anthropology, 78,* 473–484.

GalaniMoutafi, V. (2000). The self and the other: Traveler, ethnographer, tourist. *Annals of Tourism Research, 27*(1), 203–224.

Grinker, R. (2000). *In the arms of Africa: The life of Colin M. Turnbull.* New York: St. Martins Press.

Kalat, J. (2002). *Introduction to Psychology.* Pacific Grove, CA: Wadsworth.

Morris, C. *Understanding psychology* (2nd ed.). Englewood Cliffs, NJ: Prentice Hall.

Turnbull, C. (1962). *The forest people.* New York: Simon & Schuster.

TO SLEEP, NO DOUBT TO DREAM . . .

Aserinsky, E., & Kleitman, N. (1953). Regularly occurring periods of eye mobility and concomitant phenomena during sleep. *Science, 118,* 273–274. Dement, W. (1960). The effect of dream deprivation. *Science, 131,* 1705–1707.

As you can see, this section is somewhat different from the others in that there are two articles being discussed. The first study discovered a basic phenomenon about sleeping and dreaming that made the second study possible. The primary focus is William Dement's work on dream deprivation, but to prepare you for that, Aserinsky's findings must be addressed first.

In 1952, Eugene Aserinsky, while a graduate student, was studying sleep. Part of his research involved observing sleeping infants. He noticed that as these infants slept, there were periodic occurrences of active eye movements. During the remainder of the night, there were only occasional slow, rolling eye movements. He theorized that these periods of active eye movements might be associated with dreaming. However, infants could not tell him whether they had been dreaming or not. So, in order to test this idea, he expanded his research to include adults.

Aserinsky and his coauthor, Nathaniel Kleitman, employed 20 normal adults to serve as subjects. Sensitive electronic measuring devices were connected by electrodes to the muscles around the eyes of these subjects. The leads from these electrodes stretched into the next room where the subjects' sleep could be monitored. The subjects were then allowed to fall asleep normally (subjects participated on more than one night each). During the night, subjects were awakened and *interrogated,* either during periods of eye activity or during periods when little or no eye movement was observed. The idea was to wake the subjects and ask them if they had been dreaming and if they could remember the content of the dream. The results were quite revealing.

For all of the subjects combined, there were a total of 27 awakenings during periods of sleep accompanied by rapid eye movements. Of these, 20 reported detailed visual dreams. The other seven reported "the feeling of having dreamed," but could not recall the content in detail. During periods of no eye movement, there were 23 awakenings; in 19 of these instances, the subjects did not report any dreaming, while in the other four, the participants felt vaguely as if they might have been dreaming, but were not able to describe the dreams. On some occasions, subjects were allowed to sleep through the night uninterrupted. It was found that they experienced between three and four periods of eye activity during the average of seven hours of sleep.

While it may not have seemed so remarkable at the time, Aserinsky had discovered what is very familiar to most of us now: REM (rapid eye movement) sleep, or dreaming sleep. From his discovery grew a huge body of research on sleep and dreaming that continues to expand. Over the years, as research methods and physiological recording devices have become more sophisticated, we have been able to refine Aserinsky's findings and unlock many of the mysteries of sleep.

For example, we now know that after you fall asleep, you sleep in four stages, beginning with the lightest sleep (Stage 1) and progressing into deeper and deeper stages. After you reach the deepest stage (Stage 4), you begin to move back up through the stages; your sleep becomes lighter and lighter. As you approach Stage 1 again, you enter a very different kind of sleep called REM. It is during REM that you do most of your dreaming. However, contrary to popular belief, it has been found scientifically that you do not move around very much during REM. Your body is immobilized by electrochemical messages from your brain that actually paralyze your muscles. This is a survival mechanism that prevents you from acting out your dreams and possibly injuring yourself or worse!

Following a short period in REM, you proceed back into the four stages of sleep called non-rapid-eye-movement sleep (NON-REM or NREM for short). During the night, you cycle between NREM and REM about five or six times (your first REM period comes about 90 minutes after falling asleep), with NREM becoming shorter and REM becoming longer (thereby causing you to dream more toward morning). And, by the way, everyone dreams. While there is a small percentage of individuals who never remember dreams, research has determined that we all have them.

All of this knowledge springs from the discovery of REM by Aserinsky in the early 1950s. And one of the leading researchers who followed Aserinsky in giving us this wealth of information on sleeping and dreaming is William Dement. Beginning around the time of Aserinsky's findings, Dement was interested in studying the basic function and significance of dreaming.

THEORETICAL PROPOSITIONS

What struck Dement as most significant was the discovery that dreaming occurs every night in everyone. As Dement states in his article, "Since there appear to be no exceptions to the nightly occurrence of a substantial amount of dreaming in every sleeping person, it might be asked whether or not this amount of dreaming is in some way a necessary and vital part of our existence" (p. 1705). This led him to ask some obvious questions: "Would it be possible for human beings to continue to function normally if their dream life were completely or partially suppressed? Should dreaming be considered necessary in a psychological sense or a physiological sense or both?" (p. 1705).

Dement decided to try to answer these questions by studying subjects who had somehow been deprived of the chance to dream. At first he tried using depressant drugs to prevent dreaming, but the drugs themselves produced too great an effect on the subjects' sleep patterns to allow for valid results. So, he decided on "the somewhat drastic method" of waking subjects up every time they entered REM sleep during the night.

METHOD

This article reported on the first eight subjects in an ongoing sleep and dreaming research project. The subjects were all males ranging in age from 23 to 32. A participant would arrive at the sleep laboratory around his usual bedtime. Small electrodes were attached to the scalp and near the eyes to record brain-wave patterns and eye movements. As in the Aserinsky study, the wires to these electrodes ran into the next room so that the subject could sleep in a quiet, darkened room.

The procedure for the study was as follows: For the first several nights, the subject was allowed to sleep normally for the entire night. This was done to establish a baseline for each subject's usual amount of dreaming and overall sleep pattern.

Once this information was obtained, the next step was to deprive the subject of REM or dream sleep. Over the next several nights (the number of consecutive deprivation nights ranged from three to seven for the various subjects), the experimenter would awaken the subject every time the information from the electrodes indicated that he had begun to dream. The subject was required to sit up in bed and demonstrate that he was fully awake for several minutes before being allowed to go back to sleep.

An important point mentioned by Dement was that the subjects were asked not to sleep at any other times during the dream study. This was because if subjects slept or napped, they might dream, and this could contaminate the findings of the study.

Following the nights of dream deprivation, subjects entered the *recovery phase* of the experiment. During these nights (which varied from one to six), the subjects were allowed to sleep undisturbed throughout the night. Their periods of dreaming continued to be monitored electronically and the amount of dreaming was recorded as usual.

Next, each subject was given several nights off (something they were very glad about, no doubt!). Then six of them returned to the lab for another series of interrupted nights. These awakenings "exactly duplicated the dream-deprivation nights in number of nights and number of awakenings per night. The only difference was that the subject was awakened in the intervals between eye-movement (dream) periods. Whenever a dream period began, the subject was allowed to sleep on without interruption and was awakened only after the dream had ended spontaneously" (p. 1706). Finally, subjects again had the same number of recovery nights as they did following the dream-deprivation phase. These were called *control recovery*, and were included to eliminate the possibility that any effects of dream deprivation were not due simply to being awakened many times during the night, whether dreaming or not.

RESULTS

Table 1 summarizes the main findings reported. During the baseline nights, when subjects were allowed to sleep undisturbed, the average amount of sleep per night was 6 hours and 50 minutes. The average amount of time the

TABLE 1 Summary of Dream-Deprivation Results

	1. PERCENT DREAM-TIME	2. NUMBER OF DREAM DEPRIVATION	3a. NUMBER OF AWAKENINGS	3b.	4. PERCENT DREAM-TIME	5. PERCENT DREAM-TIME
SUBJECT	BASELINE	NIGHTS	FIRST NIGHT	LAST NIGHT	RECOVERY	CONTROL
1.	19.5	5	8	14	34.0	15.6
2.	18.8	7	7	24	34.2	22.7
3.	19.5	5	11	30	17.8	20.2
4.	18.6	5	7	23	26.3	18.8
5.	19.3	5	10	20	29.5	26.3
6.	20.8	4	13	20	29.0	—
7.	17.9	4	22	30	19.8 (28.1)*	16.8
8.	20.8	3	9	13	—**	—
Average	19.5	4.38	11	22	26.6	20.1

*Second recovery night.
**Subject dropped out of study before recovery nights.
(Adapted from p. 1707.)

subjects spent dreaming was 80 minutes, or 19.5% (see Table 1, column 1). Dement discovered in these results from the first several nights that the amount of time spent dreaming was remarkably similar from subject to subject. In fact, the amount of variation among the dreamers was only plus or minus 7 minutes!

The main point of this study was to examine the effects of being deprived of dreaming, or REM, sleep. The first finding to address this was the number of awakenings required to prevent REM sleep during the dream-deprivation nights. As you can see in Table 1 (column 3a), on the first night, the experimenter had to awaken the subjects between 7 and 22 times in order to block REM. However, as the study progressed, subjects had to be awakened more and more often in order to prevent them from dreaming. On the last deprivation night, the number of forced awakenings ranged from 13 to 30 (column 3b). On average, there were twice as many attempts to dream at the end of the deprivation nights.

The next and perhaps most revealing result was the increase in dreaming time after the subjects were prevented from dreaming for several nights. The numbers in Table 1 (column 4) reflect the first recovery night. The average total dream time on this night was 112 minutes, or 26.6% (compared with 80 minutes and 19.5% during baseline nights in column 1). Dement pointed out that there were two subjects who did not show a significant increase in REM (subjects 3 and 7). If they are excluded from the calculations, the average total dream time is 127 minutes, or 29%. This is a 50% increase over the average for the baseline nights.

While only the first recovery night is reported in Table 1, it was noted that most of the subjects continued to show elevated dream time (compared with baseline amounts) for five consecutive nights.

"Wait a minute!" you're thinking. Maybe this increase in dreaming has nothing to do with REM deprivation at all. Maybe it's just because these subjects were awakened so often. Well, you'll remember that Dement planned for your astute observation. Six of the subjects returned after several days of rest and repeated the procedure exactly except they were awakened between REM periods (the same number of times). This produced no significant increases in dreaming. The average time spent dreaming after the control awakenings was 88 minutes, or 20.1% of the total sleep time (column 5). When compared to 80 minutes, or 19.5%, in column 1, no significant difference was found.

DISCUSSION

Dement tentatively concluded from these findings that we need to dream. When we are not allowed to dream, there seems to be some kind of pressure to dream that increases over successive dream-deprivation nights. This was evident in his findings from the increasing number of attempts to dream following deprivation (column 3a vs. column 3b) and in the significant increase in dream time (column 4 vs. column 1). He also notes that this increase continues over several nights so that it appears to make up in quantity the approximate amount of lost dreaming. Although Dement did not use the phrase at the time, this important finding has come to be known as the *REM-rebound* effect.

Several interesting additional discoveries were made in this brief, yet remarkable article. If you return to the table for a moment, you'll see that two subjects, as mentioned before, did not show a significant REM-rebound (subjects 3 and 7). It is always important in research incorporating a relatively small number of subjects to attempt to explain these exceptions. Dement found that the small increase in subject 7 was not difficult to explain: "His failure to show a rise on the first recovery night was in all likelihood due to the fact that he had imbibed several cocktails at a party before coming to the laboratory, so the expected increase in dream time was offset by the depressing effect of the alcohol" (p. 1706).

Subject 3, however, was more difficult to reconcile. Although he showed the largest increase in the number of awakenings during deprivation (from 7 to 30), he did not have any REM rebound on any of his five recovery nights. Dement acknowledged that this subject was the one exception in his findings and theorized that perhaps he had an unusually stable sleep pattern that was resistant to change.

Finally, the eight subjects were monitored for any behavioral changes that they might experience due to the loss of REM sleep. All the subjects developed minor symptoms of anxiety, irritability, or difficulty concentrating during the REM interruption period. Five of the subjects reported a clear increase in appetite during the deprivation, and three of these gained three to five pounds. None of these behavioral symptoms appeared during the period of control awakenings.

SIGNIFICANCE OF THE FINDINGS AND SUBSEQUENT RESEARCH

More than 30 years after this preliminary research by Dement, we know a great deal about sleeping and dreaming. Some of this knowledge was discussed briefly earlier in this chapter. We know that most of what Dement reported in his 1960 article has stood the test of time. We all dream, and if we are somehow prevented from dreaming one night, we dream more the next night. There does indeed appear to be something basic in our need to dream. In fact, the REM-rebound effect can be seen in many animals.

One of Dement's accidental findings, one that he reported only as a minor anecdote, now has greater significance. One way that people may be deprived of REM sleep is through the use of alcohol or other drugs such as amphetamines and barbiturates. While these drugs increase your tendency to fall asleep, they suppress REM sleep and cause you to remain in the deeper stages of NREM for greater portions of the night. It is for this reason that many people are unable to break the habit of taking sleeping pills or alcohol in order to sleep. As soon as they stop, the REM-rebound effect is so strong and disturbing that they become afraid to sleep and return to the drug to avoid dreaming. An even more extreme example of this problem occurs with alcoholics who may have been depriving themselves of REM sleep for years. When they stop drinking, the onset of REM rebound may be so powerful that it can occur while they are *awake!* This may be an explanation for the phenomenon known as *delirium tremens* (DTs), which usually involve terrible and frightening hallucinations during withdrawal (Greenberg & Perlman, 1967).

Dement spent decades following up on his early preliminary findings regarding the behavioral effects of dream deprivation. In his later work, he deprived subjects of REM for much longer periods of time and found no evidence of harmful changes. He concluded that "[a] decade of research has failed to prove that substantial ill effects result even from prolonged selective REM deprivation" (Dement, 1974).

Finally, research with its origins in Dement's early work reported here suggests that there is a greater synthesis of proteins in the brain during REM sleep than during NREM sleep. Some believe that these chemical changes may represent the process of integrating new information into the memory structures of the brain and may even be the organic basis for new developments in personality (Rossi, 1973).

RECENT APPLICATIONS

Most experts in the field of sleep and dreaming credit Aserinsky with the discovery of REM sleep. Most studies relating to sleeping, dreaming, or sleep disorders attribute that basic fact to him. Consequently, his early work with Kleitman is frequently cited in many recent scientific articles.

Dement's extension of Aserinsky's work continues to be cited frequently in a wide range of research articles relating to sleep patterns. One such recent study found that REM sleep plays a role in people's ability to improve their performance on a newly learned task while they sleep (Stickgold et al., 2000). Another article relying on Dement's 1960 research examined REM during daytime sleep, following a night without any sleep at all (Werth et al., 2002). These researchers found, compared to nighttime sleep, daytime sleep produces significantly different REM patterns. For example, the number of awakenings needed to prevent REM only doubled at first and then stopped increasing completely. Also, subjects displayed only a small REM rebound effect (11.6% compared to 26.6% in Dement's study). These findings imply that our typically patterns of REM are associated with our natural, biological predisposition toward nighttime sleep. In other words, we humans are *diurnal,* not *nocturnal* creatures.

Dement, now at Stanford University where he began its program in sleep medicine, published his most recent book, *The Promise of Sleep: A Pioneer in Sleep Medicine Explores the Vital Connection Between Health, Happiness and a Good Night's Sleep,* in 2000. In this book, written for the nonscientist, Dement draws upon his four decades of research on sleep, and applies his vast accumulation of knowledge to helping all of us understand the vital importance of quality sleep and how to achieve it (see http://www.stanford .edu/~dement/

to learn more about Dement's work at Stanford University's Center of Excellence for the Diagnosis and Treatment of Sleep Disorders). In his book, Dement describes us as a "sleep-sick society," and set forth his goals as a sleep researcher:

> For most of my career . . . I have worked unceasingly to change the way society deals with sleep. Why? Because the current way, or nonway, is so very bad. . . . It greatly saddens me to think about the millions, possibly billions, of people, whose lives could be improved if they understood a few simple principles. Changing the way society and its institutions deal with sleep will do more good than almost anything else I can conceive, or certainly that was ever remotely in my grasp to accomplish. (Dement, 2000, pp. 4–5)

Dement. W. C. (2000). *The promise of sleep: A pioneer in sleep medicine explores the vital connection between health, happiness and a good night's sleep.* New York: Dell.

Dement, W. C. (1974). *Some must watch while some must sleep.* San Francisco, CA: Freeman.

Greenberg, R., & Perlman, C. (1967). Delirium tremens and dreaming. *American Journal of Psychiatry, 124,* 133–142.

Rossi, E. I. (1973). The dream protein hypothesis. *American Journal of Psychiatry, 130,* 1094–1097.

Stickgold, R., Whidbee, D., Schirmer, B., Patel, V., & Hobson, J. (2000). *Journal of Cognitive Neuroscience, 12*(2), 246–254.

Werth, E., Coth, K., Gallman, E., Borbely, A., & Acherman, P. (2002). Selective REM sleep deprivation during daytime—I. Time course interventions and recovery. *American Journal of Physiology: Regulatory integrative and comparative physiology, 283,* R521–R526.

UNROMANCING THE DREAM . . .

Hobson, J. A., & McCarley, R. W. (1977). The brain as a dream-state generator: An activation-synthesis hypothesis of the dream process. *American Journal of Psychiatry, 134,* 1335–1348.

The work of Aserinsky and Dement explored the apparent need for dreaming sleep in humans. Other research has examined the reasons why you dream and some of the functions dreaming might serve. The history of research on dreaming has been dominated by the belief that dreams reveal something about yourself: they are products of your inner psychological experience of the world. This view can be traced back to Sigmund Freud's psychoanalytic theories of human nature.

You'll recall that Freud believed that dreams are the expression of unconscious wishes for things we are unable to have while awake. Therefore, dreams offer insights into the unconscious that are unavailable in waking thought. However, the psychoanalytic approach also contends that many of these wishes are unacceptable to the conscious mind and, if expressed openly in dreams, would disrupt sleep and create anxiety. Thus, to protect the individual, the true desires contained in the dream are disguised in the dream's images by a hypothetical censor. Consequently, the theory asserts the true meaning of most dreams lies hidden beneath the dream's outward appearance. Freud called this surface meaning of a dream the *manifest content* and the deeper, true meaning the *latent content*. In order to reveal the meaningful information of a dream, the manifest content must be interpreted, analyzed, and penetrated.

While the validity of a great portion of Freud's work has been drawn into serious question by behavioral scientists over the past 50 years, his conceptualization of dreams remains widely accepted by psychologists and Western culture in general. (See the reading on Anna Freud for a discussion of other enduring aspects of Freud's theories.) Almost everyone has had the experience of remembering an unusual dream and thinking, "I wonder what it really means!" We believe that our dreams have deep meaning about conflicts that are hidden in the unconscious parts of our psyches.

In the late 1970s, Allan Hobson and Robert McCarley, both psychiatrists and neurophysiologists at Harvard's medical school, published a new theory of dreaming that shook the scientific community so deeply that the tremors are still being felt today. What they said, in essence, was that dreams are nothing more than your attempt to interpret random electrical impulses produced automatically in your brain during REM sleep.

They proposed that while you are asleep there is a part of your brain, located in the brain stem, that is periodically activated and produces electrical impulses. This part of your brain is related to physical movement and the processing of input from your senses while you are awake. When you are asleep, your sensory and motor abilities are shut down, but this part of your brain is not. It continues to generate what Hobson and McCarley regarded as meaningless bursts of neural static. Some of these impulses reach other parts of your brain, responsible for higher functions such as thinking and reasoning. When this happens, your brain tries to synthesize and make some sort of sense out of the impulses. To do this, you sometimes create images, ideas, and even stories with plots. If we awaken and remember this cognitive activity, we call it a dream and invest it with all kinds of significance which, according to Hobson and McCarley, was never there to begin with.

Hobson and McCarley's original article, upon which this discussion is based, is a highly technical account of the neurophysiology of sleep and dreaming. While their work can be found in nearly all textbooks that include information about dreaming, very little of the detail is offered there, due to the complex nature of the researchers' reporting. We explore their article in significantly greater detail, although for clarity and understanding, considerable distillation and simplification are unavoidable.

THEORETICAL PROPOSITIONS

Hobson and McCarley believed that modern neurophysiological evidence "permits and necessitates important revisions in psychoanalytic dream theory. The activation-synthesis hypothesis . . . asserts that many formal aspects of the dream experience may be the obligatory and relatively undistorted psychological concomitant of the regularly recurring and physiologically determined brain state called 'dreaming sleep'" (p. 1335). What they meant by this was simply that dreams are triggered automatically by basic physiological processes, and there is no *censor* distorting the true meaning to protect you from your unconscious wishes. Moreover, they contend that the strangeness and distortions often associated with dreams are not disguises, but the results of the physiology of how the brain and mind work during sleep.

The most important part of their theory was that the brain becomes activated during REM sleep and generates its own original information. This activation is then compared with stored memories in order to synthesize the activation into some form of dream content. In other words, Hobson and McCarley claim that what is referred to as REM sleep actually causes dreaming, instead of the opposing popular view that dreams produce REM sleep.

METHOD

In their article, Hobson and McCarley incorporated two methods of research. One method was to study and review previous work by many researchers in the area of sleep and dreaming. In this single article, the authors cite 37 references that pertain to their hypothesis, including several earlier studies of their own. The second method they used was research on the sleep and dreaming patterns of animals. They did not try to claim that nonhuman animals dream, since this is something no one can know for sure. (You may believe your pet dreams, but has your dog or cat ever told you what the dream was about?) However, all mammals experience stages of sleep similar to those in humans. Hobson and McCarley went one step further and claimed that there is no significant difference between humans and other animals in the physiology of dreaming sleep. So they chose cats for their experimental subjects. Using various laboratory techniques, they were able to stimulate or inhibit certain parts of the animals' brains and record the effect on dreaming sleep.

RESULTS AND DISCUSSION

The various findings detailed by Hobson and McCarley were used to demonstrate different aspects of their theory. Therefore, their results will be combined with their discussion of the findings here. The evidence generated by the researchers in support of their theory can be summarized in the following points:

1. The part of the brain in the brain stem that controls physical movement and incoming information from the senses is at least as active during dreaming sleep (which they called the *D state*) as it is when you are awake. However, while you are asleep, sensory input (information coming into your brain from the environment around you) and motor output (voluntary movement of your body) are blocked. Hobson and McCarley suggest that these physiological processes, rather than a psychological censor, may be responsible for protecting sleep.

You will remember from the previous article that you are paralyzed during dreaming, presumably to protect you from the potential danger of acting out your dreams. Hobson and McCarley reported that this immobilization actually occurs at the spinal cord and not in the brain itself. Therefore, the brain is quite capable of sending motor signals, but the body is not able to express them. The authors suggested that this may account for the strange patterns of movement in dreams, such as your inability to run from danger or the perception that you are moving in slow motion.

2. The main exception to this blocking of motor responses is in the muscles and nerves controlling the eyes. In part, this explains why rapid eye movement occurs during D state, and may also explain how visual images are triggered during dreaming.

3. Hobson and McCarley pointed out another aspect of dreaming that emerged from a physiological analysis of the D state and that could not be explained by a psychoanalytic interpretation. This was that the brain enters REM sleep at regular and predictable intervals during each night's sleep and remains in that state for specific lengths of time. There is nothing random about this sleep cycle. The authors interpreted this to mean that dreaming cannot be a response to waking events or unconscious wishes, because this would produce dreaming at any moment during sleep, according to the whims and needs of the person's psyche. Instead, the D state appeared to Hobson and McCarley to be a preprogrammed event in the brain that functions almost like a neurobiological clock.

4. The researchers pointed to findings by others that demonstrated that all mammals cycle through REM and NREM sleep. This sleep cycle varies according to the body size of the animal. A rat, for example, will shift between REM and NREM every six minutes, while for an elephant a single cycle takes two-and-a-half hours! One explanation for this difference may be that the more vulnerable an animal is to predators, the shorter are its periods of sound sleep during which it is less alert and thus in greater danger of attack. Whatever the reason, Hobson and McCarley took these findings as additional evidence that dreaming sleep is purely physiological.

5. Hobson and McCarley claimed to have found the trigger, the power supply, and the clock of the "dream state generator" in the brain. They reported this to be the pontine brain stem, located in the back and near the base of the brain. Measurements of neural activity (the frequency of firing of neurons) in this part of the brain in cats found significant peaks in activity corresponding to periods of REM sleep. When this part of the brain was artificially inhibited, the animals went for weeks without any REM sleep. Furthermore, reducing the activity of the pontine caused the length of time between periods of D state sleep to increase.

Conversely, stimulation of the brain stem caused REM sleep to occur earlier and increased the length of REM periods. Such increases in REM have been attempted through conscious behavioral techniques, but these have been mostly unsuccessful. The authors' interpretation of these findings was that since a part of the brain completely separate from the pontine brain stem is involved in consciousness, dreaming cannot be driven by psychological forces.

6. The first five points summarized from Hobson and McCarley's research focused on the *activation* portion of their theory. They maintained that the *synthesis* of this activation is what produces your experience of dreaming. The psychological implications of their theory were detailed by the authors in four basic tenets:

   (a) "The primary motivating force for dreaming is not psychological but physiological, since the time of occurrence and duration of dreaming sleep are quite constant, suggesting a preprogrammed, neurally determined genesis" (p. 1346). They did allow that dreams may have psychological meaning, but suggested that this meaning is much more basic than the psychoanalytic view imagines it to be. They further contended that dreaming should no longer be considered to have purely psychological significance.

   (b) During dreaming, the brain stem is not responding to sensory input or producing motor output based on the world around you; instead it is activating itself internally. Since this activation originates in a relatively primitive part of the brain, it does not contain any ideas, emotions, stories, fears, or wishes. It is simple electrical energy. As the activation reaches the more advanced, cognitive structures of the brain, you try to make sense out of it. "In other words, the forebrain may be making the best of a bad job in producing even partially coherent dream imagery from the relatively noisy signals sent up to it from the brain stem" (p. 1347).

   (c) Therefore, this elaboration of random signals into dreams is interpreted to be a constructive process, a synthesis, instead of a distortion process by which unacceptable wishes are hidden from your consciousness. Images are called up from your memory in an attempt to match the data generated by the brain stem's activation. It is precisely because of the randomness of the impulses, and the difficult task of the brain to try to inject them with some meaning, that dreams are often bizarre, disjointed, and seemingly mysterious.

   (d) Freud's explanation for our forgetting dreams was repression. He believed that when the content of a dream is too disturbing for some reason, you are motivated to forget it. Hobson and McCarley, acknowledging that dream recall is poor (at least 95% of all dreams are not remembered), offered a pure physiological explanation that was concordant with the rest of their activation-synthesis hypothesis. They claimed that when we awaken, there is an immediate change in the chemistry of the brain. Certain brain chemicals necessary for converting short-term memories into long-term ones are suppressed during REM sleep. So unless a dream is particularly vivid (meaning that it is produced by a large amount of activation) and you awaken during or immediately after it, the content of the dream will not be remembered.

Figure 1 illustrates Hobson and McCarley's comparison between the psychoanalytic view of the dream process and their activation-synthesis model.

IMPLICATIONS AND RECENT APPLICATIONS

Hobson and McCarley have continued to conduct research in support of their revolutionary hypothesis of dreaming. Their new conceptualization has not been universally accepted, but no psychological discussion of dreaming would be considered complete without its inclusion.

Twelve years after the appearance of Hobson and McCarley's original article on the activation-synthesis model, Allan Hobson published his book called, simply, *Sleep*. In this work, he explains his theory of dreaming in expanded and greatly simplified terms. He also elaborates on his view about what impact the theory may have on the interpretation of dream content. And, he allows, dreams are not devoid of meaning, but should be interpreted in more straightforward ways. Hobson states his view as follows:

> For all their nonsense, dreams have a clear import and a deeply personal one. Their meaning would stem, I assert, from the necessity in REM sleep for the brain-mind to act upon its own information and according to its own lights. Thus, I would like to retain the emphasis of psychoanalysis upon the power of

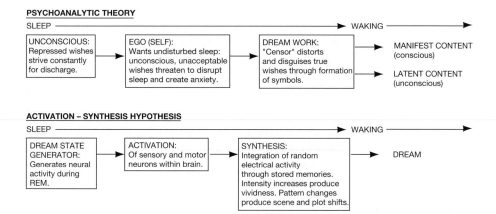

FIGURE 1 Psychoanalytic theory and activation-synthesis hypothesis compared. (Adapted from p. 1346.)

dreams to reveal deep aspects about ourselves, but without recourse to the concept of disguise and censorship or to the now famous Freudian symbols. My tendency, then, is to ascribe the nonsense to brain-mind dysfunction and the sense to its compensatory effort to create order out of chaos. That order is a function of our own personal view of the world, our current preoccupations, our remote memories, our feelings, and our beliefs. That's all. (Hobson, 1989, p. 166)

Another dream researcher took Hobson's sentiments a step further. Foulkes (1985), a leading researcher on daydreaming, also subscribes to the notion that night dreams are generated by spontaneous brain activity during sleep. He has suggested that while dreams do not contain hidden unconscious messages, they may provide us with a great deal of psychological information. Foulkes maintains that the way your cognitive system places form and sense onto the random impulses in your brain reveals information about the importance of certain of your memories and provides insight into your thinking processes. He also believes that dreams serve several useful purposes. One of these arises from dreams you have about experiences that have not actually happened to you. These dreams may assist in preparing you to encounter new or unexpected events—something like a cognitive rehearsal, or "What would I do if . . . ?"

And the research continues. Many studies seek to challenge Hobson and McCarley's conceptualization of the origin and function of dreams. One such study demonstrated how the controversy among sleep and dream theorists lives on. The Freudian-based, psychoanalytic community continues to express their annoyance that Hobson and McCarley's theories leave little room for the Freudian view that dreams are messages from the unconscious. In a journal devoted to Freudian psychoanalysis, Mancia (1999) demonstrates the differences between the psychoanalytic notion of dreaming and the theory proposed by Hobson and McCarley, often referred to as the "neuroscientific" approach. Mancia describes the clash between these two fundamental views with great clarity:

> Whereas the neuroscientists are interested in the structures involved in dream production and in dream organization and narratability; psychoanalysis concentrates on the meaning of dreams and on placing them in the context of the analytic relationship [with the analyst] in accordance with the affective [emotional] history of the dreamer. . . . The brain structures and functions of interest to the neurosciences . . . are irrelevant to their psychoanalytic understanding. (Mancia, 1999, p. 1205)

Of course, Hobson and McCarley very likely would reply that there is no psychoanalytic understanding possible, because there is no such thing as an unconscious in the Freudian conceptualization of it. That debate, while well worth having, must be saved for another time and place.

Finally, a fascinating study questioning Hobson and McCarley's theory took a new look at the specific regions of the brain that are active during REM (Solms, 2000). Until recently, most researchers, led by Hobson and Mc-

Carley, assumed that REM and dreaming are physiologically equivalent activities controlled by a single, connected brain process. However, Solms has suggested that dreaming may be generated through direct stimulation of the forebrain during *non-REM* sleep, *independently* of any brain stem involvement. Conversely, REM sleep, along with the usual brain stem activation, may occur without any dreaming taking place. Therefore, Solms suggests that brain stem activity is "just one of the many arousal triggers that can activate this forebrain mechanism. The 'REM-on' mechanism therefore stands outside the dream process itself, which is mediated by an independent, forebrain 'dream-on' mechanism" (p. 843).

CONCLUSION

Whether you are willing to accept the rather less romantic view of dreaming developed by Hobson and McCarley's research, this is an excellent example of how psychologists or scientists in any field need to remain open to new possibilities even when the *established order* has existed for decades. There is no doubt that the activation-synthesis model of dreams has changed psychology. This does not mean that we have solved all the mysteries of sleep and dreaming, and perhaps we never will. But it's bound to be a fascinating journey.

Foulkes, D. (1985). *Dreaming: A cognitive-psychological analysis.* Hillsdale, NJ: Erlbaum.

Hobson, J. A. (1989). *Sleep.* New York: Scientific American Library.

Mancia, M. (1999). Psychoanalysis and the neurosciences: A topical debate on dreams. *International Journal of Psychoanalysis, 80*(6), 1205–1213.

Solms, M. (2000). Dreaming and REM sleep are controlled by different brain mechanisms. *Behavioral and Brain Sciences, 23,* 843–850.

ACTING AS IF YOU ARE HYPNOTIZED

Spanos, N. P. (1982). Hypnotic behavior: A cognitive, social, psychological perspective. *Research Communications in Psychology, Psychiatry, and Behavior, 7,* 199–213.

The alterations in consciousness with which we are all most familiar are related to sleep and dreaming. The previous three articles have focused on several highly influential studies relating to these topics. Another phenomenon relating to altered states of consciousness is hypnosis. Hypnosis is usually seen as a mysterious and powerful process of controlling a person's mind. The phrases and words that surround hypnosis, such as *going under* and *trance*, indicate that it is commonly considered to be a separate and unique state of awareness, different from both waking and sleep. And many psychologists agree with this view. Nicholas Spanos (1942–1994), however, led the opposing view that hypnosis is, in reality, nothing more than an increased state of motivation to perform certain behaviors and can be fully explained without resorting to trances or altered states.

The beginnings of hypnosis are usually traced back to the middle of the eighteenth century, a time when mental illness was first recognized as resulting from psychological rather than organic causes. One of the many fascinating characters who helped bring psychology out of the realm of witchcraft was Franz Anton Mesmer (1733–1815). He believed that *hysterical disorders* were a result of imbalances in a universal magnetic fluid present in the body. During strange gatherings in his laboratory, soft music would play, the lights would dim, and Mesmer, clothed like a sorcerer, would take iron rods from bottles of various chemicals and touch parts of the afflicted patients' bodies. He believed that this would transmit what he called the *animal magnetism* in the chemicals into the patients and provide relief from their symptoms. Interestingly, history has recorded that in many cases this treatment appeared to be successful. It is from Mesmer that we acquired the word *mesmerize,* and many believe that his treatment included some of the techniques we now associate with hypnosis.

Throughout the history of psychology, hypnosis (named after Hypnos, the Greek god of sleep) has played a prominent role, especially in the treatment of psychological disorders, and it was a major component in Freud's psychoanalytic techniques. Ernest Hilgard has been at the forefront of modern researchers who support the position that hypnosis is an altered psychological state (Hilgard, 1978). His and others' descriptions of hypnosis have included characteristics such as increased susceptibility to suggestion, involuntary performance of behaviors, improvements in recall, increased intensity of visual imagination, dissociation (the ability to be aware of some conscious events while being unaware of others), and analgesia (lowered sensitivity to pain). Until recently, the idea that hypnosis is capable of producing thoughts, ideas, and behaviors that would otherwise be impossible and that it is an altered state of consciousness has been virtually undisputed.

However, it is the job of scientists to look upon the status quo with a critical eye and, whenever they see fit, to debunk common beliefs. Just as Hobson and McCarley proposed a new view of dreaming that was radically different from the prevailing and popular one, social psychologist Nicholas Spanos has suggested that the major assumptions underlying hypnosis, as set forth by Hilgard and others, should be questioned. In this article Spanos wrote, "The positing of special processes to account for hypnotic behavior is not only unnecessary, but also misleading. . . . Hypnotic behavior is basically similar to other social behavior and, like other social behavior, can be usefully described as strategic and goal-directed" (p. 200). In other words, Spanos contended that hypnotized subjects are actually engaging in voluntary behavior designed to produce a desired consequence. He further maintained that while such behavior may result from increased motivation, it does not involve an altered state of consciousness.

THEORETICAL PROPOSITIONS

Spanos theorized that all of the behaviors commonly attributed to a hypnotic trance state are within the normal, voluntary abilities of humans. He maintained that the only reason people define themselves as having been hypnotized is that they have interpreted their own behavior *under hypnosis* in ways that are consistent with their expectations about being hypnotized. Spanos views the process of hypnosis as a ritual that in Western culture carries a great deal of meaning. Subjects expect to relinquish control over their own behavior, and as the process of hypnotic induction develops, they begin to believe that their voluntary acts are becoming automatic, involuntary events. An example of this that Spanos offers is that early in the hypnotic procedure, voluntary instructions are given to the subject, such as, "relax the muscles in your legs," but later these become involuntary suggestions, such as, "your legs feel limp and heavy."

In collaboration with various colleagues and associates, Spanos devoted nearly a decade of research prior to this 1982 article, demonstrating how many of the effects commonly attributed to hypnotic trances could be explained just as easily (or even more easily) in less mysterious ways.

METHOD

This article does not report on a specific experiment, but rather summarizes numerous studies made by Spanos and his assoicates prior to 1982, which were designed to support his position against Hilgard's contention (and the popular belief) that hypnosis is a unique state of consciousness. Most of the findings reported were taken from 16 studies in which Spanos was directly involved, and that offered alternate interpretations of hypnotically produced behavior. Therefore, as in the previous article on dream research, results and the discussion of them are combined.

RESULTS AND DISCUSSION

Spanos claimed that there are two key aspects of hypnosis that lead people to believe it is an altered state of consciousness. One is that subjects interpret their behavior as being caused by something other than the self, thus making the action seem involuntary. The second aspect is the belief discussed previously that the hypnosis ritual creates expectations in the subject which in turn motivate the subject to behave in ways that are consistent with the expectations. The research Spanos reports in this article focuses on how these frequently cited claims about hypnosis have been drawn into question.

The Belief That Behavior Is Involuntary

As subjects are being hypnotized, they are usually asked to take various *tests* to determine if a hypnotic state has been induced. Spanos claimed that these tests are often carried out in such a way as to invite the subjects to convince themselves that something out of the ordinary is happening. Hypnotic tests involve suggestions such as, "your arm is heavy and you cannot hold it up"; your hands are being drawn together by some force and you cannot keep them apart; your arm is as rigid as a steel bar and you cannot bend it; or your body is so heavy that you cannot stand up. Spanos interpreted these test suggestions as containing two interrelated requests. One request asks subjects to do something, and the other asks them to interpret the action as having occurred involuntarily. Some subjects fail completely to respond to the suggestion. Spanos claimed that these subjects do not understand that they must voluntarily do something to initiate the suggested behavior and instead simply wait for their arms or body to begin to move. Other subjects respond to the suggestion, but are aware that they are behaving voluntarily. Finally, there are those subjects who agree to both requests; they respond to the suggestion and interpret their response as beyond their control.

Spanos suggested that whether subjects interpret their behavior to be voluntary or involuntary depends on the way the suggestion is worded. In one of his studies, Spanos put two groups of subjects through a hypnosis induction procedure. Then to one group he made various behavior suggestions, such as, "your arm is very light and is rising." To the other group he gave direct instructions for the same behaviors, such as, "raise your arm." Afterward he asked the subjects if they thought their behaviors were voluntary or involuntary. The subjects in the suggestion group were more likely to interpret their behaviors as involuntary than were those in the direct instruction group.

Right now, while you are reading this page, hold your left arm straight out and keep it there for a couple of minutes. You will notice that it begins to feel heavy. This heaviness is not due to hypnosis; it's due to gravity! So if you are *hypnotized* and given the suggestion that your outstretched arm is becoming heavy, it would be very easy for you to attribute your action of lowering your arm to involuntary forces (you want to lower it anyway!). But what if you are given the suggestion that your arm is light and rising? If you raise your arm, it should be more difficult to interpret that action as involuntary, because you would have to ignore the contradictory feedback provided by gravity. Spanos tested this idea and found that such an interpretation was more difficult. Subjects who believed they were hypnotized were significantly more likely to define as involuntary their behavior of arm-lowering than that of arm-raising. In the traditional view of hypnosis, the direction of the arm in the hypnotic suggestion should not make any difference; it should always be considered involuntary.

Suggestions made to hypnotic subjects often ask them to imagine certain situations in order to produce a desired behavior. If you were a subject, you might be given the suggestion that your arm is rigid and you cannot bend it. To reinforce this suggestion, it might be added that your arm is in a plaster cast. Spanos believed that some people may become absorbed in these *imaginal strategies* more than others, which could have the effect of leading them to believe that their response (the inability to move their arm) was involuntary. His reasoning was that if you are highly absorbed, you will not be able to focus on information that alerts you to the fact that the fantasy is not real. The more vividly you imagine the cast, its texture and hardness, how it got there, and so on, the less likely you are to remember that this is only your imagination at work. If this deep absorption happens, you might be more inclined to believe that your rigid-arm behavior was involuntary when actually it was not. In support of this, Spanos found that when subjects were asked to rate how absorbed they were in a suggested imagined scenario, the higher the absorption rating, the more likely they were to interpret their related behavior as occurring involuntarily. Spanos also noted that a person's susceptibility to hypnosis correlates with his or her general tendency to become absorbed in other activities such as books, music, or daydreaming. Consequently, these individuals are more likely to willingly cooperate with the kind of suggestions involved in hypnosis.

Creation of Expectations in Hypnotic Subjects

Spanos claims that the beliefs most people have about hypnosis are adequate in themselves to produce what is typically seen as hypnotic behavior. He further contends that these beliefs are strengthened by the methods used to induce and study hypnosis. He cites three examples of research that demonstrated how people might engage in certain behaviors under hypnosis because they think they should, rather than because of an altered state of awareness.

First, Spanos referred to a study in which a lecture about hypnosis was given to two groups of students. The lectures were identical except that one group was told that arm rigidity was a spontaneous event during hypnosis. Later both groups were hypnotized. In the group that had heard the lecture including the information about arm rigidity, some of the subjects exhibited this behavior *spontaneously*, without any instructions to do so. However, among the subjects in the other group, not one arm became rigid. According to Spanos, this demonstrated how people will enact their experience of hypnosis according to how they believe they are supposed to behave.

The second hypnotic event that Spanos used to illustrate his position involved research findings that hypnotized subjects claim the visual imagery they experienced under hypnosis was more intense, vivid, and real than similar imaginings when not hypnotized. Here, in essence, is how these studies typically have been done. Subjects are asked to imagine scenes or situations in which they are performing certain behaviors. Then, these same subjects are hypnotized and again asked to visualize the same or similar situations (the hypnotized and nonhypnotized trials can be in any order). These subjects generally report that the imagery in the hypnotized condition was significantly more intense. Spanos and his associates found, however, that when two different groups of subjects are used, one hypnotized and one not, their average intensity ratings of the visual imagery are approximately equal. Why the difference? The difference in the two methods is probably explained by the fact that when two different groups are tested, the subjects do not have anything to use for comparison. However, when the same subjects are used in both conditions, they can compare the two experiences and rate one against the other. So, since subjects nearly always rate the hypnotic imagery as more intense, this supports the idea that hypnosis is really an altered state, right? Well, if you ask Spanos, he would say, "Wrong!" In his view, the subjects who participate in both conditions expect the ritual of hypnosis to produce more intense imagery, and, therefore, they rate it accordingly.

The third and perhaps most interesting demonstration of hypnosis addressed by Spanos was the claim that hypnosis can cause people to become insensitive to pain (the analgesia effect). One way that pain can be tested in the laboratory without causing damage to the subject is by using the "cold pressor test." If you are a subject in such a study, you would be asked to immerse your arm in ice water (zero degrees centigrade) and leave it there as long as you could. After the first 10 seconds or so this becomes increasingly painful, and most people will remove their arm within a minute or two. Hilgard (1978) reported that subjects who received both waking and hypnotic training in analgesia (pain reduction) reported significantly less cold-pressor pain during the hypnotized trials. His explanation for this was that during hypnosis, a person is able to dissociate the pain from awareness. In this way, Hilgard contended, a part of the person's consciousness experiences the pain, but this part is hidden from awareness by what he called an "amnesic barrier."

Again, Spanos rejected a hypnotic explanation for these analgesic findings and offered evidence to demonstrate that reduction in perceived pain during hypnosis is a result of the subjects' motivation and expectations. All of the research on hypnosis uses subjects who have scored high on measures of hypnotic susceptibility. According to Spanos, these individuals "have a strong investment in presenting themselves in the experimental setting as good hypnotic subjects" (p. 208). The subjects know that a waking state is being compared to a hypnotic state and want to demonstrate the effectiveness of hypnosis. Spanos, working with his associate, H. J. Stam, performed a similar study involving cold-pressor pain, but with one major difference: Some subjects were told that they would first use waking analgesia techniques (such as self-distraction) and would then be tested using hypnotic pain-reduction methods, but other subjects were not told of the later hypnotic test (see also Stam and Spanos, 1980).

Figure 1 summarizes what Stam and Spanos found. When subjects expected the hypnosis condition to follow the waking trials, they rated the analgesic effect lower in order to, as the authors state, "leave room" for improvement under hypnosis. Stam and Spanos claimed that this demonstrated how even the hypnotic behavior of pain insensitivity could be attributed to the subjects' need to respond to the demands of the situation rather than automatically assuming a dissociated state of consciousness.

The most important question concerning all these findings reported by Spanos is whether we should reevaluate the phenomenon called hypnosis. And what does it mean if we were to decide that hypnosis is not the powerful

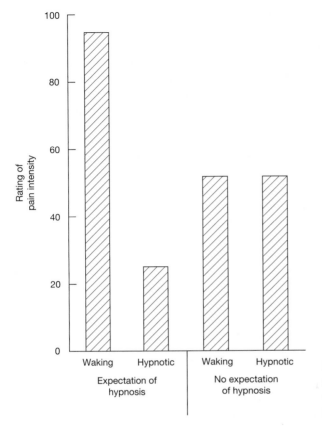

FIGURE 1 Waking versus hypnotic analgesia: expectation versus no expectation.

mind-altering force that popular culture, and many psychologists, have portrayed it to be?

IMPLICATIONS OF THE FINDINGS

In evaluating Spanos's research, you should remember that his goal was not to prove that hypnosis does not exist, but rather to demonstrate that what we call *hypnotic behaviors* are the result of highly motivated, goal-directed social behavior, not an altered and unique state of consciousness. It is well accepted among most behavioral scientists that people cannot be hypnotized against their will. Furthermore, under hypnosis, subjects will not engage in acts they believe are antisocial, and they are not able to perform feats of superhuman strength or endurance. In this article, Spanos has demonstrated how many of the more subtle aspects of hypnosis may be explained in less mysterious and more straightforward ways than that of the *hypnotic trance.*

What would be the implications of accepting Spanos's contention that hypnosis does not exist? The answer to this question is, "perhaps none."

Whether the effects of hypnosis are produced by an altered state of awareness or by increased motivation does not change the fact that hypnosis is often a useful method of helping people improve something in their lives. One reason that there continues to be such widespread and unquestioning acceptance of the power of the hypnotic trance may be that humans need to feel that there is a way out, a last resort to solve their problems if all else fails—something so omnipotent that they can even change against their own resistance to such change.

Whether hypnosis is an altered state of consciousness remains a highly controversial issue. But whatever hypnosis is, it is not the panacea most people would like to find. Several studies have shown that hypnosis is no more effective than other methods of treatment to help people stop abusing alcohol and tobacco, improve their memory, or lose weight (see Lazar & Dempster, 1981, for a review of this research).

RECENT APPLICATIONS

A citation of Spanos's 1982 article appeared in a 1997 article offering a *new* theory to explain the idea that subjects perform behaviors involuntarily under hypnosis (Lynn, 1997). This researcher contended that highly hypnotizable individuals perceive their behaviors while *under* as involuntary for several reasons. First, such people enter hypnosis with the *intention* to do what the hypnotist suggests. Second, they strongly *expect* that hypnosis has the power to mold their behavior whether they voluntarily cooperate or not. And third, "the intention to cooperate with the hypnotist as well as the expectation to be able to do so, create a heightened readiness to experience these actions as involuntary" (Lynn, 1997, p. 239). It is not surprising that this researcher relied on Spanos's work on hypnosis in that the theory mirrors and endorses the ideas set forth in the article that is the subject of this reading.

On the other hand, several recent articles have refuted Spanos's position and added support for Hilgard's findings on hypnosis and pain reduction discussed earlier (e.g., Kihlstrom, 1998, 1999; Miller & Bowers, 1993; Montgomery et al., 2000).

Finally, a recent study cited Spanos's perspectives on hypnosis to criticize certain therapeutic practices often employed by some psychotherapists to induce clients to recover ostensibly "repressed" memories of past sexual abuse (Lynn et al., 2003). The authors contended that hypnosis, along with other questionable therapeutic techniques, may distort memories or even *create* memories of abuse that never actually took place, especially in early childhood (see the reading on the work of Elizabeth Loftus in chapter 4 for more about the recovered memories issue). The researchers point out, based on Spanos's research, that, "Adults' memory reports from 24 months of age or earlier are likely to represent confabulations, condensations, and constructions of early events, as well as current concerns and stories heard about early events" (Lynn, et al., 2003, p. 42). In other words, the belief that hypnosis somehow allows clients to retrieve accurate memories of early traumatic experiences is misguided and may be subject to all the memory errors that exist in a nonhypnotized state. This, the authors contend, may lead to false memories and accusation of abuse that never happened.

Clearly the debate goes on. Spanos continued his research until his untimely death in a plane crash in June 1994 (see McConkey & Sheehan, 1995). A summary of his early work on hypnosis can be found in his 1988 book, *Hypnosis: The Cognitive-Behavioral Perspective.* Nicholas Spanos was a prolific and well-respected behavioral scientist who will be missed greatly by his colleagues and by all those who learned and benefited from his work (see Baker, 1994, for a eulogy to Nick Spanos). And, clearly, his research legacy will be carried on by others. His work on hypnosis changed psychology in that he offered a experimentally based, alternative explanation for an aspect of human consciousness and behavior that was virtually unchallenged for nearly 200 years.

Baker, R. (1994). In memoriam: Nick Spanos. *Skeptical Inquirer, 18*(5), 459.

Hilgard, E. (1978). Hypnosis and consciousness. *Human Nature, 1,* 42–51.

Kihlstrom, J. F. (1998). Attributions, awareness, and dissociation: In memoriam Kenneth S. Bowers, 1937–1996. *American Journal of Clinical Hypnosis, 40*(3), 194–205.

Kihlstrom, J. F. (1999). Personal communication.

Lazar, B., & Dempster, C. (1981). Failures in hypnosis and hypnotherapy: A review. *American Journal of Clinical Hypnosis, 24,* 48–54.

Lynn, S. (1997). Automaticity and hypnosis: A sociocognitive account. *International Journal of Clinical and Experimental Hypnosis, 45*(3), 239–250.

Lynn, S., Loftus, E., Lilienfeld, S., & Lock, T. (2003). Memory recovery techniques in psychotherapy: Problems and pitfalls. *Skeptical Inquirer, 27,* 40–46.

Montgomery, G.H., Duhamel, K.N., Redd, W. (2000). A meta-analysis of hypnotically induced analgesia: How effective is hypnosis? *International Journal of Clinical and Experimental Hypnosis 48:* 138–153

McConkey, K., & Sheehan, P. (1995). Nicholas Spanos: Reflections with gratitude. *Contemporary Hypnosis, 12,* 36–38.

Miller, M., & Bowers, K. S. (1993). Hypnotic analgesia: Dissociated experience or dissociated control? *Journal of Abnormal Psychology, 102,* 29–38.

Spanos, N., & Chaves, J. (1988). *Hypnosis: The cognitive-behavioral perspective.* New York: Prometheus.

Stam, H. J. & Spanos, N. (1980). Experimental designs, expectancy effects, and hypnotic analgesia. *Journal of Abnormal Psychology, 89,* 751–762.

3 LEARNING AND CONDITIONING

The area of psychology concerned with learning and conditioning has produced a rather well-defined body of literature explaining how animals and humans learn. Some of the most famous names in the history of psychology have devoted their entire careers to this research—names that are widely recognized even outside the behavioral sciences, such as Pavlov, Watson, Skinner, and Bandura. Picking a few of the most influential studies from this branch of psychology and from these researchers is no easy task, but the articles selected can be found in nearly every introductory psychology textbook and are representative of the mammoth contributions of these scientists.

For Pavlov, we take a journey back nearly 100 years to review his work with dogs, metronomes, salivation, and the discovery of the conditioned reflex. Second, Watson, known for many contributions, is probably most famous (notorious?) for his torturous experiment with Little Albert, which demonstrated for the first time how emotions are a product of experience. For the third study in this section, we discuss Skinner's famous explanation and demonstration of superstitious behavior in a pigeon and how humans become superstitious in exactly the same way. Finally comes an examination of the well-known "Bobo Doll Study," in which Bandura established that aggressive behaviors could be learned by children through their modeling of adult violence.

IT'S NOT JUST ABOUT SALIVATING DOGS!
Pavlov, I. P. (1927). *Conditioned reflexes.* London: Oxford University Press.

Have you ever walked into a dentist's office where the odor of the disinfectant made your teeth hurt? If you have, it was probably because the odor triggered an association that had been conditioned in your brain between that smell and your past experiences at the dentist. When you hear "The Star Spangled Banner" played at the Olympic Games, does your heart beat a little faster? This happens to most Americans. Does the same thing happen when you hear the Italian national anthem? Unless you were raised in Italy, most likely it does not, because you have been conditioned to respond to one anthem, but not to the other. And why do some people squint and become nervous if you inflate a balloon near them? It is because they have been conditioned to associate the expanding balloon with something fearful (such as a loud pop). These are just a few of countless human behaviors that exist because of a process known as *classical conditioning.*

The classical conditioning theory of learning was developed and articulated nearly 100 years ago in Russia by one of the most familiar names in the history of psychology, Ivan Petrovich Pavlov (1849–1946). Unlike most of the research presented in this book, Pavlov's name and his basic ideas of learning by association are widely recognized in popular culture (there is even a Rolling Stones song that referred to "salivatin' like Pavlov's dogs"). However, how he came to make his landmark discoveries and the true significance of his work are not so widely understood.

While Pavlov's contribution to psychology was one of the most important ever made, he was not a psychologist at all, but rather a prominent Russian physiologist studying digestive processes. For his research on digestion he was awarded the Nobel Prize for science. But the discoveries that dramatically changed his career, and the history of psychology, began virtually by accident. It is important to note that in the late 1800s, psychology was a very young science and considered by many to be less than a true science. Therefore, Pavlov's decision to make such a radical turn from the more solid and respected science of physiology to psychology was a risky career move. He wrote about the dilemma facing a physiologist whose work might involve studying the brain:

> It is logical that in its analysis of the various activities of living matter, physiology should base itself on the more advanced and more exact sciences, physics and chemistry. But if we attempt an approach from this science of psychology . . . we shall be building our superstructure on a science that has no claim to exactness. . . . In fact, it is still open to discussion whether psychology is a natural science, or whether it can be regarded as a science at all. (p. 3)

Looking back on Pavlov's discoveries, it was fortunate for the advancement of psychological science and for our understanding of human behavior that he took the risk and made the career change.

Pavlov's physiological research involved the use of dogs as subjects for studying the role of salivation on digestion. He or his assistants would introduce various food or nonfood substances into a dog's mouth and observe the rate and amount of salivation. In order to measure salivation scientifically, minor surgery was performed on the dogs so that a salivary duct was redirected through an incision in the dog's cheek and connected to a tube that would collect the saliva. Throughout this research, Pavlov made many new and interesting discoveries. For example, he found that when a dog received moist food, only a small amount of saliva would be produced, compared with a heavy flow when dry food was presented. The production of saliva under these varying conditions was regarded by Pavlov as a reflex, that is, a response that occurs *automatically* to a specific stimulus without the need for any learning. If you think about it, salivation is purely reflexive for humans, too.

Suppose I ask you, as you read this sentence, to salivate as heavily as you can. You cannot do it. But if you are hungry and find yourself sitting in front of your favorite food, you will salivate whether you want to or not!

So, Pavlov experimented with various stimuli to determine just how "intelligent" these salivary glands were. As the research continued, he began to notice certain events that were totally unexpected. The dogs began to salivate before any food reached their mouths and even before the odor of food was present. After a while, the dogs were salivating at times when no digestive stimulus was present at all. Somehow, the reflexive action of the salivary glands had been altered through the animals' experience in the lab: "Even the vessel from which the food has been given is sufficient to evoke an alimentary reflex [of salivation] complete in all its details; and, further, the secretion may be provoked even by the sight of the person who has brought the vessel, or by the sound of his footsteps" (p. 13).

This was the crossroads for Pavlov. He had observed digestive responses occurring to stimuli seemingly unrelated to digestion, and pure physiology could not provide an explanation for this. The answer had to be found in *psychology*.

THEORETICAL PROPOSITIONS

Pavlov theorized that the dogs had learned from experience in the lab to expect food following the appearance of certain signals. While these *signal stimuli* do not naturally produce salivation, the dogs came to associate them with food, and thus responded to them with salivation. Consequently, Pavlov determined that there must be two kinds of reflexes.

Unconditioned reflexes are inborn and automatic, require no learning, and are generally the same for all members of a species. Salivating when food enters the mouth, jumping at the sound of a loud noise, and the dilation of your pupils in low light are examples of unconditioned reflexes. *Conditioned reflexes*, on the other hand, are acquired through experience or learning and may vary a great deal among individual members of a species. A dog salivating at the sound of footsteps, or you feeling pain in your teeth when you smell dental disinfectant, are conditioned reflexes.

Unconditioned reflexes are formed by an *unconditioned stimulus* (UCS) producing an *unconditioned response* (UCR). In Pavlov's studies, the UCS was food and the UCR was salivation. *Conditioned reflexes* consist of a *conditioned stimulus* (CS), such as the footsteps, producing a *conditioned response* (CR), salivation. You will notice that the response in both of these examples is salivation, but when the salivation results from hearing footsteps, it is conditioning that produced it.

The question Pavlov wanted to answer was this: Since conditioned reflexes are not inborn, exactly how are they acquired? He proposed that if a particular stimulus in the dog's environment was often present when the dog was fed, this stimulus would become associated in the dog's brain with food; it would signal the approaching food. Prior to being paired with the food, the environmental stimulus did not produce any important response. In other words, to the dogs, it was a *neutral stimulus* (NS). When the dogs first arrived at the lab, the assistant's footsteps might have produced a response of curiosity (Pavlov called it the "What is it?" response), but hearing the footsteps certainly would not have caused the dogs to salivate. The footsteps, then, were a neutral stimulus. However, over time, as the dogs heard the same footsteps just prior to being fed every day, they would begin to associate the sound with food. Eventually, according to the theory, the footsteps alone would cause the dogs to salivate. So, Pavlov proposed that the process by which a neutral stimulus becomes a conditioned stimulus could be diagrammed as follows:

Step 1			UCS (food)	$\longrightarrow$	UCR (salivation)
Step 2	NS (footsteps)	+ +	UCS (food)	$\longrightarrow$	UCR (salivation)
Step 3	(Repeat step 2 several times)				
Step 4			CS (footsteps)	$\longrightarrow$	CR (salivation)

Now that he had a theory to explain his observations, Pavlov began a series of experiments to prove that it was correct. It is commonly believed that Pavlov conditioned dogs to salivate at the sound of a bell. But as you will see, his early experiments involved a metronome.

METHOD AND RESULTS

Pavlov was able to build a special laboratory at the Institute of Experimental Medicine in Petrograd (which became Leningrad and has now returned to its original name of St. Petersburg) with funds donated by "a keen and public-spirited Moscow businessman." This soundproof lab allowed for complete isolation of the subjects from the experimenters and from all extraneous stimuli during the experimental procedures. Therefore, a specific stimulus could be administered and responses could be recorded without any direct contact between the experimenters and the animals.

After Pavlov had established this controlled research environment, the procedure was quite simple. Pavlov chose food as the unconditioned stimulus. As explained previously, food will elicit the unconditioned response of salivation. Then Pavlov needed to find a neutral stimulus that was, for the dogs, completely unrelated to food. For this he used the sound of the metronome. Over several conditioning trials, the dog was exposed to the ticking of the metronome and then was immediately presented with food. "A stimulus which was neutral of itself had been superimposed upon the action of the inborn alimentary reflex. We observed that, after several repetitions of the combined stimulation, the sounds of the metronome had acquired the property of stimulating salivary secretion" (p. 26). In other words, the metronome had become a conditioned stimulus for the conditioned response of salivation.

Pavlov and his associates elaborated on this preliminary finding by using different unconditioned and neutral stimuli. For example, they presented the odor of vanilla (NS) to the subjects prior to placing a lemon juice–like solution in the dog's mouth (the UCS). The juice caused heavy salivation (UCR). After 20 repetitions of the pairing, the vanilla alone produced salivation. For a visual test, the dogs were exposed to an object that began to rotate just prior to the presentation of food. After only five pairings, the rotating object by itself (CS) caused the dogs to salivate (CR).

The importance and application of Pavlov's work extends far beyond salivating dogs. His theories of classical conditioning explained a major portion of human behavior and helped to launch psychology as a true science.

SIGNIFICANCE OF THE FINDINGS

The theory of classical conditioning (also called Pavlovian conditioning) is universally accepted and has remained virtually unchanged since its conception through Pavlov's work. It is used to explain and interpret a wide range of human behavior, including where phobias come from, why you dislike certain foods, the source of your emotions, how advertising works, why you feel anxiety before a job interview or an exam, and what arouses you sexually. Several later studies dealing with some of these applications are discussed here.

Classical conditioning focuses on reflexive behavior: those behaviors that are not under your voluntary control. Any reflex can be conditioned to occur to a previously neutral stimulus. You can be classically conditioned so that your left eye blinks when you hear a doorbell, your heart rate increases at the sight of a flashing blue light, or you experience sexual arousal when you eat strawberries. The doorbell, blue light, and strawberries were all neutral in relation to the conditioned responses until they somehow became associated with unconditioned stimuli for eye blinking (i.e., a puff of air into the eye), heart rate increase (i.e., a sudden loud noise), and sexual arousal (i.e., romantic caresses).

To experience firsthand the process of classical conditioning, here is an experiment you can perform on yourself. All you will need is a bell, a mirror, and a room that becomes completely dark when the light is switched off, to serve as your temporary laboratory. The pupils of your eyes dilate and constrict reflexively according to changes in light intensity. You have no voluntary control over this, and you did not have to learn how to do it. If I say to you, "Please dilate your pupils now," you would be unable to do so. However, when you walk into a dark theater, they dilate immediately. Therefore, a decrease in light would be considered an unconditioned stimulus for pupil dilation, the unconditioned response. In your *lab*, ring the bell and immediately after, turn off the light. Wait in the total darkness about 15 seconds and turn the light back on. Wait another 15 seconds and repeat the procedure: bell . . . light off . . . wait 15 seconds . . . light on. . . . Repeat this pairing of the neutral stimulus (the bell) with the unconditioned stimulus (the darkness) 10 to 20 times, making sure that the bell *only* rings just prior to the sudden darkness. Now, with the lights on, watch your eyes closely in the mirror, and ring the bell. You will see your pupils dilate slightly even though there is no change in light! The bell has become the conditioned stimulus and pupil dilation the conditioned response.

RELATED RESEARCH AND RECENT APPLICATIONS

Two other studies presented in this book, rest directly on Pavlov's theory of classical conditioning. In the next article, John B. Watson conditioned 11-month-old little Albert to fear a white rat (and other furry things) by employing the same principles Pavlov used to condition salivation in dogs. By doing so, Watson demonstrated how emotions, such as fear, are formed. Later, Joseph Wolpe (see chapter 9 on psychotherapy) developed a therapeutic technique for treating intense fears (phobias) by applying the concepts of classical conditioning. His work was based on the idea that the association between the conditioned stimulus and the unconditioned stimulus must be broken in order to reduce the fearful response.

This line of research on classical conditioning and phobias continues to the present. For example, studies have found that children whose parents have phobias may develop the same phobias to objects such as snakes and spiders through "vicarious" conditioning from mom and dad without any direct exposure to the feared object (Fredrikson, Annas, & Wik, 1997). Moreover, Pavlov's discoveries continue to be used to treat phobias in adults and children alike (e.g., King et al., 2000).

The countless applications of Pavlov's theory in the psychological and medical literature are far too numerous to summarize in any detail here. Instead, a few additional examples of the more notable findings are discussed.

A common problem that plagues ranchers around the world is that of predatory animals, usually wolves and coyotes, killing and eating their livestock. In the early 1970s, studies were conducted that attempted to apply Pavlovian conditioning techniques to solve the problem of the killing of sheep by coyotes and wolves without the need for killing the predators (see Gustafson et al., 1974). Wolves and coyotes were given pieces of mutton containing small amounts of lithium chloride (UCS), a chemical that if ingested makes an animal sick. When the animals ate the meat, they became dizzy, with severe nausea and vomiting (UCR). After recovering, these same hungry predators were placed in a pen with live sheep. The wolves and coyotes began to attack the sheep (CS), but as soon as they smelled their prey, they stopped and stayed as far away from the sheep as possible. When the gate to the pen was opened, the wolves and coyotes actually ran away from the sheep! Based on this and other related research, ranchers commonly use this method of classical conditioning to keep wolves and coyotes away from their herds.

A potentially vital area of research involving classical conditioning is in the field of behavioral medicine. Studies have indicated that the activity of the immune system can be altered using Pavlovian principles. Ader and Cohen (1985) gave mice water flavored with saccharine (mice love this water). They then paired the saccharine water with an injection of a drug that weakened the immune system of the mice. Later, when these conditioned mice were given the saccharine water but no injection, they showed signs of immunosuppression, a weakening of the immune response. Research is underway to study if the reverse is also possible, if immune *enhancing* responses may be classically conditioned. Overall, research is demonstrating that classical conditioning may indeed hold great promise for increasing the effectiveness of immune system responses in humans (Miller & Cohen, 2001). Just imagine: one day soon, you may be able to strengthen your resistance to illness by exposing yourself to a *nonmedical* conditioned stimulus. For example, imagine you feel the beginnings of a cold or the flu, so you slide your special classically conditioned "immune response enhancement music disk" into your CD player. As the music fills the room, your resistance rises as a conditioned response to this stimulus and stops the disease in its tracks.

As a demonstration of the continuing impact of Pavlov's discoveries on today's psychological research, consider the following. Since the previous edition of this book (2000–2003), more than 300 scientific articles cited Pavlov's work that forms the basis for this discussion. One especially fascinating recent study demonstrated how your psychological state at the time of conditioning and extinction may play a part in the treatment of classically conditioned irrational fears, called phobias (Mystkowski et al., 2003). Researchers used desensitization techniques to treat participants who were terrified of spiders. Some received the treatment after ingesting caffeine while others ingested a placebo. A week later, all subjects were retested—some receiving caffeine and others a placebo. Those who were given the placebo during treatment, but received real caffeine at the follow-up, *and* those who had received real caffeine during treatment, but received a placebo at the follow-up, experienced a relapse of the fear response. However, subjects who were in the same drug condition, either caffeine or placebo, at treatment *and* follow-up, displayed a much lower return of their fear. This finding implies that if a classically conditioned behavior is placed on extinction, it may return if the conditioned stimulus is encountered in a different context from where the extinction took place.

CONCLUSION

These examples demonstrate how extensive Pavlov's influence has been on many scientific and research disciplines. For psychology in particular, few scientists have had as much impact in any single discipline. Classical conditioning is one of the fundamental theories on which modern psychology rests. Without Pavlov's contributions, behavioral scientists still might have uncovered most of these principles over the decades. It is unlikely, however, that such a cohesive, elegant, and well-articulated theory of the conditioned reflex would ever have existed if Pavlov had not made the decision to risk his career and venture into the untested, uncharted, and highly questionable science of nineteenth-century psychology.

Ader, R., & Cohen, N. (1985). CNS-immune system interactions: Conditioning phenomena. *Behavioral and Brain Sciences, 8,* 379–394.

Fredrikson, M., Annas, P., & Wik, G. (1997). Parental history, aversive exposure, and the development of snake and spider phobias in women. *Behavior Research and Therapy, 35*(1), 23–28.

Gustafson, C. R., Garcia, J., Hawkins, W., & Rusiniak, K. (1974). Coyote predation control by aversive conditioning. *Science, 184,* 581–583.

King, N., Ollendick, T., Murphy, G., & Muris, P. (2000). Animal phobias in children: Etiology, assessment, and treatment. *Clinical Psychology and Psychotherapy, 7*(1), 11–21.

Miller, G., & Cohen, S. (2001). Psychological interventions and the immune system: A meta-analytic review and critique. *Health Psychology, 20,* 47–63.

Mystkowski, J., Mineka, S., Vernon, L., & Zinbarg, R. (2003). Changes in caffeine states enhance return of fear in spider phobia. *Journal of Consulting and Clinical Psychology, 71,* 243–250.

LITTLE EMOTIONAL ALBERT
Watson, J. B., & Rayner, R. (1920). Conditioned emotional responses. *Journal of Experimental Psychology, 3,* 1–14.

Have you ever wondered where your emotions come from? If you have, you're not alone. The source of emotions has fascinated behavioral scientists throughout psychology's history. Part of the evidence for this fascination can be found in this book; four studies are included that relate directly to emotional responses (chapter 5, Harlow, 1958; chapter 6, Ekman & Friesen, 1971; chapter 8, Seligman & Meier, 1967; and chapter 9, Wolpe, 1961). This study by Watson and Raynor on conditioned emotional responses was a strikingly powerful piece of research when it was published more than 70 years ago, and it continues to exert influence today. You would be hard pressed to pick up a textbook on general psychology or on learning and behavior without finding a summary of their findings.

The historical importance of this study is not solely due to the research findings, but also to the new psychological territory it pioneered. If we could be transported back to the turn of the century and get a feel for the state of psychology at the time, we would find it nearly completely dominated by the work of Sigmund Freud (see the reading on A. Freud in chapter 8). Freud's psychoanalytic view of human behavior was based on the idea that we are motivated by unconscious instincts and repressed conflicts from early childhood. In simplified Freudian terms, behavior, and specifically emotion, is generated internally through biological and instinctual processes.

In the 1920s, a new movement in psychology known as behaviorism, spearheaded by Pavlov and Watson, began to take hold. The behaviorist viewpoint was radically opposed to the psychoanalytic school and proposed that behavior is generated outside the person through various environmental or situational stimuli. Therefore, Watson theorized, emotional responses exist in us because we have been conditioned to respond emotionally to certain stimuli in the environment. In other words, we learn our emotional reactions. Watson believed that all human behavior was a product of learning and conditioning, as he proclaimed in his famous statement of 1913:

> Give me a dozen healthy infants, well-formed, and my own special world to bring them up in, and I'll guarantee to take any one at random and train him to become any type of specialist I might select doctor, lawyer, artist, merchant-chief, and, yes, beggarman and thief. (Watson, 1913)

This was, for its time, an extremely revolutionary view. Most psychologists, as well as public opinion in general, were not ready to accept these new ideas. This was especially true for emotional reactions, which seemed to be somehow generated from within. So Watson set out to demonstrate that emotions could be experimentally conditioned.

THEORETICAL PROPOSITIONS

Watson theorized that if a stimulus that automatically produces a certain emotion in you (such as fear) is repeatedly experienced at the same moment as something else, such as a rat, the rat will become associated in your brain with the fear. In other words, you will eventually become conditioned to be afraid of the rat. He maintained that we are not born to fear rats, but that such fears are learned through conditioning. This formed the theoretical basis for his most famous experiment, involving a subject named "Little Albert B."

METHOD AND RESULTS

The subject, Albert B., was recruited for this study at the age of nine months from a hospital where he had been raised, as an orphan, from birth. He was judged by the researchers and the hospital staff to be very healthy, both emotionally and physically. In order to see if Albert was afraid of certain stimuli, he was presented with a white rat, a rabbit, a monkey, a dog, masks with and without hair, and white cotton wool. Albert's reactions to these stimuli were closely observed. Albert was interested in the various animals and objects and would reach for them and sometimes touch them, but he never showed the slightest fear of any of them. Since they produced no fear, these are referred to as *neutral stimuli.*

The next phase of the experiment involved determining if a fear reaction could be produced in Albert by exposing him to a loud noise. All humans, and especially all infants, will exhibit fear reactions to loud, sudden noises. Since no learning is necessary for this response to occur, the loud noise is called an *unconditioned stimulus.* In this study, a steel bar four feet in length was struck with a hammer behind Albert. This noise startled and frightened him and made him cry.

Now the stage was set for testing the idea that the emotion of fear could be conditioned in Albert. The actual conditioning test was not done until the child was 11 months old. There was hesitation on the part of the researchers to create fear reactions in a child experimentally, but they made the decision to proceed based on what was, in retrospect, questionable ethical reasoning. (This is discussed in conjunction with the overall ethical problems of this study, later in this chapter.)

As the experiment began, the researchers presented Albert with the white rat and the frightening noise at the same time. At first, Albert was interested in the rat and reached out to touch it. As he did this, the metal bar was struck, which startled and frightened Albert. This process was repeated three times. One week later, the same procedure was followed. After a total of seven pairings of the noise and the rat, the rat was presented to Albert alone, without the noise. Well, as you've probably guessed by now, Albert reacted with extreme fear to the rat. He began to cry, turned away, rolled over on one side away from the rat, and began to crawl away so fast that the researchers had to rush to catch him before he crawled off the edge of the table! A fear response had been conditioned to an object that had not been feared only one week earlier.

The researchers then wanted to determine if this learned fear would transfer to other objects. In psychological terms, this transfer is referred to as *generalization*. If Albert showed fear to other similar objects, then the learned behavior is said to have generalized. The next week, Albert was tested again and was still found to be afraid of the rat. Then to test for generalization, an object similar to the rat (a white rabbit) was presented to Albert. In the author's words: "Negative responses began at once. He leaned as far away from the animal as possible, whimpered, then burst into tears. When the rabbit was placed in contact with him, he buried his face in the mattress, then got up on all fours and crawled away, crying as he went" (p. 6). Remember, Albert was not afraid of the rabbit prior to conditioning, and had not been conditioned to fear the rabbit specifically.

Little Albert was presented over the course of this day of testing with a dog, a white fur coat, a package of cotton, and Watson's own head of gray hair. He reacted to all of these items with fear. One of the most well-known tests of generalization that made this research as infamous as it is famous occurred when Watson presented Albert with a Santa Claus mask. The reaction? Yes . . . fear!

After another five days Albert was tested again. The sequence of presentations on this day are summarized in Table 1.

Another aspect of conditioned emotional responses Watson wanted to explore was whether the learned emotion would transfer from one situation to another. If Albert's fear responses to these various animals and objects occurred only in the experimental setting and nowhere else, the significance of the findings would be greatly reduced. To test this, later on the day outlined in Table 1, Albert was taken to an entirely different room with brighter lighting and more people present. In this new setting, Albert's reactions to the rat and rabbit were still clearly fearful, although somewhat less intense.

TABLE 1 Sequence of Stimulus Presentations to Albert on Fourth Day of Testing

STIMULUS PRESENTED	REACTION OBSERVED
1. Blocks	Played with blocks as usual
2. Rat	Fearful withdrawal (no crying)
3. Rat + Noise	Fear and crying
4. Rat	Fear and crying
5. Rat	Fear, crying, and crawling away
6. Rabbit	Fear, but less strong reaction than on former presentations
7. Blocks	Played as usual
8. Rabbit	Same as 6
9. Rabbit	Same as 6
10. Rabbit	Some fear, but also wanted to touch rabbit
11. Dog	Fearful avoidance
12. Dog + Noise	Fear and crawling away
13. Blocks	Normal play

The final test that Watson and Raynor wanted to make was to see if Albert's newly learned emotional responses would persist over time. Well, Albert had been adopted and was scheduled to leave the hospital in the near future. Therefore, all testing was discontinued for a period of 31 days. At the end of this time, he was once again presented with the Santa Claus mask, the white fur coat, the rat, the rabbit, and the dog. After a month, Albert was still very afraid of all these objects.

Watson and his colleagues had planned to attempt to *recondition* little Albert and eliminate these fearful reactions. However, Albert left the hospital on the day these last tests were made, and, as far as anyone knows, no reconditioning ever took place.

DISCUSSION AND SIGNIFICANCE OF FINDINGS

Watson had two fundamental goals in this study and in all his work: (a) to demonstrate that all human behavior stems from learning and conditioning and (b) to demonstrate that the Freudian conception of psychology, that our behavior stems from unconscious processes, was wrong. This study, with all its methodological flaws and serious breaches of ethical conduct (to be discussed shortly) succeeded to a large extent in convincing a great portion of the psychological community that emotional behavior could be conditioned through simple stimulus-response techniques. This finding helped, in turn, to launch one of the major schools of thought in psychology: behaviorism. Here, something as complex, personal, and human as an emotion was shown to be subject to conditioning, just as a rat in a maze learns to find the food faster and faster on each successive try.

A logical extension of this is that other emotions, such as anger, joy, sadness, surprise, or disgust, may be learned in the same manner. In other words, the reason you are sad when you hear that old song, nervous when you have a job interview or a public speaking engagement, happy when spring arrives, or afraid when you hear a dental drill is that you have developed an association in your brain between these stimuli and specific emotions through conditioning. Other more extreme emotional responses, such as phobias and sexual fetishes, may also develop through similar sequences of conditioning. These processes are the same as what Watson found with little Albert, although usually more complex.

Watson was quick to point out that his findings could explain human behavior in rather straightforward and simple terms, compared with the psychoanalytic notions of Freud and his followers. As Watson and Raynor explained in their article, a Freudian would explain thumb sucking as an expression of the original pleasure-seeking instinct. Albert, however, would suck his thumb whenever he felt afraid. As soon as his thumb entered his mouth, he ceased being afraid. Therefore, Watson interpreted thumb sucking as a conditioned device for blocking fear-producing stimuli.

An additional attack on Freudian thinking made in this article concerned how Freudians in the future, given the opportunity, might analyze Albert's fear of a white fur coat. Watson and Raynor claimed that Freudian analysts "will probably tease from him the recital of a dream which, upon their analysis, will show that Albert at three years of age attempted to play with the pubic hair of the mother and was scolded violently for it." Their main point was that they had demonstrated with little Albert that emotional disturbances in adults cannot always be attributed to sexual traumas in childhood, as the Freudian view was commonly interpreted.

QUESTIONS AND CRITICISMS

As you have been reading this, you have probably been concerned or even angered over the treatment by the experimenters of this innocent child. This study clearly violates current standards of ethical conduct in research involving humans. It would be highly unlikely that any human-subjects committee at any research institution would approve this study today. Eighty years ago, however, such ethical standards did not formally exist, and it is not unusual to find reports in the early psychological literature of what now appear to be questionable research methods. It must be pointed out that Watson and his colleagues were not sadistic or cruel people and that they were engaged in a new, unexplored area of research. They acknowledged considerable hesitation in proceeding with the conditioning process, but decided that it was justifiable, since, in their opinion, some such fears would arise anyway when Albert left the sheltered hospital environment. Even so, is it ever appropriate to frighten a child to this extent, regardless of the importance of the potential discovery? Today nearly all behavioral scientists would agree that it is not.

Another important point regarding the ethics of this study was the fact that Albert was allowed to leave the research setting and was never reconditioned to remove his fears. Watson and Raynor contend in their article that such emotional conditioning may persist over a person's lifetime. If they were correct on this point, it is extremely difficult, from an ethical perspective, to justify allowing someone to grow into adulthood fearful of all these objects (and who knows how many others!).

On a related point, several researchers have criticized Watson's assumption that these conditioned fears would persist indefinitely (Harris, 1979). Others claim that Albert was not conditioned as effectively as the authors maintained (Samelson, 1980). It has frequently been demonstrated that behaviors acquired through conditioning can be lost because of other experiences or simply because of the passage of time. Imagine, for example, that when Albert turned five, he was given a pet white rabbit for a birthday present. At first, he might have been afraid of it (no doubt baffling his adoptive parents). But as he continued to be exposed to the rabbit without anything frightening occurring (such as that loud noise), very likely he slowly became less and less afraid until the rabbit no longer caused a fear response. This is a well-established process in learning psychology called *extinction,* and it happens routinely as part of the constant learning and unlearning, conditioning and unconditioning processes we experience throughout our lives.

RECENT APPLICATIONS

Watson's 1920 article continues to be cited in research in a wide range of fields, including parenting and psychotherapy. One potentially valuable study, examined the facial expressions of emotion in infants (Sullivan & Lewis, 2003). We know that facial expressions corresponding to specific emotions are consistent among all adults and across cultures (see the reading on Ekman's research in chapter 6). This study, however, extended this research to how such expressions develop in infants and what the various expressions mean at very young ages. A greater understanding of infants' facial expressions might be of great help in adults' efforts to communicate with and care for babies. The authors noted that their goal in their research was "to provide practitioners with basic information to help them and the parents they serve become better able to recognize the expressive signals of the infants and young children in their care" (Sullivan & Lewis, 2003). This study's use of Watson's findings offers us a degree of comfort in that his questionable research tactics with Little Albert, may, in the final analysis, allow for greater sensitivity and perception into the feelings and needs of infants.

As mentioned earlier in this discussion, one emotion, fear, in its extreme form, can produce serious negative consequences known as phobias. Many psychologists believe that phobias are conditioned much like Little Albert's fear of furry animals (see the discussion of Wolpe's research on the treatment of phobias later in this book). Watson's research has been incorporated into many recent studies about the origins and treatments of phobias. One such article discussed phobias from the nature-nurture perspective and found some remarkable results. Watson's approach, of course, is rooted completely in the environmental or nurture side of the argument, and most people would view phobias as learned. However, a study by Kendler, Karkowski, and Prescott (1999) provided compelling evidence that the development of phobias may include a substantial genetic component. The researchers studied phobias and unreasonable fears in more than 1,700 female twins (see the discussion of Bouchard's twin research in the first section of this book). They claim to have found that a large percentage of the variation in phobias was due to inherited factors. The authors concluded that, while phobias may be molded by an individual's personal environmental experiences, the role of the family in phobias is primarily biological, not environmental.

Imagine: *Born to be phobic!* This view flies directly in the face of Watson's theory and should provide plenty of fuel for the ongoing nature-nurture debate in psychology and throughout the behavioral sciences.

Harris, B. (1979). What ever happened to little Albert? *American Psychologist, 34,* 151–160.

Kendler, K., Karkowski, L., & Prescott, C. (1999). Fears and phobias: reliability and heritability. *Psychological Medicine, 29*(3), 539–553.

Samelson, F. (1980). Watson's little Albert, Cyril Burt's twins, and the need for a critical science. *American Psychologist, 35,* 619–625.

Sullivan, M., & Lewis, M. (2003). Emotional expressions of young infants and children: A practitioner's primer. *Infants and Young Children, 16,* 120–142.

Watson, J. B. (1913). Psychology as the behaviorist views it. *Psychological Review, 20,* 158–177.

KNOCK WOOD!

Skinner, B. F. (1948). Superstition in the pigeon. *Journal of Experimental Psychology, 38,* 168–172.

In this reading, we examine one study from a *huge* body of research carried out by one of the most influential and most widely known psychologists ever, B. F. Skinner. Deciding how to present Skinner and which of his studies to explore was a difficult task. It is impossible to represent adequately in one short article Skinner's contributions to the history of psychology. After all, Skinner is considered by most to be the father of radical behaviorism, he was the inventor of the famous (or infamous) *Skinner Box,* and he was the author of over a dozen books and more than 70 scientific articles. This article, with the funny sounding title "Superstition in the Pigeon," has been selected from all of his work because it allows for a clear discussion of Skinner's basic theories, provides an interesting example of his approach to studying behavior, and offers a "Skinnerian" explanation of a behavior with which we are all familiar: superstition.

Skinner is referred to as a *radical behaviorist* because he believed that everything psychological is, essentially, behavioral, including public, or external behavior, and private, or internal, events such as feelings and thoughts. Although he believed that *private* behavior is difficult to study, he acknowledged that we all have our own subjective experience of these behaviors. He did not, however, view internal events, such as thoughts and emotions, as causes of behavior, but rather as part of the mix of environment and behavior that he was seeking to explain (see Schneider & Morris, 1987, for a detailed discussion of the term *radical behaviorism*). So, for Skinner, all behavior, whether internal or external, could be explained by the environmental consequences it produces.

To put Skinner's theory in very basic terms: In any given situation, your behavior is likely to be followed by consequences. Some of these consequences, such as praise, receiving money, or the satisfaction of solving a problem, will make the behavior more likely to be repeated in future similar situations. These consequences are called reinforcers. Other consequences, such as injuring yourself or feeling embarrassed, will tend to make the behavior less likely to be repeated in similar situations and are called punishers. The effects of these relationships between behavior and the environment are called reinforcement and punishment, respectively (Morris, 1997). Reinforcement and punishment are two of the most fundamental processes in what Skinner referred to as operant conditioning and may be diagrammed as follows:

Within this conceptualization, Skinner also was able to explain how learned behaviors decrease and sometimes disappear entirely. When a behavior has been reinforced and the reinforcement is then withdrawn, the likelihood of the behavior reoccurring will slowly decrease until the behavior is effectively suppressed. This process of behavior suppression is called *extinction*.

If you think about it, these ideas are not new to you. The process we use to train our pets follows these same rules. You tell a dog to sit, it sits, and you reward it with a treat. After a while the dog will sit when told to, even without an immediate reward. You have applied the principles of operant conditioning. This is a very powerful form of learning and is effective with all animals, even old dogs learning new tricks and, yes, even cats! Also, if you want a pet to stop doing something, all you have to do is remove the reinforcement, and the behavior will stop. For example, if your dog is begging at the dinner table, there is a reason for that (regardless of what you may think, dogs are not born to beg at the table!). You have conditioned this behavior in your dog through reinforcement. If you want to *put that behavior on extinction*, the reinforcement must be totally discontinued. Eventually, the dog will stop begging. By the way, if one member of the family cheats during extinction and secretly gives the beggar some food once in a while, extinction will never happen.

Beyond these fundamentals of learning, Skinner maintained that all human behavior is created and maintained in precisely the same way. It's just that with humans, the exact behaviors and consequences are not always so easy to identify. Skinner was well known for arguing that if a human behavior was interpreted by others (such as cognitive or humanistic psychologists) to be due to our highly evolved consciousness or intellectual capabilities, it was only because psychologists had been unable to pinpoint the reinforcers that had created and were maintaining the behavior. If this feels like a rather extreme position to you, remember that Skinner's position was called radical behaviorism and was always surrounded by controversy.

Skinner often met skepticism and defended his views by demonstrating experimentally that behaviors considered to be the sole property of humans could be learned by lowly creatures such as pigeons or rats. One of these demonstrations involved the contention by others that superstitious behavior is uniquely human. The argument was that superstition requires human cognitive activity (thinking, knowing, reasoning). A superstition is a belief in something, and we do not usually attribute such *beliefs* to animals. Well, Skinner said in essence that superstitious behavior could be explained as easily as any other action by using the principles of operant conditioning. He performed an experiment to prove it.

THEORETICAL PROPOSITIONS

Think back to a time when you have behaved superstitiously. Did you knock on wood, avoid walking under a ladder, avoid stepping on cracks, carry a lucky coin or other charm, shake the dice a certain way in a board game, change your behavior because of your horoscope? It is probably safe to say that everyone has done something out of superstition at some time, even if some of them might not want to admit it. Skinner said that the reason people do this is that they believe or presume that there is a connection between the superstitious behavior and some reinforcing consequence, even though, in reality, there is not. This connection exists because the behavior (such as shaking the dice that certain way) was accidentally reinforced (such as a good roll) once, twice, or several times. Skinner called this *noncontingent* reinforcement, a reward that is not contingent on any particular behavior. You believe that there is a causal relationship between the behavior and the reward, when no such relationship exists.

"If you think this is some exclusive human activity," Skinner might have said, "I'll make a superstitious pigeon!"

METHOD

In order to understand the method used in this experiment, a brief description of what has become known as the Skinner Box is necessary. The principle behind the Skinner Box (or conditioning chamber, as Skinner called it) is really quite simple. It consists of a cage or box that is empty except for a dish or tray into which food may be dispensed. This allows a researcher to have control over when the animal receives reinforcement, such as pellets of food. The early conditioning boxes also contained a lever which, if pressed, would cause some food to be dispensed. If a rat (rats were used in Skinner's earliest work) was placed in one of these boxes, it would eventually, through trial and error, learn to press the lever for food. Alternately, the experimenter could, if desired, control the food dispenser and reinforce a specific behavior. Later it was found that pigeons also made ideal subjects in conditioning experiments, and conditioning chambers were designed with disks to be pecked instead of bars to be pressed.

One of these conditioning cages was used in the study discussed here, but with one important change. In order to study superstitious behavior, the food dispenser was rigged to drop food pellets into the tray at intervals of 15 seconds, regardless of what the animal was doing at the time. You can see that this produced noncontingent reinforcement. In other words, the animal received a reward every 15 seconds, no matter what it did.

Subjects in this study were eight pigeons. These birds were fed less than their normal daily amount for several days, so that when tested they would be hungry and therefore highly motivated to perform behaviors for food. (This increased the power of the reinforcement.) Each pigeon was placed into the experimental cage for a few minutes each day and just left to do whatever a pigeon does. During this time, reinforcement was being delivered automatically every 15 seconds. After several days of conditioning in this way, two independent observers recorded the birds' behavior in the cage.

RESULTS

As Skinner reports:

> In six out of eight cases the resulting responses were so clearly defined that two observers could agree perfectly in counting instances. One bird was conditioned to turn counterclockwise about the cage, making two or three turns between reinforcements. Another repeatedly thrust its head into one of the upper corners of the cage. A third developed a tossing response as if placing its head beneath an invisible bar and lifting it repeatedly. Two birds developed a pendulum motion of the head and body in which the head was extended forward and swung from right to left with a sharp movement followed by a somewhat slower return. The body generally followed the movement and a few steps might be taken when it was extensive. Another bird was conditioned to make incomplete pecking or brushing movements directed toward but not touching the floor. (p. 168)

None of these behaviors had been observed in the birds prior to the conditioning procedure. The new behavior had nothing to do with the pigeon receiving food. Nevertheless, they behaved as if a certain action would produce the food; that is, they became superstitious.

Skinner next wanted to see what would happen if the time interval between reinforcements was extended. With one of the head-bobbing birds, the interval between the delivery of food pellets was slowly increased to one minute. When this occurred, the pigeon's movements became more energetic until finally the stepping became so pronounced that it appeared the bird was performing a kind of dance during the minute between reinforcement (such as a *pigeon food dance*).

Finally, the new behavior of the birds was put on extinction. This meant that the reinforcement in the test cage was discontinued. When this happened, the superstitious behaviors gradually decreased until they disappeared altogether. However, in the case of the *hopping* pigeon with a reinforcement interval that had been increased to a minute, over 10,000 responses were recorded before extinction occurred!

DISCUSSION

Clearly, what Skinner ended up with here was six superstitious pigeons. However, he explains his findings more carefully and modestly: "The experiment might be said to demonstrate a sort of superstition. The bird behaves as if there were a causal relation between its behavior and the presentation of food, although such a relation is lacking" (p. 171).

The next step would be to apply these findings to humans. I am sure it is not difficult for you to think of analogies in human behavior, nor was it for Skinner. He described "the bowler who has released a ball down the alley but continues to behave as if he were controlling it by twisting and turning his arm and shoulder as another case in point" (p. 171). You know, rationally, that behaviors such as these don't really have any effect on a bowling ball that is already halfway down the alley. As Skinner points out in the case of the pigeons in this study, the food was going to appear no matter what the bird did.

An additional and interesting point made by Skinner in this article was that it is not completely correct to conclude that there is no relationship between the twisting and turning of the bowler and the direction of the ball. What is true is that after the ball has left the bowler's hand, the "bowler's behavior has no effect on the ball, but the behavior of the ball has an effect on the bowler" (p. 171). In other words, it is a fact that on some occasions, the ball might happen to move in the direction of the bowler's body movements. That movement of the ball, coupled with the consequence of a strike or a spare, is enough to accidentally reinforce the twisting behavior and maintain the superstition.

Finally, the reason that superstitions are so resistant to extinction was demonstrated by the pigeon that hopped 10,000 times before giving up the behavior. When any behavior is only reinforced once in a while, it becomes very difficult to extinguish. This is because the expectation stays high that the superstitious behavior might work to produce the reinforcing consequences. You can imagine that if the connection was present every time and then disappeared, the behavior would stop quickly. However, for humans, the instances of that accidental reinforcement usually occur at large time intervals, so the superstitious behavior often may persist for a lifetime.

CRITICISMS AND SUBSEQUENT RESEARCH

Skinner's behaviorist theories and research have always been the subject of great and sometimes heated controversy. Other prominent theoretical approaches to human behavior have argued that the strict behavioral view is unable to account for many of the psychological processes that are fundamental to humans. Carl Rogers, the founder of the *humanistic* school of psychology, and well known for his debates with Skinner, summed up this criticism:

> In this world of inner meanings, humanistic psychology can investigate issues which are meaningless for the behaviorist: purposes, goals, values, choice, perceptions of self, perceptions of others, the personal constructs with which we build our world . . . the whole phenomenal world of the individual with its connective tissue of meaning. Not one aspect of this world is open to the strict behaviorist. Yet that these elements have significance for man's behavior seems certainly true. (Rogers, 1964, p. 119)

Behaviorists would argue in turn that all of these human characteristics are open to behavioral analysis. The key to this analysis is a proper interpretation of the behaviors and consequences that constitute them. (See Skinner, 1974, for a complete discussion of these issues.)

On the specific issue of superstitions, however, there appears to be less controversy and a rather wide acceptance of the learning processes involved in their formation. An experiment performed by Bruner and Revuski (1961) demonstrated how easily superstitious behavior develops in humans. Four high school students each sat in front of four telegraph keys. They were told that each time they pressed the correct key, a bell would sound, a red light would flash, and they would earn a nickel. The correct response was key number 3. However, as in Skinner's study, key number 3 would produce the desired reinforcement only after a delay interval of 10 seconds. During this interval, the students would try other keys in various combinations. Then, at some point following the delay, they would hit the third key again and receive the reinforcement. The results were the same for all the students. After a while, they had each developed a pattern of key responses (such as 1, 2, 4, 3, 1, 2, 4, 3) that they repeated over and over between each reinforcement. Pressing the 3-key was the only reinforced behavior; the other presses in the sequence were completely superstitious. Not only did they behave superstitiously, but all the students believed that the other key presses were necessary to "set up" the reinforced key. They were not aware of their superstitious behavior.

RECENT APPLICATIONS

Skinner, as one of psychology's most influential figures, still has a far-reaching substantive impact on scientific literature in many fields. His 1948 article on superstitious behavior is cited in numerous studies every year. One of these studies, for example, compared two types of reinforcement in the development of superstitious behavior (Aeschleman, Rosen, & Williams, 2003). Positive reinforcement occurs when you receive something desirable as a consequence (such as money, food, or praise). Negative reinforcement rewards you by *eliminating* something *undesirable* (such as not having to do homework or avoiding pain). The study found that greater levels of superstitious behavior (perceived control over noncontingent events) developed under conditions of negative reinforcement than under positive reinforcement. In the authors' words: "These findings . . . suggest that, relative to positive reinforcement, negative reinforcement operations may provide a more fertile condition for the development and maintenance of superstitious behaviors" (p. 37). In other words, you are more likely to employ superstitious tactics to prevent bad outcomes than to create good outcomes.

Another thought-provoking article citing Skinner's 1948 study (Sagvolden et al., 1998) examined the role of reinforcement in attention deficit/hyperactivity disorder (ADHD). The researchers asked boys with and without a diagnosis of ADHD to participate in a game in which they would receive rewards of coins or small toys. Although the reinforcement was delivered at fixed 30-second intervals (noncontingent reinforcement), all the boys developed superstitious behaviors that they *believed* were related to the rewards. In the next phase of the study, the reinforcement was discontinued. You would expect this to cause a decrease and cessation of whatever behaviors had been conditioned (extinction). This is exactly what happened with the non-ADHD boys. But the boys with ADHD, after a brief pause, became more active and began engaging impulsively in bursts of responses at an even faster pace, *as if* the reinforcement had been reestablished. The authors suggested that this overactivity and impulsiveness implied that the ADHD boys possessed significantly less ability to cope with delays of reinforcement than did the comparison group of boys. Findings such as these are important additions to our understanding and our ability to treat ADHD effectively.

CONCLUSION

Superstitions are everywhere. You probably have some, and you surely know others who have them. One study of high school and college athletes found that 40% of them engaged in superstitious behavior before or during games (Buhrmann & Zaugg, 1981). Some superstitions are such a part of a culture that they produce society-wide effects. You may be aware that most high-rise buildings do not have a thirteenth floor. Well, that's not exactly true. Obviously, a thirteenth floor exists, but no floor is *labeled* "13." This is probably not because architects and builders are an overly superstitious bunch, but rather it is due to the difficulty of renting or selling space on the thirteenth floor. Another example is that Americans are so superstitious about $2 bills that the U.S. Treasury is sitting on a pile of 4 million of these bills that people refuse to use!

Are superstitions psychologically unhealthy? Most psychologists believe that even though superstitious behaviors, by definition, do not produce the consequences that you think they do, they can serve useful functions. Often such behaviors can produce a feeling of strength and control when a person is facing a difficult situation. It is interesting to note that people who are employed in dangerous occupations tend to have more superstitions than others. This feeling of increased power and control that is sometimes created by superstitious behavior can lead to reduced anxiety, greater confidence and assurance, and improved performance.

Aeschleman, S., Rosen, C., & Williams, M. (2003). The effect of non-contingent negative and positive reinforcement operations on the acquisition of superstitious behaviors. *Behavioural Processes, 61,* 37–45.

Bruner, A., & Revuski, S. (1961). Collateral behavior in humans. *Journal of the Experimental Analysis of Behavior, 4,* 349–350.

Buhrmann, H., & Zaugg, M. (1981). Superstitions among basketball players: An investigation of various forms of superstitious beliefs and behavior among competitive basketball players at the junior high school to university level. *Journal of Sport Behavior, 4,* 163–174.

Morris, E. (1997, September). Personal communication with Professor Edward K. Morris, Human Development and Family Life, the University of Kansas.

Rogers, C. R. (1964). Toward a science of the person. In F. W. Wann (Ed.), *Behaviorism and phenomenology: Contrasting bases for modern psychology.* Chicago: Phoenix Books.

Sagvolden, T., Aase, H., Zeiner, P., & Berger, D. (1998). Altered reinforcement mechanisms in attention-deficit/hyperactivity disorder. *Behavioral Brain Research, 94*(1), 61–71.

Schneider, S., & Morris, E. (1987). The history of the term radical behaviorism: From Watson to Skinner. *Behavior Analyst, 10*(1), 27–39.

Skinner, B. F. (1974). *About behaviorism.* New York: Knopf.

SEE AGGRESSION . . . DO AGGRESSION!

Bandura, A., Ross, D., & Ross, S. A. (1961). Transmission of aggression through imitation of aggressive models. *Journal of Abnormal and Social Psychology, 63,* 575–582.

Aggression, in its overabundance of forms, is arguably the greatest social problem facing this country and the world today. Consequently, it is also one of the most heavily researched topics in the history of psychology. Over the years, the behavioral scientists who have been in the forefront of this research have been the social psychologists whose focus is on human interaction. One goal of social psychologists has been to define aggression. This may, at first glance, seem like a relatively easy goal, but such a definition turns out to be rather elusive. For example, which of the following behaviors would you define as aggression: A boxing match? A cat killing a mouse? A soldier shooting an enemy? Setting rat traps in your basement? A bullfight? The list of behaviors that may or may not be included in a definition of aggression goes on. As a result, if you were to consult ten different social psychologists, you would probably get ten different definitions of aggression.

Many researchers have gone beyond trying to agree on a definition to the more important process of examining the sources of human aggression. The question they pose is this: Why do people engage in acts of aggression? Throughout the history of psychology, many theoretical approaches have been proposed to explain the causes of aggression. Some of these contend that you are biologically preprogrammed for aggression, such that violent urges build up in you over time until they demand to be released. Other theories look to situational factors, such as repeated frustration, as the main determinants of aggressive responses. A third view, and one that may be the most widely accepted, is that aggression is learned.

One of the most famous and influential experiments ever conducted in the history of psychology demonstrated how children learn to be aggressive. This study, by Albert Bandura and his associates Dorothea Ross and Sheila Ross, was carried out in 1961 at Stanford University. Bandura is considered to be one of the founders of a school of psychological thought called "social learning theory." Social learning theorists believe that learning is the primary factor in the development of personality, and that this learning occurs through interactions with other people. For example, as you are growing up, important people such as your parents and teachers reinforce certain behaviors and ignore or punish others. Even beyond direct rewards and punishments, however, Bandura believed that behavior can be shaped in important ways through simply observing and imitating (or modeling) the behavior of others.

As you can see from the title of this chapter's study, Bandura, Ross, and Ross were able to demonstrate this modeling effect for acts of aggression. This research has come to be known throughout the field of psychology as "the Bobo doll study," for reasons that will become clear shortly. The article began with a reference to earlier research findings that demonstrated that children readily imitated the behavior of adult models while they were in the presence of the model. One of the things Bandura wanted to address in the new study was whether such imitative learning would generalize to settings in which the model was not with the child.

THEORETICAL PROPOSITIONS

The researchers proposed to expose children to adult models who behaved in either aggressive or nonaggressive ways. The children would then be tested in a new situation without the model present to determine to what extent they would imitate the acts of aggression they had observed in the adult. Based on this experimental manipulation, Bandura and his associates made four predictions:

1. Subjects who observed adult models performing acts of aggression would imitate the adult and engage in similar aggressive behaviors, even if the model was no longer present. Furthermore, this behavior would differ significantly from subjects who observed nonaggressive models or no models at all.

2. Children who were exposed to the nonaggressive models would not only be less aggressive than those who observed the aggression, but also significantly less aggressive than a control group of children who were exposed to no model at all. In other words, the nonaggressive models would have an aggression-inhibiting effect.

3. Because children tend to identify with parents and other adults of their same sex, subjects would "imitate the behavior of the same-sex model to a greater degree than a model of the opposite sex" (p. 575).

4. "Since aggression is a highly masculine-typed behavior in society, boys should be more predisposed than girls toward imitating aggression, the difference being most marked for subjects exposed to the male model" (p. 575).

METHOD

This article outlined the methods used in the experiment with great organization and clarity. Although somewhat summarized and simplified, these methodological steps are presented here.

Subjects

The researchers enlisted the help of the director and head teacher of the Stanford University Nursery School in order to obtain subjects for their study. Thirty-six boys and 36 girls, ranging in age from 3 years to almost 6 years, participated in the study as subjects. The average age of the children was 4 years and 4 months.

Experimental Conditions

Twenty-four children were assigned to the control group, which meant that they would not be exposed to any model. The remaining 48 subjects were first divided into two groups: one exposed to aggressive models and the other exposed to nonaggressive models. These groups were divided again into male and female subjects. Finally, each of these groups were divided so that half of the subjects were exposed to same-sex models and half to opposite-sex models. This created a total of eight experimental groups and one control group. A question you might be asking yourself is this: What if the children in some of the groups are already more aggressive than others? Bandura guarded against this potential problem by obtaining ratings of each subject's level of aggressiveness. The children were rated by an experimenter and a teacher (both of whom knew the children well) on their levels of physical aggression, verbal aggression, and aggression toward objects. These ratings allowed the researchers to match all the groups in terms of average aggression level.

The Experimental Procedure

Each child was exposed individually to the various experimental procedures. First, the experimenter brought the child to the playroom. On the way, they encountered the adult model who was invited by the experimenter to come and *join in the game.* The child was seated in one corner of the playroom at a table containing highly interesting activities. There were potato prints (this was 1961, so for those of you who have grown up in the high-tech age, a potato print is a potato cut in half and carved so that, like a rubber stamp, it will reproduce geometric shapes when inked on a stamp pad) and stickers of brightly colored animals and flowers that could be pasted onto a poster. Next, the adult model was taken to a table in a different corner containing a tinker toy set, a mallet, and an inflated Bobo doll 5 feet tall. The experimenter explained that these toys were for the model to play with and then left the room.

For both the aggressive and nonaggressive conditions, the model began assembling the tinker toys. However, in the aggressive condition, after a minute, the model attacked the Bobo doll with violence. For all the subjects in the aggressive condition, the sequence of aggressive acts performed by the model was identical:

> The model laid Bobo on its side, sat on it, and punched it repeatedly in the nose. The model then raised the Bobo doll, picked up the mallet, and struck the doll on the head. Following the mallet aggression, the model tossed the doll up in the air aggressively, and kicked it about the room. This sequence of physically aggressive acts was repeated three times, interspersed with verbally aggressive responses such as, "Sock him in the nose . . . , Hit him down . . . , Throw him in the air . . . , Kick him . . . , Pow . . . ," and two non-aggressive comments, "He keeps coming back for more" and "He sure is a tough fella." (p. 576)

All this took about 10 minutes, after which the experimenter came back into the room, said good-bye to the model, and took the child to another game room.

In the nonaggressive condition, the model simply played quietly with the tinker toys for the 10-minute period and completely ignored the Bobo doll. Bandura and his collaborators were careful to ensure that all experimental factors were identical for all the subjects except for the factors being studied: the aggressive versus nonaggressive model and the sex of the model.

Arousal of Anger or Frustration

Following the 10-minute play period, all subjects from the various conditions were taken to another room that contained very attractive toys, such as a fire engine, a jet fighter, a complete doll set including wardrobe, a doll carriage, and so on. The researchers believed that in order to test the subjects for aggressive responses, the children should be somewhat angered or frustrated, which would make such behaviors more likely to occur. To accomplish this, they allowed the subjects to begin playing with the attractive toys, but after a short time told them that the toys in this room were reserved for the other children. The subjects were also told, however, that they could play with some other toys in the next room.

Test for Imitation of Aggression

The final experimental room was filled with both aggressive and nonaggressive toys. Aggressive toys included a Bobo doll (of course!), a mallet, two dart guns, and a tether ball with a face painted on it. The nonaggressive toys included a tea set, crayons and paper, a ball, two dolls, cars and trucks, and plastic farm animals. Each subject was allowed to play in this room for 20 minutes. During this period, judges behind a one-way mirror rated each child's behavior on several measures of aggression.

Measures of Aggression

A total of eight different responses were measured in the subjects' behavior. In the interest of clarity, only the four most revealing measures will be summarized here. First, all acts that imitated the physical aggression of the model were recorded. These included sitting on Bobo, punching it in the nose, hitting it with the mallet, kicking it, and throwing it into the air. Second, imitation of the models' verbal aggression was measured by counting the subjects' repetition of the phrases, "Sock him, Hit him down, Pow," and so on. Third, other mallet aggression (i.e., hitting objects other than the doll with the mallet) were recorded. Fourth, nonimitative aggression was documented by tabulating all subjects' acts of physical and verbal aggression that had not been performed by the adult model.

RESULTS

The findings from these observations are summarized in Table 1. If you examine the results carefully, you will discover that three of the four hypotheses presented by Bandura, Ross, and Ross in the introduction were supported.

The children who were exposed to the violent models tended to imitate the exact violent behaviors they observed. There were an average of 38.2 instances of imitative physical aggression for each of the male subjects, and 12.7 for the female subjects who had been exposed to the aggressive models. Additionally, the models' verbally aggressive behaviors were imitated an aver-

TABLE 1 Average Number of Aggressive Responses from Children in Various Treatment Conditions

	TYPE OF MODEL				
TYPE OF AGGRESSION	AGGRESSIVE MALE	NON-AGGRESSIVE MALE	AGGRESSIVE FEMALE	NON-AGGRESSIVE FEMALE	CONTROL GROUP
Imitative Physical Aggression					
Boys	25.8	1.5	12.4	0.2	1.2
Girls	7.2	0.0	5.5	2.5	2.0
Imitative Verbal Aggression					
Boys	12.7	0.0	4.3	1.1	1.7
Girls	2.0	0.0	13.7	0.3	0.7
Mallet Aggression					
Boys	28.8	6.7	15.5	18.7	13.5
Girls	18.7	0.5	17.2	0.5	13.1
Nonimitative Aggression					
Boys	36.7	22.3	16.2	26.1	24.6
Girls	8.4	1.4	21.3	7.2	6.1

(Adapted from p. 579.)

age of 17 times by the boys and 15.7 times by the girls. These specific acts of physical and verbal aggression were virtually never observed in the subjects exposed to the nonaggressive models or in the control subjects who were not exposed to any model.

As you will recall, Bandura and his associates predicted that nonaggressive models would have a violence-inhibiting effect on the children. In order for this hypothesis to be supported, the results should show that the subjects in the nonaggressive conditions averaged significantly fewer instances of violence than those in the no-model control group. In Table 1, if you compare the nonaggressive model columns with the control group averages, you'll see that the findings were mixed. For example, boys and girls who observed the nonaggressive male exhibited far less nonimitative mallet aggression than controls, but boys who observed the nonaggressive female aggressed more with the mallet than did the boys in the control group. As the authors readily admit, these results were so inconsistent in relation to the aggression-inhibiting effect of nonaggressive models that they were inconclusive.

The predicted gender differences, however, were strongly supported by the data in Table 1. Clearly, boys' violent behavior was influenced more by the aggressive male model than by the aggressive female model. The average total number of aggressive behaviors by boys was 104 when they had observed a male aggressive model, compared with 48.4 when a female model had been observed. Girls, on the other hand, while their scores were less consistent, averaged 57.7 violent behaviors in the aggressive female model condition, compared with 36.3 when they observed the male model. The authors point out that in same-sex aggressive conditions, girls were more likely to imitate verbal aggression while boys were more inclined to imitate physical violence.

Finally, boys were significantly more physically aggressive than girls in nearly all the conditions. If all the instances of aggression in Table 1 are tallied, there were 270 violent acts by the boys, compared with 128 by the girls.

DISCUSSION

Bandura, Ross, and Ross claimed that they had demonstrated how specific behaviors—in this case, violent ones—could be learned through the process of observation and imitation without any reinforcement provided to either the models or the observers. They concluded that children's observation of adults engaging in these behaviors sends a message to the child that this form of violence is permissible, thus weakening the child's inhibitions against aggression. The consequence of this observed violence, they contended, is an increased probability that a child will respond to future frustrations with aggressive behavior.

The researchers also addressed the issue of why the influence of the male aggressive model on the boys was so much stronger than the female aggressive model was on the girls. They explained that in our culture, as in most, aggression is seen as more typical of males than females. In other words, it is a masculine-typed behavior. So, a man's modeling of aggression carried with it the weight of social acceptability and was, therefore, more powerful in its ability to influence the observer.

SUBSEQUENT RESEARCH

At the time this experiment was conducted, the researchers probably had no idea how influential it would become. By the early 1960s, television had grown into a powerful force in American culture and consumers were becoming concerned about the effect of televised violence on children. This has been and continues to be hotly debated. In the past 30 years, there have been no fewer than three congressional hearings on the subject of television violence, and the work of Bandura and other psychologists has been included in these investigations.

These same three researchers conducted a follow-up study two years later that was intended to examine the power of aggressive models who are on film, or who are not even real people. Using a similar experimental method involving aggression toward a Bobo doll, Bandura, Ross, and Ross designed an experiment to compare the influence of a live adult model with the same model on film and to a cartoon version of the same aggressive modeling. The results demonstrated that the live adult model had a stronger influence than the filmed adult, who, in turn, was more influential than the cartoon. However, all three forms of aggressive models produced significantly more violent behaviors in the children than was observed in children exposed to nonaggressive models or control subjects (Bandura, Ross, & Ross, 1963).

On an optimistic note, Bandura found in a later study that the effect of modeled violence could be altered under certain conditions. You will recall that in his original study, no rewards were given for aggression to either the models or the subjects. But what do you suppose would happen if the model behaved violently and was then either reinforced or punished for the behavior while the child was observing? Bandura (1965) tested this idea and found that children imitated the violence more when they saw it rewarded, but significantly less when the model was punished for aggressive behavior.

Critics of Bandura's research on aggression have pointed out that aggressing toward an inflated doll is not the same as attacking another person, and that children know the difference. Building on the foundation laid by Bandura and his colleagues, other researchers have examined the effect of modeled violence on real aggression. In a study using Bandura's Bobo doll method (Hanratty, O'Neil, & Sulzer, 1972), children observed a violent adult model and were then exposed to high levels of frustration. When this occurred, they often aggressed against a live person (dressed like a clown), whether that person was the source of the frustration or not.

RECENT APPLICATIONS

Bandura's research discussed in this chapter made at least two fundamental contributions to psychology. First it demonstrated dramatically how children can acquire new behaviors simply by observing adults, even when the adults are not physically present. Social learning theorists believe that much, if not most, of the behaviors that comprise human personality are formed through this modeling process. Second, this research laid the groundwork for hundreds of studies over the past 40 years on the effects on children of viewing violence in person or in the media. (For a summary of Bandura's many contributions to psychology see http://www.ship.edu/~cgboeree/bandura .html, 1998.)

Within the past decade the U.S. Congress has held new rounds of hearings on media violence focusing on the potential effects of TV, movies, video games, computer games, and the Internet. In 2000, a joint statement to Congress from six national medical associations including the American Medical Association, the American Academy of Pediatrics, and the American Psychological Association stated:

> At this time, well over 1000 studies . . . point overwhelmingly to a causal connection between media violence and aggressive behavior in some children. The conclusion of the public health community, based on over 30 years of research, is that viewing entertainment violence can lead to increases in aggressive attitudes, values and behavior, particularly in children. Its effects are measurable and long-lasting. Moreover, prolonged viewing of media violence can lead to emotional desensitization toward violence in real life (American Medical Association, 2000).

Broadcasters and multimedia developers, feeling increased pressure to respond to public and legislative attacks, are working to reduce media violence or put in place parental advisory rating systems warning of particularly violent content.

Perhaps of even greater concern is the mounting evidence demonstrating that the effects of violent media on children may continue into adulthood (Heusmann et al., 2003). One study found "that childhood exposure to media violence predicts young adult aggressive behavior for both males and females. Identification with aggressive TV characters and perceived realism of TV violence also predict later aggression. These relations persist even when the effects of socioeconomic status, intellectual ability, and a variety of parenting factors are controlled" (Heusmann et al., 2003, p. 201).

As children acquire easier access to quickly expanding media channels and formats, concerns over the effects of violence embedded in the media are bound to increase as well. Because preventing children's access to violent media is probably an impossible task, research is increasingly focusing on strategies for preventing media violence from translating into real life aggression among children. These efforts have been stepped up considerably in the wake of school shootings at Columbine and other locations throughout the United States, and are likely to continue on many research fronts for the foreseeable future.

American Medical Association. (2000). Media violence *is* harmful to kids—and to public health. Retrieved October 3, 2003 from, http://www.ama-assn.org/sci-pubs/amnews/pick_00/hlsb0814.htm.

Bandura, A. (1965). Influence of models' reinforcement contingencies on the acquisition of imitative responses. *Journal of Personality and Social Psychology, 1,* 589–595.

Bandura, A., Ross, D., & Ross, S. (1963). Imitation of film mediated aggressive models. *Journal of Abnormal and Social Psychology, 66,* 3–11.

Hanratty, M., O'Neil, E., & Sulzer, J. (1972). The effect of frustration on the imitation of aggression. *Journal of Personality and Social Psychology, 21,* 30–34. http://www.ship.edu/~cgboeree/bandura.html (1998).

Huesmann, L. R., Moise, J., Podolski, C. P., & Eron, L. D. (2003). Longitudinal relations between childhood exposure to media violence and adult aggression and violence: 1977–1992. *Developmental Psychology, 39(2),* 201–221.

4 INTELLIGENCE, COGNITION, AND MEMORY

The branch of psychology most concerned with the topics in this section is known as *cognitive psychology*. Cognitive psychologists study human mental processes. Our intelligence, our ability to think and reason in complex ways, and our ability to store and retrieve symbolic representations of our experiences all combine to make humans uniquely different from other animals. And, of course, how we do these things greatly affects our behavior. However, studying these mental processes is much more difficult than studying observable behavior, so a great deal of creativity and ingenuity has been necessary.

The studies included here have changed the way psychologists view our internal mental behavior. The first article discusses the famous Pygmalion study, which demonstrated that not only performance in school, but actual IQ scores of children, can be influenced by the expectations of others, such as teachers. The second reading discusses a body of work that has transformed how we perceive another fundamental human attribute: our intelligence. In the early 1980s Howard Gardner proposed that humans do not possess one general intelligence, but at least seven distinct intelligences. His idea has become widely known as *Mulitple Intelligence (MI) Theory*. Third, we encounter an early groundbreaking study in cognitive psychology that examined how animals and humans form mental images of the environment around them called *cognitive maps*. And fourth is an examination of research that revealed how our memories don't work exactly as we think they do, and the implication of this for eyewitness testimony in court.

WHAT YOU EXPECT IS WHAT YOU GET
Rosenthal, R., & Jacobson, L. (1966). Teachers' expectancies: Determinates of pupils' IQ gains. *Psychological Reports, 19*, 115–118.

We are all familiar with the idea of the self-fulfilling prophecy. One way of describing this concept is to say that if we expect something to happen in a certain way, our expectation will tend to make it so. Whether self-fulfilling prophecies really do occur in a predictable way in everyday life is open to scientific study, but psychological research has demonstrated that in some areas they are a reality.

93

The question of the self-fulfilling prophecy in scientific research was first brought to the attention of psychologists in 1911 in the famous case of "Clever Hans," the horse of Mr. von Osten (Pfungst, 1911). Clever Hans was a horse that was famous for being able to read, spell, and solve math problems by stomping out answers with his front hoof. Naturally there were many skeptics, but when Hans's abilities were tested by a committee of experts, they were found to be genuinely performed without prompting from Mr. von Osten. But how could any horse (except possibly for Mr. Ed!) possess such a degree of human intelligence? Well, a psychologist, O. Pfungst, performed a series of careful experiments and found that Hans was receiving subtle unintentional cues from his questioners. For example, after asking a question, people would look down at the horse's hoof for the answer. As the horse approached the correct number of hoofbeats, the questioners would raise their eyes or head very slightly in anticipation of the horse completing his answer. The horse had been conditioned to use these subtle movements from the observers as signs to stop stomping, and this usually resulted in the correct answer to the question.

So, you might ask, how is a trick horse related to psychological research? Well, the Clever Hans findings pointed out the possibility that observers often have specific expectations or biases that may cause them to send covert and unintentional signals to a subject being studied. These signals, then, may cause the subject to respond in ways that are consistent with the observers' bias and, consequently, confirm their expectations. What all this finally boils down to is that an experimenter may think a certain behavior results from his or her scientific treatment of one subject or one group of subjects compared with another. Actually the behavior may result from nothing more than the experimenter's own biased expectations. If this occurs, it renders the experiment invalid. This threat to the validity of a psychological experiment is called the *experimenter expectancy effect*.

Robert Rosenthal, a leading researcher on this methodological issue, has demonstrated the experimenter expectancy effect in laboratory psychological experiments. In one study (Rosenthal & Fode, 1963), psychology students in a learning and conditioning course unknowingly became subjects themselves. Some of the students were told they would be working with rats that had been specially bred for high intelligence, as measured by their ability to learn mazes quickly. The rest of the students were told that they would be working with rats bred for dullness in learning mazes. The students then proceeded to condition their rats to perform various skills, including maze learning. The students who had been assigned the maze-bright rats reported significantly faster learning times than those reported by the students with the maze-dull rats. In reality, the rats given to the students were standard lab rats and were randomly assigned. These students were not cheating or purposefully slanting their results. The influences they exerted on their animals were apparently unintentional and unconscious.

As a result of such research, the threat of experimenter expectancies to scientific research has been well established. Properly trained researchers, using careful procedures (such as the double-blind method, in which the experimenters who come in contact with the subjects are unaware of the hypotheses of the study) are usually able to avoid most of these expectancy effects.

Beyond this, however, Rosenthal was concerned about how such biases and expectancies might occur outside the laboratory, such as in school classrooms. Because teachers in public schools may not have the opportunity to learn about the dangers of expectancies, how great an influence might this tendency have on the students' potential performance? After all, teachers have historically been given students' IQ scores beginning in the first grade. Could this information set up biased expectancies in the teachers' minds and cause them to unintentionally treat "bright" students (as judged by high IQ scores) differently from those seen as less bright? And if so, is this fair? Those questions formed the basis of Rosenthal and Jacobson's study.

THEORETICAL PROPOSITIONS

Rosenthal labeled this expectancy effect, as it occurs in natural interpersonal settings outside the laboratory, the *Pygmalion effect*. In the Greek myth, a sculptor (Pygmalion) falls in love with his sculpted creation of a woman. Most people are more familiar with the modern Shaw play *Pygmalion* (*My Fair Lady* is the musical version) about the blossoming of Eliza Doolittle because of the teaching, encouragement, and *expectations* of Henry Higgins. Rosenthal suspected that when an elementary school teacher is provided with information (such as IQ scores) that creates certain expectancies about students' potential, whether strong or weak, the teacher might unknowingly behave in ways that subtly encourage or facilitate the performance of the students seen as more likely to succeed. This, in turn, would create the self-fulfilling prophecy of actually causing those students to excel, perhaps at the expense of the students for whom lower expectations exist. In order to test these theoretical propositions, Rosenthal and his colleague Jacobson obtained the assistance of an elementary school (called Oak School) in a predominantly lower middle-class neighborhood in a large town.

METHOD

With the cooperation of the Oak School administration, all the students in grades one through six were given an IQ test (called the Tests of General Ability, or TOGA) near the beginning of the academic year. This test was chosen because it was a nonverbal test for which a student's score did not depend primarily upon school-learned skills of reading, writing, and arithmetic. Also, it was a test with which the teachers in Oak School probably would not be familiar. The teachers were told that the students were being given the Harvard Test of Inflected Acquisition. Such deception was important in this case in order for expectancies to be created in the minds of the teachers, a necessary ingredient for the experiment to be successful. It was further explained to the teachers that the Harvard Test was designed to serve as a predictor of academic *blooming* or *spurting*. In other words, teachers believed that students who scored high on the test were ready to enter a period of increased learning abilities within the next year. This predictive ability of the test was also, in fact, not true.

At Oak School, there were three classes at each of the six grade levels. All of the 18 teachers (16 women, 2 men) for these classes were given a list of names of students in their classes who had scored in the top 20% on the Harvard Test and were therefore identified as potential academic bloomers during the academic year. But here's the key to this study: The children on the teachers' top 10 lists had been assigned to this experimental condition purely at random. The only difference between these children and the others (the controls) was that they had been identified to their teachers as the ones who would show unusual intellectual gains.

Near the end of the school year, all children at the school were measured again with the same test (the TOGA), and the degree of change in IQ was calculated for each child. The differences in IQ changes between the experimental group and the controls could then be examined to see if the expectancy effect had been created in a real-world setting.

RESULTS

Figure 1 summarizes the results of the comparisons of the IQ increases for the experimental versus the control groups. For the entire school, the children for whom the teachers had expected greater intellectual growth averaged significantly greater improvement than did the control children (12.2 and 8.2 points, respectively). However, if you examine Figure 1, it is clear that this difference was accounted for by the huge differences in grades one and

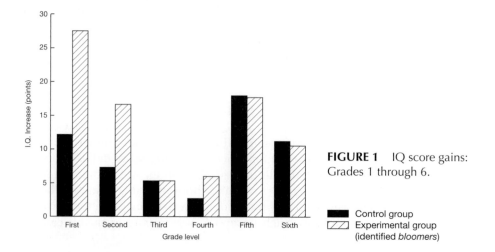

FIGURE 1   IQ score gains: Grades 1 through 6.

■ Control group
▨ Experimental group
(identified *bloomers*)

two. Possible reasons for this are discussed shortly. Rosenthal and Jacobson offered another useful and revealing way to organize the data for these first and second graders. Figure 2 illustrates the percentage of the children in each group who obtained increases in IQ of at least 10, 20, or 30 points.

Two major findings emerged from this early study. First, the expectancy effect previously demonstrated in formal laboratory settings also appears to function in less experimental, real-world situations. Second, the effect was very strong in the early grades, yet almost nonexistent for the older children. What does all this mean?

DISCUSSION

As Rosenthal suspected from his past research, the teachers' expectations of their students' behavior became a self-fulfilling prophecy. "When teachers expected that certain children would show greater intellectual development, those children did show greater intellectual development" (Rosenthal & Jacobson, 1968, p. 85). Remember that the data reported are averages of three classes and three teachers for each grade level. It is difficult to think of other explanations for the differences in IQ gains besides the teachers' expectations.

However, Rosenthal felt it was important to try to explain *why* the self-fulfilling prophecy was not demonstrated in the higher grade levels. Both in the article that is the focus of this chapter and in later writings, Rosenthal and Jacobson offered several possible reasons for this finding:

1. Younger children are generally thought of as being more malleable or "transformable." If this is true, then the younger children in the study may have experienced greater change simply because they were easier to change than the older children were. Related to this is the possibility that even if younger children are not more malleable, teachers may have believed that they were. This belief alone may have been enough to create differential treatment and produce the results that were reported.

2. Younger students in an elementary school tend to have less well-established reputations. In other words, if the teachers had not yet had a chance to form an opinion of a child's abilities, the expectancies created by the researchers would have carried more weight.

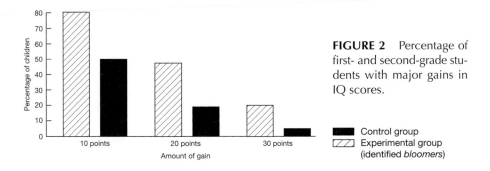

FIGURE 2 Percentage of first- and second-grade students with major gains in IQ scores.

Control group
Experimental group (identified *bloomers*)

3. Younger children may be more easily influenced by and more susceptible to the subtle and unintentional processes that teachers use to communicate performance expectations to them:

> Under this interpretation, it is possible that teachers react to children of all grade levels in the same way if they believe them to be capable of intellectual gain. But perhaps it is only the younger children whose performance is affected by the special things the teacher says to them; the special ways in which she says them; the way she looks, postures, and touches the children from whom she expects greater intellectual growth. (Rosenthal & Jacobson, 1968, p. 83)

4. Teachers of these lower grades may differ from upper-grade teachers in ways that produce greater communication of their expectations to the children. Rosenthal and Jacobson did not speculate as to exactly what these differences might be if indeed they exist.

SIGNIFICANCE OF FINDINGS AND SUBSEQUENT RESEARCH

The real importance of Rosenthal and Jacobson's findings at Oak School relates to the potential long-lasting effects of teachers' expectations on the scholastic performance of students. This, in turn, feeds directly into one of the most controversial topics in psychology and education today: the question of the fairness of IQ tests. We'll return to this discussion shortly, but first, it is of interest to explore some later research that examined the ways in which teachers unconsciously communicate their higher expectations to the students whom they believe possess greater potential.

A study conducted by Chaiken, Sigler, and Derlega (1974) involved videotaping teacher-student interactions in a classroom situation in which the teachers had been informed that certain children were extremely bright (these *bright* students had been chosen at random from all the students in the class). Careful examination of the videos indicated that teachers favored the identified *brighter* students in many subtle ways. They smiled at these students more often, made more eye contact, and had more favorable reactions to these students' comments in class. These researchers go on to report that students for whom these high expectations exist are more likely to enjoy school, receive more constructive comments from teachers on their mistakes, and work harder to try to improve. What this and other studies indicate is that teacher expectancies, while their influence is not the only determinant of a child's performance in school, can affect more than just IQ scores.

Imagine for a moment that you are an elementary school teacher with a class of 20 students. On the first day of class, you receive a class roster on which is printed the IQ scores for all of your students. You notice that five of your pupils have IQ scores over 145, well into the genius range. Do you think that your treatment and expectations of those children during the school year would be the same as your other students? What about your expectations of those students compared with another five students with IQ scores in the low to normal range? If you answered that your treatment and expectations would be the same, I'd be willing to bet that you'd be wrong. As a matter of fact, they probably *shouldn't* be the same! The point is that if your expectations became self-fulfilling prophecies, that might be unfair to some of the students. Now consider another, more crucial point. Suppose the IQ scores you received on your class roster were *wrong*. If these erroneous scores created expectations that benefited some students over others, it would clearly be unfair and probably unethical. This is one of the major issues fueling the IQ controversy that rages today.

For many years, many researchers have charged that the standard IQ tests used to assess the intelligence of children contain a racial or cultural bias. The argument is that since the tests were designed primarily by white, upper middle-class males, they contain ideas and information to which other ethnic groups are not exposed. Children from various minority groups in the United States traditionally score lower on these tests than white children do. Since it would be ridiculous to assume that these nonwhite children possess less basic intelligence than white children, the reason for these differences in scores must lie in the tests themselves. Traditionally, however, teachers in grades K through 12 were given this IQ information on all their students. If you stop and think about this fact in relation to the research by Rosenthal and Jacobson, you'll see what a potentially dangerous situation may have been created. Besides the fact that children have been categorized in school according to their IQ scores (advanced placement, remedial classes, etc.), teachers' unintended expectations, based on this possibly biased information, may have been creating unfair self-fulfilling prophecies. The arguments supporting this idea are convincing enough that most states have instituted a moratorium on IQ testing and the use of IQ scores until such testing can be shown to be bias-free. And at the core of these arguments has been the research addressed in this chapter (see also the related work by Howard Gardner on *multiple intelligences* in the next reading).

RECENT APPLICATIONS

Due in large part to Rosenthal and Jacobson's research, the power of teachers' expectations on students' performance has become an integral part of our understanding of the educational process. Furthermore, Rosenthal's theory of interpersonal expectancies has exerted its influence in numerous areas other than education. In 2002, Rosenthal himself reviewed the literature on expectancy effects using meta-analysis techniques (explained in the Smith and Glass study in chapter 9). He demonstrated how "the expectations of psychological researchers, classroom teachers, judges in the courtroom, business executives, and health care providers can unintentionally affect the responses of their research participants, pupils, jurors, employees, and patients" (Rosenthal, 2002, p. 839).

An uncomfortably revealing article incorporating Rosenthal's expectancy research examined the criteria school teachers use to refer their students to school psychologists for assessment and counseling (Andrews, et al, 1997). The researchers found that teachers referred African American children for developmental handicap assessment at rates significantly higher than the rates of Caucasian students in their classrooms. In addition, boys were referred in equally disproportionate numbers over girls for problems of classroom and playground behavior problems. The researchers suggested that the differences among the various student groups may have revealed more about teachers' expectancies than real individual differences.

Finally, Rosenthal's Pygmalion studies have not been without critics. Richard Snow at Stanford University has questioned Rosenthal's findings for over 30 years and the debate between them continues today (Rosenthal is at The University of California). A concise, pithy, and rather rancorous dialogue between them on this very topic appeared in a 1994 issue of *Current Directions in Psychological Science,* the journal of the American Psychological Society (Rosenthal, 1994; Snow, 1994). It's a revealing and enjoyable read!

Andrews, T., Wisniewski, J., & Mulick, J. (1997). Variables influencing teachers' decisions to refer children for school psychological assessment services. *Psychology in Schools, 34*(3), 239–244.

Chaiken, A., Sigler, E., & Derlega, V. (1974). Nonverbal mediators of teacher expectancy effects. *Journal of Personality and Social Psychology, 30,* 144–149.

Pfungst, O. (1911). *Clever Hans (the horse of Mr. von Osten): A contribution to experimental, animal, and human psychology.* New York: Holt, Rinehart and Winston.

Rosenthal, R. (2002). Covert communication in classrooms, clinics, courtrooms, and cubicles. *American Psychologist, 57,* 839–849.

Rosenthal, R. (1994). Critiquing *Pygmalion:* A 25-year perspective. *Current Directions in Psychological Science, 4*(6), 171–172.

Rosenthal, R., & Fode, K. (1963). The effect of experimenter bias on the performance of the albino rat. *Behavioral Science, 8,* 183–189.

Rosenthal, R., & Jacobson, L. (1968). *Pygmalion in the classroom: Teacher expectations and pupils' intellectual development.* New York: Holt, Rinehart and Winston.

Snow, R. (1994). Pygmalion and intelligence? *Current Directions in Psychological Science, 4*(6), 169–171.

JUST *HOW* ARE YOU INTELLIGENT?
Gardner, H. (1983) *Frames of mind: The theory of multiple intelligences.* New York: Basic Books.

The heading for this chapter is an intentional play on words. The usual form of the question, "Just how intelligent *are* you?" implies that you have a certain amount of intelligence. The question here, "Just *how* are you intelligent?" is entirely unrelated to an *amount,* and is asking you instead about the nature of your particular *kinds* of intelligence. This discussion is about how many types of intelligence might exist in humans.

Many of you reading this probably have taken at least one intelligence test in your life (even if you don't remember it), and some of you may have taken several. For the most part, intelligence tests developed over the past 100 years have been designed to produce a single score. That score was called your *Intelligence Quotient* (IQ). If tests of intelligence are designed to produce a single score, a person's intelligence must also be conceptualized as a single, overall, *general* mental ability. That is exactly how intelligence was interpreted throughout most of the twentieth century. In fact, intelligence was often referred to as "g" for this general mental ability. Each individual's IQ score was used widely to judge, categorize, and describe people in various settings, including school, the workplace, and the military.

However, in the 1970s and 1980s, researchers began to question the validity of the unitary, "IQ-score approach" to human intelligence. Many of the tests themselves were shown to be biased in favor of certain economic classes and ethnic groups, and children's educational opportunities were often being dictated by their IQ scores alone (see the earlier chapter on the work of Robert Rosenthal for an example of this problem.

As criticisms of this conceptualization of intelligence grew in number and influence, IQ tests began to be used less and less. At the same time, a new, and, at the time, radically different, view of intelligence was making its way into scientific and popular thinking about how our minds work. In stark contrast to the notion of a single, generalized intelligence, this emerging approach expanded the notion of intelligence into many *different* mental abilities, each possessing, in itself, the characteristics of a complete, "free-standing" intelligence. Howard Gardner, as the most prominent proponent of this new view of *multiple intelligences,* introduced it to the world in his 1983 book, *Frames of Mind,* which forms the basis of this chapter.

THEORETICAL PROPOSITIONS

Gardner's theory of multiple intelligences was based on much more than simply observing the various, diverse mental skills people can demonstrate. His ideas stem from his research on the structure of the brain itself. Prior to launching his work on intelligence per se, Gardner had spent most of his career studying the biology and functioning of the brain. Gardner expanded on previous research demonstrating that the human brain is not only diverse in its abilities, but is also extremely specialized in its functioning. In other words, different regions of your brain are "assigned" to carry out specific tasks related to thinking and knowing. This brain specialization may be demonstrated by observing, as Gardner has done, exactly what abilities are lost or diminished when a person experiences damage to a particular region of the brain. For example, in most people language abilities reside primarily in one section of the brain's left hemisphere, vision is centered in the occipital cortex at the rear of the brain, and one specific brain structure located at the base of the visual cortex is responsible for your ability to recognize and discriminate among human faces (see the reading on Michael Gazzaniga's split-brain research earlier in this book for more on brain specialization).

Carrying the theory of brain specialization a step further, Gardner contends that different parts of the human brain are responsible for different aspects of intelligence, or, more correctly, different intelligences altogether. To defend scientifically his theory of multiple intelligences, Gardner drew upon evidence from many sources and developed criteria for defining a certain set of abilities as a unique intelligence. Gardner described his sources of data as follows:

> In formulating my brief on multiple intelligences, I have reviewed evidence from a large and hitherto unrelated group of sources: studies of prodigies, gifted individuals, brain-damaged patients, *idiot-savants* [a rare form of mental retardation or autism accompanied by extraordinary talent or ability in one or two mental areas], normal children, normal adults, experts in different lines of work, and individuals from diverse cultures. (p. 9)

METHOD

Incorporating information from all of these sources, Gardner then developed a set of eight indicators or "signs" that define an intelligence. Any intellectual ability, or set of abilities, must map onto most of these criteria, if it is to be considered a separate, autonomous intelligence:

1. *Potential isolation of the intelligence by brain damage.* Gardner contended that if a specific mental ability can be destroyed through brain damage, or if it remains relatively intact when other abilities have been destroyed, this provides convincing evidence that the ability may be a separate intelligence unto itself.

2. *The existence of savants, prodigies, and other exceptional individuals relating to the intelligence.* You are aware that certain individuals possess an extreme level of intellectual skill in one particular ability. Some mentally retarded and autistic people demonstrate "strokes of genius," and some people with normal intelligence are *prodigies,* with abilities far beyond others of their age or experience. Gardner believed that the exceptional skills of these individuals lend significant support for considering an ability as a separate intelligence.

3. *A clear set of information-processing (thinking) operations linked to the intelligence.* This refers to mental abilities that are specific to the ability under consideration. For an ability to qualify as an intelligence it must involve a specific set of mental processes, which Gardner calls *core operations,* that exist in specific areas of the brain and are triggered by certain kinds of information. Table 1 lists the core operations for the various intelligences proposed by Gardner.

4. *A distinctive developmental history of the intelligence and the potential to reach high levels of expertise.* Gardner believes that an intelligence must include a developmental path that starts with simple and basic steps and progresses through incremental milestones of increased skill levels.

5. *Evidence that the intelligence has developed through evolutionary time.* Human intelligence has evolved over millions of years as one of many adaptive mechanisms that have allowed us to survive as a species. If a particular set of abilities is to be defined as an intelligence, Gardner believed the skills involved should show evidence of evolutionary development,

TABLE 1 Core Operations and Famous Examples of Gardner's Eight Intelligences

INTELLIGENCE	CORE OPERATIONS	FAMOUS EXAMPLES
Linguistic	Syntax (word phrasing), phonology (the sounds speech), semantics (the meaning of words), pragmatics (word usage)	Shakespeare, J.K. Rowling, Dr. Seuss, Woody Allen
Musical	Pitch (frequency of sounds), rhythm, timbre (quality of sounds)	Mozart, Lauryn Hill, Andrea Boccelli, Paul McCartney
Logical-mathematical	Numbers, quantities, categorization, causal relations	Albert Einstein, Carl Sagan, Marie Curie, B.F. Skinner
Spatial	Accurate visualization, mental rotation and transformation of images	Picasso, Frank Lloyd Wright, Leonardo DaVinci, van Gogh
Bodily-kinesthetic	Control of one's own body, control in handling objects	Charlie Chaplin, LeBron James, Serena and Venus Williams
Interpersonal	Awareness of others' feelings, emotions, goals, motivations	Ghandi, Abraham Maslow, Oprah Winfrey
Intrapersonal	Awareness of one's own feelings, emotions, goals, motivations	Plato, Hermann Rorschach, Helen Keller, Bill Gates
Naturalist	Recognition and classification of objects in the environment; sensitivity to the natural world	Charles Darwin, Jane Goodall, Rachel Carson

based on cross-cultural research, and observations of similar types of abilities in nonhuman animals (such as the "mental maps" in the rats in Tolman's research discussed in the previous reading in this chapter).

6. *Ability to study the intelligence with psychological experiments.* Gardner maintains that any ability proposed as an intelligence must be able to be confirmed using solid experimental techniques. An example of this might be an experiment to determine a person's speed and accuracy in a *mental rotation task* as a sign of spatial relationships skills. Figure 1 contains a demonstration of this task. How fast can you figure it out?

7. *Ability to measure the intelligence with existing standardized tests.* Here, Gardner was acknowledging the potential value of IQ and other tests of intelligence that had gone before. However, the value he saw was not in the tests' ability to produce a single intelligence score, but in the fact that some of the tests contain various subscales they may, in fact, measure different intelligences.

8. *Aspects of the intelligence may be represented by a system of symbols.* Finally, Gardner proposed that any human intelligence should incorporate a system of symbols. The most obvious of these, of course, are human language and math. Other examples of symbol systems include notation for musical ability and pictures for spatial skills.

In the next section we look at a summary of the intelligences Gardner proposed as part of his original theory in his 1983 book. Each intelligence he included was subjected to analysis using his eight criteria. If an ability failed to meet most of the criteria, it was rejected. Through this process of elimination, Gardner originally suggested seven distinct human intelligences, and later added an eighth.

RESULTS

Gardner discussed each of his original seven intelligences in detail in his 1983 book. Here, we provide brief descriptions of each intelligence, along with a few of Gardner's own words, to give you the "flavor" of the abilities involved. Additionally, Table 1 summarizes the core operations of each intelligence and provides several well-known individuals who may be seen as scoring high on the abilities that comprise each intelligence. Although Gardner does not endorse any single test for measuring multiple intelligences, many have been developed. You can try some of these yourself online simply by searching for "test of multiple intelligence."

Linguistic Intelligence.   If you are high is linguistic intelligence, you are able to use words in ways that are more skillful, useful, and creative than the average person. You are able to use language to convince others of your position; you can memorize and recall detailed or complex information; you are better than most at explaining and teaching concepts and ideas to others; and you enjoy using language to talk about language itself. Gardner suggested that talented poets are good examples of individuals possessing high linguistic intelligence:

> In the poet's struggles over the wording of a line or stanza, one sees at work some central aspects of linguistic intelligence. The poet must be superlatively sensitive to the shades of meanings of words and must try to preserve as many of the sought-after meanings as possible. . . . A sensitivity to the order among words, the capacity to follow the rules of grammar, and, on carefully selected occasions, to violate them. At a somewhat more sensory level—a sensitivity to the sounds, rhythms, inflections, and meters of words—that ability to make poetry even in a foreign tongue beautiful to hear. (pp. 77–78)

Musical Intelligence.   You are probably already guessing some of the components of musical intelligence: gifted abilities involving sound, especially, pitch, timbre, and rhythm. Gardner claimed that this is the earliest of all intelligences to emerge. Musical child prodigies serve as examples of individuals are "musical geniuses." Gardner points to the musical composer to illustrate musical intelligence:

> [A] composer can be readily identified by the facts that he constantly has "tones in his head"—that is, he is always, somewhere near the surface of consciousness, hearing tones, rhythms, and larger musical patterns. (p. 101)

Logical-Mathematical Intelligence.   This intelligence enables you to think about, analyze, and compute various relationships among abstract objects, concepts, and ideas. High levels of this intelligence may be found among mathematicians, scientists, and philosophers, but may also be present in those individuals who are obsessed with sports statistics, design computer code, or develop algorhythms as a hobby:

What characterizes [this] individual is a love of dealing with abstraction. . . . The mathematician must be absolutely rigorous and perennially skeptical: no fact can be accepted unless it has been proved rigorously by steps that are derived from universally accepted first principles. . . . One obvious source of delight attends the solution of a problem that has long been considered insoluble. (pp. 138–141)

Spatial Intelligence.　You would score high in spatial intelligence if you are better than most people in creating, visualizing, and manipulating mental images. These are skills that come naturally and easily to those in various visually oriented professions or avocations such as artists, sculptors, interior decorators, engineers, and architects. To be more specific, Gardner explained that spatial intelligence entails:

The ability to recognize instances of the same element; the ability to transform or to recognize a transformation of one element into another; the capacity to conjure up mental imagery and then to transform that imagery; the capacity to produce a graphic likeness of spatial information; and the like. (p. 176)

The object rotation task in Figure 1 is an example of a skill with which someone high in spatial intelligence would have very little difficulty.

Bodily Kinesthetic Intelligence.　These abilities might be called "physical intelligence." If you are high in bodily kinesthetic intelligence, you are very aware of your own body and bodily movements and are skilled in using and controlling your body to achieve various goals or effects. As you might imagine, dancers, athletes, surgeons, potters, and many actors possess a high degree of bodily intelligence. Gardner goes on to explain:

Characteristic of such an intelligence is the ability to use one's body in highly differentiated and skilled ways, for expressive as well as goal-directed purposes. . . . Characteristic as well is the capacity to work skillfully with objects, both those that involve fine motor movements of one's fingers and hands and those that exploit gross motor movements of the body. (pp. 206–207)

The next two intelligences Gardner proposed, while separate, fell into a single category that Gardner called the *personal intelligences*. One type of personal

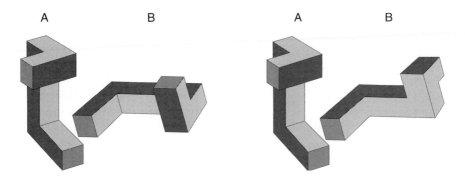

FIGURE 1 Example of Mental Rotation Task to Assess Spatial Intelligent. Are the two figures in each set the same or different?

intelligence is focused inward, while the other is focused outward. He referred to these as *intrapersonal intelligence* and *interpersonal intelligence* respectively.

Intrapersonal Intelligence. How well do you "know yourself"? Gardner proposed that the ability to be aware of and understand who you are, your emotions, your motivations, and the sources of your actions exist in varying degrees among humans. Gardner describes a high degree of intrapersonal intelligence as follows:

> The core capacity here is *access to one's own feeling life* – one's range of emotions: the capacity instantly to effect discriminations among these feelings and, eventually, to label them, to enmesh them in symbolic codes, to draw upon them as a means of understanding and guiding one's behavior. (p. 239)

Interpersonal Intelligence. This intelligence is contrasted with intrapersonal intelligence by asking "How well do you know *others?*" Interpersonal intelligence involves skills similar to those of intrapersonal intelligence, but they are outward-directed; focused on the feelings, motivations, desires, and behaviors of other people:

> The core capacity here is the ability to notice and make distinctions among other individuals and, in particular, among their moods, temperaments, motivations, and intentions. In an advanced form, interpersonal knowledge permits a skilled adult to read the intentions and desires—even when these have been hidden—of many other individuals and, potentially to act upon this knowledge. (p. 239)

These, then, are the seven sets of abilities that comprised Gardner's original conceptualization of multiple intelligences. He states very clearly in *Frames of Mind* that these formed a working, and somewhat preliminary, list, and, through further study and research, other intelligences might be added or a convincing argument might be made to remove one or more of the original seven. What has happened over the years is that these seven intelligences have maintained their positions in the theory, and, as we shall see, Gardner has added an eighth intelligence.

SUBSEQUENT RESEARCH AND CRITICISMS

Gardner's theory of multiple intelligences, now often referred to as MI Theory, was immediately seized upon by educators, parents, and society in general as proof of a belief they had always held: *people are smart in different ways.* Finally, here was an explanation for those children (and adults, too) who performed poorly on tests and in some subjects in school, but were clearly exceptionally bright in other ways.

MI Theory mapped well onto growing concerns and research about learning disabilities and was largely responsible for the reformulation in education of "learning disabilities" into "learning differences." Indeed, MI Theory has exercised its greatest influence in the area of education, and Gardner's research following the publication of *Frames of Mind* focused on applying his ideas to enhancing the educational process for children and adults.

As Gardner was revisiting his original theory ten years after its original publication, he considered the possibility of other sets of abilities that might qualify as intelligences. Several candidates had been suggested to him by colleagues in various fields, such as a spiritual intelligence, a sexual intelligence, and a digital intelligence (Gardner, 2003). Although Gardner concedes that selecting a certain set of skills that qualify as an intelligence is open to different interpretations, he believed that these and many other suggestions did not meet his eight criteria adequately to be added to his MI Theory. Gardner did, however, find one additional ability that he felt clearly met the criteria for an intelligence. Gardner was asked by a colleague to describe the abilities of history's most influential biologists, and when he attempted to do so, he realized that none of the other seven intelligences fit those individuals very well. This sparked the addition of an eighth ability that he called, *naturalist intelligence.* Gardner explains

> The naturalist intelligence refers to the ability to recognize and classify plants, minerals, and animals, including rocks and grass and all variety of flora and fauna. Darwin is probably the most famous example of a naturalist because he saw so deeply into the nature of living things. (quoted in Checkley, 1997)

So, currently, eight intelligences comprise Gardner's MI Theory. Over the years, Gardner has suggested two additional possibilities: *spiritual intelligence* and *existential intelligence,* but has not yet determined that these meet his criteria adequately to be added fully to the list of intelligences. Since the 1983 release of *Frames of Mind,* Gardner has published numerous books and articles refining his theory and applying it in relevant educational settings. Indeed, MI Theory has been applied in educational settings, especially K-12, more than in any other learning or thinking environment. Only one year after the publication of *Frames of Mind,* the *Key School* in Indianapolis had begun redesigning their curriculum completely around MI theory, and today most schools incorporate the theory to varying degrees.

Although MI Theory is an extremely popular approach to human intelligence and has found widespread support in various research and educational domains, it has certainly not gone uncriticized. New, influential theories that challenge long-standing views in any science are typically targets for intense controversy within the field. MI Theory has been no different. One common objection to MI Theory suggests that Gardner's eight intelligences are not really separate intelligences, but rather merely describe different "thinking styles," all of which may be seen as existing within earlier unified intelligence views discussed at the beginning of this reading (Morgan, 1996). Another criticism contends that the theory contains embedded contradictions that make it too ambiguous to be valid (Klein, 1998). Moreover, Klein contends, because of its ambiguity, MI Theory can be molded "conveniently" to explain virtually any cognitive activity, rendering it impossible to prove or disprove. Finally, some researchers have argued that not enough rigorous scientific research has been done to demonstrate the validity of the intelligences and the effectiveness of applying MI Theory in real world settings. These critics suggest, if future research finds that MI Theory is not a valid or effective tool, a great deal of time and effort will have been wasted and learning thought to have been taking place, in reality, was not (Collins, 1998). These and other criticisms notwithstanding, MI Theory continues to influence strongly the field of human intelligence.

RECENT APPLICATIONS

Between 2000 and the middle of 2003, as this edition was being prepared, approximately 70 scientific articles cited Gardner's book, *Frames of Mind.* If we extend this search to include his other books and articles relating to MI Theory, the number of citations approaches several hundred. Clearly, Gardner's work in this area continues to have a powerful and widespread impact on research and thinking about learning and intelligence. To give you an idea of the diverse applications of MI Theory, here is a brief description of just two of these recent applications.

A cross-cultural study of Gardner's seven intelligences compared British and Iranian students' self-ratings and rating of parents' levels of each intelligence (Furnham et al., 2002). Some of the most interesting findings were (a) Iranian students rated themselves lower in logical-mathematical intelligence, but higher in spatial, musical, and intrapersonal intelligence than did the British students; (b) Iranians perceived their fathers' mathematical and spatial intelligence to be lower, but their fathers' interpersonal and intrapersonal intelligence to be higher than did the British students; (c) the Iranian students rated their mothers' level of intelligence *lower* than did the British students on all but one (intrapersonal) of the seven intelligences; and (d) the Iranians rated their brothers *higher* than the British on all but one scale (mathematical).

Another fascinating study relating Gardner's theory to Sandra Bem's research on androgyny (discussed in the *Personality* section of this book) found that people's estimates of their own intelligence was linked to their gender-identity (Rammstedt & Rammsayer, 2002). Researchers asked subjects to estimate their own level on various intelligences, and also complete the *Bem Sex Role Inventory* measuring their level of masculinity, femininity, and androgyny. Not only were gender differences found for the logical-mathematical intelligence (masculine) versus musical intelligences (feminine), but also the males' degree of self-perceived masculinity, femininity, or androgyny significantly influenced their estimates of their own level of various intelligences.

CONCLUSION

Gardner's MI Theory has survived over two decades and shows no signs of fading from view. Whether the ideas of the theory continue to grow in importance and influence or are overshadowed by new conceptualizations of intelligence remains to be seen. Whatever its future, however, one point is certain: MI Theory has changed forever how the world looks at learning, teaching, and intelligence. However, Gardner himself cautions that MI Theory is a means to an end and should not be an end in itself:

> Educational goals should reflect one's own values, and these can never come simply or directly from a scientific theory. Once one reflects on one's educational values and states one's goals, however, then the putative existence of our multiple intelligences can prove very helpful. And, in particular, if one's educational goals encompass disciplinary understanding, then it is possible to mobilize our several intelligences to help achieve that lofty goal. . . . I have come to realize that once one releases an idea into the world, one cannot completely control its behavior—anymore than one can control those products of our genes called children. Put succinctly, MI has and will have a life of its own, over and above what I might wish for it, my most widely known intellectual offspring. (Gardner, 2002)

Checkley, K. (1997). The first seven . . . and the eighth. *Educational Leadership, 55*, 8–13.

Collins, J. (1998). Seven kinds of smart. *Time, 152*, 94–96.

Furnham, A., Shahidi, S., & Baluch, B. (2002). Sex and cultural differences in perceptions of estimated multiple intelligence for self and family: A British-Iranian comparison. *Journal of Cross Cultural Psychology, 33*, 270–285.

Gardner, H. (2003). Multiple intelligences after twenty years. Paper presented at the American Educational Research Association, Chicago, IL, April 21, 2003.

Klein, P. (1998). A response to Howard Gardner: Falsifiability, empirical evidence, and pedagogical usefulness in educational psychologies. *Canadian Journal of Education, 23*, 103–112.

Morgan, H. (1996). An analysis of Gardner's theory of multiple intelligence. *Roeper Review, 18*, 263–269.

Rammstedt, B., & Rammsayer, T. (2002). Gender differences in self-estimated intelligence and their relation to gender-role orientation. *European Journal of Personality, 16*, 369–382.

MAPS IN YOUR MIND

Tolman, E. C. (1948). Cognitive maps in rats and men. *Psychological Review, 55*, 189–208.

Many of the studies in this book were included because the theoretical propositions underlying them and their findings contradicted the prevailing view and conventional wisdom of their time. Watson's study of Little Albert, Hobson and McCarley's conceptualization of dreams, Harlow's theory of infant attachment, Bouchard's revelations concerning genetic influences on personality, and LaPiere's observations of attitudes versus behavior, among others, all challenged the status quo of psychological thinking and thereby opened up new and often revolutionary interpretations of human behavior. Edward C. Tolman's theories and studies of learning and cognition made just such a contribution. During the years when psychology was consumed with strict stimulus-response learning theories that dismissed *unobservable* internal mental activity, Tolman, at the University of California at Berkeley, was doing experiments demonstrating that complex internal cognitive activity occurred even in rats and that these mental processes could be studied without the necessity of observing them directly. Due to the significance of his work, Tolman is considered to be the founder of a school of thought about learning that is today called *cognitive-behaviorism.*

In order to experience something of what Tolman proposed, imagine for a moment that you want to make your way from your present location to the nearest post office or video store. You probably already have an image in your mind of where these are located. Now think about the route you would take to get there. You know you have to take certain streets or highways, make certain turns, and eventually enter the building. This picture in your mind of your location relative to the post office or video store and the route you would follow to travel between them is called a *mental representation.* Tolman called these representations *cognitive maps.* Tolman maintained that not only do humans use cognitive maps, but also animals, including rats, think about their world in ways similar to cognitive maps. Why does anyone care how a rat thinks? Well, if you were a learning theorist in the 1930s and 1940s, the main research method being used was rats in mazes.

THEORETICAL PROPOSITIONS

In the first half of the twentieth century, learning theorists were on the front lines of psychology. In addition to trying to explain the mechanisms involved in learning, they were invested in demonstrating the respectability of psychology as a true science. Since psychology had been emerging as a science from its roots in philosophy for only a few decades, many researchers felt that the best way to prove psychology's scientific potential was to emulate the *hard* sciences such as physics. This notion led the learning theorists to propose that the only proper subject for study was, as in physics, observable, measurable events. A certain stimulus applied to an organism could be measured. And the organism's behavior in response to that stimulus could be measured. What went on inside the organism between these two events was not observable or measurable and, therefore, not *studyable* and, for that matter, not important. So, according to this view, when a rat learned to run through a maze faster and faster and with fewer and fewer errors, the learning process consisted of a succession of stimuli to which a succession of correct responses led to the reward of food at the end of the maze. This limited stimulus-response connectionist view of behavior formed the core of behaviorism and dominated the first 50 years or so of psychology's short history.

However, led by Tolman, a small band of renegades appeared during the 1930s and 1940s who maintained that much more was going on inside the learning organism than mere responses to stimuli. In fact, Tolman proposed two main modifications to the prevailing view. One was that the true nature and complexity of learning could not be fully understood without an examination of the internal mental processes that accompany the observable stimuli and responses. As Tolman stated in the famous 1948 article that is the subject of this discussion:

> We believe that in the course of learning something like a field map of the environment gets established in the rat's brain. We agree with the other [stimulus-

response] school that the rat running a maze is exposed to stimuli and is finally led as a result of these stimuli to the responses which actually occur. We feel, however, that the intervening brain processes are more complicated, more patterned, and often . . . more autonomous than do the stimulus-response psychologists. (p. 192)

The second proposal made by Tolman was that even though internal cognitive processes could not be directly observed, they could be objectively and scientifically inferred from observable behavior.

METHOD AND RESULTS

Tolman presented numerous studies in his 1948 article to support his views, all of which involved maze learning by rats. Two of the studies that clearly and concisely demonstrated his theoretical position are included here.

The first was called the *latent learning* experiment. For this study, rats were divided into three groups. Group C, the control group, was exposed to a complex maze using the standard procedure of one run through the maze each day with a food reward at the end of the maze. Group N (no reward) was exposed to the maze for the same amount of time each day but found no food and received no reward for any behavior in the maze. Group D (delayed reward) was treated exactly like group N for the first 10 days of the study, but then on day 11 found food at the end of the maze and continued to find it each day thereafter. Figure 1 summarizes the results for the three groups based on the average number of errors (running down blind alleys) made by each group of rats.

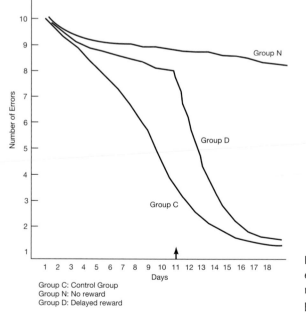

Group C: Control Group
Group N: No reward
Group D: Delayed reward

FIGURE 1 Latent learning experiment error rates in maze learning. (Adapted from p. 195.)

As you can easily see in the graph, the rats in groups N and D did not learn much of anything about the maze when they were not receiving any reward for running through the maze. The control rats learned the maze to near-perfection in about two weeks. However, when the rats in group D discovered a reason to run the maze (food!), they learned it to near-perfection in only about three days (day 11 to day 13). The only possible explanation for these findings was that during those 10 days when the rats were wandering around in the maze, they were learning much more about the maze than they were showing. As Tolman explained, "Once . . . they knew they were to get food, they demonstrated that during the preceding nonreward trials, they had learned where many of the blinds were. They had been building up a 'map' and could utilize [it] as soon as they were motivated to do so" (p. 195).

The second study to be discussed here was called the "spatial orientation" experiment. Stimulus-response theorists had maintained that a rat only "knows" where the food reward is by running the maze (and experiencing all the S-R connections) to get to it. This is very much like saying you only know where your bedroom is by walking out of the kitchen, across the living room, down the hall, past the bathroom, and into your room. In reality, you have a mental representation of where your bedroom is in the house without having to "run the maze." Tolman's spatial orientation technique was designed to show that rats trained in a maze actually know the location in space of the food reward relative to their starting position even if the elements of the maze are radically changed or even removed.

First, rats learned to run the simple maze shown in Figure 2. They would enter the maze at the start, run across a round table and into the path leading, in a somewhat circuitous route, to a food reward at the end. This was a relatively simple maze and no problem for the rats who learned it to near perfection in 12 trials.

Then the maze was changed to a sunburst pattern, similar to that shown in Figure 3. Now when the trained rats tried to run their usual route, they

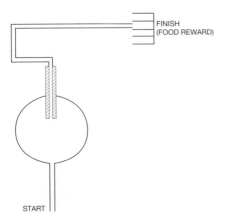

FINISH
(FOOD REWARD)

START

FIGURE 2   Spatial orientation experiment: Simple maze. (Adapted from p. 202.)

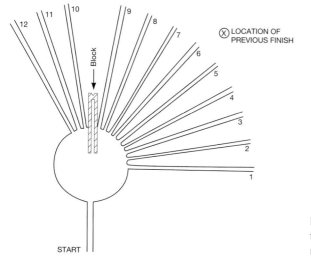

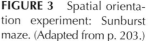

(X) LOCATION OF
PREVIOUS FINISH

FIGURE 3 Spatial orientation experiment: Sunburst
maze. (Adapted from p. 203.)

found it blocked and had to return to the round table. There they had a
choice of 12 possible alternate paths to try to get to where the food had been
in the previous maze. Figure 4 shows the number of rats choosing each of the
12 possible paths.

As you can see, path 6, which ran to about four inches from where the
food reward box had been placed in the previous maze, was chosen by significantly more rats than any other possible route. Stimulus-response theory
might have predicted that the rats would choose the path most closely in
the direction of the first turn in the original maze (path 11), but this was not
the case. "The rats had, it would seem, acquired not merely a strip-map to the

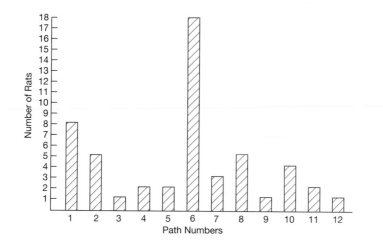

FIGURE 4 Spatial orientation experiment: Number of rats choosing each path.
(Adapted from p. 204.)

effect that the original specifically trained-on path led to food, but rather a wider, comprehensive map to the effect that food was located in such and such a direction in the room" (p. 204). Here, Tolman was expanding his theory beyond the notion that rats, and potentially other organisms including humans, produce cognitive maps of the route from point A to point Z. He was demonstrating that the maps that are produced are not mere *strip maps* represented as A to B to C and so on, to Z, but are much broader, comprehensive or conceptual maps that give organisms a cognitive *lay of the land.*

DISCUSSION

Tolman's concluding remarks in his 1948 article focused on this distinction between narrow strip maps and broader comprehensive maps. In applying his findings to humans, Tolman theorized that comprehensive maps of our social environment are advantageous to humans, while narrow, striplike maps can lead to negative human conditions such as mental illness or prejudice and discrimination. His reasoning was based on findings related to the studies described earlier indicating that when rats were overmotivated (i.e., too hungry) or overfrustrated (too many blind alleys), they tended to develop very narrow maps and were less likely to acquire the comprehensive cognitive mapping skills of the rats described in his studies. Acknowledging that he was not a clinical or social psychologist, Tolman offered this as a possible explanation for some of society's social problems. In Tolman's words:

> Over and over again men are blinded by too violent motivations and too intense frustrations into blind . . . haters of outsiders. And the expression of their hates ranges all the way from discrimination against minorities to world conflagrations.
>
> What in the name of Heaven or Psychology can we do about it? My only answer is to preach again the virtue of reason—of, that is, broad cognitive maps. . . . We dare not let ourselves or others become so over-emotional, so hungry, so ill-clad, so over-motivated that only narrow strip-maps will be developed. All of us . . . must be made calm enough and well-fed enough to be able to develop truly comprehensive maps. . . . We must, in short, subject our children and ourselves (as the kindly experimenter would his rats) to the optimal conditions of moderate motivation and an absence of unnecessary frustrations, whenever we put them and ourselves before that great God-given maze which is our human world. (p. 208)

SUBSEQUENT RESEARCH AND RECENT APPLICATIONS

Over the decades since Tolman's early studies, a great deal of research has supported his theories of cognitive learning. Perhaps the most notable outgrowth of Tolman's ideas and reasoning is the fact that today, one of the most active and influential subfields of the behavioral sciences is *cognitive psychology*. This branch of psychology is in the business of studying internal, unobservable cognitive processes. From a time only a few decades ago when the entire concept of "mind" was rejected as subject matter for scientific investigation, psychology has made a nearly complete reversal. Now it is generally accepted that the way a stimulus is processed mentally through perceiving, attending, thinking, expecting, remembering, and analyzing is at least as important in determining a behavioral response as the stimulus itself, if not more so.

Tolman's theory of cognitive mapping has influenced another area of psychology known as *environmental psychology*. This field is concerned with the relationship between human behavior and the environment in which it occurs. A key area of research in environmental psychology is concerned with how you experience and think about your life's various surroundings, such as your city, your neighborhood, your school campus, or the building in which you work. The study of your conceptualizations of these places is called *environmental cognition*, and your precise mental representations of them have been given Tolman's term, *cognitive maps*. Using Tolman's basic concepts, environmental psychologists have been influential not only in our understanding of how people understand their environments, but also in how environments should be designed or adapted to create the optimal *fit* with our cognitive mapping processes.

One of the leading environmental psychologists in applying Tolman's ideas to humans was Lynch (1960). Lynch proposed five categories of environmental features that we make use of in forming our cognitive maps. *Paths* are perceived arteries that carry traffic, whether it be in cars, on foot, on bicycles, or in boats. *Edges* are boundaries we use in our cognitive mapping to divide one area from another, but do not function as paths, such as a canyon, a wall, or the shore of a lake. *Nodes* are focal points, such as city parks, traffic circles, or a fountain, where paths or edges meet. *Districts* take up large spaces on our mental representations and are defined by some common characteristic, such as the theater district or restaurant row. Finally, *landmarks* are structures that you use as points of reference within your map and that are usually visible from a distance. Examples of these would be a clock tower, a church steeple, or a tall or especially unusual building.

This early article by Tolman articulating his theory of cognitive mapping has been cited consistently and frequently throughout the 50 years since its publication in a wide array of diverse studies. Between 2000 and 2003, as this book entered production, this study was cited in over 115 studies in various social science fields. For example, a recent study applied Tolman's model of cognitive maps to understanding how birds rely on the location of the sun to locate landmarks and create cognitive maps for their remarkable migratory treks over hundreds or even thousands of miles (Bingman & Able, 2002). Another study from the field of tourism cited Tolman's ideas in an examination of how travelers to undeveloped wilderness areas (called *nature-based tourists*) develop their knowledge of the terrain they are exploring (Young, 1999). The author found that several factors influenced the quality of the subjects' mental maps, including mode of transportation, whether they had visited the region before, number of days in the area, where the tourists were from, their age, and their gender.

Today, much of our traveling does not require going anywhere at all, at least in a physical sense. We can now travel anywhere in the world in the

Internet. Tolman's conceptualization of cognitive maps has found a place in research on the psychology of the World Wide Web. Imagine for a moment what you do when you are on the Internet: You explore; you jump from place to place; you surf; you navigate. You don't really go anywhere physically, you often feel as if you had been on a journey. And chances are, most of you could go there again using the approximately same route, right? So, if you think about it, you have formed a mental map of a small part of the Web! A study in a journal devoted to research on human-computer relationships examined Internet search behavior and the strategies people use to navigate the Web (Hodkinson et al., 2000). The researchers were able to translate Web search behavior into graphic form, identify individual search strategies, and suggest possible methods for improving Internet search effectiveness.

Finally, a revealing test of a theory's endurance over time is its ability to continue to generate controversy and debate. Tolman's theories proposed in his 1948 article have passed this test with high marks as evidenced by an article by Bennett (1996). This author claims, in a rather bold statement appearing in a biology journal, that

> No animal has been conclusively shown to have a cognitive map . . . because simpler explanations of the crucial novel short-cutting results are invariably possible. . . . I argue the cognitive map is no longer a useful hypothesis for elucidating the spatial behavior of animals and that the use of the term should be avoided. (p. 219)

So, according to Bennett, the 50-year history of Tolman's influence on the fields of cognitive and environmental psychology should be discarded. Not likely.

Bennett, A. (1996). Do animals have cognitive maps? *Journal of Experimental Biology, 199*(1), 219–224.
Bingman, V., & Able, K. (2002). Maps in birds: Representation mechanisms and neural bases. *Current Opinion in Neurobiology, 12,* 745–750.
Hodkinson, C., Kiel, G., & McColl-Kennedy, J. (2000). Consumer web search behavior: Diagrammatic illustration of wayfinding on the web. *International Journal of Human-Computer Studies, 52*(5), 805–830.
Lynch, K. (1960). *The image of the city.* Cambridge, MA: MIT Press.
Young, M. (1999). Cognitive maps of nature-based tourists. *Annals of Tourism Research, 26*(4), 817–839.

THANKS FOR THE MEMORIES!

Loftus, E. F. (1975). Leading questions and the eyewitness report. *Cognitive Psychology, 7,* 560–572.

PERRY MASON: Hamilton, I believe that my client is telling the truth when she says she was nowhere near the scene of the crime.

HAMILTON BURGER: Perry, why don't we let the jury decide?

PERRY MASON: Because, Hamilton, I don't believe there is going to
be a trial. You haven't got a case. All you have is
circumstantial evidence.

HAMILTON BURGER: Well, Perry, I suppose this is as good a time as any
to tell you. We have someone who saw the whole
thing, Perry. We have an *eyewitness!*

And as the mysterious music crescendos, we know that this is going to be another difficult case for Perry Mason. Even though we are reasonably certain
he will prevail in the end, the presence of a single eyewitness to the crime has
changed a weak case into a nearly airtight one for the district attorney. Why
do eyewitness reports provide such strong evidence in criminal cases? The
reason is that attorneys, judges, juries, and the general public believe that the
way in which a person remembers an event, must be the way it actually happened. In other words, memory is thought of as a process of replaying an
event similar to a video or DVD. However, psychologists who study memory
have now drawn into question that and many other common beliefs about
the reliability of human memory.

One of the leading researchers in the area of memory is Elizabeth Loftus at the University of Washington. She has found that when an event is recalled it is not accurately re-created. Instead, what is recalled is a memory
that is a reconstruction of the actual event. Loftus's research has demonstrated that reconstructive memory is a result of your use of new and existing
information to fill in the gaps in your recall of an experience. She maintains
that your memories are not stable, as we commonly believe, but that they are
malleable and changeable over time. So if you tell someone a story from your
vacation five years ago, you think you are re-creating the experience just as it
happened, but you probably are not. Instead, you have reconstructed the
memory using information from many sources, such as the previous times
you've told it, other experiences from the same or later vacations, perhaps a
movie you saw last year that was shot in the same place as your vacation, and
so on. You know this is true if you have ever recounted an experience in the
presence of another person who was with you at the time. You are often surprised by how your stories can totally disagree about an event you both experienced at the same time!

Usually, these alterations in memory are harmless. However, in legal
proceedings, when a defendant's fate may rest on the testimony of an eyewitness, memory reconstructions can be crucial. For this reason, most of Loftus's
research in the area of memory has been connected to legal eyewitness testimony. In her early research, she found that very subtle influences in how a
question is worded can alter a person's memory for an event. For example, if
witnesses to an automobile accident are asked, "Did you see a broken headlight?" or "Did you see the broken headlight?" the question using the word
the produced more positive responses than the question using the word *a*,
even when there had been no broken headlight. The use of *the* presupposes

the presence of a broken headlight and this, in turn, causes witnesses to add a new feature to their memories of the event.

The article that is the focus of this discussion is one of the most often cited studies by Loftus because it reports on four related studies that took her theory one major step further. In these studies, she demonstrated that the wording of questions asked of eyewitnesses could alter their memories of events when they were asked other questions about the events at a later time. Keep in mind that this research influenced both memory theory and criminal law.

THEORETICAL PROPOSITIONS

This research focused on the power of questions containing presuppositions to alter a person's memory of an event. Loftus defines a presupposition as a condition that must be true in order for the question to make sense. For example, suppose you have witnessed an automobile accident and I ask you, "How many people were in the car that was speeding?" The question *presupposes* that the car was speeding. But what if the car was not actually speeding? Well, you might answer the question anyway because it was not a question about the speed of the car. Loftus proposed, however, that because of the way the question was worded, you might add the speeding information to your memory of the event. Consequently, if you are asked other questions later, you will be more likely to say the car was speeding. Loftus hypothesized that if eyewitnesses are asked questions that contain a false presupposition about the witnessed event, the new *false* information may be incorporated into the witness's memory of the event and appear subsequently in new testimony by the witness.

METHOD AND RESULTS

For each of the four experiments reported, the method and results will be summarized together.

Experiment 1

In the first study, 150 students in small groups saw a film of a five-car chain-reaction accident that occurs when a driver runs through a stop sign into oncoming traffic. The accident takes only four seconds and the entire film runs less than a minute. After the film, the subjects were given a questionnaire containing 10 questions. For half of the subjects, the first question was, "How fast was Car A [the car that ran the stop sign] going when it ran the stop sign?" For the other half of the subjects, the question read, "How fast was Car A going when it turned right?" The remaining questions were of little interest to the researchers until the last one, which was the same for both groups: "Did you see a stop sign for Car A?"

In the group that had been asked about the stop sign, 40 subjects (53%) said they saw a stop sign for Car A, while only 26 (35%) in the turned-right group claimed to have seen it. This difference was found to be statistically significant.

Experiment 2

The second study Loftus reported was the first in this series to involve a delayed memory test and was the only one of the four not to use an automobile accident as the witnessed event. For this study, 40 subjects were shown a three-minute segment from the film *Diary of a Student Revolution*. The clip showed a class being disrupted by eight demonstrators. After they viewed the film, the subjects were given questionnaires containing 20 questions relating to the film clip. For half of the subjects, one of the questions asked, "Was the leader of the four demonstrators who entered the classroom a male?" For the other half, the question asked, "Was the leader of the 12 demonstrators who entered the classroom a male?" All remaining questions were identical for the two groups.

One week after this initial test, the subjects from both groups returned and answered 20 new questions about the film (without seeing it again). The one question that provided the results of the study was, "How many demonstrators did you see entering the classroom?" Remember, both groups of subjects saw the same film and answered the same questions, except for the reference to 12 versus 4 demonstrators.

The group that had received the question presupposing 12 demonstrators reported seeing an average of 8.85. Those who had received the question asking about 4 demonstrators averaged 6.40. This was also a significant difference. Some of the subjects recalled the correct number of 8. However, this experiment showed that, on average, the wording of one question altered the way subjects remembered the basic characteristics of a witnessed event.

Experiment 3

This experiment was designed to see if false presuppositions inherent in questions could cause witnesses to reconstruct their memory of an event to include objects that were not there. The subjects (150 university students) watched a short video of an accident involving a white sports car and then answered 10 questions about the content of the video. One question included for half of the subjects was, "How fast was the white sports car going when it passed the barn while traveling along the country road?" The other half of the subjects were asked, "How fast was the white sports car going while traveling along the country road?" As in the previous study, the subjects returned a week later and answered 10 new questions about the accident. The question addressing the issue under study was, "Did you see a barn?"

Of those subjects who had previously answered a question in which a barn was mentioned, 13 (17.3%) of them answered *Yes* to the test question a week later, compared with only 2 (2.7%) in the no-barn group. Once again, this was a statistically significant difference.

Experiment 4

The final experiment reported in this article was a somewhat more elaborate study designed to meet two goals. First, Loftus wanted to further demonstrate the memory reconstruction effects found in Experiment 3. Second, she wondered if perhaps just the mention of an object, even if it was not included as part of a false presupposition, might be enough to cause the object to be added to memory. For example, you are asked directly, "Did you see a barn?" when there was no barn in the film. You will probably answer *No*. But if you are asked again a week later, might that barn have crept into your memory of the event? This was the idea Loftus tested in the fourth experiment.

Three groups of 50 subjects viewed a three-minute film shot from the inside of a car that ends with the car colliding with a baby carriage pushed by a man. The three groups then received booklets containing questions about the film. These booklets differed as follows:

> *Group D:* The direct question group received booklets containing 40 "filler" questions and five key questions directly asking about nonexistent objects; for example, "Did you see a barn in the film?"
>
> *Group F:* The false presupposition group received the same 40 filler questions and five key questions that contained presuppositions about the same nonexistent objects, such as, "Did you see a station wagon parked in front of the barn?"
>
> *Group C:* The control group received only the 40 filler questions.

One week later all the subjects returned and answered 20 new questions about the film. Five of the questions were the exact same key questions as were asked of the direct-question group a week before. So group D saw those five questions twice. The measurement used was the percentage of subjects in each group who claimed to remember the nonexistent objects.

Table 1 summarizes the findings for all three groups. Remember, there was no school bus, truck, center line on the road, woman pushing the carriage, or barn in the film. Combining all the questions, the overall percentages of those subjects answering "yes" to the direct questions one week later were 29.2% for the false-presupposition group, 15.6% for the direct-question group, and 8.4% for the control group. The differences between the direct-question group and the false-presupposition group for each item as well as for all the items combined were statistically significant. However, while there is a trend to indicate a similar effect of the direct questions over controls, these differences were not large enough to reach statistical significance.

DISCUSSION

Based on these and other studies, Loftus argued that an accurate theory of memory and recall must include a process of reconstruction that occurs when new information is integrated into the original memory of an event. The findings of these studies cannot be explained by assuming that recall sim-

TABLE 1 Appearance of Nonexistent Objects in Subjects' Recall of Filmed Accident Following Direct Questions and False Presuppositions

DIRECT QUESTION	FALSE PRESUPPOSITION	PERCENT OF "YES" RESPONSES TO DIRECT QUESTION ONE WEEK LATER		
		C	D	F
Did you see a school bus in the film?	Did you see the children getting on the school bus?	6	12	26
Did you see a truck in the beginning of the film?	At the beginning of the film, was the truck parked beside the car?	0	8	22
Did you see a center line on the country road?	Did another car cross the center line on the country road?	8	14	26
Did you see a woman pushing the carriage?	Did the woman pushing the carriage cross into the road?	26	36	54
Did you see a barn in the film?	Did you see a station wagon parked in front of the barn?	2	8	18

C = control group
D = direct-question group
F = false-presupposition group
(From p. 568.)

ply involves a mental replaying of an event, even with varying degrees of accuracy. To illustrate, Figure 1 compares the traditional view of recall with the reformulated process proposed by Loftus. As you can see, the extra step of integrating new information into memory has been added. This new information, in turn, causes your representation of the original memory to be altered or *reconstructed*. Later, if you are asked a question about the event, your recall will not be of the actual original event, but of your reconstruction of it. Loftus contended that this reconstruction process was the reason that barns, school busses, trucks, women pushing baby carriages, and center lines in roads were all conjured up in subjects' memories when they were not part of the original experience. The false presupposition in the questions, provided a subtle form of new information that was unintentionally integrated into the original memory of the event.

In applying this idea to eyewitnesses in criminal investigations, Loftus pointed out that often witnesses are questioned more than once. They might be asked questions by police at the scene of the crime, interviewed by the prosecuting attorney assigned to the case, and again examined if they testify in court. During these various sessions of questions, it is not unlikely that false presuppositions will be made, probably unintentionally. There are innumerable ways in which this might happen. Common, innocent-sounding questions such as "What did the guy's gun look like?" or "Where was the get-

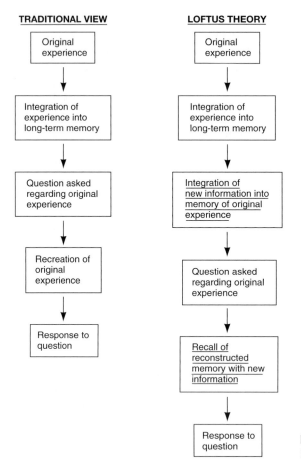

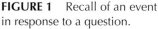

FIGURE 1   Recall of an event in response to a question.

away car parked?" have been shown to increase the chances that witnesses will remember a gun or a getaway car whether or not they were actually there (Smith & Ellsworth, 1987). So, while the attorneys, the judge, and the jury are making the assumption that the witness is re-creating what was actually seen, Loftus contends that what is being remembered by the witness is a "regenerated image based on the altered memorial representation" (p. 571).

RECENT APPLICATIONS

Several studies represent the ongoing influence of Loftus's impressive body of work on eyewitness testimony. One study citing her 1975 article examined how lawyers' complicated questions negatively affect eyewitness accuracy and confidence (Kebbell & Giles, 2000). All subjects watched identical videotaped events and were questioned a week later about what they saw. Half of the subjects were asked questions in confusing language (you know, that lawyer-speak of "Is it not true that . . . ?"), while others were asked the same questions in simple language. The results were clear: the subjects receiving the confusing form of the questions were less accurate in their eyewitness reports and were also less confident of their answers than those in the straightforward-question condition.

Another fascinating study applied Loftus's work to reports of "fantastic memories," that is, memories that bear greater similarity to fantasy than reality, such as alien abductions, out-of-body experiences, ESP events, encounters with ghosts, and so on (French, 2003). Clearly, if these reports of memories were true, they would provide proof that these "paranormal" occurrences are real. However, research tells us time and time again that such events have never been scientifically demonstrated. So, what accounts for the memories? The answer may be the fallibility and unreliability of human memory as discussed in this reading and, perhaps, the ability of our brains to *create* memories of events that never actually happened. As French points out, "a number of psychological variable that have been shown to correlate with susceptibility to false memories (e.g., hypnotic susceptibility, tendency to dissociate, etc.) also correlate with the tendency to report paranormal . . . experiences" (p. 153). We discuss this false memory issue next.

In addition to her ongoing work in the area of eyewitness testimony, Elizabeth Loftus is currently one of the leading experts in the heated controversy over repressed childhood memories. On one side of this new debate are those people who claim to have been abused, usually sexually, sometime in their past, but who have only recently, often with the help of a therapist, remembered the abuse because the traumatic memories have been repressed in their unconscious. On the other side are those who have been accused of this abuse, but who categorically deny it and claim that these memories have been either fantasized or implanted through the therapeutic process (see Garry & Loftus, 1994, for a popular press review of the controversy). This falls squarely into the area of Loftus's memory research.

Loftus's book *The Myth of Repressed Memories: False Memories and Allegations of Sexual Abuse* (Loftus & Ketcham, 1994; also, see Pope, 1995, for a review) summarized her findings in this area and combined them into a cohesive argument. Basically, Loftus contends, and appears to have demonstrated in numerous studies, that repressed memories simply do not exist. In fact, she is at the forefront of psychologists who question the entire notion and existence of an unconscious. A main feature of Loftus's argument is that experimental evidence repeatedly demonstrates that especially traumatic memories tend to be the ones we remember *best*. And yet, clinicians often report these instances of repressed memories of abuse that rise to the surface during specific and intense forms of therapy. How can these two seemingly opposing views be reconciled? Well, Loftus suggests three possible memory distortions that might explain what clinicians see as repression (Loftus,

Joslyn, & Polage, 1998). First, early sexual abuse may simply be forgotten, not repressed. She cites research demonstrating that when children do not understand the sexual nature of a potentially abusive event, it tends to be remembered poorly. Second, it is possible that people in therapy say they had forgotten a traumatic event, but, in reality, they never actually forgot it. Avoiding thinking about something is different from forgetting it. And finally, Loftus contends that some "people may *believe* that a particular traumatic event occurred and was repressed when, if, fact, it did not happen in the first place. Under some circumstances, some combination of these distortions could lead to situations that are interpreted as repression" (p. 781).

You can imagine that Loftus's position on repressed and recovered memories is not without critics (e.g., Pezdek & Roe, 1997 Steinberg, 2000). After all, her rejection of the power of repression is directly opposed to models of psychology and the mind that have been around since Freud. Moreover, many therapists and victims have a very personal stake in the belief that one's memories of abuse can be repressed for years and later recovered. However, a careful reading of Loftus's thorough and careful scientific work should cause anyone to question this belief.

CONCLUSION

Elizabeth Loftus is considered by most to be the leading researcher in the areas of memory reconstruction and eyewitness inaccuracy. Her research in these areas continues. Her findings over the years have held up quite well to challenges and have been supported by other researchers in the field.

There is little doubt within the psychological and legal professions today that eyewitness reports are subject to many sources of error such as postevent information integration. It is because of the body of research by Loftus and others that the power and reliability of eyewitnesses in judicial proceedings is being seriously questioned. Loftus herself is one of the most sought-after expert witnesses (usually for the defense) to demonstrate to juries the care they must use when evaluating the testimony of eyewitnesses.

As Loftus herself puts it in her recent book, "I study memory and I am a skeptic" (Loftus & Ketcham, 1994, p. 7). Perhaps we all should be.

French, C. (2003). Fantastic memories: The relevance of research into eyewitness testimony and false memories for reports of anomalous experiences. *Journal of Consciousness Studies, 10,* 153–174.

Garry, M., & Loftus, E. (1994). Repressed memories of childhood trauma: Could some of them be suggested? *USA Today magazine, 122,* 82–85.

Kebbell, M., & Giles, C. (2000). Some experimental influences of lawyers' complicated questions on eyewitness confidence and accuracy. *Journal of Psychology, 134*(2), 129–139.

Loftus, E., Joslyn, S., & Polage, D. (1998). Repression: A mistaken impression? *Development and Psychopathology, 10*(4), 781–792.

Loftus, E., & Ketcham, K. (1994). *The myth of repressed memories: False accusations and allegations of sexual abuse.* New York: St. Martin's Press.

Pezdek, K., & Roe, C., (1997). The suggestibility of children's memory for being touched: Planting, erasing, and changing memories. *Law and Human Behavior, 21,* 95–107.

Pope, K. (1995). What psychologists better know about recovered memories, research: Lawsuits, and the pivotal experiment. *Clinical Psychology: Science and Practice, 2*(3), 304–315.

Smith, V., & Ellsworth, P. (1987). The social psychology of eyewitness accuracy: Leading questions and communicator expertise. *Journal of Applied Psychology, 72,* 294–300.

Steinberg, M. (2000). The stranger in the mirror. *Psychology Today, 33,* 34.

5 HUMAN DEVELOPMENT

This subfield of psychology is concerned with the developmental changes everyone goes through from birth to death. This is one of the largest and most complex specialties in the behavioral sciences. Although we grow up to be unique individuals, a great deal of our development is similar and predictable, and occurs according to certain relatively fixed schedules. Included among the most influential areas of research in developmental psychology are the processes of attachment or bonding between infant and mother, the development of intellectual abilities, and the changes relating to the aging process.

Some of the most famous and influential research ever conducted in psychology is discussed in this section. Dr. Harry Harlow's work with monkeys demonstrated the importance of early infant attachments in later psychological adjustment. The sweeping discoveries of Jean Piaget formed the entire foundation of what we know today about cognitive development. A small sample of his research is included here in detail so that you may glimpse the ingenuity of his methods and clarity of his findings. Next is a famous body of research by Lawrence Kohlberg focusing on how moral character develops and why some people appear to behave at a higher moral level than others. In addition, since human development is a lifelong process, a well-known project by Ellen Langer and Judith Rodin (often referred to as *the plant study*) is included to illustrate how everyone, no matter how old, needs to feel in control of their own lives, activities, and destinies.

DISCOVERING LOVE
Harlow, H. F. (1958). The nature of love. *American Psychologist, 13,* 673–685.

Sometimes it seems that research psychologists have gone too far. How can something such as love be studied scientifically? Well, however you define love, you'll have to agree that it influences a huge amount of our behavior. If we make that assumption, then it follows that psychologists would have to be interested in what it is, where you get it, and how it works.

Harry Harlow (1906–1981), a developmental psychologist, is considered by many to have made the greatest contribution since Freud in studying how

126

our early life experiences affect adulthood. Most psychologists agree that your experiences as an infant with closeness, touching, and attachment to your mother (or primary caregiver) have an important influence on your abilities to love and be close to others later in life. After all, if you think about it, what was your first experience with love? It was the bond between you and your mother beginning at the moment of your birth. But what exactly was it about that connection that was so crucial? The Freudians believed that it was the focus around the importance of the breast and the instinctive oral tendencies during the first year of life (the famous *oral stage*). Later, the behaviorists countered that notion with the view that all human behavior is associated with our so-called primary needs, such as hunger, thirst, and avoidance of pain. Since the mother can fill these needs, the infant's closeness to her is constantly reinforced by the fact that she provides food for the infant. Consequently, the mother becomes associated with pleasurable events and, therefore, love develops. In both of these conceptualizations, love was seen as something secondary to other instinctive or survival needs. However, Harlow discovered that love and affection may be primary needs that are just as strong as or even stronger than those of hunger or thirst.

One way to begin to uncover the components of the love between an infant and mother would be to place infants in situations where the mother does not provide for all of the infant's needs and where various components of the environment can be scientifically manipulated. According to previous theories, we should be able to prevent or change the quality and strength of the bond formed between the infant and mother by altering the mother's ability to meet the infant's primary needs. For ethical reasons, however, it is obvious that such research could not be done on humans. Since Harlow had been working with rhesus monkeys for several years in his studies of learning, it was a simple process to begin his studies of love and attachment with these subjects. Biologically, rhesus monkeys are very similar to humans. Harlow also believed that the basic responses of the rhesus monkey relating to bonding and affection in infancy (such as nursing, contact, clinging, etc.) are the same for the two species. Whether such research with nonhuman subjects is ethical is addressed later in this section.

THEORETICAL PROPOSITIONS

In Harlow's previous studies, infant monkeys were raised carefully by humans in the laboratory so that they could be bottle-fed better, receive well-balanced nutritional diets, and be protected from disease more effectively than if they were raised by their monkey mothers. Harlow noticed that these infant monkeys became very attached to the cloth pads (cotton diapers) that were used to cover the bottoms of their cages. They would cling to these pads and would become extremely angry and agitated when the pads were removed for cleaning. This attachment was seen in the baby monkeys as early as one day old and was even stronger over the monkeys' first several months of life. Apparently, as Harlow states, "the baby, human or monkey, if it is to survive, must clutch at more than a straw" (p. 675). If a baby monkey was in a cage without this soft covering, it would thrive very poorly even though it received complete nutritional and medical care. When the cloth was introduced, the infant would become healthier and seemingly content. Therefore, Harlow theorized that there must be some basic need in these infant monkeys for close contact with something soft and comforting in addition to primary biological needs such as hunger and thirst. In order to test this theory, Harlow and his associates decided to "build" different kinds of experimental monkey mothers.

METHOD

The first surrogate mother they built consisted of a smooth wooden body covered in sponge rubber and terry cloth. It was equipped with a breast in the chest area that delivered milk and contained a lightbulb inside for warmth. They then constructed a different kind of surrogate mother that was less able to provide soft comfort. This mother was made of wire mesh shaped about the same as the wooden frame, so that an infant monkey could cling to it in a similar way as to the cloth mother. This wire mother also came equipped with a working nursing breast and also was able to provide heat. In other words, the wire mother was identical to the cloth mother in every way except for the ability to offer what Harlow called *contact comfort.*

These manufactured mothers were then placed in separate cubicles that were attached to the infant monkeys' living cage. Eight infant monkeys were randomly assigned to two groups. For one group, the cloth mother was equipped with the feeder (a nursing bottle) to provide milk, and for the other group, the wire mother was the milk provider. I'm sure you can already see what Harlow was testing here. He was attempting to separate the influence of nursing from the influence of contact comfort on the monkeys' behavior toward the mother. The monkeys were then placed in their cages and the amount of time they spent in direct contact with each mother was recorded for the first five months of their lives. The results were striking, but we'll get to those shortly.

Following these preliminary studies, Harlow wanted to explore the effects of attachment and contact comfort in greater detail. Common knowledge tells us that when children are afraid, they will seek out the comfort of their mothers (or other primary caregivers). To find out how the young monkeys with the wire and cloth mothers would respond in such situations, Harlow placed in their cages various objects that caused a fearful reaction in them, such as a wind-up drum-playing toy bear. (To a baby monkey this bear, which is as big as the monkey itself, is very frightening.) The responses of the monkeys in these situations were observed and recorded carefully.

Another study Harlow developed was called the *open field test* and involved placing young monkeys in a small, unfamiliar room containing various objects (wooden blocks, blankets, containers with lids, a folded piece of paper) that, under normal conditions, monkeys like to play with and manipulate. The monkeys who were raised with both the cloth and wire mothers were placed in the room with either the cloth mother present, no mother present, or the wire mother present. The idea here was to examine the tendency of the young monkeys to adapt to and explore this strange situation with or without the presence of the mother.

Finally, Harlow wanted to find out if the attachments formed between the monkeys and their surrogate mothers would persist after periods of separation. When the monkeys reached 6 months of age and were on solid food diets, they were separated for short periods from the mother, and then reunited in the open-field situation.

RESULTS

In the original experiment, you will remember that all the monkeys had access to both the cloth mother and the wire mother. For half the monkeys the cloth mother provided the milk and for the other half the wire mother did so. By now you've probably guessed that the monkeys preferred the cloth mother (wouldn't you?), but what was so surprising was the extreme strength of this preference even among those monkeys who received their milk from the wire mother. Contrary to the popular theories at the time of this research, the fulfilling of biological needs such as hunger and thirst was of almost no importance in the monkeys' choice of a mother. The huge influence of contact comfort in producing an attachment between infant and mother monkey was clearly demonstrated. Figure 1 graphically illustrates this effect. After the

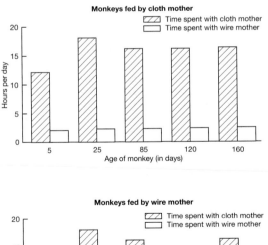

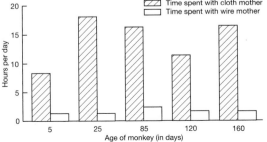

FIGURE 1 Amount of time spent each day on the cloth and wire mothers.

first few days of adjustment, all the monkeys, regardless of which mother had the milk, were spending nearly all their time each day on the cloth mother. Even those monkeys who were fed by the wire mother would only leave the comfort of the cloth mother to nurse briefly and then return to the cloth-covered surrogate immediately.

The two groups of monkeys that were raised with only a cloth or wire mother further demonstrated the importance of contact comfort. While both groups of these infants ate the same amount and gained weight at the same rate, the infants in the wire mother condition did not digest the milk as well and experienced frequent bouts of diarrhea. This suggests that the lack of the soft mother was psychologically stressful to these infants.

The results of the frightening-object tests provided additional evidence of the young monkeys' attachment to the cloth mother. Whenever the monkeys found themselves faced with something frightening they would run to the cloth mother and cling to it for comfort and protection. As the monkeys' age increased, this response became even stronger. Again, it made no difference whether a monkey had received its milk from the wire or the cloth mother; when afraid, they all sought the security of the soft, cloth-covered surrogate.

You may have noticed in humans that when children feel safe and secure because of the presence of a parent, they are more curious and more willing to explore their environment. Often, they will investigate everything around them, provided they are still able to see the parent. Harlow's strange-situation or open-field tests were designed to simulate this behavior in the monkeys in relation to the surrogate mothers. When placed into this strange room, all the monkeys immediately rushed to the cloth mother, clutched it, rubbed their bodies against it, and manipulated its body and face. After a while these infants "began to use the mother surrogate as a source of security, a base of operations. . . . They would explore and manipulate a stimulus and then return to the mother before adventuring again into the strange new world" (p. 679).

However, when the infant monkeys were placed into the same room without the soft mother, their reactions were completely different. They would freeze with fear and engage in emotional behaviors such as crying, crouching, and thumb sucking. Sometimes they would run to the part of the room where the mother usually was and then run from object to object, screaming and crying. When the wire mother was present, they behaved exactly the same as in the no-mother condition. This was once again true of all the monkeys, regardless of the nursing condition (cloth vs. wire) in which they had been raised.

In the last part of this study, the monkeys were separated from the mother for various periods of time after they stopped nursing and were on solid-food diets (about five to six months of age). After the longest separation (30 days), when the monkeys were reunited with the cloth mother in the same open-field situation, the monkeys rushed to the mother, climbed on it, clutched it tightly, and rubbed their heads and faces on its body. They then played with the surrogate mother, which included biting and tearing at the cloth cover. The main difference was that the monkeys did not leave the mother to explore and play with the objects in the room as they had done before. Apparently, according to Harlow, the need for contact comfort was greater than the natural tendency for exploration. It should be pointed out, however, that these reunions only lasted about three minutes and that such exploration may have occurred if the sessions had been extended.

DISCUSSION

As Harlow points out, the studies reported in this article demonstrate the overwhelming importance of contact comfort in the development of attachment between infant monkeys and their mothers. In fact, this factor in bonding appears to be considerably more important than the mother's ability to provide life-sustaining milk to the infant.

One of the many reasons this research changed psychology is that the findings went against the grain of the popular beliefs of the behaviorists at that time, who focused on the reinforcement qualities of feeding as the driving force behind the infant-mother bond. However, as Harlow stated about his findings, "the primary function of nursing as an affectional variable is that of ensuring frequent and intimate body contact of the infant with the mother. Certainly, man cannot live by milk alone" (p. 677).

There is little question that Harlow believed that his results could be applied to humans, a question that is discussed shortly. In fact, he offered the possibility of his findings' practical applications to humans. He contended that as socioeconomic demands on the family increase, women would be entering the workplace with increasing frequency. This was of concern to many at the time of Harlow's research, since it was widely believed that the mother's presence for nursing was necessary for attachment and proper child rearing. He went on to state that, since the key to successful parenting is contact comfort and not the *mammalian capabilities* of women, the American male is able to participate on equal terms in the rearing of infants. This view may be widely accepted today, but when Harlow wrote this in 1958, it was revolutionary.

CRITICISMS AND SIGNIFICANCE OF THE FINDINGS

Harlow's claims notwithstanding, do you think it's appropriate to view humans as having the same attachment (or love) processes as monkeys? There has been some research to support the view that the attachment of human babies to their caregivers does indeed go well beyond simply fulfilling biological needs. It has been shown that greater skin-to-skin contact between a mother and her very young infant enhances attachment (Klaus & Kennell, 1976). However, the attachment process develops much more slowly in humans: over the first six months compared with the first few days for monkeys. In addition, only approximately 70% of children appear to be securely attached to an adult at one year old (Sroufe, 1985).

There are many people, past and present, who would offer criticisms of Harlow's work based on the ethics of performing such experiments on infant monkeys. The question raised is this: Do we as humans have the right to subject monkeys (or any animal) to potentially harmful situations for the sake of research? In the case of Harlow's research, there are sensible arguments on both sides. One of the ways science judges the ethics of such research is by examining the potential benefits to people and society. Whether you feel that this study was ethical or not, the findings have affected humans in several positive ways. Some of these relate to issues of institutionalized children, adoption, and child abuse.

Unfortunately, many children in our culture are forced to spend portions of their lives in institutional settings, either because their parents are unable to keep and care for them (orphanages), or because of their own various illnesses and other physical difficulties (hospital settings). Harlow's research has influenced the kind of care we try to provide for those children. There is now general acceptance that basic biological care in institutional settings is inadequate and that infants need to be in physical contact with other humans. Institutionalized children need to be touched and held by staff members, nurses, and volunteers as much as possible. Also, when not precluded by medical conditions, these children are often placed in situations where they can see and touch each other, thereby gaining additional contact comfort. While such attempts at filling attachment needs will never replace real parental care, they are clearly a vast improvement over simple custodial care.

The work of Harlow offered encouragement and optimism for nonmaternal caregivers to be effective parents. Since it appeared that nursing was secondary to contact comfort in the development and adjustment of infants, the actual mother of a child was no longer seen as the only proper person to provide care. Now fathers could feel more adequate to assume a larger role in the process. But beyond this, other nonparental caregivers, such as babysitters or day care–center workers, when necessary, could be seen as acceptable options. Moreover, these discoveries greatly enhanced the prospect of adoption, since it was recognized that an adoptive parent could offer a child just as much contact comfort as a biological parent could.

Finally, Harlow's early studies shed light on the terrible problem of child abuse. One surprising aspect of such abusive relationships is that in nearly all cases, the abused child seems to love and to be firmly attached to the abusive parent. According to a strict behaviorist interpretation, this is difficult to understand. But if attachment is the strongest basic need, as Harlow suggested, then this would far outweigh the effects of the abusive punishment. Harlow actually tested this in later studies. He designed surrogate mother monkeys that were able to reject their infants. Some emitted strong jets of air, while others had blunt spikes that would pop out and force the baby monkeys away. The way the monkeys would respond to this treatment would be to move a small distance away until the rejection ended. They would then return and cling to the mother as tightly as ever (Rosenblum & Harlow, 1963).

RECENT APPLICATIONS

Harlow's research continues to be cited frequently in studies on the influence of touch, bonding, attachment, and the effects of human contact on emotional and physical health. One such study examined the connection between social isolation (lack of opportunities for close, meaningful, social contact with others) and physical health among adults who live in life situations marked by loneliness (Cacioppo & Hawkley, 2003). Findings indicated that adults lacking in social contact experienced everyday life events as more stressful, were at greater risk of high blood pressure, healed from injuries more slowly, and slept more poorly than people with healthy social connections.

Another study citing Harlow work demonstrated how skin-to-skin contact (cleverly referred to as *kangaroo care*) is critically important in the survival and development of premature infants and in establishing the infant-mother bond following premature births (Feldman & Eidelman, 1998). This is an important finding, in that hospitals caring for high-risk premature infants must work to balance a baby's need for physical contact and touch with other, equally compelling safeguards against potentially life-threatening infections that a premature baby's undeveloped immune system might be unable to fight.

Harlow's ideas have also been applied to psychotherapeutic settings. As humanistic and holistic approaches to counseling have developed over the past 40 years, the healing qualities of touch have played an increasingly central role (see LaTorre, 2000). As one psychotherapist explains:

> I have found that when touch is focused and intentioned, particularly in touch therapies such as acupressure and therapeutic touch, it becomes an important aspect in the therapeutic interaction. It deepens awareness and supports change. Rather than creating confusion, touch therapies when used appropriately enhance the psychotherapeutic interaction instead of detracting from it. The key word here is appropriate. Touch is a very powerful tool and should not be used lightly. (LaTorre, 2000, p. 105)

CONCLUSION

It would be a mistake to assume that Harlow had a monopoly on the definition of the nature of love. It is unmistakable, however, that his discoveries changed the way we view the connection between infant and mother. Perhaps, if this research has permeated, at least a little, into our culture, some good has come from it. For example, Harlow tells the story of a woman who, after hearing Harlow present his research, came up to him and said, "Now I know what's wrong with me! I'm just a wire mother" (p. 677).

Cacioppo, J., & Hawkley, L. (2003). Social isolation and health with an emphasis on underlying mechanisms. *Perspectives in Biology and Medicine, 46,* S39–S52.

Feldman, R., & Eidelman, A. (1998). Intervention programs for premature infants: How and do they affect development? *Clinics in Perinatology, 25*(3), 613–629.

Klaus, M. H., & Kennell, J. H. (1976). *Maternal infant bonding.* St. Louis MO: Mosby Press.

LaTorre M. (2000). Integrative perspectives. Touch and psychotherapy. *Perspectives in Psychiatric Care 36,* 105–106.

Rosenblum, L. A., & Harlow, H. (1963). Approach-avoidance conflict in the mother surrogate situation. *Psychological Reports, 12,* 83–85.

Sroufe, A. (1985). Attachment classification from the perspective of the infant-caregiver relationships and infant temperament. *Child Development, 56,* 1–14.

OUT OF SIGHT, BUT NOT OUT OF MIND

Piaget, J. (1954). *The development of object concept: The construction of reality in the child* (pp. 3–96). New York: Basic Books.

How did you progress from an infant, with a few elementary thinking skills, to the adult you are now, with the ability to reason and analyze the world in many complex ways involving language, symbols, and logic? Your first reaction to this question may very likely be to say, "Well, I acquired these intellectual abilities through learning: the process of interacting with my environment and the teaching I received from adults as I developed."

While this explanation seems intuitively correct to most people, many developmental psychologists believe that there is much more to acquiring intellectual abilities than simple learning. The prevailing view about intellectual development is that it is a process of maturation, much like physical development, that occurs in a predictable fashion from birth through adulthood.

Do you look at an infant and see a person who, with enough learning, is capable of adult physical behaviors? Of course not. Instead you know that there is a process of physical maturation that will enable the child to behave in increasingly complex ways over time. Until the child achieves a given level of development, all the learning in the world cannot produce certain behaviors. For example, consider the behavior of walking. You probably think of walking as a learned behavior. But imagine trying to teach a six-month-old to walk. You could place the infant on an Olympic schedule of eight hours of practice every day, and the child will not learn to walk. This is because the child has not yet reached the physical maturity to be able to perform the behavior of walking.

Intellectual, or cognitive, development is seen by most researchers in much the same way. There are certain levels of thinking and reasoning ability that cannot be understood until an appropriate stage of cognitive development has been reached, no matter how much learning takes place. Psychology owes its realization and understanding of this conceptualization of cognitive development to the work of the Swiss psychologist Jean Piaget (1896–1980).

Piaget is one of the most influential figures in the history of psychology. His work not only revolutionized developmental psychology, but also is the foundation of all subsequent investigations in the area of the formation of the intellect. Piaget was originally trained as a biologist and studied the inborn ability of animals to adapt to new environments. While Piaget was studying at the Sorbonne in Paris, he accepted a job (to earn extra money) at the

Alfred Binet Laboratory, where the first intelligence tests had been developed. He was hired to standardize a French version of a reasoning test that had been developed in English. It was during his employment in Paris that Piaget began to formulate his theories about cognitive development.

THEORETICAL PROPOSITIONS

The work at the Binet Laboratory was tedious and not very interesting to Piaget at first. But then he began to notice some interesting patterns in the answers given by children at various ages to the questions on the test. Children at similar ages appeared to be making the same mistakes. That is, they were using the same reasoning to reach the same answers. And what fascinated Piaget was not the correct answers, but the thinking that produced the wrong answers. Based on these observations, he theorized that older children had not just learned more than the younger ones, but were thinking differently about the problems. This led him to question the current prevailing definition of intelligence, based on a test score, in favor of one that involved a more complete understanding of the cognitive strategies used by children at various ages (Ginzburg & Opper, 1979).

Piaget devoted the next 50 years of his life and career to studying intellectual development in children. His work led to his famous theory of cognitive development, which for decades was a virtually undisputed explanation for how humans acquire their complex thinking skills. His theory holds that all humans develop through four stages of cognitive development that always occur in the same sequence and at approximately the same ages. These are summarized in Table 1.

As important as his theory itself were the techniques Piaget used to study the thinking abilities in children. At the Binet Laboratory, he realized that if his new conceptualization of intelligence were to be explored, new methods had to be developed. Instead of the usual, overly rigid standardized tests, he proposed an interview technique that allowed the child's answers to influence the direction of the questioning. In this way, the processes underlying the child's answers could be best explored.

One of the most remarkable aspects of Piaget's research is that in reaching many of his conclusions, he studied his *own* children, Lucienne, Jacqueline, and Laurent. By today's scientific standards, this method would be highly questionable because of the rather extreme possibility of bias and lack of objectivity. However, as there are always exceptions to rules, Piaget's findings from his children have been successfully applied to all children universally.

Obviously a single chapter in this book is far too little space to explore more than a small fraction of Piaget's work. Therefore, we will focus on his discovery of a key intellectual skill called *object permanence*. This ability provides an excellent example of one of Piaget's most important findings, as well as ample opportunity to experience his methods of research.

Object permanence refers to your ability to know that an object exists even when it is hidden from your senses. If someone walks over to you now

TABLE 1 Piaget's Stages of Cognitive Development

STAGE	AGE RANGE	MAJOR CHARACTERISTICS
Sensori-motor	0–2 years	• All knowledge is acquired through senses and movement (such as looking and grasping) • Thinking is at the same speed as physical movement • Object permanence develops
Preoperational	2–7 years	• Thinking separates from movement and increases greatly in speed • Ability to think in symbols develops • Nonlogical, "magical" thinking • Animism: all objects have thoughts and feelings • Egocentric thinking: unable to see world from others' points of view
Concrete operations	7–11 years	• Logical thinking develops, including classifying objects and mathematical principles, but only as they apply to real, concrete objects • Conservation of liquid, area, volume • Ability to infer what others may be feeling or thinking
Formal operations	11 and up	• Logical thinking extends to hypothetical and abstract concepts • Ability to reason using metaphors and analogies • Ability to explore values, beliefs, philosophies • Ability to think about past and future • Not everyone uses formal operations to the same degree, and some not at all

and takes this book out of your hands and runs into the next room, do you think that the book or the book-snatcher has ceased to exist? Of course not. You have a *concept* of the book and the person in your mind even though you cannot see, hear, or touch them. However, according to Piaget, this was not always true for you. He demonstrated that your cognitive ability to conceive of objects as permanent and unchanging was something you, and everyone else, developed during your first two years of life. The reason this ability is important is that without it, problem solving and internal thinking are impossible. Therefore, before a child can leave the sensori-motor stage (0 to 2 years; see Table 1) and enter the preoperational period (2 to 7 years), object permanence must be mastered.

METHOD AND RESULTS

Piaget studied the process of developing object permanence using *unstructured evaluation methods.* For infants and very young children, these techniques often took the form of games he would play with his children. Through observing their problem-solving ability and the errors they made in the games, Piaget identified six substages of development that occur during the sensori-motor period and are involved in the formation of the object concept. For you to experience the flavor of his research, these six stages are summarized here with examples of Piaget's interactions with his children from his own observational journals:

- *STAGE 1 (Birth to 1 month)* This stage is concerned primarily with reflexes relating to feeding and touching. There is no evidence of object permanence during this first month of life.

- *STAGE 2 (1 to 4 months)* During stage 2, while there is still no sign of an object concept, there are behaviors that Piaget interprets as preparing the infant for this ability. The child begins to repeat purposely behaviors that center on the infant's own body. For example, if an infant's hand accidentally comes in contact with its foot, it might reproduce the same movements over and over again to cause the event to be repeated. Piaget called these *primary circular reactions.* Also, at this stage, infants are able to follow moving objects with their eyes. Often, if an object leaves the child's visual field and fails to reappear, the child will turn its attention to other visible objects and show no signs of searching for the "vanished" object. Piaget called this behavior *passive expectation.* The following interaction between Piaget and his son, Laurent, illustrates this:

  > Observation 2. Laurent at 0;2 [0 years, 2 months]. I look at him through the hood of his bassinet and from time to time I appear at a more or less constant point; Laurent then watches that point when I am out of his sight and obviously expects me to reappear. (p. 9)
  > The child limits himself to looking at the place where the object vanished: Thus he merely preserves the attitude of the earlier perception and if nothing reappears, he soon gives up. If he had the object concept . . . he would actively search to find out where the thing could have been put. . . . But this is precisely what he does not know how to do, for the vanished object is not yet a permanent object which has been moved; it is a mere image which reenters the void as soon as it vanishes, and emerges from it for no objective reason. (p. 11)

- *STAGE 3 (4 to 10 months)* It is during this stage that children begin to purposefully and repeatedly manipulate objects they encounter in their environment (*secondary circular reactions*). The child begins to reach for and grasp things, to shake them, bring them closer to look at or place in the mouth, and to acquire the ability of rapid eye movements to follow quickly moving or falling objects. Late in this stage, the first signs of object permanence appear. For example, children begin to search for objects that are obscured from view if a small part of the object is visible.

  > Observation 23. At 0;9 I offer Lucienne a celluloid goose which she has never seen before; she grasps it at once and examines it all over. I place the goose beside her and cover it before her eyes, sometimes completely, sometimes revealing the head. Two very distinct reactions. . . . When the goose disappears completely, Lucienne immediately stops searching even when she is on the point of grasping it. . . . When the beak protrudes, not

> only does she grasp the visible part and draw the animal to her, but . . .
> she sometimes raises the coverlet beforehand in order to grasp the whole
> thing! . . . Never, even after having raised the coverlet several times on
> seeing the beak appear, has Lucienne tried to raise it when the goose was
> completely hidden! Here . . . is proof of the fact that the reconstruction of
> a totality is much easier than search for an invisible object. (pp. 29–30)

Still, however, Piaget maintains that the object concept is not fully
formed. To the child at this stage, the object does not have an independent existence, but is tied to the child's own actions and sensory perceptions. In other words, "it would be impossible to say that the half-hidden
objective is conceived as being masked by a screen; it is simply perceived
as being in the process of disappearing" (p. 35).

- *STAGE 4 (10 to 12 months)* During the later weeks of stage 3 and early in
  stage 4, children have learned that objects continue to exist even when
  they are no longer in sight. A child will search actively and creatively for
  an object that has been completely hidden from view. While on the surface this may indicate a fully developed object concept, Piaget found
  that this cognitive skill is still incomplete because the child still lacks the
  ability to understand *visible displacements*. To understand what Piaget
  meant by this, consider the following example (you can try this yourself). If you sit with an 11-month-old and hide a toy completely under a
  towel (call this place A), the child will search for and find it. However, if
  you then openly hide the toy under a blanket (place B), the child will
  probably go back to searching where it was previously found, in place A.
  Furthermore, you can repeat this process over and over and the child
  will continue to make the same error, called the *A-not-B effect*.

  > Observation 40. At 0;10 Jacqueline is seated on a mattress . . . I take her
  > parrot from her hands and hide it twice in succession under the mattress,
  > on her left, in A. Both times Jacqueline looks for the object immediately
  > and grabs it. Then I take it from her hands and move it very slowly before
  > her eyes to the corresponding place on her right, under the mattress, in
  > B. Jacqueline watches the movement very attentively, but at the moment
  > when the parrot disappears in B she turns to her left and looks where it
  > was before, in A. (p. 51)

  Piaget's interpretation of this error in stage 4 was not that children
  are absentminded, but that the object concept is not the same for them
  as it is for you or me. To 10-month-old Jacqueline, her parrot is not an
  individual, permanent, separate thing that exists independently of her
  actions. When it was hidden and successfully found in A it became a
  parrot-in-A, a thing that was defined not only by its *parrotness*, but also by
  its hiding place. In other words, the parrot is just a piece of the overall
  picture in the child's mind and not a separate object.

- *STAGE 5 (12 to 18 months)* Beginning around the end of the first year of
  life, the child gains the ability to follow visible sequential displacements
  and searches for an object where it was last visibly hidden. When this

happens, Piaget claimed that the child had entered stage 5 of the sensori-motor period.

> Observation 54. Laurent, at 0;11, is seated between two cushions, A and B. I hide the watch alternately under each; Laurent constantly searches for the object where it has just disappeared, that is sometimes in A, sometimes in B, without remaining attached to a privileged position as during the preceding stage. (p. 67)

However, Piaget points out that true object permanence remains incomplete because the child is unable to understand what he called *invisible displacements*. Imagine the following example. You watch someone place a coin in a small box and then, with their back to you, they walk over to the dresser and open a drawer. When they return you discover that the box is empty. This is an invisible displacement of the object. Naturally, you would go to the dresser and look in the drawer. Well, as Piaget demonstrated, perhaps it is not so "natural."

> Observation 55. At 1;6 Jacqueline is sitting on a green rug and playing with a potato, which interests her very much (it is a new object for her). She . . . amuses herself by putting it into an empty box and taking it out again. I then take the potato and put it in the box while Jacqueline watches. Then I place the box under the rug and turn it upside down, thus leaving the object hidden by the rug without letting the child see my maneuver, and I bring out the empty box. I say to Jacqueline, who has not stopped looking at the rug and who realized that I was doing something under it: "Give Papa the potato." She searches for the object in the box, looks at me, again looks at the box minutely, looks at the rug, etc., but it does not occur to her to raise the rug in order to find the potato underneath. During the five subsequent attempts the reaction is uniformly negative. (p. 68)

- *STAGE 6 (18 to 24 months)* Finally, as the child approaches the end of the sensori-motor period (refer back to Table 1), the concept of the permanent object becomes fully realized. Entry into this stage is determined by the child's ability to represent mentally objects that undergo invisible displacements.

> Observation 66. At 1;7 Jacqueline reveals herself to be . . . capable of conceiving of the object under a series of superimposed or encasing screens. . . . I put the pencil in the box, put a piece of paper around it, wrap this in a handkerchief, then cover the whole thing with the beret and the coverlet. Jacqueline removes these last two screens, then unfolds the handkerchief. She does not find the box right away, but continues looking for it, evidently convinced of its presence; she then perceives the paper, recognizes it immediately, unfolds it, opens the box, and grasps the pencil. (p. 81)

Piaget considered this cognitive skill of object permanence to be the beginning of true thought: the ability to use insight and mental symbolism to solve problems. This, then, prepares the child to move into the next full stage of cognitive development: the preoperational period, during which thought separates from action, which allows the speed of mental operations to increase greatly. In other words, object permanence is the foundation for all subsequent advances in intellectual ability. As Piaget stated:

> The conservation of the object is, among other things, a function of its localization; that is, the child simultaneously learns that the object does not cease to exist when it disappears and he learns where it does go. This fact shows from the outset that the formation of the schema of the permanent object is closely related to the whole spatio-temporal and causal organization of the practical universe. (Piaget & Inhelder, 1969)

DISCUSSION

This method of exercises and observation of behavior formed the basis of Piaget's work throughout his formulation of all four stages of cognitive development. Piaget contended that all of his stages applied universally to all children, regardless of cultural or family background. Additionally, he stressed several important aspects relating to the stages of development of the object concept during the sensori-motor period (see Ginzburg & Opper, 1979, for an elaboration of these points).

1. The ages associated with each stage are approximate. Since Piaget's early work only involved three children, it was difficult for him to predict age ranges with a great deal of confidence. For example, certain abilities he observed in Jacqueline at age 1;7 were present in Lucienne at 1;3.
2. Piaget maintained, however, that the sequence of the stages was invariant. All children must pass through each stage before going on to the next, and no stage can ever be skipped.
3. Changes from one stage to the next occur gradually over time so that the errors being made at one stage slowly begin to decrease as new intellectual abilities mature. Piaget believed that it is quite common and normal for children to be between stages and exhibiting abilities from earlier and later stages at the same time.
4. As a child moves into the next higher stage, the behaviors associated with the lower stages do not necessarily disappear completely. It would not be unusual for a child in stage 6 to apply intellectual strategies used in stage 5. Then when these prove unsuccessful, the child will invoke new methods for solving the problem typical of stage 6 reasoning.

CRITICISMS AND RECENT APPLICATIONS

Although Piaget's conceptualization of cognitive development has dominated the field of developmental psychology for the last 40 years, he has certainly not been without critics. Some of them have focused primarily on questioning Piaget's basic notion that cognitive development happens in discrete stages. Many learning theorists have disagreed with Piaget on this issue and contend that intellectual development is continuous, without any particular sequence built into the process. They believe that cognitive abilities, like all other behaviors, are a result of modeling and a person's learning and conditioning history.

Other critics of Piaget's ideas have claimed that the age ranges at which he asserted specific abilities appear are incorrect, and some even argue that certain cognitive skills may already be present at birth. Object permanence is one of those abilities that has been drawn into question. In a series of ingenious studies, using newly developed research methodology, developmental psychologist Renee Baillargeon and her associates have demonstrated that infants as young as two and one-half months of age appear to possess early forms of object permanence (Aguilar & Baillargeon, 1999; Baillargeon, 1987). She and others assert that the methods used by Piaget were inadequate to measure accurately the abilities of very young infants. Additional evidence of the possibility that object permanence may indeed be an inborn skill comes from a study by Wilcox, Nadel, and Rosser (1996) in which premature infants were tested using methods similar to those in Baillargeon's work to see if they could remember the correct location of a disappearing and reappearing toy lion. Their findings indicated that not only did infants as young as two and one-half months correctly remember the toy's location, but the premature infants' performance on these tasks did not differ significantly from full-term babies.

Piaget's concepts and discoveries are influencing research discoveries in an ever-widening variety of fields. This is evidenced by the large number of recent articles that have cited Piaget's book that forms the basis for this discussion: more than 170 between 2000 and 2003. For example, one study compared six and one-half-month-old infants' tendency to search for objects hidden by darkness to their tendency to search for objects hidden under a cloth in the light, as in Piaget's games with his children (Shinskey & Munakata, 2003). Interestingly, the researchers found that "infants have a genuine advantage in searching for objects hidden in the dark" (p. 281) compared to objects hidden by coverlets in the light. However, the authors were unsure as to why this difference may exist. One explanation may be that the appearance of the coverlet interferes with the infants' new, tenuous ability of representing the object mentally. An alternate explanation may be that our ability to think about, and search for, objects in the dark is more important from an evolutionary, survival perspective than doing so when items are merely hidden beneath something in the light.

Another study citing Piaget's work on object permanence found an association between development of the object concept and sleep in nine-month-old infants (Scher, Amir, & Tirosh, 2000). The findings indicated that infants with a more advanced grasp of object permanence experienced significantly fewer sleep difficulties than those with lower levels of the object concept. This makes a certain intuitive sense, if you think about it. After all, if you weren't sure all your stuff would still be there in the morning, you probably wouldn't sleep very well either!

CONCLUSION

As new methods for studying infants' cognitive abilities have been developed, such as preference-looking and habituation-dishabituation techniques, some of Piaget's discoveries are being drawn into question (see Dworetzky, 1996 for a discussion of such research methods). In fact, there are numerous ongoing controversies surrounding his theory of cognitive development. This controversy is healthy in that it motivates research that will eventually lead to even greater improvements in our knowledge about our intellectual abilities.

Controversy notwithstanding, Piaget's theory remains the catalyst and foundation for all related research. His work continues to guide enlightened people's ideas about research with children, methods of education, and styles of parenting. Piaget's contribution was and is immeasurable.

Aguilar, A., & Baillargeon, R. (1999). 2.5-month-old infants' reasoning about when objects should and should not be occluded. *Cognitive Psychology, 39*(2), 116–157.

Baillargeon, R. (1987). Object permanence in 3-and-a-half- and 4-and-a-half-month-old infants. *Developmental Psychology, 23,* 655–664.

Dworetzky, J. (1996). *Introduction to child development,* 6th ed., New York: West.

Ginzburg, H., & Opper, S. (1979). *Piaget's theory of intellectual development.* Englewood Cliffs, NJ: Prentice-Hall.

Piaget, J., & Inhelder, B. (1969). *The psychology of the child.* New York: Basic Books.

Scher, A., Amir, T., & Tirosh, E. (2000). Object concept and sleep regulation. *Perceptual and Motor Skills, 91*(2), 402–404.

Shinskey, J., & Munakata, Y. (2003). Are infants in the dark about hidden objects? *Developmental Science, 6,* 273–282.

Wilcox, T., Nadel, L., & Rosser, R. (1996). Location memory in healthy preterm and full-term infants. *Infant Behavior and Development, 19*(3), 309–323.

HOW MORAL ARE YOU?

Kohlberg, L. (1963). The development of children's orientations toward a moral order: Sequence in the development of moral thought. *Vita Humana, 6,* 11–33.

Have you ever really thought about your personal morality? What are the moral principles guiding your decisions in life? If you stop to think about it, experience tells you that people vary a great deal in terms of the morality of their thought and actions. Morals are generally defined by psychologists as attitudes and beliefs that people hold that help them decide what is right and wrong. Your concept of morality is determined by the rules and norms of conduct that are set forth by the culture in which you have been raised and that have been internalized by you. Morality is not part of your *standard equipment* at birth: You were born without morals. As you developed through childhood into adolescence and adulthood, you developed your ideas about right and wrong. Every normal adult has a conception of morality. But where did this conception originate? What was the process by which it went from being a set of cultural rules to being part of who you are?

Probably the two most famous and influential figures in the history of research on the formation of morality were Jean Piaget (discussed previously) and Lawrence Kohlberg (1927–1987). Following Piaget's work, and before Kohlberg's, a period of 20 to 30 years passed during which child psychologists paid little attention to morality. Kohlberg's research at the University of Chicago incorporated and expanded upon many of Piaget's ideas about intellectual development and sparked renewed interest in this area of study. As others had done in the past, Kohlberg was addressing this question: "How does the amoral infant become capable of moral reasoning?"

Using the work of Piaget as a starting point, Kohlberg theorized that the uniquely human ability to make moral judgments develops in a predictable way during childhood. Moreover, he believed that there are specific, identifiable *stages* of moral development, related and similar in concept to Piaget's stages of intellectual development. As Kohlberg explained, "The child can internalize the moral values of his parents and culture and make them his own only as he comes to relate these values to a comprehended social order and to his own goals as a social self" (Kohlberg, 1964). In other words, a child must reach a certain stage of intellectual ability in order to develop a certain level of morality.

With these ideas in mind, Kohlberg set about formulating a method for studying children's abilities to make moral judgments. From that research came his widely recognized theory of moral development.

THEORETICAL PROPOSITIONS

When Kohlberg asserted that morality is acquired in developmental stages, he was using the concept of stage in a precise and formal way. It is easy to think of nearly any ability as occurring in stages, but psychologists draw a clear distinction between changes that develop gradually over time (such as a person's height) and those that develop in distinct and separate stages. So when Kohlberg referred to "structural moral stages in childhood and adolescence," he meant that (1) each stage is a uniquely different kind of moral thinking and not just an increased understanding of an adult concept of morality; (2) the stages always occur in the same step-by-step sequence so that no stage is ever skipped and there is never backward progression; and (3) the stages are prepotent, meaning that children comprehend all stages below their own and perhaps have some understanding of no more than one stage above. Children are incapable of understanding higher stages, regardless of encouragement, teaching, or practice. Furthermore, they prefer to function at the highest moral stage they have reached. Also implied in this stage formulation of moral development is the notion that the stages are universal and they occur in the same order, regardless of individual differences in experience and culture.

Kohlberg believed that his theory of the formation of morality could be explored by giving children at various ages the opportunity to make moral judgments. If the reasoning they used to make moral decisions could be found to progress predictably at increasing ages, this would be evidence that his stage theory was essentially correct.

METHOD

Kohlberg's research methodology was really quite simple. He presented children of varying ages with 10 hypothetical moral dilemmas. Each child was interviewed for two hours and asked questions about the moral issues presented in the dilemmas. The interviews were tape recorded for later analysis of the moral reasoning used. Two of Kohlberg's most widely cited moral dilemmas were as follows:

> *The Brother's Dilemma.* Joe's father promised he could go to camp if he earned the $50 for it, and then changed his mind and asked Joe to give him the money he had earned. Joe lied and said he had only earned $10 and went to camp using the other $40 he had made. Before he went, he told his younger brother, Alex, about the money and about lying to their father. Should Alex tell their father? (p. 12)

> *The Heinz Dilemma.* In Europe, a woman was near death from a special kind of cancer. There was one drug that the doctors thought might save her. It was a form of radium that a druggist in the same town had recently discovered. The drug was expensive to make, but the druggist was charging 10 times what the drug cost him to make. He paid $200 for the radium and charged $2,000 for a small dose of the drug. The sick woman's husband, Heinz, went to everyone he knew to borrow the money, but he could only get together about $1,000, which is half of what it cost. He told the druggist that his wife was dying and asked him to sell it cheaper or let him pay later. But the druggist said, "No, I discovered the drug and I'm going to make money from it." So Heinz got desperate and broke into the man's store to steal the drug for his wife. Should the husband have done this? (p. 17)

The subjects in Kohlberg's original study were 72 boys living in the Chicago suburbs. The boys were in three different age groups: 10, 13, and 16 years. Half of each group were from lower middle-class socioeconomic brackets; the other half were from the upper middle-class brackets. During the course of the two-hour interviews, the children expressed between 50 and 150 moral ideas or statements.

Following are four examples quoted by Kohlberg of responses made by children of different ages to these dilemmas.

> *Danny, age 10, The Brother's Dilemma.* "In one way it would be right to tell on his brother, or [else] his father might get mad at him and spank

him. In another way it would be right to keep quiet, or [else] his brother might beat him up." (p. 12)

Don, age 13, The Heinz Dilemma. "It really was the druggist's fault, he was unfair, trying to overcharge and letting someone die. Heinz loved his wife and wanted to save her. I think anyone would. I don't think they would put him in jail. The judge would look at all sides and see the druggist was charging too much." (p. 19)

Andy, age 13, The Brother's Dilemma. "If my father finds out later, he won't trust me. My brother wouldn't either, but I wouldn't [feel so bad] if he (the brother) didn't." (p. 20)

George, age 16, The Heinz Dilemma. "I don't think so, since it says the druggist had a right to set the price. I can't say he'd actually be right; I suppose anyone would do it for a wife, though. He'd prefer to go to jail than have his wife die. In my eyes he'd have just cause to do it, but in the law's eyes he'd be wrong. I can't say more than that as to whether it was right or wrong." (p. 21)

Based on such statements, Kohlberg and his associates defined six stages of moral development and assigned the statements to one of the six stages. Additionally, there were six types of motives the subjects used to justify their reasoning, which corresponded to the six stages. It should be noted that each of the six stages of moral reasoning delineated by Kohlberg was intended to apply universally to any situation the child might encounter. The stages do not predict a specific action a child might take when faced with a real dilemma, but rather the reasoning the child would use in determining a course of action.

RESULTS

Kohlberg grouped the six stages he had found into three *moral levels,* outlined in Table 1. The early stages of morality, which Kohlberg called the "premoral" level, are characterized by egocentrism and personal interests. In stage 1, the child fails to recognize the interests of others and behaves morally out of fear of punishment for *bad* behavior. In stage 2, the child begins to recognize the interests and needs of others, but behaves morally in order to get moral behavior back. Good behavior is, in essence, a manipulation of a situation to meet the child's own needs.

In level 2, conventional morality that is a part of a recognition of one's role in interpersonal relationships comes into play. In stage 3, the child behaves morally in order to live up to the expectations of others and maintain relationships that contain trust and loyalty. It is during this stage, according to Kohlberg, that Golden Rule thinking begins and the child becomes concerned about the feelings of others. Stage 4 begins the child's recognition of and respect for law and order. Here a person takes the viewpoint of the larger social system and sees good behavior in terms of being a law-abiding citizen.

TABLE 1 Kohlberg's Six Stages of Moral Development

LEVEL 1. PREMORAL LEVEL	
Stage 1.	Punishment and obedience orientation (consequences for actions determine right and wrong)
Stage 2.	Naive instrumental hedonism (satisfaction of one's own needs defines what is good)
LEVEL 2. MORALITY OF CONVENTIONAL ROLE-CONFORMITY	
Stage 3.	"Good boy–nice girl" orientation (what pleases others is good)
Stage 4.	Authority maintaining morality (maintaining law and order, doing one's duty is good)
LEVEL 3. MORALITY OF SELF-ACCEPTED MORAL PRINCIPLES	
Stage 5.	Morality of agreements and democratically determined law (society's values and individual rights determine right and wrong)
Stage 6.	Morality of individual principles of conscience (right and wrong are a matter of individual philosophy according to universal principles)

(Adapted from p. 13.)

There is no questioning of the established social order, but rather the belief that whatever upholds the law is good.

When a person enters level 3, judgments about morality begin to transcend formal societal laws. In stage 5, a recognition takes place that some laws are better than others. Sometimes what is moral may not be legal, and vice versa. The individual still believes that laws should be obeyed to maintain social harmony, but may seek to change laws through due process. At this stage, Kohlberg maintained, a person will experience conflict in attempting to integrate morality with legality.

Finally, if a person reaches stage 6, his or her moral judgments will be based upon the belief that there are universal ethical principles. When laws violate these principles, the person behaves according to his or her ethical principles, regardless of the law. Morality is determined by the individual's own conscience. Kohlberg was to find in this and later studies that very few individuals actually reach stage 6. He eventually ascribed this level of reasoning to great leaders of conscience such as Gandhi, Thoreau, and Martin Luther King. Kohlberg claimed that

> a motivational aspect of morality was defined by the motive mentioned by the subject in justifying moral action. Six levels of motive were isolated, each congruent with one of the developmental types. They were as follows: (1) punishment by another; (2) manipulation of goods or rewards by another; (3) disapproval by others; (4) censure by legitimate authorities followed by feelings of guilt; (5) community respect and disrespect; (6) self-condemnation. (p. 13)

Finally, it was crucial to Kohlberg's stage theory that the different levels of moral reasoning advance with the age of the person. To test this, he analyzed the various stages corresponding to the children's answers according to the ages of the children. Figure 1 summarizes these findings: As the age of the subjects increased, the children used increasingly higher stages of moral reasoning to respond to the dilemmas. Other statistical analyses demonstrated that the ability to use each stage appeared to be a prerequisite to moving to the next-higher level.

DISCUSSION

In Kohlberg's discussion of the implications of his findings, he pointed out that this new conceptualization clarified how children actively organize the morality of the world around them in a series of predictable, sequential stages. For the child, this was not seen simply as an assimilation and internalization of adult moral teachings through verbal explanation and punishment, but as an emergence of cognitive moral structures that developed as a result of the child's interaction with the social and cultural environment. In this view, children do not simply learn morality, they construct it. What this means is that a child is literally incapable of understanding or using stage 3 moral reasoning before passing through stages 1 and 2. And a person would not apply the moral concepts of basic human rights found in stage 5 to solve a dilemma unless that person had already experienced and constructed the

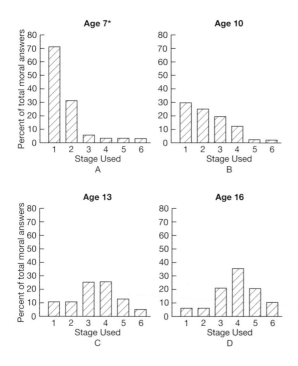

FIGURE 1 Stages of moral reasoning by age. Kohlberg notes that the data for the asterisked group of 7-year-old boys were acquired from an additional group of 12. (Figures adapted from data on p. 15 of original study.)

patterns of morality inherent in the first four stages. Further implications of this and later work of Kohlberg are discussed shortly.

CRITICISMS AND RECENT APPLICATIONS

As Kohlberg expanded and revised his stage theory of moral development over more than 30 years following this original study, it has received criticism from several perspectives. One of the most often cited of those is that even if Kohlberg was correct in his ideas about moral reasoning, this does not mean they can be applied to moral behavior. In other words, what a person says is moral may not be reflected in the person's moral actions. Several studies have demonstrated a lack of correspondence between moral reasoning and moral behavior, while others have found evidence that such a relationship does exist. One interesting line of research related to this criticism focused on the importance of situational factors, minimally addressed by Kohlberg, in determining whether someone will act according to his or her stage of moral reasoning (see Kurtines, 1986). Although some validity may attend this criticism, Kohlberg acknowledged that his theory was intended to apply to moral reasoning. The fact that situational forces may sometimes alter moral behavior does not imply that moral reasoning does not progress through the stages he described.

Another criticism of Kohlberg's work has focused on his claim that the six stages of moral reasoning are universal. These critics claim that Kohlberg's stages represent an interpretation of morality that is uniquely found in Western individualistic societies and, therefore, would not apply to the non-Western cultures that make up most of the world's population (i.e., Simpson, 1974). However, in defense of the universality of Kohlberg's ideas, 45 separate studies conducted in 27 different cultures were reviewed by Snarey (1987). In every study, researchers found that their subjects all passed through the stages in the same sequence, without reversals, and that stages 1 through 5 were present in all the cultures studied. Interestingly, however, in the more collectivist cultures (Taiwan, Papua New Guinea, and Israel), some of the moral judgments did not fit into any of Kohlberg's six stages. These were judgments based on the welfare of the entire community. Such reasoning was not found in the judgments made by American male subjects (see the reading on Triandis's research on individualistic and collectivist cultures later in this book).

Finally, a third area of criticism deals with the belief that Kohlberg's stages of moral development may not apply equally to males and females. The researcher leading this line of questioning has been Carol Gilligan (1982). She maintained that women and men do not think about morality in the same way. In her own research, she found that, in making moral decisions, women talked more than men about interpersonal relationships, responsibility for others, avoiding hurting others, and the importance of the connections among people. She called this foundation upon which women's morality rests a *care orientation*. Based on this gender difference, Gilligan has argued that women will score lower on Kohlberg's scale because the lower stages deal more with these relationship issues (such as stage 3, which is based primarily on building trust and loyalty in relationships). Men, on the other hand, Gilligan says, make moral decisions based on issues of justice, which fit more easily into Kohlberg's highest stages. She contends that neither of these approaches to morality is superior, and that if women are judged by Kohlberg to be at a lower moral level than men, it is because of an unintentional gender bias built into the theory.

Other researchers, for the most part, have failed to find support for Gilligan's assertion. Several studies have found no significant gender differences in moral reasoning using Kohlberg's methods. Gilligan has responded to those negative findings by acknowledging that although women are capable of using all levels of moral reasoning, in their real lives they choose not to. Instead, women focus on the human relationship aspects discussed in the preceding paragraph. This has been demonstrated by research (not employing Kohlberg's methods specifically) showing how girls are willing to make a greater effort to help another person in need and tend to score higher on tests of emotional empathy (see Hoffman, 1977, for a more complete discussion of these gender issues).

Kohlberg's early work on the development of moral judgment continues to be cited in studies from a wide range of disciplines. Not surprisingly, a significant proportion of current studies employing Kohlberg's model are found in the area of law and criminal justice. One very provocative study examined groups of individuals that you might logically expect to have very poorly developed moral reasoning abilities: rapists, child molesters, and incest offenders (Valliant et al., 2000). The researchers found that these criminals actually demonstrated fairly advanced levels of moral reasoning abilities, but also scored high on test for psychopathic deviance and paranoia. The authors interpret their findings as follows: "These results imply that rapists and child molesters have the ability to understand moral issues; however, given their personality orientation, they ignore these interpersonal values" (p. 67).

Another study citing Kohlberg's theory examined the accuracy of eyewitness testimony given by children (Bottoms et al., 2002). Children between the ages of three and six participated in a play session with their mothers. Half of the children were told not to play with certain toys in the room. However, when the researcher left the children's mothers urged them to play with the "forbidden" toys, but to "keep it a secret." Later the researchers interviewed the children and asked if they had played with the prohibited toys. "Results indicated that older children who were instructed to keep events secret withheld more information than did older children not told to keep events secret. Younger children's reports were not significantly affected by the secret manipulation" (p. 285). Often, children are told by adults to keep secrets about adults' illegal or injurious activities. Understanding when their understanding of the use and meaning of secrecy may play an important role in the use of child eyewitness testimony in legal proceedings (see the reading on Loftus's research on eyewitness testimony elsewhere in this book).

CONCLUSION

Dialogue and debate on Kohlberg's work within the behavioral sciences has continued to the present and shows every sign of continuing vigorously into the future. Its ultimate validity and importance remain to be clearly defined. However, few new conceptualizations of human development have produced the amount of research, speculation, and debate that surrounds Kohlberg's theory of moral development. And its usefulness to society, in one sense, was predicted by Kohlberg in this statement from 1964:

> While any conception of moral education must recognize that the parent can-not escape the direct imposition of behavior demands and moral judgments upon the child, it may be possible to define moral education primarily as a mat-ter of stimulating the development of the child's own moral judgment and its control of action. . . . [I] have found teachers telling 13-year-olds not to cheat "because the person you copied from might have it wrong and so it won't do you any good." Most of these children were capable of advancing much more mature reasons for not cheating. . . . Children are almost as likely to reject moral reasoning beneath their level as to fail to assimilate reasoning too far above their level. (p. 425)

Bottoms, B., Goodman, G., Schwartz-Kenney, B., & Thomas, S. (2002). Children's use of secrecy in the context of eyewitness reports. *Law and Human Behavior, 26,* 285–313.

Gilligan, C. (1982). *In a different voice: Psychological theory and women's development.* Cambridge, MA: Harvard University Press.

Hoffman, M. L. (1977). Sex differences in empathy and related behavior. *Psychological Bulletin, 84,* 712–722.

Kohlberg, L. (1964). Development of moral character and moral ideology. In H. Hoffman & L. Hoffman (Eds.), *Review of child development research* (Vol. 1). New York: Russell-Sage Foundation.

Kurtines, W. (1986). Moral behavior as rule-governed behavior: Person and situation effect on moral decision making. *Journal of Personality and Social Psychology, 50,* 784–791.

Simpson, E. (1974). Moral development research: A case of scientific cultural bias. *Human Development, 17,* 81–106.

Snarey, J. (1987). A question of morality. *Psychological Bulletin, 97,* 202–232.

Valliant, P., Gauthier, T., Pottier, D., & Kosmyna, R. (2000). Moral reasoning, interpersonal skills, and cognition of rapists, child molesters, and incest offenders. *Psychological Reports, 86*(1), 67–75.

IN CONTROL AND GLAD OF IT!

Langer, E. J., & Rodin, J. (1976). The effects of choice and enhanced personal responsibility for the aged: A field experiment in an institutional setting. *Journal of Personality and Social Psychology, 34,* 191–198.

Control. This seemingly small psychological concept may be the single most important influence on all of human behavior. What we are talking about here is not your ability to control the actions of others, but the personal power you possess over your own life and the events in it. Related to this ability are your feelings of competence and personal power and the availability of choices in any given situation. Most of us feel that we have at least some control over our individual destinies. You have made choices in your life—some good ones, and maybe some poor ones—and they have brought you to where you are today. And while you may not consciously think about it, you will make many more choices in your life. Each day you make choices and decisions about your behavior. When your sense of control is threatened, you experience negative feelings (anger, outrage, indignation) and will rebel by behaving in ways that will restore your perception of personal freedom. It's the well-worn idea that if someone tells you that you have to do something, you very likely will either refuse or do exactly the opposite. Or, conversely, forbid someone to do something and they will find that activity more attractive than they did before it was forbidden (remember Romeo and Juliet?). This tendency to resist any attempt to limit our freedom is called *reactance.*

If our need to control our personal environment is as basic to human nature as it appears to be, what do you think would happen if that control were taken away from you and you were unable to get it back? You would very likely experience psychological distress that could take the form of anxiety, anger, outrage, depression, helplessness, and even physical illness. Studies have shown that when people are placed in stressful situations, the negative effects of the stress can be reduced if the subjects believe they have some control over the stressful event. For example, people in a crowded elevator perceive the elevator to be less crowded and feel less anxiety if they are standing next to the control panel in the elevator car; they believe they have a greater sense of control over their environment (Rodin, Solomon, & Metcalf, 1979). Another well-known study exposed subjects to loud bursts of noise and then had them perform problem-solving tasks. One group had no control over the noise. Another group was told that they could press a button and stop the noise at any time. However, they were asked not to press the button if they could avoid it. Subjects in the no-control group performed significantly worse on the tasks than the subjects who believed they could exert control over the noise. By the way, none of the subjects in this latter group actually pressed the button, so they were exposed to just as much noise as the group that had no perception of control.

What this all boils down to is that we are happier and more effective people when we have the power to choose. Unfortunately, in our society, many people's lives reach a stage when they lose this power when they are no longer allowed to make even the simplest of choices for themselves. This life stage is called old age. Many of us have heard about or experienced firsthand the tragic sudden decline in health and alertness of an elderly person when he or she is placed in a retirement home or nursing home. Many illnesses such as colitis, heart disease, and depression have been linked to feelings of helplessness and loss of control that occur prior to the illness. One of the most difficult transitions elderly people must go through when entering a nursing home is the loss of the personal power to control their daily activities and influence their own destinies. Langer and Rodin, who had been studying these issues of power and control for some time prior to the study we are considering here, decided to put these ideas to the test in a real nursing home.

THEORETICAL PROPOSITIONS

If the loss of personal responsibility for one's life causes a person to be less happy and healthy, then increasing control and power should have the opposite effect. Langer and Rodin wanted to test this theoretical idea directly by enhancing personal responsibility and choice for a group of nursing home residents. Based on previous literature and their own earlier studies, they predicted that the patients who were to be given this control should demonstrate improvements in mental alertness, activity level, satisfaction with life, and other measures of behavior and attitude.

METHOD

Subjects

Langer and Rodin obtained the cooperation of a Connecticut nursing home called Arden House. This facility was rated by the state as one of the finest care units in the area, offering quality medical care, recreational facilities, and residential conditions. It was a large and modern home with four residential floors. The residents in the home were all of generally similar physical and psychological health and came from similar socioeconomic backgrounds. When a new resident entered the home, he or she was assigned to a room on the basis of availability. Consequently, the characteristics of the residents on all floors were, on average, equivalent. Two floors were randomly selected for the two treatment conditions. Fourth-floor residents (8 men and 39 women) received the *increased-responsibility* treatment. The second floor was designated as the comparison group (9 men and 35 women). These 91 subjects ranged in age from 65 to 90.

Procedure

The nursing home administrator agreed to work with the researchers in implementing the two experimental conditions. He was described as an outgoing and friendly 33-year-old who interacted with the residents daily. He called a meeting of the two floors and spoke with them in order to give them some new information about the home. The two messages informed the residents of the home's desire that their lives there be as comfortable and pleasant as possible and discussed several of the services that were available to them. However, within these messages there were some important differences for the two groups.

The responsibility-induced group (fourth floor) was told that they had the responsibility of caring for themselves and deciding how they should spend their time. He went on to explain the following:

You should be deciding how you want your room arranged—whether you want it to be as it is or whether you want the staff to help you rearrange the furniture. . . . It's your responsibility to make your complaints known to us, to tell us what you would like to change, to tell us what you would like. Also, I wanted to take this opportunity to give each of you a present from Arden House. [A box of small plants was passed around and the patients were given two decisions to make: first, whether or not they wanted a plant at all, and second, to choose which one they wanted. All residents did select a plant.] The plants are yours to keep and take care of as you'd like.

One last thing: I wanted to tell you that we're showing a movie two nights next week, Thursday and Friday. You should decide which night you'd like to go, if you choose to see it at all. (p. 194)

The comparison group (second floor) was told how much the home wanted to make their lives fuller and more interesting. He explained the following to them:

We want your rooms to be as nice as they can be and we've tried to make them that way for you. We want you to be happy here. We feel that it's our responsibility to make this a home you can be proud of and happy in and we'll do all we can to help you. . . . Also, I wanted to take this opportunity to give you each a present from Arden House. [The nurse walked around with a box of plants and each patient was handed one.] The plants are yours to keep. The nurses will water and care for them for you.

One last thing: I wanted to tell you that we're showing a movie next week on Thursday and Friday. We'll let you know later which day you're scheduled to see it. (p. 194)

Three days later, the director went around to each resident's room and reiterated the same message.

It's not difficult to see what the important difference was between these two messages. The fourth-floor group was given the opportunity to make choices and exercise control over their lives in various ways. The second-floor group, while other factors were basically the same, was given the message that most of their decisions would be made for them. These policies were then followed on these two floors for the next three weeks. (It should be noted that the level of control given to the fourth-floor residents was always available to all residents at the home. For this experiment, it was simply reiterated and made clearer to the experimental group.)

Measuring the Outcomes

Several methods of measurement (dependent variables) were used in this study to determine if the different responsibility conditions would make a difference. There were two questionnaires administered one week before the director's talk and again three weeks after. One questionnaire was given to the residents; it asked questions about how much control they felt they had and how active and happy they were at the home. The other questionnaire was given to nurses on each floor (who were not aware of the research being conducted), asking them to rate patients on 10-point scales for how happy, alert, dependent, sociable, and active they were and about their sleeping and eating habits. There were also two measures of the residents' actual behavior. Records were kept of the attendance at the movie that was being shown the next week. Also, there was a contest held for patients to guess how many jelly beans there were in a large jar. If residents wished to enter the contest, they simply wrote their guess and their name on a slip of paper and placed it in a box next to the jar.

RESULTS

Table 1 summarizes the results of the two questionnaires. As can be seen clearly, the differences between the groups were striking, and supported Langer and Rodin's predictions about the positive effects of choice and personal power. The residents in the increased-responsibility group reported that they felt happier and more active than those in the comparison group. Also the interviewer's rating of alertness was higher for the fourth-floor residents. All these differences were statistically significant. Even greater differences were seen on the nurses' ratings. Keep in mind that the nurses who rated the patients were "blind" (uninformed) as to the two treatment conditions to avoid any bias in their ratings. They determined that, overall, the increased-responsibility group's condition improved markedly over the three weeks of the study, while the comparison group in general was seen to decline. In fact, "93% of the experimental group (all but one subject) were considered improved, whereas only 21% of the comparison group (six subjects) showed this positive change" (p. 196). Fourth-floor residents took to visiting others more and spent considerably more time talking to various staff mem-

TABLE 1 Summary of Questionnaire Responses

QUESTIONNAIRE ITEM	DIFFERENCE BETWEEN FIRST AND SECOND ADMINISTRATION		
	INCREASED-RESPONSIBILITY GROUP	COMPARISON GROUP	SIGNIFICANT DIFFERENCE?
RESIDENT'S SELF-REPORT:			
• Happy	+0.28	−0.12	YES
• Active	+0.20	−1.28	YES
• Interviewer's rating			
of alertness	+0.29	−0.37	YES
NURSES' RATINGS:			
• General improvement	+3.97	−2.39	YES
• Time spent:			
—visiting other patients	+6.78	−3.30	YES
—visiting others	+2.14	−4.16	YES
—talking to staff	+8.21	+1.61	YES
—watching staff	−2.14	+4.64	YES

(Adapted from p. 195.)

bers. On the other hand, the increased-responsibility residents began to spend less time engaged in passive activities such as simply watching the staff.

The behavioral measures that were taken added further support to the positive effects of control. Significantly more subjects from the experimental group attended the movie. This difference in attendance was not found for a movie shown one month previously. While the jelly-bean guessing contest may have seemed a somewhat silly measurement for a scientific study, the results were quite interesting. Ten residents on the fourth floor participated in the game, but only one second-floor patient did so.

DISCUSSION

Langer and Rodin pointed out that their study, combined with other previous research, demonstrated that when people who have been forced to give up their control and decision-making power are given a greater sense of personal responsibility, their lives and attitudes improve. As to the practical applications of this research, the authors are succinct and to the point:

> Mechanisms can and should be established for changing situational factors that reduce real or perceived responsibility in the elderly. Furthermore, this study adds to the body of literature suggesting that senility and diminished alertness are not an almost inevitable result of aging. In fact, it suggests that some of the negative consequences of aging may be retarded, reversed, or possibly prevented by returning to the aged the right to make decisions and a feeling of competence. (p. 197)

SIGNIFICANCE OF FINDINGS AND SUBSEQUENT RESEARCH

Probably the best example of the significance of the findings of this study was provided by the authors in a subsequent study of the same residents in the same nursing home (Rodin & Langer, 1977). Eighteen months after their first study, Langer and Rodin returned to Arden House for a follow-up to see if the increased-responsibility conditions had any long-term effects. For the patients still in residence, ratings were taken from doctors and nurses and a special talk on psychology and aging by one of the authors (J. Rodin) was given to the residents. The number of residents in each of the original conditions who attended the talk was recorded and the frequency and type of questions asked were noted.

Ratings from the nurses demonstrated continued superior condition of the increased-responsibility group. The average total ratings (derived by adding all their ratings together and averaging this total over all patients) for the experimental group was 352.33 versus 262.00 for the comparison group (a highly significant statistical difference). The health ratings from doctors also indicated an increase in overall health status for the experimental group compared with a slight decline in health for the control residents. While there was no significant difference in the number of residents attending the lecture, most of the questions were asked by the increased-responsibility subjects and the content of the questions related to autonomy and independence. Probably the most important finding of all was that 30% of the subjects in the comparison group had died during the 18-month interval. For the experimental group, only 15% had died during that time.

One important criticism of research such as this was pointed out by Langer and Rodin themselves. The consequences of intervention by researchers in any setting where the well-being of the participants is involved must be very carefully considered. For example, it could be dangerous and clearly unethical to provide the elderly with certain kinds of power and control only to have this responsibility taken away again when the research is completed. A study by Schulz (1976) allowed nursing home residents to have varying amounts of control over when they would be visited by local college students. Those having the most control over when and for how long the visits would take place showed significantly improved functioning, just as Langer and Rodin found. However, when the study was completed and the students discontinued their visits, this (inadvertently on the part of the researchers) led to greater debilitation in health of the experimental group than of those residents who were never exposed to the increased-control situation. In Langer and Rodin's study, this did not happen, because feelings of general control over normal day-to-day decision making were fostered among the residents. This, then, was a positive change that was able to be continued over time with sustained positive results.

RECENT APPLICATIONS

As mentioned earlier in this chapter, personal power and control over one's life is a key factor in a happy and productive life. Old age is a time when the potential exists for this power to be lost. Langer and Rodin's studies and the subsequent work of Judith Rodin (see Rodin, 1986) have made it clear that the greater our sense of control, the healthier, happier, and smoother our process of aging. Awareness of this is growing even today as nursing homes, state nursing home certification boards, hospitals, and other institutional settings encourage and require increased choice, personal power, and control for the elderly.

Many studies incorporating Langer and Rodin's 1976 research have continued to support the need for, and value of, personal control as we age. For example, a 2003 study of depression among elderly residents in senior citizen homes in Germany found that a lack of perceived freedom and personal choice were predictors of depressive symptoms along with poor physical fitness and a lack of social support (Krampe et al., 2003). The authors concluded that "therapy and prevention of depression among inhabitants of old people's residences should include both promotion of volitional self-regulation [personal choice] and improvement of perceived freedom because each of these factors contribute independently to the explanation of depression" (p. 117).

On the other hand, can a person have *too* many choices? A fascinating study examined the effects of offering people a limited number of choices compared to a large array of choices (Iyengar & Lepper, 2000). In both field and lab settings, subjects were offered an opportunity to purchase gourmet jams or chocolates or to write an extra credit essay in a class. Some participants were given 6 choices of items or topics while others were given 24 or 30 options. The results were strikingly clear. People were up to 10 times more likely to buy jam or chocolates when they had 6 choices compared to 30. In addition, significantly more students opted to write the extra credit exam when they were given the smaller number of topic choices. "Moreover, participants actually reported greater subsequent satisfaction with their selection and wrote better essays when their original set of options had been limited" (p. 995). Whether findings about jam and student essays may be applied to nursing home empowerment programs has yet to be investigated; however, common sense suggests that similar effects might well be obtained if elderly people (or anyone) were to be overwhelmed with too many choices.

CONCLUSION

You can see that personal power and control not only affects your happiness, but it also can make you healthier. It is not difficult to apply Langer and Rodin's ideas to your own life. Think for a moment about events, settings, and experiences in which very little personal control over your behavior was allowed. You probably remember those experiences as more uncomfortable, more unpleasant and significantly less enjoyable than events where you could choose what to do and how to act. In most of life's situations, increasing your degree of behavioral choice, and that of others, is a goal clearly worth pursuing.

Iyengar, S., & Lepper, M. (2000). When choice is demotivating: Can one desire too much of a good thing? *Journal of Personality and Social Psychology, 79*, 995–1006.

Krampe, H., Hautzinger, M., Ehrenreich, H., & Kroner-Herwig, B. (2003). Depression among elderly living in senior citizen homes: Investigation of a multifactorial model of depression. *Zeitschrift fur klinische psychologie und psychotherapie, 32*, 117–128.

Rodin, J. (1986). Aging and health: Effects of the sense of control. *Science, 233*, 1271–1276.

Rodin, J., & Langer, E. J. (1977). Long-term effects of a control relevant intervention with the institutionalized aged. *Journal of Personality and Social Psychology, 35*, 897–902.

Rodin, J., Solomon, S., & Metcalf, J. (1979). Role of control in mediating perceptions of density. *Journal of Personality and Social Psychology, 36*, 988–999.

Schulz, R. (1976). Effects of control and predictability on the psychological well-being of the institutionalized aged. *Journal of Personality and Social Psychology, 33*, 563–573.

6 EMOTION AND MOTIVATION

This section deals with our inner experiences of emotion and motivation. Many nonpsychologists have trouble with the idea of the scientific exploration of these issues. There is a popular belief that our emotions and motivations just sort of happen, that we don't have much control over them, and that they are part of our standard equipment from birth. However, psychologists have always been fascinated with the issues of where your emotions come from and what causes you to act the way you do. Emotion and motivation are basic and powerful influences on behavior, and a great deal of research has been done to allow us to understand them better.

The first study in this section may surprise you in that it focuses on Masters and Johnson's work relating to human sexual response. The reason it is included here is that human sexual feelings and behaviors are strongly influenced by our emotions and they can also serve as powerful motivational forces. The second reading examines a famous, fascinating study about facial expressions of emotions and demonstrates that our expressions for basic emotions are the same for everyone in all cultures throughout the world. The third study in this section presents research about how extreme emotions, or what we might call stress, can affect your health. The fourth reading allows you to experience the process of one of the most, if not the most, famous experiments in the area of motivation: the original demonstration of a psychological event called *cognitive dissonance*.

A SEXUAL MOTIVATION ...
Masters, W. H., & Johnson, V. E. (1966). *Human sexual response.* Boston: Little, Brown.

You may not immediately think so, but human sexuality is very psychological. Many people might logically place the study of sexual behavior into the disciplines of biology or physiology, and it is true that these sciences certainly connect to the topic in various ways and are the central focus of sexual behavior of animals. However, for humans, sex is a distinctly psychological event. Think about it: Sexual attraction, sexual desire, and sexual functioning are all largely dependent upon psychology. If you doubt this, just consider a cou-

158

ple of obvious facts. You know that most people engage in sexual behavior for many reasons other than reproduction. Those reasons are usually psychological. Also, humans are the only species on earth to suffer from sexual problems such as inhibited sexual desire, anorgasmia, erectile dysfunction, premature ejaculation, inhibited orgasm, vaginismus, and so on. These problems often have psychological causes.

Having said that, however, you should be aware at the outset of this discussion that the full enjoyment of our sexuality, as well as successful treatment of sexual problems, depends on a clear and thorough understanding of our sexual functioning: the physiology of our human sexual response. This is what Masters and Johnson have given us.

Prior to the 1960s, the definitive work on the sexual behavior of humans was the large-scale surveys of Americans published by Alfred Kinsey in the late 1940s and early 1950s. The famous *Kinsey Reports* asked thousands of men and women about their sexual behavior and attitudes and covered topics ranging from frequency of intercourse to masturbation habits to homosexual experiences. With the publication of these reports, suddenly we had a yardstick with which to compare our own sexual lifestyles and make relative judgments of our personal sexual behaviors. Self-report data such as Kinsey obtained must, of course, always be interpreted with caution, since people will tend to answer in ways that appear to be socially acceptable (especially when answering questions of a highly personal nature). Nevertheless, the *Kinsey Reports* offered a rare glimpse into the sexuality of humans, and they are still cited today as a source of statistical information about sexual behavior. However, the accuracy of Kinsey's work notwithstanding, his research only provided information about what people do sexually. There remained a conspicuous information gap relating to what happens to us when we engage in sexual behavior and what to do if we are experiencing some kind of sexual problem.

Enter Masters and Johnson. These are names that have become synonymous with human sexuality research and are recognized by millions throughout the world. As the decade of the 1960s began, the United States was launched into what has now become known as the sexual revolution. The sweeping social changes that were taking place provided an opportunity for open and frank scientific exploration of our sexuality that would not have been possible previously. Until the 1960s, lingering Victorian messages that sexual behavior is something secretive, hidden, and certainly not a topic of discussion, much less study, would have precluded virtually all support, social and financial, from Masters and Johnson's project. But as men and women began to more openly acknowledge the fact that we are sexual beings, with sexual feelings and desires, the social climate became one that was ready not only to accept the explicit research of Masters and Johnson, but to demand it. Statistics were no longer enough. People were ready to learn about their physical responses to sexual stimulation.

It was within this social context that Masters and Johnson set about studying human sexual response. Their early work culminated in the book that is the subject of this discussion. While this work was carried out over three decades ago, it continues to form the foundation of our current knowledge of the physiology of sexual response.

PARTICIPANT PROPOSITIONS

The most important proposition in Masters and Johnson's research was that to understand human sexuality we must study actual sexual behavior in response to sexual stimulation, rather than simply record what people perceive or believe their sexual experiences to be.

Their objective in proposing this theory was a therapeutic one: to help people overcome sexual problems that they might be experiencing. Masters and Johnson expressed this goal as follows:

> [The] fundamentals of human sexual behavior cannot be established until two questions are answered: What physical reactions develop as the human male and female respond to effective sexual stimulation? Why do men and women behave as they do when responding to effective sexual stimulation? If human sexual inadequacy ever is to be treated successfully, the medical and behavioral professions must provide answers to these basic questions. (p. 4)

Combined with this objective, Masters and Johnson also proposed that the only method by which such answers could be obtained was direct systematic observation and physiological measurements of men and women in all stages of sexual responding.

METHOD

Subjects

As you might imagine, the first hurdle in a research project such as this is obtaining subjects. The project required human subjects who would be willing to engage in sexual acts in the laboratory while being closely observed and monitored. There was concern on the part of the researchers that such a requirement might create the impossibility of finding subjects who would be willing to participate and who would also statistically represent the general population. Another concern was that the strange and artificial environment of the research lab might cause subjects who did volunteer for the study to be unable to respond in their usual ways.

During the early phases of their study, Masters and Johnson employed prostitutes as subjects. This decision was based on their assumption that individuals from more average and typical lifestyles would refuse to participate. Eight female and three male prostitutes were studied extensively for nearly two years. The researchers described the contributions of these first 11 subjects as being crucial to the development of the methods and research techniques used throughout the entire study.

These subjects, however, did not constitute an appropriate group on which to base an extensive study of human sexual response. This was because their lifestyle and sexual experiences did not even remotely represent the population at large. Therefore, the researchers knew that any findings based on this subject group could not be credibly applied to people in general. It was necessary, therefore, to obtain a more representative sample of subjects. Contrary to their earlier assumption, the researchers did not find this as difficult as they had anticipated.

Through their contacts in the academic, medical, and therapeutic communities in a large metropolitan area, Masters and Johnson were able to obtain a large group of volunteers from a wide range of socioeconomic and educational backgrounds. The age, gender, and educational demographics of the subjects who were eventually chosen are summarized in Table 1. All volunteers were carefully interviewed to determine their reasons for participating and their ability to communicate on issues of sexual responsiveness. The prospective subjects also agreed to a physical exam to determine *reproductive normalcy.*

Procedures

In order to study in detail the physiological responses during sexual activity and stimulation, rather elaborate methods of measurement and observation had to be developed. These included standard measures of physiological response such as pulse, blood pressure, and rate of respiration. Additionally, specific sexual responses were to be observed and recorded. For this the "sexual activity of study subjects included, at various times, manual and mechanical manipulation, natural coition with the female partner in supine, superior, or knee-chest position, and, for many female study subjects, artificial coition in the supine or knee-chest positions" (p. 21). What all that means is that sometimes subjects were observed and measured having intercourse in various positions, and other times they were observed and measured during masturbation either manually or with mechanical devices specially designed to allow for clear recording of response.

These special devices, designed by physicists, were, basically, clear plastic artificial penises that allowed for internal observations without distortion. These could be adjusted in size for the woman's comfort and were controlled

TABLE 1 Distribution of Subjects by Age, Gender, and Educational Level

AGE	NO. MALES	NO. FEMALES	HIGH SCHOOL	COLLEGE	GRAD. SCHOOL
18–20	2	0	2	0	0
21–30	182	120	86	132	84
31–40	137	111	72	98	78
41–50	27	42	18	29	22
51–60	23	19	15	15	12
61–70	8	14	7	11	4
71–80	3	4	3	3	1
81–90	0	2	0	2	0
Totals	382	312	203	290	201

(Adapted from pp. 13–15.)

completely by the woman for depth and rate of movement in the vagina throughout the response cycle.

PARTICIPANT ORIENTATION AND COMFORT

You can imagine that all these expectations, observations, and devices might create real emotional difficulties for many of the subjects. And Masters and Johnson were acutely aware of these difficulties. To help place subjects at ease with the study's procedures, they insured that

> sexual activity was first encouraged in privacy in the research quarters and then continued with the investigative team present until the study subjects were quite at ease in their artificial surroundings. No attempt was made to record reactions . . . until the study subjects felt secure in their surroundings and confident of their ability to perform. . . . This period of training established a sense of security in the integrity of the research interest and in the absolute anonymity embodied in the program. (pp. 22–23)

Some subjects were involved in only one recording session, while others participated actively for many years. For the research included in the book that is the topic of discussion here, Masters and Johnson estimated that 10,000 complete sexual response cycles were studied with female response outnumbering male by a ratio of 3 to 1. In their words, "a minimum of 7,500 complete cycles of sexual response have been experienced by female study subjects cooperating in various aspect of the research program, as opposed to a minimum total of 2,500 male orgasmic (ejaculatory) experiences" (p. 15).

RESULTS

From this research, Masters and Johnson discovered a wealth of information about human sexual response, and selected findings are summarized shortly. However, another aspect of their research to keep in mind is that what they found from their subjects is true of nearly everybody. Of course, there are rare exceptions, anomalies, and abnormalities in the population as a whole, but with those few exceptions, everyone's physiological responses to sexual stimulation is quite similar. That fact is part of what has made Masters and Johnson's research so invaluable. It has the potential to improve everyone's sexual life. You must remember, though, as you read about their early findings, that they were not addressing issues relating to sexual attitudes, emotions, values, morality, preferences, orientations, or likes or dislikes. These, clearly, are not similar for everyone, and it is the individual variations that create the great and wondrous diversity that exists in human sexuality. Let's look at some of Masters and Johnson's most influential findings.

The Sexual Response Cycle

After studying approximately 10,000 sexual events, Masters and Johnson found that human sexual response could be divided into four stages which they termed the human sexual response cycle. These stages are excitement, plateau, orgasm, and resolution (Table 2). While they acknowledge in their

TABLE 2 Stages of the Sexual Response Cycle

STAGE	FEMALE RESPONSES	MALE RESPONSES
Excitement	First sign: vaginal lubrication. Clitoral glans becomes erect. Nipples become erect, breasts enlarge. Vagina increases in length and inner two-thirds of vagina expands.	First sign: erection of penis. Time to erection varies (with person, age, alcohol/drug use, fatigue, stress, etc.). Skin of scrotum pulls up toward body, testes rise. Erection may be lost if distracted, but usually regained readily.
Plateau	Outer one-third of vaginal walls swell, reducing opening by up to 50 percent. Inner two-thirds of vagina continues to balloon or "tent." Clitoris becomes erect and retracts towards body and under hood. Lubrication decreases. Minor lips engorge with blood and darken in color, indicating orgasm is near. Muscle tension and blood pressure increase.	Full erection attained; not lost easily if distracted. Penile glans enlarges further. Cowper's glands secrete pre-ejaculate fluid. Testes elevate farther, and enlarge slightly, indicating orgasm is near. Muscle tension and blood pressure increase.
Orgasm	Begins with rhythmic contractions in pelvic area at intervals of 0.8 seconds, especially in muscles behind the lower vaginal walls. Uterus contracts rhythmically as well. Muscle tension increased throughout body. Some woman report ejaculation of fluid from the urethra.	Begins with pelvic contractions 0.8 seconds apart. Ejaculation, the expelling of semen, occurs in two phases: (1) emission: semen builds up in urethral bulb, producing sensation of ejaculatory inevitability; (2) expulsion: genital muscles contract, forcing semen out through urethra.
Resolution	Clitoris, uterus, vagina, nipples, etc., return to unaroused state typically in less than one minute. Clitoris often remains very sensitive to touch. This process may take several hours if woman has not experienced an orgasm.	Approximately a 50% loss of erection within one minute; more gradual return to fully unaroused state. Testes reduce in size and descend. Scrotum relaxes.

book that the stages were arbitrarily defined, these divisions made the discussion of sexual response easier and clearer. Today, human sexual response is rarely discussed in academic or professional settings without reference to these four stages. Both men and women experience the same four stages, although there are some differences in them that are discussed later.

Sexual Anatomy

One of the great contributions made by Masters and Johnson in their research on sexual response was the dispelling of sexual myths. And one area of widespread misunderstanding that the researchers attempted to correct relates to sexual anatomy—specifically, the penis and the vagina. Throughout history, one of the most common sexual concerns expressed by men has been worry over penis size. Well, Masters and Johnson studied a lot of penises and could finally shed some scientific light on these concerns. They called them "phallic fallacies." The two worries men have expressed are these: (1) larger penises are more effective in providing satisfying sexual stimulation for the woman, and (2) their own penis is too small. Masters and Johnson proved both concerns to be misguided by discussing actual average sizes found in their research and reporting on their revolutionary finding comparing erect size with flaccid (unerect) size.

The researchers found that the normal range for flaccid penile length in this study population (80 men) was between 2.8 inches and 4.3 inches, with an average length of about 3 inches. For erect penises the average length ranged from about 5.5 inches to just under 7 inches, with an average of about 6 inches. These numbers were significantly smaller than the commonly held beliefs about what constitutes a large versus a small penis. But what was even more surprising was that when they measured the size of erect penises, the researchers found that a larger flaccid penis does not predict a larger erect penis. In fact, overall, they discovered that smaller flaccid penises tend to enlarge more upon sexual excitement than do penises that are larger in their flaccid state. Looking at averages, a flaccid penis of 3 inches increased to a length of 6 inches, while a 4-inch flaccid penis only added about 2.5 inches to reach a length of 6.5 inches. To further illustrate this finding, Masters and Johnson reported the largest and smallest observed change from flaccid to erect state. One male subject was found to have a flaccid penile length of 2.8 inches. The increase that was observed in this subject upon erection was 3.3 inches, creating an erect length of 6.1 inches. Another subject who was measured flaccid at 4 inches increased only 2.1 inches, for an identical erect length of 6.1 inches.

More important than all these measurements of penises is the notion that a woman's sexual enjoyment and satisfaction depend on penis size. Masters and Johnson's research, as explained in a section in their book titled Vagina Fallacies, found that idea to be totally without merit. In their careful observations using the artificial penis technique described earlier, they determined that the vagina is an extremely elastic structure capable of accommodating penises of varying size. "Full accommodation usually is accomplished with the first few thrusts of the penis regardless of penile size" (p. 194). Furthermore, they found that during the plateau stage of the response cycle (see Table 2), the walls of the vaginal opening swell to envelop a penis of virtually any size. Therefore, as the authors conclude, "it becomes obvious that penile size usually is a minor factor in sexual stimulation of the female partner" (p. 195).

Female and Male Differences in Sexual Response

While there are many similarities in the sexual response cycles of men and women, Masters and Johnson also discovered important differences. The most famous and most revolutionary difference they found concerns the orgasm and resolution stages of the cycle. Following orgasm, both men and women enter the resolution stage, when sexual tension decreases rapidly and sexual structures return to their unaroused states (this is also known as detumescence). Masters and Johnson found that during this time, a man experiences a refractory period, during which he is physically incapable of experiencing another orgasm regardless of the type or amount of stimulation he receives. This refractory period may last from several minutes to several hours or even a day, and tends to lengthen with a man's age.

Masters and Johnson found that women do not appear to have a refractory period and that with effective stimulation are capable of experiencing one or more additional orgasms following the first without any loss of sexual arousal. Through this process, women, unlike men, are "capable of maintaining an orgasmic experience for a relatively long period of time" (p. 131).

While this multiorgasmic capacity was not news to many women, it was not widely known. Prior to Masters and Johnson's work, it was commonly believed that men had the greater orgasmic capabilities. Consequently, this one finding, as well as many others in Masters and Johnson's research, had a far-reaching impact on cultural and societal attitudes about male and female sexuality. It should be noted here that while women are physiologically capable of multiple orgasms, not all women seek or even desire them. Indeed, many women have never experienced multiple orgasms and are completely satisfied with their sexual lives. Also, many women who have had multiple orgasms find that they are usually satisfied with one. The important point is that individuals vary greatly in terms of what is physically and emotionally satisfying sexually. Masters and Johnson were attempting to address the full range of physiological possibilities.

CRITICISMS

Most of the criticisms of Masters and Johnson's early research focus either on the arbitrary nature of their four stages of sexual response or on the fact that they spent little time discussing the cognitive and emotional aspects of sexuality. Both of these lines of criticism are somewhat misplaced, since Masters and Johnson addressed them in their early writings.

As mentioned earlier, the authors were fully aware that their divisions of the cycle were purely arbitrary, but those divisions were helpful in researching and explaining the complex process of sexual response in humans. Other researchers over the years have suggested different stage theories. For example, Helen Singer Kaplan (Kaplan, 1974) has proposed a three-stage model that includes desire, vasocongestion (engorgement of the genitals), and muscle contractions (orgasm). These stages reflect Kaplan's belief that an analysis of sexual response should begin with sexual desire before any sexual stimulation begins, and she suggests that no distinction can or need be drawn between excitement and plateau. Her focus on the desire aspect of sexuality leads into the other main criticism of Masters and Johnson's original work: the lack of attention to psychological factors.

Again, Masters and Johnson clearly stated that an examination of such factors was not the goal of the project. They did believe, however, that a complete understanding of the physiological side of sexual behavior was an absolute prerequisite for a satisfying and fulfilling sex life. And they demonstrated this belief in subsequent books dealing with the psychological and emotional aspects of our sexuality.

Finally, there has been some research over the 30 years since Masters and Johnson's first book appeared that has questioned some of their findings as they apply to all humans. For example, it has been found that a small percentage of women may experience a refractory period during which time they are incapable of experiencing additional orgasms, and a small percentage of men may be capable of multiple orgasms with little or no refractory period in between. Also, while ejaculation was thought to be entirely the domain of men, there is some tentative, and controversial, evidence to suggest that some women (again, a small percentage) may, on occasion, ejaculate upon orgasm (see Zaviacic, 2002 for a discussion of this research).

CONCLUSIONS

You'll recall from the beginning of this discussion that the main goal of Masters and Johnson's research was to address problems of sexual inadequacy—to help people solve their sexual problems. There is little question that they have done that. Virtually all sex therapy, whether for erectile problems, inhibited orgasm, premature ejaculation, arousal difficulties, or any other problem, rests on the foundation of Masters and Johnson's research. It is impossible to overestimate the contributions of Masters and Johnson in our understanding and study of human sexuality. An examination of any recent sexuality textbook will reveal more citations for and more space devoted to the work of Masters and Johnson than any other researchers. But beyond this, William Masters and Virginia Johnson have, over the decades since the publication of *Human Sexual Response,* continued to research and apply their own findings to helping people find sexual fulfillment. Four years after the publication of their first book, they released *Human Sexual Inadequacy* (1970), which took their earlier research and applied it directly to solutions for sexual problems. Their continuous attention to their chosen field is easily demonstrated by a list of their subsequent books: *The Pleasure Bond* (1970); *Homosexuality in Perspective* (1979); *Human Sexuality,* 5th edition (1995); *Crisis: Heterosexual Behavior in the Age of AIDS* (1988); *Masters and Johnson on Sex and Human Loving* (1986); and *Heterosexuality* (1998).

RECENT APPLICATIONS

It would be impossible to list here even a representative sample of the numerous articles and books published each year that refer substantively to Masters and Johnson's early work on human sexual response. These publications range from basic core texts in human sexuality (e.g., King, 2004; Strong, et al., 2004) to very specific, cutting-edge articles in psychology and sexuality journals. To demonstrate this wide influence, consider the following sampling of recent studies citing Masters and Johnson's 1966 book.

One study incorporated Masters and Johnson's pioneering work in designing, administering, and analyzing responses to a national survey of sexual satisfaction among nearly 1,000 women, aged 20–65 years, in heterosexual relationships (Bancroft et al., 2003). The goal of the study was to examine whether women's sexual problems may be viewed as similar to men's sexual problems, and to what extent pharmacological treatments, such as Viagra, might be helpful. Interestingly, the study found that the physical side of sexual response (arousal, vaginal lubrication, orgasm) was *not* strongly related to sexual distress among the respondents: "The overall picture is that lack of emotional well-being and negative emotional feelings during sexual interaction with the partner are more important determinants of sexual distress than impairment of the more physiological aspects of female sexual response. Although we do not have directly comparable data for men, we can predict that the pattern would be different, with greater importance attached to genital response" (Bancroft et al., 2003, p. 202). In other words, solutions to women's most common sexual problems may be considerably more complex than just a "little *pink* pill."

Another study relying on Masters and Johnson's early work focused on sexuality and aging in women (Gelfand, 2000). This author pointed out that as of the turn of the twenty-first century, the average life expectancy for women was 79 years and argued that sex for older women is an integral component of their quality of life. While acknowledging certain inevitable age-related physical changes associated with hormonal decreases and some common illnesses, the author argued that the sexual side of elderly women's quality of life must play a central role in medical decisions. This study and others in the same vein are targeted directly at the members of medical professions who must make clinical decisions for the treatment of various diseases and conditions among their older patients. More and more, research is urging physicians and other health care professionals to acknowledge that sex remains an important part of life and should never be neglected in caring for their adult patients, no matter what their age.

In an important and fascinating study relying on Masters and Johnson's model, sexual responses of women with spinal cord injuries were compared to women without such injury (Whipple, Gerdes, & Komisaruk, 1996). Sexual arousal and orgasm during self-stimulation of the vagina, cervix, and a *hypersensitive area* were assessed using physiological and self-report measures. In the past, most researchers believed that women with spinal cord injuries could not achieve orgasm. In this study, however, women with spinal cord injuries became sexually aroused and several reported experiencing orgasm. In fact, *more* of the women with spinal cord injuries reported orgasm during the study than the uninjured women!

So, it appears that humans are born to be sexual and are "designed" to remain sexually active throughout our lives, even in the face of serious nerve damage. Thanks in large part to the work of Masters and Johnson, our understanding of the physical processes involved in human sexual pleasure and response is quite advanced compared to a half a century ago, but we still have a great deal to learn. William Masters continued as director of the Masters and Johnson Institute in St. Louis until his retirement in 1994. He died from complications of Parkinson's disease on February 16, 2001, at the age of 85.

Bancroft, J., Loftus, J., & Long, J. (2003). Distress about sex: A national survey of women in heterosexual relationships. *Archives of Sexual Behavior, 32*, 193–208.

Gelfand, M. (2000). Sexuality among older women. *Journal of Women's Health and Gender-Based Medicine, 9* (Suppl. 1), S15–S20.

Kaplan, H. S. (1974). *The new sex therapy.* New York: Brunner/Mazel.

King, B. (2004). *Human sexuality today.* Upper Saddle River, NJ: Prentice Hall.

Whipple, B., Gerdes, C., & Komisaruk, B. (1996). Sexual response to self-stimulation in women with complete spinal-cord injury. *Journal of Sex Research, 33*(3), 231–240.

Zaviacic, Milan (2002). Female urethral expulsions evoked by local digital stimulation of the g-spot: Differences in the response patterns. *The Journal of Sex Research, 24,* 311–18.

I CAN SEE IT ALL OVER YOUR FACE!

Ekman, P., & Friesen, W. V. (1971). Constants across cultures in the face and emotion. *Journal of Personality and Social Psychology, 17,* 124–129.

Think of something funny. What is the expression on your face? Now think of something in your past that made you sad. Did your face change? Chances are it did. Undoubtedly, you are aware that certain facial expressions coincide with specific emotions. And, most of the time, you can probably tell how people are feeling emotionally from the expressions on their faces. Now, consider this: Could you be equally successful in determining someone's emotional state based on facial expression if that person is from a different culture—say, Romania, Sumatra, or Mongolia? In other words, do you believe facial expressions of emotion are universal? Most people believe that they are, until they stop and consider how radically different other cultures are from their own. Think of the multitude of cultural differences in gestures, personal space, rules of etiquette, religious beliefs, attitudes, and so on. With all these differences influencing behavior, it would be rather amazing if there are any human characteristics, including the emotional expressions that are identical across all cultures.

Paul Ekman is considered the leading researcher in the area of the facial expression of emotion. This early article details his research, which was designed to demonstrate the universality of these expressions. While the authors acknowledged in their introduction that previous researchers had found some evidence that facial behaviors are determined by culturally variable learning, they argued that this evidence was weak and that expressions of basic emotions are equivalent in all cultures.

Several years prior to this study, Ekman and Friesen had conducted research in which they showed photographs of faces to college-educated people in Argentina, Brazil, Chile, Japan, and the United States. All the subjects from every country successfully identified the same facial expressions as corresponding to the same emotions. The researchers presented their findings as evidence of universality in these expressions. However, as Ekman and Friesen themselves pointed out, these findings were open to criticism, since members of the cultures studied had all been exposed to international mass media (movies, magazines, television), which is full of facial expressions. What was needed to prove the universality of emotional expression was a culture that had not been exposed to any of these things. Imagine how difficult (perhaps impossible!) it would be to find such a culture today. Well, even in 1971 it wasn't easy.

Ekman and Friesen traveled to the Southeast Highlands of New Guinea to find subjects for their study among the Fore people who existed then as an isolated Stone Age society. Many of the members of this group had experienced little or no contact with Western or Eastern modern cultures. Therefore, they had not been exposed to emotional facial expressions other than those of their own people.

THEORETICAL PROPOSITIONS

The theory underlying Ekman and Friesen's study was that the specific facial expressions corresponding to basic emotions are universal. Ekman and Friesen stated it quite simply:

> The purpose of this paper was to test the hypothesis that members of a preliterate culture who had been selected to ensure maximum visual isolation from literate cultures will identify the same emotion concepts with the same faces as do members of literate Western and Eastern cultures. (p. 125)

METHOD

The subgroup of the Fore who were the most isolated were among those referred to as the South Fore. The individuals selected to participate in the study had seen no movies, did not speak English or Pidgin, had never worked for a Westerner, and had never lived in any of the Western settlements in the area. There were 189 adults and 130 children chosen to participate, out of a total South Fore population of about 11,000. For comparison, there were also 23 adults chosen who had experienced a great deal of contact with Western society through watching movies, living in the settlements, and attending missionary schools.

Through trial and error, the researchers found that the most effective method of asking the subjects to identify emotions was to present them with three photographs of different facial expressions and read a brief description of an emotion-producing scene or story that corresponded to one of the photographs. The subject could then simply point to the expression that best matched the story. The stories used were selected very carefully to be sure that each scene was related to only one emotion and that it was recognizable to the Fore people. Table 1 lists the six stories developed by Ekman and Friesen. The authors explained that the fear story had to be longer to prevent the subjects from confusing it with surprise or anger.

TABLE 1 Ekman and Friesen's Stories Corresponding to Six Emotions

EMOTION	STORY
1. Happiness	His (her) friends have come and he (she) is happy.
2. Sadness	His (her) child (mother) has died and he (she) feels very sad.
3. Anger	He (she) is angry and about to fight.
4. Surprise	He (she) is just now looking at something new and unexpected.
5. Disgust	He (she) is looking at something he (she) dislikes; or he (she) is looking at something that smells bad.
6. Fear	He (she) is sitting in his (her) house all alone and there is no one else in the village. There is no knife, ax, or bow and arrow in the house. A wild pig is standing in the door of the house and the man (woman) is looking at the pig and is very afraid of it. The pig has been standing in the doorway for a few minutes, and the person is looking at it very afraid, and the pig won't move away from the door, and he (she) is afraid the pig will bite him (her).

(Adapted from p. 126.)

Forty photographs of 24 different people, including men, women, boys, and girls, were used as examples of the six emotional expressions. These photographs had been validated previously by showing them to members of various other cultures. Each photograph had been judged by at least 70% of observers in at least two literate Western or Eastern cultures to be representative of the emotion being expressed.

The actual experiment was conducted by teams consisting of one member of the research group and one member of the South Fore tribe, who explained the task and translated the stories. Each adult subject was shown three photographs (one correct and two incorrect), was told the story that corresponded to one of them, and was asked to choose the expression that best matched the story. The procedure was the same for the children, except that they only had to choose between two photographs, one correct and one incorrect. Each subject was presented with various sets of photographs so that no single photograph ever appeared twice in the comparison.

The translators were given careful training to ensure that they would not influence the subjects. They were told that there was no absolutely correct response and were asked to not prompt the subjects. Also, they were taught how to translate the stories exactly the same way each time and to resist the temptation to elaborate and embellish them. To avoid unintentional bias, the Western member of the research team avoided looking at the subject and simply recorded the answers given.

Remember that these were photographs of Western facial expressions of emotions. So, could the Fore people correctly identify the emotions in the photographs, even though they may never have seen a Western face before?

RESULTS

First, analyses were conducted to see if there were differences between males and females or between adults and children. The adult women were found to be more hesitant to participate and were considered to have had less contact with Westerners than the men. However, no significant differences in ability to correctly identify the emotions in the photographs were found between any of the groups.

Tables 2 and 3 summarize the percentage of correct responses for the six emotions by the least Westernized adults and the children, respectively. Not all subjects were exposed to all emotions, and sometimes subjects were exposed to the same emotion more than once. Therefore, the number of subjects in the tables do not equal the overall total number of participants. All of the percentages were statistically significant except when subjects were asked to distinguish fear from surprise. When this situation existed, many errors were made, and, for one group, surprise was actually selected a significant 67% of the time when the story described fear.

Comparisons were made between the Westernized and non-Westernized adults. No significant differences were found between these two groups on the number who chose the correct photographs matching the emotion stories. There were also no differences found between younger and older children. As you can see in Table 3, the children appeared to perform better than the adults, but Ekman and Friesen attributed this to the fact that they only had to choose between two photographs instead of three.

DISCUSSION

Ekman and Friesen did not hesitate to draw a confident conclusion from their data: "The results for both adults and children clearly support our hypothesis that particular facial behaviors are universally associated with particular emotions" (p. 128). This conclusion was based on the fact that the South Fore had no opportunity to learn anything about Western expressions and, thus, had no way of identifying them unless the expressions were universal.

As a way of double-checking their findings, the researchers videotaped members of the isolated Fore culture portraying the same six facial expressions. Later, when these tapes were shown to college students in the United

TABLE 2 Percent of Adults Correctly Identifying Emotional Expressions in Photographs

EMOTION IN STORY	NUMBER OF SUBJECTS	PERCENT CHOOSING CORRECT PHOTOGRAPH
Happiness	220	92.3
Anger	98	85.3
Sadness	191	79.0
Disgust	101	83.0
Surprise	62	68.0
Fear	184	80.5
Fear (with surprise)	153	42.7

(Adapted from p. 127.)

TABLE 3 Percent of Children Correctly Identifying Emotional Expressions in Photographs

EMOTION IN STORY	NUMBER OF SUBJECTS	PERCENT CHOOSING CORRECT PHOTOGRAPH
Happiness	135	92.8
Anger	69	85.3
Sadness	145	81.5
Disgust	46	86.5
Surprise	47	98.3
Fear	64	93.3

(Adapted from p. 127.)

States, the students correctly identified the expressions corresponding to each of the emotions.

> The evidence from both studies contradicts the view that all facial behavior associated with emotion is culture-specific, and that posed facial behavior is a unique set of culture-bound conventions not understandable to members of another culture. (p. 128)

The one exception to their consistent findings, that of the confusion subjects seemed to experience in distinguishing between expressions of fear and surprise, Ekman and Friesen explained by acknowledging that there are certainly some cultural differences in emotional expression, but this did not detract from the preponderance of evidence that nearly all the other expressions were correctly interpreted across the cultures. They speculated that fear and surprise may have been confused "because in this culture fearful events are almost always also surprising; that is, the sudden appearance of a hostile member of another village, the unexpected meeting of a ghost or sorcerer, etc." (p. 129).

IMPLICATIONS OF THE RESEARCH

This study by Ekman and Friesen served to demonstrate scientifically what you already suspected: that facial expressions of emotions are universal. However, you might still be asking yourself, "What is the significance of this information?" Well, part of the answer to that question relates to the nature–nurture debate about which human behaviors are present at birth and which are acquired through learning. Since facial expressions for the six emotions used in this study appear to be influenced very little by cultural differences, it is possible to conclude that they must be innate, that is, biologically *hard-wired* in at birth.

Another reason behavioral scientists find the notion of universal emotional expressions interesting is that it addresses issues about how humans evolved. In 1872, Darwin published a now-famous book called *The Expression of Emotion in Man and Animals*. He maintained that facial expressions were adaptive mechanisms that assisted animals in adapting to their environment and, therefore, increased their ability to survive. The idea behind this was that if certain messages could be communicated within and across species of animals through facial expressions, survival would be enhanced. For example, an expression of fear would provide a silent warning of imminent danger from predators; an expression of anger would warn less dominant members of the group to stay away from more powerful ones; and an expression of disgust would communicate a message of, "Yuck! Don't eat that, whatever you do," and prevent a potential poisoning. These expressions, however, would do the animals no good if they weren't universal among all the individuals making up the various species. Even though these expressions may now be less important to humans in terms of their survival-enhancement value, the fact that they are universal among us would indicate that they have been passed on to us from our evolutionary ancestors and have assisted us in reaching our present position on the evolutionary ladder.

A fascinating study demonstrated this *leftover* survival value of facial expressions in humans. The researchers (Hansen & Hansen, 1988) reasoned that if facial expressions could warn of impending danger, then humans should be able to recognize certain expressions, such as anger, more easily than other, less threatening expressions. To test this, they presented subjects with photographs of crowds of people with different facial expressions. In some of the photographs, all of the people's expressions were happy except for one that was angry. In other photographs, all of the expressions were angry, except for one that was happy. The subjects' task was to pick out the face that was different. The amount of time it took the subjects to find a single happy face in a crowd of angry faces, was significantly longer than when they were to search a crowd of happy faces for a single angry face. Furthermore, as the size of the crowds in the photographs increased, the time for subjects to find the happy face also increased, but finding the angry face did not take significantly longer. This and other similar findings have indicated that humans may be biologically programmed to respond to the information provided by certain expressions better than others because they offered more survival information.

RECENT APPLICATIONS

Other more recent studies in various areas of research have relied on Ekman's early findings in attempting to improve our understanding of children and adults with developmental or learning disabilities. One such study found that children diagnosed with autism (a pervasive developmental disorder marked by language deficits, social withdrawal, and repetitive self-stimulation behaviors) appear to have difficulty recognizing the facial expressions that correspond to basic emotions (Bolte & Poustka, 2003). This difficulty was even more pronounced in families with more than one autistic child, and may help explain why many autistic individuals typically show difficulty interpreting emotional responses from others.

Ekman's research on facial expressions has also played a fundamental role in cross-cultural psychology research. David Matsumoto, one of the leading researchers in this area, has made frequent use of Ekman's concepts in his studies of intercultural interpretations of emotions and behavioral expectations (e.g., Matsumoto, Kasri, & Kooken, 1999). In addition, Matsumoto and Ekman have collaborated with other researchers on a study of cross-cultural gender differences in facial expressions (Biehl et al., 1997).

The influence of Ekman's research, however, is not limited to humans. Ekman's 1971 study has been cited in research on emotions in *farm animals* (Desire, Boissy, & Veissier, 2002). These researchers suggest that the welfare of farm animals depends, in part, on their emotional reactions to their environment. When individual animals feel in harmony with their environment, their welfare is maximized; however, "any marked deviation from the state, if perceived by the individual, results in a welfare deficit due to negative emotional experiences" (p. 165). Clearly one group of farm animals feels very harmonious with their environment because, as the ad campaign says, "great cheese comes from happy cows, and happy cows come from California."

Finally, another study citing Ekman's 1971 article attempted to shed light on exactly how one specific facial feature, the eyebrows, contributes to facial recognition (Sadr, Jarudi, & Sinha, 2003). Previous research had centered more on the eyes and mouth, but these researchers found that the eyebrows may be more important than the eyes themselves. The authors concluded "that the absence of eyebrows in familiar faces leads to a very large and significant disruption in recognition performance. In fact, a significantly greater decrement in face recognition is observed in the absence of eyebrows than in the absence of eyes" (p. 285). So, if you are ever in need of an effective disguise, be sure to cover your eyebrows!

CONCLUSION

During the two decades following the early cross-cultural research on emotional expressions, Ekman has continued his emotion research both individually and in collaboration with Friesen and several other researchers. Within this body of work, many fascinating discoveries have been made. One further example of Ekman's research involved what is called the *facial feedback theory* of emotional expressions. The theory states that the expression on your face actually feeds information back to your brain to assist you in interpreting the emotion you are experiencing. Ekman tested this idea by identifying the exact facial muscles involved in each of the six basic emotions. He then instructed subjects to tense these muscles into expressions resembling the various emotions. When they did this, Ekman was able to measure physiological responses in the subjects that corresponded to the appropriate emotion resulting from the facial expression alone, and not from the actual presence of the emotion itself (Ekman, Levensen, & Friesen, 1983).

Ekman has also extended his research into the area of deception and how the face and the body *leak* information to others about whether someone is telling the truth. In general, his findings have indicated that people are able to detect when others are lying at a slightly better than chance level when observing their facial expressions. However, when allowed to observe another's entire body, subjects were much more successful in detecting lies, indicating that the body may provide better clues to certain states of mind than the face alone (see Ekman, 1985, for a complete discussion of this issue).

Ekman and his associates have provided us with a large literature on the nonverbal communication provided by facial expressions (see Ekman, 2003). And research in this area continues. There is little doubt that the studies will continue until we are successful in accomplishing the goal that was the title of Ekman and Friesen's 1975 book *Unmasking the Face*.

Biehl, M., Matsumoto, D., Ekman, P., Hearn, V., Heider, K., Kudoh, T., & Ton, V. (1997). Japanese and Caucasian facial expressions of emotions: Reliability data and cross-national differences. *Journal of Nonverbal Behavior, 21*(1), 3–23.

Bolte, S., & Poustka, F. (2003). The recognition of facial affect in autistic and schizophrenia subjects and their first-degree relatives. *Psychological Medicine, 33*, 907–915.

Desire, L., Boissy, A., & Veissier, I. (2002). Emotions in farm animals: A new approach to animal welfare in applied ethology. *Behavioural Processes, 60*, 165–180.

Ekman, P. (2003). *Emotions revealed: Recognizing faces and feelings to improve communication and emotional life.* New York: Times Books.

Ekman, P. (1985). *Telling lies.* New York: Norton.

Ekman, P., & Friesen, W. (1975). *Unmasking the face.* Englewood Cliffs, NJ: Prentice-Hall.

Ekman, P., Levensen, R., & Friesen, W. (1983). Autonomic nervous system activity distinguishes between emotions. *Science, 164*, 86–88.

Hansen, C., & Hansen, R. (1988). Finding the face in the crowd: An anger superiority effect. *Journal of Personality and Social Psychology, 54*, 917–924.

Matsumoto, D., Kasri, F., & Kooken, K. (1999). American-Japanese cultural differences in judgements of statement intensity and subjective experience. *Cognition and Emotion, 13*(2), 201–218.

Sadr, J., & Sinha, P. (2003). The role of eyebrows in face recognition. *Perception, 32*, 285–293.

LIFE, CHANGE, AND STRESS
Holmes, T. H., & Rahe, R. H. (1967). The Social Readjustment Rating Scale. *Journal of Psychosomatic Research, 11*, 213–218.

Everyone knows about stress. For most of you, most of the time, stress is an unpleasant, negative experience. Stress is not easy to define, but one way of looking at it is to think of stress as any emotion in its extreme form. In this sense, extreme fear, anger, sadness, or even happiness could produce stress. Think for a moment about the last time you were under a heavy amount of stress: the kind of stress that lasts more than a few hours or even a few days. Maybe you had to move to a new city, had a legal problem, had difficulties in a relationship with another person, had a job change, lost your job, experienced the death of someone close to you, were injured, or experienced some other major stressful change. You know the kind of stress I mean—it goes on for a while and you have to cope with it every day. What happened to you? How well did you cope? Did you find that your health deteriorated in some way?

The connection between stress and illness is the focus of this chapter and this famous article by Thomas Holmes and Richard Rahe. Take a moment to answer this question: Do you believe in a clear connection between stress and illness? I bet you answered with a resounding "Yes!" But if I had asked this same question of people 20 or 30 years ago, only a few would have believed that such an association existed. Together, psychology and medicine over the past couple of decades have established with a high degree of certainty that this connection does indeed exist, and they have worked to understand it and intervene in it. For the behavioral sciences, those who are primarily concerned with this issue are called health psychologists. Notice that the journal in which the article appears deals with psychosomatic illness. Psychosomatic illness refers to health problems that are caused primarily by psychological factors rather than physical ones. Such illnesses are real; the discomfort, pain, and suffering exist medically. Victims of psychosomatic problems should not be confused with *hypochondriacs*, who suffer from imaginary or exaggerated illnesses.

Many studies by health psychologists have established that when certain external changes occur in people's lives requiring them to make major internal, psychological adjustments, there is a tendency for a higher incidence of illness. These changes have been termed *life stress*. The amount of life stress you experience varies over time. There may have been some periods in your past (or present) when many changes were occurring, while at other times things were relatively stable. Life stress also varies greatly from person to person. The overall number of changes that occur in your life is different from the number in someone else's. So if I were to ask you how much life stress you have experienced over the past year, what would you say? A lot? Not much? A moderate amount? These kinds of vague judgments were not much use to scientists who wanted to study the relationship between life stress and illness. Therefore, the first question in this area of research that needed to be answered was this: How can life stress be measured?

Obviously, researchers could not bring people into a laboratory, expose them to stressful events for a short time, and then expect to see a sudden appearance of illness. First, this would be unethical, and second, it would not represent how stress works in real life. To tackle this problem, Holmes and Rahe developed a written scale to measure life stress. They acknowledged in their article that previous attempts to examine a person's level of stress only determined the number and types of stressful events. They proposed to take this line of reasoning one step further and develop a way to measure the size or magnitude of various stressful life experiences. The idea behind this was that if such a measure could be developed, then it would be possible to obtain a person's score in terms of life stress and relate this to the status of the person's health.

METHOD

From their clinical experiences, Holmes and Rahe compiled a list of 43 life events that people commonly feel are stressful, in that they require a person to make psychological adjustments in order to adapt to the event. This list was then presented to nearly 394 subjects, who were asked to rate each item on the list for the amount of stress produced by the event. The actual instructions that were given to the subjects read, in part:

> In scoring, use all of your experience in arriving at your answer. This means personal experience where it applies as well as what you have learned to be the case for others. Some persons accommodate to change more readily than others; some persons adjust with particular ease or difficulty to only certain events. Therefore, strive to give your opinion of the average degree of adjustment necessary for each event rather than the extreme. . . . "Marriage" has been given an arbitrary value of 500. As you complete each of the remaining events, think to yourself, "Is this event indicative of more or less readjustment than marriage? Would the readjustment take longer or shorter to accomplish?" (p. 213)

Subjects were then instructed to assign a point value to each event relative to the 500 value given to marriage. If they saw an event as requiring more readjustment than marriage, the point value would be higher, and vice versa. All the subjects' ratings for each item were averaged and then divided by 10 to arrive at a score for the individual items.

This was a study with a rather simple and straightforward method. The importance and value of the research was in the results and the applications of the measuring device, which they called the *Social Readjustment Rating Scale* (SRRS).

RESULTS

Table 1 lists the 43 life events in order by rank, and the average point value assigned to each one by the subjects in the study. You can see that *death of a spouse* was rated the most stressful, whereas *minor violations of the law* was rated as the least stressful of the items included on the list. You might notice that not all the items are what you might consider to be negative. However, events such as Christmas, marriage, and, yes, even a vacation, can be stressful in terms of Holmes and Rahe's definition of *stress:* need for psychological readjustment to the event.

In order to check for consistency in the ratings, the researchers divided the subjects into several subgroups and correlated their ratings of the items. Some of these subgroups compared were male versus female, single versus married, college-educated versus no college, white versus black, younger versus older, higher socioeconomic versus lower socioeconomic, religious versus nonreligious, and so on. For all the subgroup comparisons, the correlations were very high, indicating a strong degree of agreement among the subjects. What this meant was that Holmes and Rahe could assume with a reasonable amount of confidence that this scale could be applied to all people with an approximately equal degree of accuracy.

TABLE 1 The Social Readjustment Rating Scale

RANK	LIFE EVENT	MEAN VALUE
1	Death of spouse	100
2	Divorce	73
3	Marital separation	65
4	Jail term	63
5	Death of close family member	63
6	Personal injury or illness	53
7	Marriage	50
8	Fired at work	47
9	Marital reconciliation	45
10	Retirement	45
11	Change in health of family member	44
12	Pregnancy	40
13	Sex difficulties	39
14	Gain of new family member	39
15	Business readjustment	39
16	Change in financial state	38
17	Death of close friend	37
18	Change to different line of work	36
19	Change in number of arguments with spouse	35
20	Large mortgage	31
21	Foreclosure of mortgage or loan	30
22	Change in responsibilities at work	29
23	Son or daughter leaving home	29
24	Trouble with in-laws	29
25	Outstanding personal achievement	28
26	Wife begins or stops work	26
27	Begin or end school	26
28	Change in living conditions	25
29	Revision of personal habits	24
30	Trouble with boss	23
31	Change in work hours or conditions	20
32	Change in residence	20
33	Change in schools	20
34	Change in recreation	19
35	Change in church activities	19
36	Change in social activities	18
37	Small mortgage	17
38	Change in sleeping habits	16
39	Change in number of family get-togethers	15
40	Change in eating habits	15
41	Vacation	13
42	Christmas	12
43	Minor violations of the law	11

(Adapted from p. 216.)

DISCUSSION

Holmes and Rahe note in their discussion a clear common theme applied to all the life events listed on their scale. Every time one of these stressful events occurs in someone's life, they explained, it requires some degree of adaptation, change, or coping. "The emphasis," they wrote, "is on change from the existing steady state and not on psychological meaning, emotion, or social desirability" (p. 217). This explains why some of the items may be interpreted as positive by some and negative by others, but either way, change is required and stress is produced.

Remember, this article explains the research behind the development of a method for measuring life stress. If you want to try it yourself, just look down the list and circle the life changes that have occurred in your life over the past 12 months. Each change has a certain number of points assigned to it, called *life change units* (LCUs). Calculate your LCU total. This gives you an estimate of your amount of life stress. Take a moment now to find your score. Now that you've done this, it probably feels as if something is missing, doesn't it? Well, what's missing is what your score means about your health. This, after all, was the researchers' whole point in developing the scale to begin with.

To address this, Holmes and Rahe didn't stop with developing the SRRS, but went on together and separately to examine the relationship between their scale and the probability of illness.

SUBSEQUENT RESEARCH

In the late 1960s, the SRRS began to be used in many studies as a tool for examining the stress-illness relationship. The value of the scale rested on its ability to predict illness based on people's total LCU scores.

In early studies, several thousand people were asked to fill out the SRRS and to report their histories of illness. Figure 1 graphically illustrates the overall findings of these studies (see Holmes & Masuda, 1974). In another study of 2,500 naval personnel, LCUs for the past six months were recorded using the SRRS just prior to shipboard tours of duty. During the six-month tour, those with fewer than 100 LCUs reported an average of 1.4 illnesses, those with between 300 and 400 averaged 1.9 illnesses, and those with between 500 and 600 suffered 2.1 illnesses (Rahe, Mahan, & Arthur, 1970). These and other studies over the years have generally supported Holmes and Rahe's contention that the SRRS can be helpful in predicting stress-related illness. The findings reported here will also give you an idea of what your score on the scale means.

Think of your score (especially if it's high) as an important indicator of how stressful your life is and what impact this stress could have on your health. However, before you become too worried, there have been several meaningful criticisms of the SRRS and its ability to predict illness that need to be discussed.

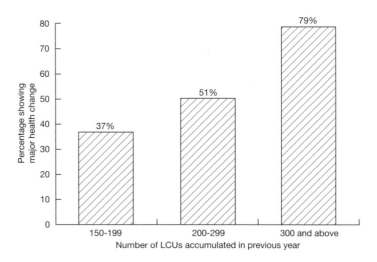

FIGURE 1   Relationship between life change units and illness.

CRITICISMS

Since Holmes and Rahe developed their SRRS, many researchers have expressed serious concerns about its accuracy and usefulness (see Taylor, 2002, for a complete review of these criticisms). One of the most widely expressed criticisms regards the inclusion of both positive and negative life events in the same scale, as well as both events that are in your control (events of choice, such as marriage) and events over which you have no control (such as the death of a friend). Research has demonstrated that certain events such as those that are sudden, negative, and out of your control are much more predictive of illness than are positive, controllable life changes.

Others have maintained that the scale is flawed in that it does not take into account your *interpretation* of a particular event. For example, retirement for one person may mean an end of a career, being *forced out to pasture*, while to another it is escape from drudgery into freedom. One researcher has suggested that a more accurate scale would be one that allows a person to check an event and also rate it on some measure of severity. Cohen, Kamarck, & Mermelstein, developed a scale designed to do this called the *Perceived Stress Scale* (1983).

In addition, the way the research has related the SRRS to illness has been questioned. When carefully analyzed statistically, the predictive relationship between your LCU score and illness is rather weak. In fact, SSRI scores account for only about 10% of the total variation among people who become ill. In other words, if you examine 1,000 people to see who becomes sick over a six-month period, there will be a great variation in the individual factors leading to their illness or lack of illness. If you have them all complete an SRRS, you will find that out of all the possible reasons for health variation, their LCU scores explain about 10% of it. This is, nevertheless, a statistically significant correlation that confirms the ability of the SRRS to predict illness. However, it also says that many *other* factors are involved in illness. Another way to look at it is, if you know someone's LCU score, your chances of predicting the future of that person's health are significantly better than if you did *not* have their score.

So, you might ask, if the SRRS has been so severely criticized, why is it so important and why is it in this book? Good question. Remember, some of the breakthroughs in the history of psychology were subsequently found to be lacking in some way, but that doesn't diminish the impact they had on our view of human behavior. This work of Holmes and Rahe, the SRRS, *in spite of* its limitations, continues to hold its place as a popular stress-research tool, more than 30 years after its inception.

RECENT APPLICATIONS

Although other tools for measuring stress have been, and are being, developed, the SRRS is still chosen frequently by researchers. As proof of the scale's ongoing popularity, a tally of the studies citing Holmes and Rahe's scale between 2000 and the middle of 2003 as this edition was being prepared, totaled 315 articles! This was more citations than any other study in this book, and similar statistics on the influence of Holmes and Rahe's scale can be found for virtually any year throughout the last three decades. It is impossible to discuss here even a representative sampling of these studies, so a brief mention will be made of several recent articles to convey the wide variety of research areas still making use of the SRRS.

One study incorporating the SRRS, examined the relationship between life events and feelings of hopelessness (Haatainen et al., 2003). The researchers followed adults among the general population (without any diagnosed mental illness) over two years. Four percent of those who were not feeling hopeless at the beginning of the two years and 56% of who were experiencing hopelessness at the beginning of the two years reported hopelessness at the end of the two-year period. The life events most responsible for continuing or developing hopelessness were, worsening of financial situation and interpersonal conflicts at work. However, the authors point out that positive changes in the subjects' living situations appeared to *protect* them from becoming hopeless (for more on the topic see the study by Seligman on learned helplessness in the *Psychopathology* section of this book).

A study comparing alcoholics with nonalcoholics adapted Holmes and Rahe's scale to examine the link between stress and alcohol abuse (Fouquereau et al., 2003). The participants were asked to contemplate imagined scenarios involving two, combined life-change events or a stressful social situation. The alcoholics and nonalcoholics rated the scenarios as equally stressful, but rated the urge to drink alcohol in response to the situation very differently. "The nonalcoholics reported little stimulus to drink from any combination of items, whereas the alcoholics not only perceived the individual items as stimulating an urge to drink, but also used the same cognitive rule in judging the combined urge to drink as they used in judging the combined stress" (p. 669). The authors suggest that these findings may be important in helping recovering alcoholics find ways of reducing stress in their lives and using strategies other than drinking for coping with stressful life events.

Finally, an important cross-cultural study questioned the validity of applying Western definitions and theories about stress to other cultures (Laungani, 1996). Using India as an example, the author found that even the word "stress" itself does not translate well into other languages. He further contends that trying to overlay Western conceptualizations of stress, such as those tapped by the SRRS, onto other cultures, may not provide an accurate picture of the nature and experience of stress for large portions of the world's population. For example, people in cultures that are described as more *collectivistic,* such as India, Japan, or Israel, where the welfare of the larger group takes precedence over the welfare of a single person, may experience less life stress or may perceive entirely different life events as stressful than members of Western "individualistic" cultures, such as the United States, where the SRRS was developed (for a more complete discussion of these cultural variations, see the reading on Triandis's work in chapter 7 of this book).

Other applications of the SRRS in the study of human behavior include, but are not limited to, cigarette smoking, immune response, posttraumatic stress disorder, police officer burnout, child abuse, breast cancer, diabetes, medical school success, chronic illnesses, effects of war on spouses and children of deployed soldiers, HIV infection and AIDS, the psychological effects of natural disasters, divorce, and the aging process.

CONCLUSION

The relationship between stress and illness, while real, is complex and not a simple matter to study. Rahe himself has suggested that in addition to a simple LCU score, several factors present in each individual must be considered to predict psychosomatic illness:

1. How much experience you have had in the past with stressful events.
2. Your coping skills; that is, your ability to psychologically defend yourself in times of life stress.
3. The strength of your physiological systems (such as your immune system) to defend you against the life stress that you are unable to cope with psychologically.
4. How you deal with illness when it does occur (such as practicing recuperative behaviors and seeking medical help).

Psychology and medicine, working together, are closing in on an understanding of the psychological component of illness. It has become clear to both fields that successful treatment of illness must involve the entire person: mind and body.

Cohen S., Kamarck T., & Mermelstein R. (1983). A global measure of perceived stress. *Journal of Health and Social Behavior, 24,* 385–396.

Fouquereau, E., Fernandez, A., Mullet, E., & Sorum, P. (2003). Stress and the urge to drink. *Addictive Behaviors, 28,* 669–685.

Haatainen, K., Tanskanen, A., Kylmä J., Antikainen, R., Honkalampi, K., Koivumaa-Honkanen, H., Viinamäki, H., & Hintikka, J. (2003). Life events are important in the course of hopelessness—a 2-year follow-up study in a general population. *Social Psychiatry and Psychiatric Epidemiology, 38,* 436–441.

Holmes, T. H., & Masuda, M. (1974). Life change and illness susceptibility. In B. S. Dohrenwend & B. P. Dohrenwend (Eds.), *Stressful life events: Their nature and effects.* New York: Wiley.

Laungani, P. (1996). Cross-cultural investigations of stress: Conceptual and methodological considerations. *International Journal of Stress Management, 3*(1), 25–35.

Rahe, R. H., Mahan, J., & Arthur, R. (1970). Prediction of near-future health change from subjects' preceding life changes. *Journal of Psychosomatic Research, 14,* 401–406.

Taylor, S. (2002). *Health psychology,* 5th ed. New York: McGraw-Hill.

THOUGHTS OUT OF TUNE

Festinger, L., & Carlsmith, J. M. (1959). Cognitive consequences of forced compliance. *Journal of Abnormal and Social Psychology, 58,* 203–210.

Have you ever been in a position of having to do or say something that was contrary to your attitudes or private opinions? Chances are you have; everyone has at some time. When you behaved that way, what happened to your true attitude or opinion? Nothing? Well, maybe nothing. However, studies have shown that in some cases, when your behavior is contrary to your attitude, your attitude will change in order to bring it into alignment with your behavior. For example, if a person is forced (by the demands of an experiment) to deliver a speech in support of a viewpoint or position opposed to his or her own opinion, the speaker's attitudes will shift toward those given in the speech.

In the early 1950s, various studies explained this opinion shift as a result of (1) mentally rehearsing the speech and (2) the process of trying to think of arguments in favor of the forced position. In performing those mental tasks, the early theories argued, subjects convince themselves of the position they were about to take. In pursuing this line of reasoning further, additional studies were conducted that offered monetary rewards to subjects for giving convincing speeches contrary to their own views. It was expected that the greater the reward, the greater would be the resulting opinion change in the speaker. (Seems logical, doesn't it?) However, as one of many examples of how common sense is a poor predictor of human behavior, just the opposite was found to be true. Larger rewards produced *less* attitude change than smaller rewards. Based on the theories of learning that were popular at the time (operant conditioning, reinforcement theory, etc.), such findings were difficult for researchers to explain.

A few years later, Leon Festinger (1919–1989), a research psychologist at Stanford University, proposed the highly influential and now famous theory of *cognitive dissonance*, which could account for the seemingly discrepant findings. The word *cognitive* refers to any mental processes, such as thoughts, ideas, units of knowledge, attitudes, or beliefs; dissonance simply means *out of tune.* Therefore, Festinger suggested, you will experience cognitive dissonance when you simultaneously hold two or more cognitions that are psychologically inconsistent. When this condition exists, it creates discomfort and stress to varying degrees, depending on the importance of the dissonance to your life. This discomfort then motivates you to change something in order to reduce it. Since you cannot change your behavior (because you have already done it, or because the situational pressures are too great), you change your attitudes.

Festinger's theory grew out of reports of the rumors that spread throughout India following a 1934 earthquake there. In the areas outside the disaster zone, the rumors predicted that there would be additional earthquakes of even greater proportions and throughout an even greater portion of the country. These rumors were without any scientific foundation. Festinger wondered why people would spread such catastrophic and anxiety-increasing ideas. It occurred to him over time that perhaps the rumors were not anxiety-increasing, but *anxiety-justifying.* That is, these people were very frightened, even though they lived outside the danger area. This created cognitive dissonance: The cognition of fear was out of tune with the lack of any scientific basis for their fear. So, their spreading the rumors of greater disasters justified their fears and reduced their dissonance. They made their view of the world fit with what they were feeling and how they were behaving.

THEORETICAL PROPOSITIONS

Festinger theorized that normally in our society what you publicly state will be substantially the same as your private opinion or belief. Therefore, if you believe *X,* but publicly state *not X,* you will experience the discomfort of cognitive dissonance. However, if you know that the reasons for your statement of not X were clearly justified by pressures, promises of rewards, or threats of punishment, then dissonance will be reduced or eliminated. Therefore, the more you view your inconsistent behavior to be of your own choosing, the greater will be your dissonance.

One way for you to reduce this unpleasant dissonance is to alter your private opinion to bring it into agreement or consonance with your behavior (making the statement). Festinger contended that changes in attitudes and opinions will be greatest when dissonance is large. Think about it for a moment. Suppose someone offers you a great deal of money to state, in public, views that are the opposite of your true views, and you agree to do so. Then suppose someone else makes the same request, but offers you just a little money, and even though it hardly seems worth it, you agree anyway. In which case will your dissonance be the greatest? Logically, you would experience more dissonance in the less-money situation, because of insufficient justification for your attitude-discrepant behavior. Therefore, according to Festinger's theory, your private opinion will shift more in the little-money condition. Let's see how Festinger (with the help of his associate James Carlsmith) set about testing this theory.

METHOD

Imagine you are a university student enrolled in an introductory psychology course. One of your course requirements is to participate for three hours during the semester as a subject in psychology experiments. You check the bulletin board that posts the various studies being carried out by professors and graduate students, and you sign up for one that lasts two hours and deals with *measures of performance*. In this study by Festinger and Carlsmith, as in many psychology experiments, the true purpose of the study cannot be revealed to the subjects, since this could seriously bias their responses and invalidate the results. The actual original group of subjects consisted of 71 male, lower division, psychology students.

You arrive at the laboratory at the appointed time (here, the laboratory is nothing more than a room). You are told that this experiment takes a little over an hour, so it had to be scheduled for two hours. Since there will be some time remaining, the experimenter informs you that some people from the psychology department are interviewing subjects about their experiences as subjects, and asks you to talk to them after participating. Then you are given your first task.

A tray containing 12 spools is placed in front of you, and you are told to empty the tray onto the table, refill the tray with the spools, empty it again, refill it, and so on. You are to work with one hand and at your own speed. While the experimenter looks on with a stopwatch and takes notes, you do this over and over for 30 minutes. Then the tray is removed and you are given a board with 48 square pegs. Your task now is to turn each peg a quarter of a turn clockwise, and repeat this over and over for 30 minutes more! If this sounds incredibly boring to you, that was precisely the intention of the researchers. This part of the study was, in the authors' words, "intended to provide, for each subject uniformly, an experience about which he would have a somewhat negative opinion." Undoubtedly, you would agree that this objective was accomplished. Following completion of the tasks, the experiment really began.

The subjects were randomly assigned to one of three conditions. In the control condition, the subjects, after completing the tasks, were taken to another room where they were interviewed about their reactions to the experiment they had just completed. The rest of the subjects were lured a little further into the experimental manipulations. Following the tasks, the experimenter spoke to them as if to explain the purpose of the study. He told each of them that they were among the subjects in group A, who performed the tasks with no prior information, while subjects in group B always received descriptive information about the tasks prior to entering the lab. He went on to say that the information received by group B subjects was that the tasks were fun and interesting and that this message was delivered by an undergraduate student posing as a subject who had already completed the tasks. It is important to keep in mind that none of this was true. It was a fabrication intended to make the next crucial part of the study realistic and believable. This was, in other words, the cover story.

The experimenter then left the room for a few minutes. Upon returning, he continued to speak, but now appeared somewhat confused and uncertain. He explained, a little embarrassed, that the undergraduate who usually gives the information to group B subjects had called in sick, there was a subject from group B waiting, and they were having trouble finding someone to fill in for him. He then very politely asked the subject if he would be willing to join in on the experiment and be the one to inform the waiting subject.

The experimenter offered some of the subjects a dollar each for their help, while others were offered $20. After a subject agreed, he was given a sheet of paper marked *For Group B* on which was written, "It was very enjoyable, I had a lot of fun, I enjoyed myself, it was intriguing, it was exciting." The subject was then paid either $1 or $20 and taken into the waiting room to meet the incoming *subject.* They were left alone in the waiting room for 2 minutes, after which time the experimenter returned, thanked the subject for his help, and led him to the interview room, where he was asked his opinions of the tasks exactly as had been asked of the subjects in the control condition.

If this whole procedure seems a bit complicated, it really is not. The bottom line is that there were three groups: one group who received $1 each to lie about the tasks, one group who were paid $20 each to lie about the tasks, and a control group who did not lie at all. The data from 11 of the subjects were not included in the final analysis because of procedural errors, so there were 20 subjects in each group.

RESULTS

The results of the study were reflected in how each of the subjects actually felt about the boring tasks in the final interview phase of the study. They were asked to rate the experiment as follows:

1. Were the tasks interesting and enjoyable? Measured on a scale of −5 (extremely dull and boring) to +5 (extremely interesting and enjoyable). The 0 point indicated the tasks were neutral, neither interesting nor uninteresting.

2. How much did you learn about your ability to perform such tasks? Measured on a 0 to 10 scale, where 0 means nothing learned and 10 means a great deal learned.

3. Do you believe the experiment and tasks were measuring anything important? Measured on a 0 to 10 scale, where 0 means no scientific value and 10 means great scientific value.

4. Would you have any desire to participate in another similar experiment? Measured on a scale of −5 (definitely dislike to participate) to +5 (definitely like to participate), with 0 indicating neutral feelings.

The averages of the answers to the interview questions are presented in Table 1. Questions 1 and 4 were designed to address Festinger's theory of cognitive dissonance, and the differences indicated are clearly significant. Contrary to previous research interpretations in the field, and contrary to what most of us might expect using common sense, those subjects who were paid $1 for lying about the tasks were the ones who later reported liking the tasks more, compared with both those paid $20 to lie and those who did not lie. This finding is reflected both in the first direct question and also in the $1 group's greater willingness to participate in another similar experiment (question 4).

DISCUSSION

The theory of cognitive dissonance states, in Festinger's words:

1. If a person is induced to do or say something that is contrary to his private opinion, there will be a tendency for him to change his opinion to bring it into correspondence with what he has said or done.

2. The larger the pressure used to elicit the overt behavior, the weaker will be the above-mentioned tendency.

Festinger and Carlsmith's findings clearly support this theory. Festinger's explanation for this was that when people engage in attitude-discrepant behavior (the lie), but have strong justification for doing so ($20), they will experience only a small amount of dissonance and, therefore, not feel particularly motivated to make a change in their opinion. On the other hand, people who have insufficient justification ($1) for their attitude-discrepant behavior will experience greater levels of dissonance and, therefore, alter their opinions more radically in order to reduce the resultant discomfort. The theory may be presented graphically as follows:

Attitude-discrepant → *Sufficient justification for* → *Dissonance* → *Attitude change*
behavior → *behavior* → *small* → *small*

Attitude-discrepant → *Insufficient justification for* → *Dissonance* → *Attitude change*
behavior → *behavior* → *large* → *large*

TABLE 1 Average Ratings on Interview Questions for Each Experimental Condition

QUESTION	CONTROL GROUP	$1 GROUP	$20 GROUP
1. How enjoyable tasks were (−5 to +5)*	−0.45	+1.35	−0.05
2. How much learned (0 to 10)	3.08	2.80	3.15
3. Scientific importance (0 to 10)	5.60	6.45	5.18
4. Participate in similar experiences (−5 to +5)*	−0.62	+1.20	−0.25

*Questions relevant to Festinger and Carlsmith's hypothesis. (from p. 207)

QUESTIONS AND CRITICISMS

Festinger himself anticipated that previous researchers whose theories were threatened by this new idea would attempt to criticize the findings and offer alternate explanations for them (such as mental rehearsal and thinking up better arguments, as discussed at the beginning of this chapter). In order to counter these criticisms, the sessions in which the subject lied to the incoming subject were recorded and rated by two independent raters who had no knowledge of which condition ($1 vs. $20) they were rating. Statistical analyses of these ratings showed no differences in the content or persuasiveness of the lies between the two groups. Therefore, the only apparent explanation remaining for the findings is what Festinger termed cognitive dissonance.

Over the years since cognitive dissonance was demonstrated by Festinger and Carlsmith, other researchers have refined—but not rejected—the theory. The refinements were summarized by Cooper and Fazio (1984), who outlined four necessary steps for an attitude change to occur through cognitive dissonance. The first step is that the attitude-discrepant behavior must produce unwanted negative consequences. Festinger and Carlsmith's subjects had to lie to fellow students and convince them to participate in a very boring experiment. This produced the required negative consequences. This also explains why when you compliment someone on their clothes even though you can't stand them, your attitude toward the clothes probably doesn't change.

The second step is that personal responsibility must be taken for the negative consequences. This usually involves a choice. If you choose to behave in an attitude-discrepant way resulting in negative consequences, you will experience dissonance. However, if someone forces you to behave in that way, you will not feel personally responsible and no cognitive dissonance will result. Although Festinger and Carlsmith's article uses the phrase *forced compliance* in the title, the subjects actually believed that their actions were voluntary.

It has also been demonstrated that physiological arousal (the third step) is a necessary component of the process of cognitive dissonance. Festinger felt that dissonance is an uncomfortable state of tension that motivates us to change our attitudes. Studies have shown that, indeed, when subjects freely behave in attitude-discrepant ways, they experience physiological arousal. Festinger and Carlsmith did not measure this with their subjects, but it is safe to assume that physiological arousal was present.

Finally, the fourth step is that the person must be aware that the arousal experienced is being caused by the attitude-discrepant behavior. The discomfort the subjects felt in Festinger and Carlsmith's study would have been easily and clearly attributed to the fact that they were lying about the experiment to a fellow student.

Festinger and Carlsmith's conceptualization of cognitive dissonance has become a widely accepted and well-documented psychological phenomenon. Most psychologists agree that two fundamental processes are responsible for changes in our opinions and attitudes. One is persuasion—when other people actively work to convince you to change your views—and the other is cognitive dissonance.

RECENT APPLICATIONS

Social science research continues to rely on, demonstrate, and confirm Festinger and Carlsmith's theory and findings. One interesting study found that you may experience cognitive dissonance and change your attitude about an issue simply by *observing* people whom you like and respect engaging in attitude discrepant behavior, without any personal participation on your part at all (Norton et al., 2003). The authors referred to this process as *vicarious dissonance.* In the study, college students heard speeches disagreeing with their attitudes on a controversial issue (a college fee increase). For some, the speech in favor of the increase was given by a member of their own college (their "ingroup"), while for others, the speech was made by a member of another college (their "outgroup"). When an ingroup member delivered the speech, the subjects' experienced cognitive dissonance and decreased their negative attitudes toward the increase. In an even stronger demonstration of vicarious dissonance, the researchers found that the subjects did not even have to hear the speech itself; simply *knowing* that the ingroup member agreed to make the speech created enough dissonance to cause the hypothesized attitude change.

A fascinating study in a completely different vein used the theory of cognitive dissonance to explain why drug abusers continue to drive while under the influence, *after* completing a court-mandated treatment program for previous drug-and-driving infractions (Albery et al., 2000). Results indicated that offenders who continued to use drugs and drive, believed only alcohol posed a significantly greater risk behind the wheel, but not other drugs. Again, Festinger and Carlsmith's theory plays a central role in these findings, because driving while using drugs, after enduring a lengthy treatment program, would likely create a great deal of uncomfortable cognitive dissonance that could only be resolved by a major attitude shift about the drugs' effects (in this case, it would be called *denial*).

Finally, very important research based on Festinger's theory of cognitive dissonance, conducted by the psychologist Elliot Aronson at the University of California, Santa Cruz, focused on changing students' risky sexual behaviors (Shea, 1997). Sexually active students were asked to make videotapes about how condom use can reduce the risk of HIV infection. After making the tapes, half of the students were divided into groups and encouraged to discuss why college students resist using condoms and to reveal their own experiences of not using condoms. In other words, these subjects had to admit that they did not always adhere to the message they had just promoted in the videos; they had to face their own hypocrisy. The other students who engaged in making the videos did not participate in the follow-up discussions. When all the students were then given the opportunity to buy condoms, a significantly higher proportion of those in the hypocrisy group purchased them compared to the video-only group. More importantly, three months later, when the subjects were interviewed about their sexual practices, 92% of the students in the hypocrisy group said they had been using condoms every time they had intercourse compared to only 55% of those who participated in making the videotapes, but who were not required to publicly admit their attitude-discrepant behavior. This is a clear example of cognitive dissonance at work. The more you are forced to confront the discrepancy between your beliefs and your behavior, the more dissonance you experience, and the more you are motivated to change your behavior. Aronson, a strong proponent of the importance of cognitive dissonance in bringing about real-life behavioral change, explains that, "Most of us engage in hypocritical behavior all the time, because we can blind ourselves to it. But if someone comes along and forces you to look at it, you can no longer shrug it off" (Shea, 1997, p. A15).

Albery, I., Strang, J., Gossop, M., & Griffiths, P. (2000). Illicit drugs and driving: Previewence, beliefs, and accident involvement among a cohort of current out-of-treatment drug users. *Drug and Alcohol Dependence, 58*(1–2), 197–204.

Cooper, J., & Fazio, R. (1984). A new look at dissonance theory. In L. Berkowitz (Ed.), *Advances in experimental social psychology*. New York: Academic Press.

Norton, M. I., Monin, B., Cooper, J., & Hogg, M. A. (2003). Vicarious dissonance: Attitude change from the inconsistency of others. *Journal of Personality and Social Psychology, 85*, 47–62.

Shea, C. (1997, June 20). A University of California psychologist investigates new approaches to changing human behavior. *Chronicle of Higher Education, 43*(41), A15.

7 PERSONALITY

If you ask yourself the question "Who am I?" you are asking the same question posed by personality psychologists. Research on personality seeks to reveal those human characteristics that make each person unique and to determine where those characteristics came from. When behavioral scientists speak of personality, they are usually referring to qualities that are relatively stable across situations and consistent over time. Who you are does not change each day, each week, or, usually, even each year. Instead, certain characteristics about you are constant and predictable. This predictability is of great interest to those who study personality. Psychologists have theorized hundreds of personality traits over the years. Most of these have been debated and argued so much, it is often unclear whether they truly measure meaningful differences among individuals. However, a few factors have been repeatedly shown to predict specific behaviors reliably. These are the focus of this section.

The first reading discusses Julian Rotter's famous research into how people view the location of power in their lives. Some believe that their lives are controlled by external factors, such as fate, while others feel the control is internal—in their own hands. This quality of externality versus internality has been shown to be a consistent and important factor in who you are. Second, you will read about research by Sandra Bem from the 1970s that quite literally revolutionized the way most of the world views a fundamental and powerful component of who you are: your gender. Third comes the highly influential study that first identified what many of you now know as *Type A* and *Type B* personalities and how Type A individuals may be more prone to heart disease. Finally, comes a study that has influenced virtually all subfields of psychology by reminding all of us that human behavior must always be considered within a *cultural* context. This reading discusses the work of Harry Triandis, who, over the past 30 years, has carefully and convincingly developed his theory that most human societies fall within one of two categories: *collectivist* cultures and *individualistic* cultures. This single (though certainly not simple) dimension may explain a great deal about how the culture in which you are raised has a profound effect on who you are.

ARE YOU THE MASTER OF YOUR FATE?

Rotter, J. B. (1966). Generalized expectancies for internal versus external control of reinforcement. *Psychological Monographs, 80,* 1–28.

Are the consequences of your behavior under your personal control or determined by forces outside of yourself? Think about it for a moment: When something good happens to you, do you take credit for it or do you think how lucky you were? When something negative occurs, is it usually your responsibility or do you just chalk it up to fate? The same question may be posed in more formal psychological language: Do you believe that there is a causal relationship between your behavior and its consequences?

Julian Rotter, one of the most influential behaviorists in psychology's history, proposed that individuals differ a great deal in where they place the responsibility for what happens to them. When people interpret the consequences of their behavior to be controlled by luck, fate, or powerful others, this indicates a belief in what Rotter called an *external locus of control* (locus simply means location). Conversely, he maintained that if people interpret their own behavior and personality characteristics as responsible for behavioral consequences, they have a belief in an *internal locus of control.* In his frequently cited 1966 article, Rotter explained that a person's tendency to view events from an internal versus an external locus of control can be explained from a social learning theory perspective.

In this view, as a person develops from infancy through childhood, behaviors are learned because they are followed by some form of reinforcement. This reinforcement increases the child's expectancy that a particular behavior will produce the desired reinforcement. Once this expectancy is established, the removal of reinforcement will cause the expectancy of such a relationship between behavior and reinforcement to fade. Therefore, reinforcement sometimes is seen as contingent upon behavior, and sometimes it is not (see the discussion of contingencies in the reading on work of B. F. Skinner). As children grow, some will have frequent experiences in which their behavior directly influences reinforcement, while for others, reinforcement will appear to result from actions outside of themselves. Rotter claimed that the totality of your specific learning experiences creates in you a generalized expectancy about whether reinforcement is internally or externally controlled.

"These generalized expectancies," Rotter wrote, "will result in characteristic differences in behavior in a situation culturally categorized as chance-determined versus skill-determined, and may act to produce individual differences within a specific condition" (p. 2). In other words, you have developed an internal or external interpretation of the consequences for your behavior that will influence your future behavior in almost all situations. Rotter believed that your locus of control, whether internal or external, is an important part of who you are, a part of your personality.

Look back at the questions posed at the beginning of this chapter. Which do you think you are, an internal or an external? Rotter wanted to study differences among people on this dimension and, rather than simply ask them, he developed a test that measures a person's locus of control. Once he was able to measure this characteristic in people, he could then study how it influenced their behavior.

THEORETICAL PROPOSITIONS

Rotter proposed to demonstrate two main points in his research. First, he predicted that a test could be developed to measure reliably the extent to which individuals possess an internal or an external locus-of-control orientation toward life. Second, he hypothesized that people will display stable individual differences in their interpretations of the causes of reinforcement in the same situations. He proposed to demonstrate his hypothesis by presenting research comparing behavior of *internals* with that of *externals* in various contexts.

METHOD

Rotter designed a scale containing a series of many pairs of statements. Each pair consisted of one statement reflecting an internal locus of control and one reflecting an external locus of control. Those taking the test were instructed to select "the one statement of each pair (and only one) which you more strongly believe to be the case as far as you're concerned. Be sure to select the one you actually believe to be more true rather than the one you think you should choose or the one you would like to be true. This is a measure of personal belief: Obviously there are no right or wrong answers" (p. 26). The test was designed so that subjects were forced to choose one statement for each pair and could not designate *neither* or *both*.

Rotter's measuring device endured many revisions and alterations. In its earliest form, it contained 60 pairs of statements, but by using various tests for reliability and validity, it was eventually refined and streamlined down to 23 items. Added to these were six *filler items*, which were designed to disguise the true purpose of the test. Such filler items are often used in tests such as this because if subjects were able to guess what the test is trying to measure, they might alter their answers in some way in an attempt to *perform better*.

Rotter called his test the *I-E Scale*, which is the name it is known by today. Table 1 includes examples of typical items from the I-E Scale, plus samples of the filler items. If you examine the items, you can see quite clearly which statements reflect an internal or external orientation. Rotter contended that his test was a measure of the extent to which a person possesses the personality characteristic of internal or external locus of control.

Rotter's next step was to demonstrate that he could actually use this characteristic to predict people's behavior in specific situations. To do this he reported on several studies (by Rotter and others) in which scores on the I-E Scale (in various forms) were examined in relation to individuals' interactions with various events in their lives. These studies found significant correlations

TABLE 1 Sample Items and Filler Items from Rotter's I-E Scale

ITEM #	STATEMENTS
2a.	Many of the unhappy things in people's lives are partly due to bad luck.
2b.	People's misfortunes result from the mistakes they make.
11a.	Becoming a success is a matter of hard work; luck has little or nothing to do with it.
11b.	Getting a good job depends mainly on being in the right place at the right time.
18a.	Most people don't realize the extent to which their lives are controlled by accidental happenings.
18b.	There is really no such thing as "luck."
23a.	Sometimes I can't understand how teachers arrive at the grades I get.
23b.	There is a direct connection between how hard I study and the grades I get.
	FILLER ITEMS
1a.	Children get into trouble because their parents punish them too much.
1b.	The trouble with most children nowadays is that their parents are too easy with them.
14a.	There are certain people who are just no good.
14b.	There is some good in everybody.

(Adapted from pp. 13–14.)

between I-E scores and situations such as those involving gambling, political activism, persuasion, smoking, achievement motivation, and conformity.

RESULTS

Following is a brief summary of the findings reported by Rotter of research in the areas mentioned in the previous paragraph. (See pp. 19–24 in the original study for complete discussion and citation of specific references.)

Gambling

Rotter reported on studies that looked at betting behavior in relation to locus of control. These found that individuals identified as internals by the I-E Scale tended to prefer betting on *sure things* and liked intermediate odds over the long shots. Externals, on the other hand, would wager more money on risky bets. In addition, externals would tend to engage in more unusual shifts in betting called the *gambler's fallacy* (such as betting more on a number that has not come up for a while on the basis that it is *due*).

Persuasion

An interesting study cited by Rotter used the I-E Scale to select two groups of students, one highly internal and the other highly external. Both groups shared similar attitudes, on average, about the fraternity and sorority system on the campus. Both groups were asked to try to persuade other students to change their attitudes about these organizations. The internals were found to be significantly more successful than externals in altering the attitudes of others. Conversely, other studies demonstrated that internals were more resistant to manipulation of their attitudes by others.

Smoking

An internal locus of control appeared to relate to self-control as well. Two studies discussed by Rotter found that (1) smokers tended to be significantly more external than nonsmokers, and (2) individuals who quit smoking after the original surgeon general's warning appeared on cigarette packs were more internally oriented, even though both internals and externals believed the warning was true.

Achievement Motivation

If you believe your own actions are responsible for your successes, it is logical to assume that you should be more motivated to achieve success than someone who believes success is more a matter of fate. Rotter pointed to a study of 1,000 high school students that found a positive relationship between an internal score on the I-E Scale and 15 out of 17 indicators of this achievement motivation. These included plans to attend college, amount of time spent on homework, and how interested the parents were in the students' school work. Each of these achievement-oriented factors were more likely to be found for students with an internal locus of control.

Conformity

One study was cited that exposed subjects to the conformity test developed by Solomon Asch, in which a subject's willingness to agree with a majority's incorrect judgment was evidence for conforming behavior (see the reading on Asch's conformity study). Subjects were allowed to bet (with money provided by the experimenters) on the correctness of their judgments. Under this betting condition, those found to be internals conformed significantly less to the majority and bet more money on themselves when making judgments contrary to the majority than did the externals.

DISCUSSION

As part of his discussion, Rotter posed possible sources for the individual differences he found on the dimension of internal-external locus of control. He referred to several studies that addressed the issue of possible causes. Three potential sources for the development of an internal or external orientation were suggested: cultural differences, socioeconomic differences, and variations in styles of parenting.

One study cited found differences in locus of control among various cultures. In an isolated community in the United States, three distinct groups could be compared: Ute Indians, Mexican Americans, and Caucasians. It was found that those individuals of Ute heritage were, on average, the most external, while the whites were the most internal. The Mexican Americans scored between the other two groups on the I-E Scale. These findings, which appeared to be independent of socioeconomic level, suggested ethnic differences in locus of control.

Rotter also referred to some early and tentative findings indicating that socioeconomic level even within a particular culture may relate to locus of control findings. These findings suggested that a lower socioeconomic position predicts greater externality.

Styles of parenting were implicated by Rotter as an obvious source for learning to be internal or external. While he did not offer supportive research evidence at the time, he suggested that parents who administer rewards and punishments to their children in ways that are unpredictable and inconsistent would likely encourage the development of an external locus of control (this is discussed in greater detail shortly).

Rotter summarized his findings by pointing out that the consistency of the results leads to the conclusion that locus of control is a definable characteristic of individuals that operates fairly consistently across various situations. Furthermore, the influences on behavior produced by the internal-external dimension are such that it will influence different people to behave differently when faced with the same situation. In addition, Rotter contended that locus of control can be measured, and that the I-E Scale is an effective tool for doing so.

Finally, Rotter hypothesized that those with an internal locus of control (i.e., those who have a strong belief that they can control their own destiny) are more likely than externals to (1) gain information from the situations in their life in order to improve future behavior in those situations or similar ones, (2) take the initiative to change and improve their condition in life, (3) place greater value on inner skill and achievement of goals, and (4) be more able to resist manipulation by others.

SUBSEQUENT RESEARCH

Since Rotter developed his I-E Scale, hundreds of studies have examined the relationship between locus of control and various behaviors. Following is a brief sampling of a few of those as they relate to rather diverse human behaviors.

In his 1966 article, Rotter touched on how locus of control might relate to health behaviors. Since then, other studies have examined the same relationship. In a review of locus-of-control research, Strickland (1977) found that individuals with an internal focus generally take more responsibility for their own health. They are more likely to engage in more healthy behaviors (such as not smoking and adopting better nutritional habits) and practice greater care in avoiding accidents. Additionally, studies have found that internals generally have lower levels of stress and are less likely to suffer from stress-related illnesses.

Rotter's hypotheses regarding the relationship between parenting styles and locus of control have been at least partially confirmed. Research has shown that parents of children who are internals tend to be more affectionate, more consistent with discipline, and more concerned with teaching children to take responsibility for their actions. Parents of externally oriented children have been found to be more authoritarian and restrictive, and do not allow their children much opportunity for personal control (see Davis & Phares, 1969, for a discussion of those findings).

A fascinating study demonstrated how the concept of locus of control may have sociological and even catastrophic implications. Sims and Baumann (1972) applied Rotter's theory to explain why more people die in tornados in Alabama than in Illinois. These researchers noticed that the death rate from tornados was five times greater in the South than in the Midwest, and they set out to determine why. One by one they eliminated all of the explanations related to the physical locations, such as storm strength and severity (the storms are actually stronger in Illinois), time of day of the storms (an equal number occur at night in both regions), type of business and residence construction (masonry is as dangerous as wood-frame, but for different reasons), and the quality of warning systems (even before warning systems existed, Alabama had the same higher death rate).

With all the obvious environmental reasons ruled out, Sims and Baumann suggested that the difference might be due to psychological variables and proposed the locus-of-control concept as a likely possibility. Questionnaires containing a modified version of Rotter's I-E Scale were administered to residents of four counties in Illinois and Alabama that had experienced a similar incidence of tornados and tornado-caused deaths. They found that the respondents from Alabama demonstrated a significantly greater external locus of control than did those from Illinois. From this finding, as well as from responses to other items on the questionnaire relating to tornado behavior, the researchers concluded that an internal orientation promotes behaviors that are more likely to save lives in the event of a tornado (such as paying attention to the news media or alerting others). This stems directly from the internals' belief that their behavior will be effective in changing the outcome of the event. In this study, Alabamians were seen as "less confident in themselves as causal agents, less convinced of their ability to engage in effective action. . . . The data . . . constitute a suggestive illustration of how man's personality is active in determining the quality of his interaction with nature" (Sims & Baumann, 1972, p. 1391).

RECENT APPLICATIONS

To say that hundreds of studies have incorporated Rotter's Locus of Control theory since his article appeared in 1966 may have been a serious understatement. In reality, there may have been thousands! A search of the three years prior to the publication of this text reveals 110 citations of this study in the professional literature; looking at the previous six years, the total is over 700. Such a great reliance on Rotter's theory speaks clearly to the broad acceptance of the impact and validity of the internal-external personality dimension. Following are a few representative examples from the great variety of recent studies citing his pioneering work.

Do you tend to feel sorry for yourself when you are stressed and things don't go your way? Psychologists call such a response, *self-pity*. A study by Stober (2003) examined how self-pity is linked to other personality characteristics such as, anger, loneliness, and internal-external control beliefs. One of the study's strongest findings was a connection between self-pity and locus of control. "With respect to control beliefs, individuals high in self-pity showed generalized externality beliefs, seeing themselves as controlled by both chance and powerful others" (p. 183). In addition, self-pity was shown to be associated with depression, which is linked, in turn, to an external locus of control (Yang & Clum, 2000). This connection is addressed in greater detail in the discussion of Seligman's *learned helplessness* study later in this section.

Often, when Rotter's research on locus of control is being discussed, the subject of religious faith arises. Many religious people believe that it is desirable and proper at times to place their fate in God's hands, yet within Rotter's theory, this would indicate an external locus of control with its negative connotations. A fascinating recent study in the *Journal of Psychology and Religion* addressed this very issue (Welton, Adkins, Ingle, & Dixon, 1996). Using various locus-of-control scales and subscales, subjects were assessed on their degree of internal locus of control, perceived control by *powerful others*, belief in chance, and belief in *God control*. The advantages associated with an internal locus of control were also found in the subjects scoring high on the God-control dimension. The authors contend that if a person has an external locus of control as measured by Rotter's scale, but the external power is perceived as a strong faith in a supreme being, they will be less subject to the typical problems associated with externals (i.e., powerlessness, depression, low achievement, low motivation for change).

A great deal of important cross-cultural research has relied heavily on Rotter's conceptualization of the internal-external locus of control dimension of personality. For example, one study from Russian researchers examined locus-of-control and right-wing authoritarian attitudes in Russian and American college students (D'yakonova & Yurtaikin, 2000). Results indicated that among the American students greater internal locus of control was correlated with higher levels of authoritarianism, while no such connection was found for the Russian subjects. Another cross-cultural study relied on Rotter's I-E Scale to examine the psychological adjustment to the diagnosis of cancer in a highly superstitious collectivist culture (Sun & Stewart, 2000). Interestingly, findings from this study indicated that "even in a culture where supernatural beliefs are widespread, an [internal locus of control] relates positively and 'chance' beliefs relate negatively with adjustment" to a serious illness such as cancer (p. 177). Research areas other than those discussed earlier that have cited Rotter's study include posttraumatic stress disorder, issues of control and aging, childbirth methods, coping with anticipatory stress, the effects of environmental noise, academic performance, white-collar crime, adult children of alcoholics, child molestation, mental health following natural disasters, contraceptive use, and HIV and AIDS prevention research.

CONCLUSION

The dimension of internal-external locus of control has been generally accepted as a relatively stable aspect of human personality that has meaningful implications for predicting behavior across a wide variety of situations. The phrase *relatively stable* is used because a person's locus of control can change under certain circumstances. Those who are externally oriented often will become more internal when their profession places them in positions of greater authority and responsibility. People who are highly internally oriented may shift toward a more external focus during times of extreme stress and uncertainty. Moreover, it is possible for individuals to learn to be more internal, if given the opportunity.

Implicit in Rotter's concept of locus of control is the assumption that internals are better adjusted and more effective in life. Although most of the research confirms this assumption, Rotter, in his later writings, sounded a note of caution (see Rotter, 1975). Everyone, especially internals, must be attentive to the environment around them. If a person sets out to change a situation that is not changeable, frustration, disappointment, and depression are the potential outcomes. When forces outside of the individual are *actually* in control of behavioral consequences, the most realistic and healthy approach to take is probably one of an external orientation.

Davis, W., & Phares, E. (1969). Parental antecedents of internal-external control of reinforcement. *Psychological Reports, 24,* 427–436.

D'yakonova, N., & Yurtaikin, V. (2000). An authoritarian personality in Russia and in the USA: Value orientation and locus of control. *Voprosy Psikhologii, 4,* 51–61.

Rotter, J. (1975). Some problems and misconceptions related to the construct of internal versus external reinforcement. *Journal of Consulting and Clinical Psychology, 43,* 56–67.

Sims, J., & Baumann, D. (1972). The tornado threat: Coping styles in the North and South. *Science, 176,* 1386–1392.

Stober, J. (2003). Self-pity: Exploring the links to personality, control beliefs, and anger. *Journal of Personality, 71,* 183–220.

Strickland, B. (1977). Internal-external control of reinforcement. In T. Blass (Ed.), *Personality variables in social behavior.* Hillsdale, NJ: Erlbaum.

Sun, L., & Stewart, S. (2000). Psychological adjustment to cancer in a collective culture. *International Journal of Psychology, 35*(5), 177–185.

Welton, G., Adkins, A., Ingle, S., & Dixon, W. (1996). God control—The 4th dimension. *Journal of Psychology and Theology, 24*(1), 13–25.

Yang, B., & Clum, G. (2000). Childhood stress leads to later suicidality via its effects on cognitive functioning. *Suicide and Life-Threatening Behavior, 30*(3), 183–198.

MASCULINE OR FEMININE . . . OR BOTH?

Bem, S. L. (1974). The measurement of psychological androgyny. *Journal of Consulting and Clinical Psychology, 42,* 155–162.

Are you male or female? Are you a man or a woman? Are you masculine or feminine? Three seemingly similar questions, yet the range of possible answers may surprise you. As for the first question, the answer is usually fairly clear: it is a biological answer based on a person's chromosomes, hormones, and sexual anatomical structures. Most people also have little trouble answering the second question with confidence. Virtually all of you are quite sure about which sex you perceive yourself to be, and you've been sure since you were about four years old. Odds are good you did not have to stop for even a split second to think about whether you perceive yourself to be a man or a woman.

However, the third question might not be quite so easy to answer. Different people possess varying amounts of "maleness" and "femaleness," or masculinity and femininity. If you think about people you know, you can probably place some on the extremely feminine side of this dimension (they are more likely to be women), others fit best on the extremely masculine side (they are more likely to be men), and still others seem to fall somewhere in between the two, possessing both masculine and feminine characteristics (they may be either men or women). These "categories" are not intended to be judgmental, they simply define variations in one important characteristic among people. This masculinity-femininity dimension forms the basis of what psychologists usually refer to as *gender*, and your perception of your own maleness and femaleness is your *gender identity*. Your gender identity is one of the most basic and most powerful components comprising your personality: your self-concept and others' perceptions about *who you are.*

Prior to the 1970s, behavioral scientists (and most nonscientists as well) usually assumed a mutually exclusive view of gender: that people's gender identity was either primarily masculine or primarily feminine. Masculinity and femininity were seen as opposite ends of a one-dimensional gender scale. If you were to complete a test measuring your gender identity based on this view, your score would place you somewhere along a single scale, either more toward the masculine or toward the feminine side of the scale. Furthermore, researchers and clinicians presumed that psychological adjustment was, in part, related to how well a person "fit" into one gender category or the other, based on their biological sex. In other words, for optimal psychological health, men should be as masculine as possible and women should be as feminine as possible.

Then, in the early 1970s this one-dimensional view of gender was challenged in an article by Anne Constantinople (1973) claiming that masculinity and femininity are not two ends of a single scale, but rather, are best described as two *separate* dimensions on which individuals could be measured. In other words, a person could be high or low in masculinity and high or low in femininity *at the same-time.* Figure 1 illustrates the comparison of a one-dimensional and a two-dimensional concept of gender.

This may not seem particularly surprising to you, but at the time, it was revolutionary. This two-dimensional view of gender was seized upon at the time by Sandra Bem of Stanford University. Bem challenged the prevailing notion that healthy gender identity is represented by behaving predominantly according to society's expectations for one's biological sex. She proposed that a more balanced person, who is able to incorporate both masculine and feminine behaviors, may actually be happier and more well

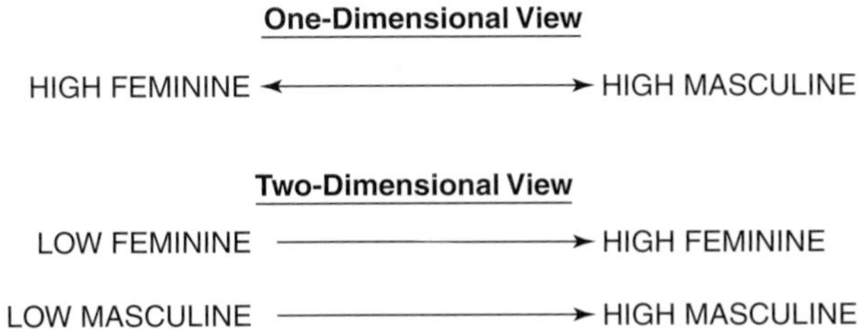

One-Dimensional View

HIGH FEMININE ◄─────────────► HIGH MASCULINE

Two-Dimensional View

LOW FEMININE ─────────────► HIGH FEMININE

LOW MASCULINE ─────────────► HIGH MASCULINE

FIGURE 1 Comparison of the traditional one-dimensional and the more recent two-dimensional model of gender.

adjusted than someone who is strongly sex-typed as either masculine or feminine. Bem took the research a step further and set out to develop a method for measuring gender on a two-dimensional scale. In the article that forms the basis for this chapter, Bem coined the term *androgynous* (from "andro" meaning male, and "gyn" referring to female) to describe individuals who embrace both masculine and feminine characteristics, depending on which behaviors best fit a particular situation. Moreover, Bem contended that not only are some people androgynous, but androgyny offers an *advantage* of greater behavioral flexibility as a person moves from situation to situation in life. Bem explained it in this way:

> The highly sex-typed individual is motivated to keep [his or her] behavior consistent with an internalized sex-role standard, a goal that [he or she] presumably accomplishes by suppressing any behavior that might be considered undesirable or inappropriate for [his or her] sex. Thus, whereas a narrowly masculine self-concept might inhibit behaviors that are stereotyped as feminine, and a narrowly feminine self-concept might inhibit behaviors that are stereotyped as masculine, a mixed, or androgynous, self-concept might allow an individual to engage freely in both "masculine" and "feminine" behaviors. (p. 155)

For example, you may know a woman who is gentle, sensitive, and soft-spoken (traditional feminine characteristics), but she is also ambitious, self-reliant, and athletic (traditional masculine characteristics). On the other hand, a male friend of yours may be competitive, dominant, and risk-taking (masculine traits), but displays traditional feminine characteristics as well, such as affectionate, sympathetic, and cheerful. When a person displays a balance of masculine and feminine traits, Bem described that person as *androgynous*. This article explains the theories and processes Bem used to develop a scale for assessing gender, called the *Bem Sex-Role Inventory* (BSRI).

THEORETICAL PROPOSITIONS

Whenever scientists propose new and novel theories that challenge the prevailing views of the time, they must bear the responsibility of demonstrating the validity of their revolutionary ideas. If Bem wanted to explore the notion of androgyny and demonstrate differences between androgynous people and those who are highly masculine or feminine, she needed to find a way to establish the existence of androgynous individuals. In other words, she had to *measure it.*

Bem's contended that measuring androgyny would require a scale that was fundamentally different from masculinity-femininity scales that had gone before. With this goal in mind, her scale contained the following innovations:

1. Bem's first concern was to develop a gender scale that did not assume a one-dimensional view: that masculinity and femininity were opposite ends of a single dimension. So, her test incorporated two separate scales, one measuring masculinity and another measuring femininity (see Figure 1).

2. Her scale was based on masculine and feminine traits that were *perceived* as desirable for men and women respectively. Previous gender scales were based on the behaviors most commonly *observed* in men and women, rather than those judged by American society to be more desirable.

   > A characteristic qualified as masculine if it was judged to be more desirable for a man than for a woman, and it qualified as feminine if it was judged to be more desirable for a woman than for a man. (pp. 155–156)

3. The BSRI was designed to differentiate among masculine, feminine, and androgynous individuals by looking at the *difference* in the score on the feminine section of the scale and the score on the masculine section. In other words when a person's feminine trait score is subtracted from his or her masculine trait score, the difference would determine the degree of masculinity, femininity, or androgyny.

Bem decided that her scale would be comprised of a list of personality characteristics or traits. To arrive at a gender score, each characteristic could simply be rated on a scale of 1 to 7 indicating the degree to which respondents perceived a particular trait described themselves. Let's take a look at how the scale was developed.

METHOD
Item Selection

Remember, Bem's idea was to use masculine and feminine characteristics that are seen by society as desirable in one sex or the other. To arrive at her final scale, she began with long lists of positively valued characteristics that seemed to her and several of her psychology students to be either masculine, feminine, or neither masculine or feminine. Each of these three lists of traits contained about 200 items. She then asked 100 undergraduate students (half male and half female) at Stanford University to serve as judges and rate whether the characteristics were more desirable for a man or for a woman on a 7-point scale from 1 ("not at all desirable") to 7 ("extremely desirable") in American society.

Using these ratings from the student judges, Bem selected the "top twenty" highest rated characteristics for the masculinity scale and for the femininity scale. She also selected items that were rated no more desirable for men than for women, but equally desirable for *anyone* to possess regardless of sex (these are not androgynous items, but simply gender-neutral). She selected 10 positive items and 10 negative gender-neutral items. These items were included in the final scale to ensure that respondents would not be overly influenced by seeing all masculine and feminine descriptors or all desirable items. So, the final scale consisted of 60 items. A sampling of the final selection of traits on the BSRI is shown in Table 1. Note that in the actual scale, the items are not divided according to sex-type, but are mixed up in random order.

Scoring

As mentioned earlier, a person completing the BSRI simply needs to respond to each item using a 7-point scale indicating how well the descriptor describes him- or herself. The response scale is as follows: *1 = Never or almost never true; 2 = Usually not true; 3 = Sometimes, but infrequently; true; 4 = Occasionally true;*

TABLE 1 Modified Sex Role Inventory

RATING	FEMININE ITEMS	RATING	MASCULINE ITEMS	RATING	NEUTRAL ITEMS
_____	Affectionate	_____	Acts as a leader	_____	Adaptable
_____	Yielding	_____	Willing to take risks	_____	Conceited
_____	Cheerful	_____	Ambitious	_____	Unpredictable
_____	Flatterable	_____	Willing to take a stand	_____	Truthful
_____	Compassionate	_____	Analytical	_____	Inefficient
_____	Understanding	_____	Strong Personality	_____	Tactful
_____	Gentle	_____	Assertive	_____	Jealous
_____	Feminine	_____	Self-sufficient	_____	Sincere
_____	Loves children	_____	Masculine	_____	Moody
_____	Soft spoken	_____	Independent	_____	Reliable

Modified, based on Table 1, p. 156

Rate items using the following scale as they apply to you:

1 = Never or almost never true
2 = Usually not true
3 = Sometimes but infrequently true
4 = Occasionally true
5 = Often true
6 = Usually true
7 = Always or almost always true

Scoring

Femininity Score: Total of Feminine ratings ÷ 10 =   _____
Masculinity Score: Total of Masculine ratings ÷ 10 =   _____
Androgyny Score: Subtract Masculine from Feminine = _____

Interpretation:

Feminine = 1.00 or greater
Near Feminine = +.50 to +1.00
Androgynous = −.50- to +.50
Near Masculine = −1.00 to −.50
Masculine = −1.00 or less

5 = *Often true;* 6 = *Usually true;* 7 = *Always or almost always true.* After respondents complete the scale, they receive three scores: a masculinity score, a femininity score, and, most important for this article, an androgyny score. The masculinity score is determined by adding up all the scores on the masculine items and dividing by 20 to obtain the average rating on those items. The femininity score is likewise determined. The average score on each of these scales may be anywhere from 1.0 to 7.0. So, have you figured out how an androgyny score might be calculated from these averages? Remember, the scale taps into masculinity and femininity independently, but it does not contain androgynous items per se. If you are thinking androgyny could be determined by looking at the degree of *difference* between a person's masculine and feminine scores, you are right: that is exactly what Bem did. Androgyny was determined by subtracting the masculinity score from the femininity score. Androgyny scores, then, could range from −6 to +6. It's simple, really. Here are three rather extreme examples to illustrate a masculine sex-typed person, a feminine sex-typed person, and an androgynous person:

Jennifer's masculinity score is 1.5 and her femininity score is 6.4. Subtracting 1.5 from 6.4 gives Jennifer an androgyny score of 4.9. Richard's masculinity score is 5.8 and his femininity score is 2.1. So, Richard's androgyny score is −3.7. Dana receives a masculinity score of 3.9 and a femininity score of 4.3. Dana's androgyny score, then, is 0.4.

<u>Jennifer</u>: Femininity Score = 6.4
Minus Masculinity score = −1.5
_____
Androgyny score = 4.9

<u>Richard</u>: Femininity Score = 2.1
Minus Masculinity score = −5.8
_____
Androgyny score = −3.7

<u>Dana</u>: Femininity Score = 4.3
Minus Masculinity score = −3.9
_____
Androgyny score = 0.4

Looking at the numbers, which of our three examples scored the *highest* in androgyny? The answer is Dana. Why? Because Dana's scores for masculine and feminine characteristics were about the same and did not show much bias in either direction, unlike Jennifer and Richard. Therefore, Dana's score reflected a *lack* of sex-typed self-perception, and more of a balance between masculine and feminine, which is the *definition* of androgyny.

So, the scoring on the BSRI is interpreted like this: scores closest to zero (whether positive or negative) indicate androgyny; as scores move farther away from zero in the plus direction greater femininity is indicated; as scores move farther away from zero in the minus direction, greater masculinity is indicated.

You may want to try completing the scale for yourself. Of course, at this point, you are *not* the ideal respondent, because you now know too much about how the scale works! Also, you will be rating feminine, masculine, and neutral traits separately, rather than all mixed up as they would be in the actual scale. Nevertheless, with those cautions in mind, you should feel free to give it a try. Table 1 provides simplified scoring and interpretation guidelines.

RESULTS

Any measuring device must be both reliable and valid. *Reliability* refers to a scale's consistency of measurement, that is, how well the various items tap into the same characteristic being measured, and the scale's ability to produce similar results over repeated administrations. *Validity* refers to how well the scale truly measures what it is intended to measure—in the case of the BSRI, masculinity and femininity.

Reliability of the BSRI

Statistical analyses on the scores from the student samples demonstrated that the internal consistency of the BSRI was very high for both scales. This implies that the 20 masculine items were all measuring a single trait (presumably masculinity), and the 20 feminine items were measuring a single trait (presumably femininity). To determine the scale's consistency of measurement over time, Bem administered the BSRI a second time to about 60 of the original respondents four weeks later. Their scores for the first and second administrations correlated very highly, thereby suggesting a high level of "test-retest" reliability.

Validity of the BSRI

To ensure that the BSRI was valid, the masculinity and femininity scales must be analyzed to be sure they are not measuring the *same* trait. This was important, because a basic theoretical proposition of Bem's study was that masculinity and femininity are *independent* dimensions of gender and should be able to be measured separately. Bem demonstrated this by correlating scores on the masculine scale and the feminine scale of the BSRI. The correlations showed that the scales were clearly *unrelated* and functioned independently from each other.

Next, Bem needed to verify that the scale was indeed measuring masculine and feminine gender characteristics. To confirm this, Bem analyzed average scores on the masculine and feminine scales for men and women separately. You would expect such an analysis should show that men scored higher on the masculine items and women scored higher on the feminine items. This is exactly what Bem found for respondents from both colleges, and the difference was highly statistically significant.

Finally, Bem divided her sample of respondents into the gender categories listed earlier in this discussion: masculine, feminine, and androgynous. She found a large number of people who had very small differences in their feminine and masculine scores. In other words, they were androgynous. Table 2 shows the percentages of masculine, feminine, and androgynous respondents in Bem's study.

TABLE 2 Percentages of Feminine, Masculine, and Androgynous Respondents

CATEGORY	MALES	FEMALES
Feminine	7%	35%
Near Feminine	6%	17%
Androgynous	35%	29%
Near Masculine	19%	11%
Masculine	33%	8%

Number of respondents = 917
Adapted from Table 7, p. 161 (samples combined)

DISCUSSION

The discussion section of Bem's article is short, succinct, and cogent. The best way to represent it is to quote it directly, in its entirety:

> It is hoped that the development of the BSRI will encourage investigators in the areas of sex differences and sex roles to question the traditional assumption that it is the sex-typed individual who typifies mental health and to begin focusing on the behavioral and societal consequences of the more flexible sex-role concepts. In a society where rigid sex-role differentiation has already outlived its utility, perhaps the androgynous person will come to define a more human standard of psychological health. (p. 162)

This statement from Bem illustrates how this study changed psychology. Over the decades since Bem's article, Western cultures have become increasingly accepting of the idea that some people are more androgynous than others, and that possessing some characteristics of both traditionally masculine and feminine characteristics is not only acceptable, but may provide certain advantages. More men and women than ever before are choosing to engage in vocations, avocations, sports activities, and family activities that have traditionally been seen as "limited" to their opposite gender. From women corporate executives to stay-at-home dads, from female firefighters and soldiers to male nurses and schoolteachers, and from women taking charge to men exploring their sensitive sides, the social changes in gender roles and expectations are everywhere you look.

This is not to say, by any means, that the culture has become "gender-blind." On the contrary, sex-role expectations still exert powerful influences over our choices of behaviors and attitudes, and discrimination based on gender continues to be a significant social problem. In general, males are still expected to be more assertive and women more emotionally expressive; the vast majority of airline pilots still are men (96%) and nearly all dental hygienists still are women (98%); but the *degree* of cultural differentiation along gender lines has decreased and is continuing to do so.

A great deal of research was generated by Bem's new conceptualization of gender. As discussed earlier, prior to the 1970s, the prevailing belief was that people would be most well adjusted in life if their "gender matched their sex," that is, boys and men should display masculine attitudes and behaviors and girls and women should display feminine attitudes and behaviors. However, the "discovery" of androgyny shifted this focus, and studies began to explore gender differences among masculine, feminine, *and* androgynous individuals.

CRITICISMS AND SUBSEQUENT RESEARCH

Research has shown that androgynous children and adults tend to have higher levels of self-esteem and are more adaptable in diverse settings (Taylor & Hall, 1982). Other research has suggested that androgynous individuals have greater success in heterosexual intimate relationships, probably due to their greater ability to understand and accept each other's differences (Coleman & Ganong, 1985). More recent research has even revealed that people with the most positive traits of androgyny are psychologically healthier and happier (Woodhill & Samuels, 2003). However the basic theory of androgyny as developed by Bem and others has undergone various changes and refinements over the years.

Numerous researchers have suggested that the psychological advantages experienced by people who score high in androgyny may be due more to the presence of masculine traits rather than a balance between male and female characteristics (Whitley, 1983). If you think about it, this makes sense. Clearly, many traditional feminine traits, such as dependent, self-critical, overly emotional are seen by society as undesirable. So it stands to reason that people who possess more masculine than feminine characteristics will receive more favorable treatment by others which, in turn creates greater levels of self-confidence and self-esteem in the individual. However, not all masculine qualities are positive and not all feminine qualities are negative. Positive and negative traits exist for both genders.

This has led researchers to propose a further refinement of the androgyny concept to include *four* dimensions: desirable femininity, undesirable femininity, desirable masculinity, and undesirable masculinity (see Ricciardelli & Williams, 1995). Qualities such as firm, confident, and strong are seen as desirable masculine traits, while bossy, noisy, and sarcastic are undesirable masculine traits. On the feminine side, patient, sensitive, and responsible are desirable traits, and nervous, timid, and weak are undesirable traits. So, depending on how someone's set of personality traits line up, a person could be seen as *positive masculine, negative masculine, positive feminine, negative feminine, positive androgynous,* or *negative androgynous.*

When gender characteristics are more carefully defined to consider both positive and negative traits, the advantages for positive androgynous individuals become even more pronounced (i.e., Woodhill & Samuels, 2003). People who possess the best of male and female gender qualitites are more likely to be more well-rounded, happier, more popular, better liked, more flexible and adaptable, and like themselves more than those who are able to draw on only one set of gender traits, or who combine negative aspects of both genders. Just imagine someone (male or female) who is patient, sensitive, responsible, firm, confident, and strong (positive androgyny) compared to a person who is nervous, timid, weak, bossy, noisy, and sarcastic (negative androgyny) and you'll get the idea behind this enhancement of Bem's theory.

Sandra Bem continues to be a leading researcher in the field of gender roles. She has applied her theories and research to the ongoing debates about gender inequality which she discusses in detail in her 1994 book, *The Lenses of Gender.* More recently, she has mapped her ideas onto the complexities of marriage, family, and child rearing, in her book, *An Unconventional Family* (1998). In this book, Bem drew from her own experiences with her former husband, Daryl Bem (the noted Cornell Psychologist) to explore how a couple might attempt to avoid gender stereotyped expectations, function as two truly equal partners, and raise their children as "gender-liberated," positive-androgynous individuals.

RECENT APPLICATIONS

One question that might have occurred to you as you were reading this chapter was whether or not the items used to measure masculinity and femininity are still valid, that is still able to discriminate between people who are masculine and feminine. In fact, you may have disagreed with some or many of them. After all, this study is several decades old and society's expectations of sex-typed behaviors are bound to change over time, right? Well, the answer to that question is a resounding "maybe!" One study from the late 1990s reexamined all of the items on the BSRI with a sample of students from a mid-sized southern U.S. university. The researchers were able to demonstrate all but two items from Bem's scale still distinguished masculinity and femininity to a statistically significantly degree (Holt & Ellis, 1998). The two exceptions—"childlike" and "loyal"—were both feminine descriptors on the BSRI, but were not rated as more desirable for women than for men in the 1998 study.

Another study, however, found strikingly conflicting results. When students from an urban university in the northeastern U.S. were asked to validate the BSRI's descriptors, results were quite different (Konrad & Harris, 2002). These researchers found that (a) women rated only *one* masculine item out of 20 ("masculine") more desirable for men than for women; (b) men rated only 13 out of the 20 masculine items more desirable for men than for women; (c) women rated only 2 of the feminine items more desirable for women than for men ("feminine" and "soft spoken"); and (d) men rated just 7 feminine items more desirable for women than for men.

How can we reconcile these discrepancies? One possibility is that people's views of gender vary significantly according to geographic region. Holt and Ellis's data were from the southern United States (and a relatively small town) while Konrad and Ellis's participants were from the northeastern United States (and a large city). Alternatively, the authors acknowledge that the participants in their study may have "guessed" the purpose of the study and slanted their answers accordingly:

> Specifically, despite the fact that respondents were asked to rate only one sex or the other, merely specifying the sex of the target could have cued respondents to the study's purpose. Given this possibility, respondents might have provided more egalitarian responses than they actually had in order to present a positive self-image. (Konrad and Ellis, 2002, p. 270)

The BSRI continues to exert a powerful influence in studies involving sexuality and gender. In fact it has formed the basis for gender assessment in hundreds of studies on a wide range of topics. For example, the BSRI has been used in studies on the effects of men's attitudes toward women after viewing sexually explicit films (Mulac, Jansma, & Linz, 2002); how people change their gender behaviors depending on the sex of the person with whom they are interacting (Pickard & Strough, 2003); cross-cultural variations in gender roles (Sugihara & Katsurada, 2000); and how gender identity affects eating disorders such as bulimia and anorexia nervosa (Klingenspor, 2002).

CONCLUSION

This study by Sandra Bem changed psychology because it altered the way psychologists, individuals, and entire societies view one of the most basic human characteristics: gender identity. Bem's research has played a pivotal role in broadening our view of what is truly meant to be male or female, masculine or feminine and, in doing so, has allowed everyone the opportunity to expand their range of activities, choices, and life goals.

Bem, S. L. (1993). *The Lenses of Gender: Transforming the Debate on Sexual Inequality.* New Haven, CT: Yale University Press.

Bem, S. L. (1998). *An Unconventional Family.* New Haven, CT: Yale University Press.

Constantinople, A. (1973). Masculinity-femininity: An exception to a famous dictum? *Psychological Bulletin, 80,* 389–407.

Holt, C., & Ellis, J. (1998). Assessing the current validity of the Bem Sex Role Inventory. *Sex Roles: A Journal of Research, 39,* 929–941.

Klingenspor, B. (2002). Gender-related self-discrepancies and bulimic eating behavior. *Sex Roles: A Journal of Research, 24,* 51–64.

Konrad, A., & Harris, C. (2002). Desirability of the Bem Sex-Role Inventory for women and men: A comparison between African Americans and European Americans. *Sex Roles: A Journal of Research, 47,* 259–271.

Mulac, A., Jansma, L., & Linz, D. (2002). Men's behavior toward women after viewing sexually-explicit films: Degradation makes a difference. *Communication Monographs, 69,* 311–328.

Pickard, J., & Strough, J. (2003). The effects of same-sex and other-sex contexts on masculinity and femininity. *Sex Roles: A Journal of Research, 48,* 421–432.

Ricciardelli, L., & Williams, R. (1995). Desirable and undesirable gender traits in three behavioral domains. *Sex Roles, 33,* 637–655

Sugihara, Y., & Katsurada, E. (2000). Gender-role personality traits in Japanese culture. *Psychology of Women Quarterly, 24,* 309–318.

Taylor, M., & Hall, J. (1982). Psychological androgyny: Theories, methods and conclusions. *Psychological Bulletin, 92,* 347–366.

Whitley, B. (1983). Sex role orientation and self esteem: A critical meta-analytic review. *Journal of Personality and Social Psychology, 44,* 773–786.

Woodhill, B., & Samuels, C. (2003). Positive and negative androgyny and their relationship with psychological health and well-being. *Sex Roles, 48,* 555–565.

RACING AGAINST YOUR HEART

Friedman, M., & Rosenman, R. H. (1959). Association of specific overt behavior pattern with blood and cardiovascular findings. *Journal of the American Medical Association, 169,* 1286–1296.

Who are you? If someone were to ask you that question, you would probably respond by describing some of your more obvious or dominant characteristics. Such characteristics, often referred to as traits, are important in making you the unique person that you are. Traits are assumed to be consistent across situations and over time. Psychologists who have supported the trait theory of personality (and not all have) have proposed that personality consists of various groups of traits that exist in all of us, but in varying amounts (such as androgyny or locus of control discussed earlier in this section). Most interesting to psychologists (and everyone, really) is the ability of a person's traits to predict their behavior in given situations and over time. In other words, trait theorists believe that insight into your unique profile of traits will allow us to predict various behavioral outcomes for you now and in the future. Therefore, it is easy to imagine how dramatically this interest would increase if certain personality characteristics were found to predict how healthy you will be or even predict your chances of dying from a heart attack.

You are probably aware of one group of personality characteristics related to health, popularly known as the *Type A personality*. To be precise, *Type A* refers to a specific *pattern* of behaviors rather than the overall personality of an individual. This behavior pattern was first reported in the late 1950s by two cardiologists, Meyer Friedman (1911–2001) and Ray Rosenman. Their theory and findings have exerted a huge influence in linking psychology and health and in our understanding of the role of personality in the development and prevention of illness.

THEORETICAL PROPOSITIONS

The story about how these doctors first realized the idea for their research demonstrates how careful observation of small, seemingly unimportant details can lead to major scientific breakthroughs. Dr. Friedman was having the furniture in his office waiting room reupholstered. The upholsterer pointed out how the material on the couches and chairs had worn out in an odd way. The front edges of the seat cushions had worn away faster than the rest. It was as if Dr. Friedman's cardiac patients were literally "sitting on the edge of their seats." This observation prompted Friedman to wonder if his patients (people with heart disease) were different in some important characteristic, compared to those of doctors in other specialties.

Through surveys of executives and physicians, Friedman and Rosenman found a common belief that people exposed over long periods of time to chronic stress stemming from excessive drive, pressure to meet deadlines, competitive situations, and economic frustration are more likely to develop heart disease. They decided to put these ideas to a scientific test.

METHOD

Using their earlier research and clinical observations, the two cardiologists developed a *model* or set of characteristics for a specific overt (observable) behavior pattern that they believed was related to increased levels of cholesterol and consequently to coronary heart disease (CHD). This pattern, labeled *pattern A*, consisted of the following characteristics (see p. 1286 of the original study): (1) an intense, sustained drive to achieve one's personal goals; (2) a profound tendency and eagerness to compete in all situations; (3) a persistent desire for recognition and advancement; (4) continuous involvement in multiple activities that are constantly subject to deadlines; (5) habitual tendency to rush to finish activities; and (6) extraordinary mental and physical alertness.

The researchers then developed a second set of overt behaviors, labeled *pattern B*. Pattern B was described as essentially the opposite of pattern A, and was characterized by a relative absence of the following: drive, ambition, sense of time urgency, desire to compete, or involvement in deadlines.

Friedman and Rosenman next needed to find subjects for their research who fit the descriptions of patterns A and B. To do this they contacted managers and supervisors of various large companies and corporations. They explained the behavior patterns and asked the managers to select from among their associates those who most closely fit the particular patterns. The groups that were finally selected consisted of various levels of executives and nonexecutives, all males. There were 83 men in each group, with an average age in group A of 45 and in group B, 43. All subjects were given several tests relating to the goals of the study.

First, the researchers designed interviews to assess the history of CHD in the subjects' parents; the subjects' own history of heart trouble; the number of hours of work, sleep, and exercise each week; and smoking, alcohol, and dietary habits. Also during these interviews, the researchers determined if a subject had a fully or only partially developed behavior pattern in his group (either A or B), based on body movements, tone of conversation, teeth clenching, gesturing, general air of impatience, and the subjects' own admission of drive, competitiveness, and time urgency. It was determined that 69 of the 83 men in group A exhibited this fully developed pattern, while 58 of the 83 subjects in group B were judged to be of the fully developed Type B.

Second, all subjects were asked to keep a diary of everything they ate or drank over one week's time. Code numbers were assigned to the subjects so that they would not feel reluctant to report alcohol consumption honestly. The diets of the subjects were then broken down and analyzed by a hospital dietitian who was not aware of the subjects' identities or to which group they belonged.

Third, research assistants took blood samples from all subjects to measure cholesterol levels and clotting time. Instances of coronary heart disease were determined through careful questioning of the subjects about past coronary health and through standard electrocardiogram readings. Rosenman and an cardiologist not involved in the study interpreted these findings independently (to avoid bias). With one exception, their interpretations agreed for all subjects.

Finally, the researchers determined the number of subjects with *arcus senilis*, through illuminated inspection of the subjects' eyes. *Arcus senilis* refers to the formation of an opaque ring around the cornea of the eye caused by the breakdown of fatty deposits in the bloodstream.

Now, let's try to boil down all of Friedman and Rosenman's data and see what they found.

RESULTS

The interviews indicated that the men chosen for each group fit the profiles developed by the researchers. Group A subjects were found to be chronically harassed by commitments, ambitions, and drives. Also, they were clearly eager to compete in all of their activities, both professional and recreational. In addition, they also admitted a strong desire to win. The men in group B were found to be strikingly different from those in group A, especially in their lack of the sense of time urgency. The men in group B appeared to be satisfied with their present positions in life and avoided pursuing multiple goals and competitive situations. They were much less concerned about advancement and typically spent more time with their families and in noncompetitive recreational activities.

Table 1 is a summary of the most relevant comparisons for the two groups on the characteristics from the tests and surveys. Table 2 summarizes the outcome measurements relating to blood levels and illnesses. As can be seen in Table 1, the two groups were similar on nearly all of the measured characteristics. Although the men in group A tended to be a little higher on most of the measurements, the only differences that were statistically significant were the number of cigarettes smoked each day and the percentage of men whose parents had a history of coronary heart disease.

However, if you take a look at the cholesterol and illness levels in Table 2, some very convincing differences emerge. First, though, considering the overall results in the table, it appears that no meaningful difference in blood clotting time was found for the two groups. The speed at which your blood coagulates relates to your potential for heart disease and other vascular illness. The slower your clotting time, the less your risk. In order to examine this statistic more closely, Friedman and Rosenman compared the clotting times for those subjects who exhibited a *fully developed* Type A pattern (6.8 minutes) with those judged as *fully developed* Type Bs (7.2 minutes). This difference in clotting time was statistically significant.

The other findings in Table 2 are unambiguous. Cholesterol levels were clearly and significantly higher for group A subjects. This difference was even greater if the subjects with the fully developed patterns were compared. The

TABLE 1 Comparison of Characteristics for Group A and Group B (Averages)

	WEIGHT	WORK HOURS/ WEEK	EXERCISE HOURS/ WEEK	NUMBER OF SMOKERS	CIGARETTES/ DAY	ALCOHOL CALORIES/ DAY	TOTAL CALORIES	FAT CALORIES	PARENTS WITH CHILDREN
Group A	176	51	10	67	23	194	2,049	944	36
Group B	172	45	7	56	15	149	2,134	978	27

(Compiled from data on pp. 1289–1293.)

TABLE 2 Comparisons of Blood and Illness for Group A and Group B

	AVERAGE CLOTTING TIME (MINUTES)	AVERAGE SERUM CHOLESTEROL	ARCUS SENILIS (PERCENT)	CORONARY HEART DISEASE (PERCENT)
Group A	6.9	253	38	28
Group B	7.0	215	11	4

(Compiled from data on p. 1293.)

incidence of arcus senilis was three times greater for group A and five times greater in the fully developed comparison groups.

Finally, the key finding of the entire study, and the one that secured its place in history, was the striking difference in the incidence of clinical coronary heart disease found in the two groups. In group A, 23 of the subjects (28%) exhibited clear evidence of CHD, compared with three men (4%) in group B. When the researchers examined these findings in terms of the fully developed subgroups, the evidence became even stronger. All 23 of the CHD cases in group A came from those men with the fully developed Type A pattern. For group B, all three of the cases were from those subjects exhibiting the incomplete Type B pattern.

DISCUSSION OF FINDINGS

The conclusion implied by the authors was that the Type A behavior pattern was a major cause of CHD and related blood abnormalities. However, if you carefully examine the data in the tables, you will notice a couple of possible alternative explanations for those results. One was that group A men reported a greater incidence of CHD in their parents. Therefore, maybe something *genetic* rather than the behavior pattern accounted for the differences found. The other rather glaring difference was the greater number of cigarettes smoked per day by group A subjects. Today we *know* that smoking contributes to CHD. So, perhaps it was not the Type A behavior pattern that produced the results, but rather the heavier smoking.

Friedman and Rosenman responded to both of those potential criticisms in their discussion of the findings. First, they found that within group A, an equal number of light smokers (10 cigarettes or fewer per day) had CHD as did heavy smokers (more than 10 cigarettes per day). Second, in group B there were 46 men who smoked heavily, yet only two exhibited CHD. These findings led the authors to suggest that cigarette smoking may have been a characteristic of the Type A behavior pattern, but not a direct cause of the CHD that was found. It is important to remember that this study was done over 30 years ago, before the link between smoking and CHD was as firmly established as it is today.

As for the possibility of parental history creating the differences, "the data also revealed that of the 30 group A men having a positive parental history, only eight (27%) had heart disease and of 53 men without a parental history, 15 (28%) had heart disease. None of the 23 group B men with a positive parental history exhibited clinical heart disease" (p. 1293). Again, more recent research that controlled carefully for this factor has demonstrated a family link in CHD. However, it is not clear whether it is a tendency toward heart disease or toward a certain behavior pattern (such as Type A) that is inherited.

SIGNIFICANCE OF THE RESEARCH AND SUBSEQUENT FINDINGS

This study by Friedman and Rosenman was of crucial importance to the history of psychological research for three basic reasons. First, this was one of the earliest systematic studies to establish clearly that specific behavior patterns characteristic of some individuals can contribute in dramatic ways to serious illness. This sent a message to physicians that to consider only the physiological aspects of illnesses may be wholly inadequate for successful prognosis, treatment, intervention, and prevention. Second, this study began a new line of scientific inquiry into the relationship between behavior and CHD that has produced scores of research articles. The concept of the *Type A personality* and its connection to CHD has been refined to the point that it may be possible to prevent heart attacks in high-risk individuals before the first one occurs.

The third long-range outcome of Friedman and Rosenman's research is that it has played an important role in the creation and growth of a relatively new branch of the behavioral sciences called health psychology. Health psychologists study all aspects of health and medicine in terms of the psychological influences that exist in health promotion and maintenance, the prevention and treatment of illness, the causes of illness, and the health care system.

One subsequent study is especially important to report here. In 1976, Rosenman and Friedman published the results of a major eight-year study of over 3,000 men who were diagnosed at the beginning of the study as being free of heart disease and who fit the Type A behavior pattern. Compared with the subjects with Type B behavior pattern, these men were twice as likely to develop CHD, suffered significantly more fatal heart attacks, and reported five times more coronary problems. What was perhaps even more important, however, was that the Type A pattern predicted who would develop CHD independently of other predictors such as age, cholesterol level, blood pressure, or smoking habits (Rosenman et al., 1976).

One question you might be asking yourself by now is, Why? What is it about this Type A pattern that causes CHD? The most widely accepted theory answers that Type As respond to stressful events by becoming nonintensely physiologically aroused than non-Type-As. This extreme arousal causes the body to produce more hormones such as adrenaline and also increases heart rate and blood pressure. Over time these exaggerated reactions to stress damage the arteries which, in turn, leads to heart disease (Matthews, 1982).

RECENT APPLICATIONS

Both Friedman and Rosenman, together and separately, have continued in their role of leading researchers in the field of personality and behavioral variables in CHD. Their research along with many others' has spawned a new research niche referred to as *cardiopsychology* which focuses on the psychological factors involved in the development, course, rehabilitation, and coping mechanisms of CHD (Jordan, Barde, & Zeiher, 2001). Their original article discussed here, as well as more recent research, is cited in a broad range of studies published in many countries. The Type A concept has been refined, strengthened, and applied to numerous research areas, some of which follow quite logically, while others might surprise you.

For example, one study examined the relationship between Type A behavior and driving (Perry & Baldwin, 2000). The results left little doubt that "Friends should not let Type A friends drive!" The study found a clear association between Type A personality and an increase in driving-related incidents: more traffic accidents, more tickets, greater impatience on the road, more displays of road rage, and overall riskier driving behaviors. You might want to respond to the Type A assessment items at the end of this reading before you get behind the wheel next time.

A study from the field of health psychology applied the Type A concept in exploring the link between stress and burnout to coronary heart disease in working women (Hallman et al., 2003). As you are probably aware, as women have entered the professional workforce in increasing numbers over the past 40 years, they have also become more prone to many stress-related health problems previously found mainly in men. This study confirms that women with CHD did indeed report higher levels of burnout and lesser coping abilities. The authors suggest that "in order to optimize the outcome of rehabilitation and prevention, we need more research on women, of women, and especially from women's point of view" (p. 433).

Finally, Friedman and Rosenman's 1959 article was incorporated into a study of the relationships between parents and their adolescent children (Forgays, 1996). In this study, Type A characteristics and family environments of over 900 subjects were analyzed. Results indicated that teenage children of Type A parents tend to be Type As themselves. Not surprising, but, once again, this brings up the nature–nurture question. Do kids inherit a genetic tendency toward Type A behavior, or do they learn it from being raised by Type A parents? Forgays addressed this in his study: "Further analyses indicated an *independent* contribution of perceived family environment to the development of TABP [Type A Behavior Pattern] in adolescents" (p. 841, emphasis added). However, it would not be particularly surprising in light of recent research trends, if adoption and twin studies reveal a significant inherited, genetic influence on the Type A and Type B personality dimension (see the study by Bouchard in the first chapter of this book for a discussion of genetic influences on personality).

CONCLUSION

Do you have a Type A personality? How would you know? As with your level of introversion or extroversion, mentioned at the beginning of this chapter, your *Type A-ness* versus your *Type B-ness* is a part of who you are. Tests have been developed to assess people's Type A or Type B behavior patterns. You can get a rough idea by examining the list of Type A characteristics below to see how many apply to you:

1. Frequently doing more than one thing at a time.
2. Urging others to hurry up and finish what they are saying.
3. Becoming very irritated when traffic is blocked or when you are waiting in line.

4. Gesturing a lot while talking.

5. Having a hard time sitting with nothing to do.

6. Speaking explosively and using obscenities often.

7. Playing to win all the time, even in games with children.

8. Becoming impatient when watching others carry out a task.

If you suspect that you are a Type A, you may want to consider a more careful evaluation by a trained physician or a psychologist. Several successful programs to intervene in the connection between Type A behavior and serious illness have been developed, largely in response to the work of Friedman and Rosenman (e.g., George et al., 1998).

Forgays, D. (1996). The relationship between Type-A parenting and adolescent perceptions of family environment. *Adolescence, 34*(124), 841–862.

George, I., Prasadaro, P., Kumaraiah, V., & Yavagal, S. (1998). Modification of Type A behavior pattern in coronary heart disease: A cognitive-behavioral intervention program. *NIMHANS Journal, 16*(1), 29–35.

Hallman, T., Thomsson, H., Burell, G., Lissers, J., & Setterlind, S. (2003). Stress, burnout, and coping: Differences between women with coronary heart disease and healthy matched women. *Journal of Health Psychology, 8,* 433–445.

Jordan, J., Barde, B., & Zeiher, A. (2001). Cardiopsychology today. *Herz, 26,* 335–344.

Matthews, K. A. (1982). Psychological perspectives on the Type A behavior pattern. *Psychological Bulletin, 91,* 293–323.

Perry, A., & Baldwin, D. (2000). Further evidence of associations of Type A personality scores and driving-related attitudes and behaviors. *Perceptual and Motor Skills, 91*(1), 147–154.

Rosenman, R. H., Brond, R., Sholtz, R., & Friedman, M. (1976). Multivariate prediction of CHD during 8.5-year follow-up in the Western Collaborative Group Study. *American Journal of Cardiology, 37,* 903–910.

THE ONE; THE MANY . . .

Triandis, H., Bontempo, R., Villareal, M., Asai, M., & Lucca, N. (1988). Individualism and collectivism: Cross-cultural perspectives on self-ingroup relationships. *Journal of Personality and Social Psychology, 54,* 323–338.

If one characteristic of human nature might be agreed upon by virtually all psychologists, it is that *behavior never occurs in a vacuum.* Even those who place the greatest emphasis on internal motivations, dispositional demands, and genetic drives make allowances for various external, environmental forces to enter the equation that ultimately leads to what you do and who you are. Over the past 30 to 40 years, the field of psychology has increasingly embraced the belief that one very powerful environmental influence on humans is the culture in which they live. In fact, researchers *rarely* find observable patterns of human behavior that are consistent and stable in all, or even most, cultures (see the discussion of Ekman's research on facial expressions elsewhere in this book for an extended analysis of cross-cultural consistency). This is especially true of behaviors relating to human interactions and relationships. Interpersonal attraction, sex, touching, personal space, friendship, family dynamics, parenting styles, childhood behavior expectations, court-ship rituals, marriage, divorce, cooperation versus competition, crime, love, and hate are all subject to profound cultural influences. So, it is safe to say, that an individual simply cannot be understood with any degree of complete-ness or precision, without careful consideration of the culture in which he or she lives.

Conceptually, that's all well and good, but in practice, culture is a tough nut. Think about it. How would you go about unraveling all of the cultural factors that have combined to influence who you have become? Most cultures are way too complex to draw many valid conclusions. For example, colon can-cer rates in Japan are a fraction of American rates. Well, Japan and the United States are diverse cultures, so what cultural factors might account for this dif-ference? Differences in amount of fish consumed? Amount of rice? Amount of alcohol? What about differences in stress levels and the pace of life? Per-haps differences in religious practices of the two countries have effects on health? Could variations in the support of family relations and friendships contribute to health and wellness? Or, as is more likely, does the answer lie in a combination of two or three or all of these factors plus many others? The point is, if you are going to include culture in a complete understanding of human nature, you will need reliable and valid ways of defining cultural dif-ferences. This is where Harry Triandis enters psychology's recent history.

Since the 1960s, and throughout his career in the psychology depart-ment at the University of Chicago, Urbana-Champaign, Triandis has worked to develop and refine fundamental attributes of cultures and their members that allow them to be differentiated and studied in meaningful ways. This ar-ticle, published in 1988, explains and demonstrates what is probably his most influential contribution to cross-cultural psychology, the delineation of *indiv-idualistic* versus *collectivist* cultures. Today, this dimension of fundamental cul-tural variation forms the basis for literally hundreds of studies each year in psychology, sociology, and several other fields. In this article, Triandis pro-poses that the degree to which a particular culture can be defined as individ-ualistic or collectivist determines the behavior and personalities of its members in complex and pervasive ways.

In very basic terms, a collectivist culture is one in which the individual's needs, desires, and outcomes, are *secondary* to the needs, desires, and goals of the larger group to which the individual belongs, called an *ingroup*. Ingroups may include a family, a tribe, a village, a professional organization, or even an entire country depending on the situation. In these cultures a great deal of the behavior of individuals is motivated by what is good for the larger group as a whole, rather than that which provides maximum personal achievement for the individual. The ingroups to which people belong tend to remain sta-ble over time, and individual commitment to the group is often extremely high even when a person's role in the group becomes difficult or unpleasant for him or her. Individuals look to their ingroup to help meet their emo-tional, psychological, and practical needs.

Individualistic cultures, on the other hand, place a higher value on the welfare and accomplishments of the individual than on the needs and goals of the larger ingroups. In these cultures, the influence of the ingroup on a member's individual behavior is likely to be small. Individuals feel less emotional attachment to the group and are willing to leave an ingroup if it becomes too demanding and join or form a new ingroup. Because of this minimal commitment of individuals to groups in individualistic cultures, it is quite common for a person to assume membership in numerous ingroups, while no single group exerts more than a little influence on his or her behavior. In this article, Triandis, and his associates from several diverse cultures, describe a multitude of distinguishing characteristics of collectivist and individualistic cultures. These are summarized in Table 1. Such distinctions are, of course, broad generalizations and there are always exceptions in any culture whether individualistic or collectivist.

In general, according to Triandis, individualistic cultures tend to be in Northern and Western Europe and in those countries that have been influenced by Northern Europeans historically. In addition, highly individualistic cultures appear to share several characteristics: possessing a frontier, large numbers of immigrants, and rapid social and geographical mobility, "all of which tend to make the control of ingroups less certain. The high levels of individualism . . . in the United States, Australia, and Canada are consistent with this point" (p. 324). Most other regions of the world, he maintains, are collectivistic cultures.

THEORETICAL PROPOSITIONS

Triandis states at the beginning of this article:

> Culture is a fuzzy construct. If we are to understand the way culture relates to social psychological phenomena, we must analyze it by determining dimensions of cultural variation. One of the most promising such dimensions is individualism—collectivism. (p. 323)

So, his assumption underlying this and many of his studies and publications is that when cultures are defined and interpreted according to the individualism-collectivism model, we can explain a large portion of the variation we see in human behavior, social interaction, and personality. In this article, Triandis was attempting to summarize the extensive potential uses of his theory (see Table 1) and to report on three scientific studies he undertook to test and demonstrate his individualism-collectivism theory.

METHOD

As mentioned earlier, this article reported on three separate studies. The first study employed only American participants and was designed to define the concept of individualism more clearly as it applies to the United States. The second study's goal was to begin to compare an individualistic culture, the United States, with cultures assumed to be fundamentally collectivist, specifically Japan and Puerto Rico. In Study 2, the focus was on comparing the rela-

TABLE 1 Differences between Collectivist and Individualistic Cultures

COLLECTIVIST CULTURES	INDIVIDUALISTIC CULTURES
• Sacrifice: emphasize personal goals over ingroup goals	• Hedonism: focus on personally satisfying goals over ingroup goals
• Interpret self as extension of group	• Interpret self as distinct from group
• Concern for group is paramount	• Self-reliance is paramount
• Rewards for achievement of group	• Rewards for personal achievement
• Less personal and cultural affluence	• Greater personal and cultural affluence
• Greater conformity to clear group norms	• Less conformity to group norms
• Greater value on love, status, and service	• Greater value on money and possessions
• Greater cooperation with in group, but less with outgroup members	• Greater cooperation with members of ingroup and members of various outgroups
• Higher value on "vertical relationships" (child-parent, employer-employee)	• Higher value on "horizontal relationships" (friend-friend, husband-wife)
• Parenting through frequent consultation and intrusion into child's private life	• Parenting through detachment, independence, and privacy for the child
• More people oriented in reaching goals	• More task oriented in reaching goals
• Prefer to hide interpersonal conflicts	• Prefer to confront interpersonal conflicts (leading to more lawsuits)
• Many individual obligations to the ingroup, but high level of social support, resources, and security in return	• Many individual rights with few obligations to the group, but less support, resources, and security from the group in return
• Fewer friends, but deeper, lifelong friendships with many obligations	• Make friends easily, but friends are less intimate acquaintances
• Few ingroups and everyone else is perceived as one large outgroup	• Many ingroups, but less perception of all others as outgroup members
• Great harmony within groups, but potential for major conflict with members of outgroups	• Ingroups tend to be larger and interpersonal conflicts more likely to occur within the ingroup
• Shame (external) used more as punishment	• Guilt (internal) used more as punishment
• Slower economic development and industrialization	• Faster economic development and industrialization
• Less social pathology (crime, suicide, child abuse, domestic violence, mental illness)	• Greater levels of all categories of social pathology
• Less illness	• Higher illness rates
• Happier marriages; less divorce	• Less happy marriages; higher divorce rates
• Less competition	• More competition
• Focus on family group rather than larger public good	• Greater concern for greater public good

Summarized from Triandis, 1988, pp. 323–335.

tionships of individuals to their ingroups in the two types of cultures. The third study was undertaken to test the hypothesis that members of collectivist cultures perceive that they receive better social support and enjoy more consistently satisfying relationships with others, whereas those in individualistic cultures report that they are often lonely. All the studies gathered data from participants through the use of questionnaires. Each study and its findings will be summarized briefly here.

Study 1

Participants in Study 1 were 300 undergraduate psychology students at the University of Chicago where Triandis is a professor of psychology. Each student was given a questionnaire consisting of 158 items structured to measure his or her tendency toward collectivist versus individualistic behaviors and beliefs. Agreement with a statement such as, "Only those who depend on themselves get ahead in life," represented an individualistic stance, while support for an item such as, "When my colleagues tell me personal things about themselves, we are drawn closer together," was evidence for a more collectivist perspective. Also included in the questionnaire were five scenarios that placed subjects in hypothetical social situations and asked them to predict their behavior. The example provided in the article was for the subjects to imagine they wanted to go on a long trip that various ingroups opposed. The participants were asked how likely they were to consider the opinions and wishes of parents, spouses, close relations, close friends, acquaintances, neighbors, and coworkers in deciding whether to take the trip.

When the response data were analyzed, nearly 50% of the variation in the participants' responses could be explained by three factors: "self-reliance," "competition," and "distance from ingroups." Only 14% of the variation was explained by the factor called "concern for ingroup." More specifically, Triandis summed up the results of Study 1 as follows:

> These data suggest that U.S. [individualism] is a multifaceted concept. The ingredients include more concern for one's own goals than the ingroup goals, less attention to the views of ingroups, self-reliance combined with competition, detachment from ingroups, deciding on one's own rather than asking for the views of others, and less general concern for the ingroup. (p. 331)

He also suggested that the items comprising the questionnaire and the scenarios are effective ways to measure the degree of individualism in one individualistic culture, the United States, but that this scale may or may not produce equally valid results in other cultural settings.

Study 2

The question asked in this study was, "Do people in collectivist cultures indicate more willingness to subordinate their personal needs to the needs of the group?" The participants were 91 University of Chicago students, 97 Puerto Rican and 150 Japanese university students, and 106 older Japanese individuals. A 144-item questionnaire designed to measure collectivist characteristics was translated into Spanish and Japanese and completed by all subjects. Items from the scale had been shown in previous research to tap into three collectivist-related tendencies: "concern for ingroup," "closeness of self to ingroup," and "subordination of own goals to ingroup goals."

In this study, the findings were a fascinating mixed bag with some results supporting the individualistic-collectivist theory and others seeming to refute it. For example, the Japanese students were significantly more concerned with the views of coworkers and friends than were the Illinois students, but this difference was not observed for the Puerto Rican students. Also, the Japanese subjects expressed feeling personally honored when their ingroups are honored, but they paid attention to the views of and sacrifice their personal goals to only *some* ingroups in their lives, but not others. And, while conformity is a common attribute of collectivist cultures, very little conformity was found for the Japanese participants—less, in fact, than the American students. One finding suggested that as collectivist cultures become more affluent and westernized, they may undergo a shift to greater individualism. As evidence of this, the older Japanese participants perceived themselves to be more similar to their ingroups than did the Japanese university students.

So, you might be asking, how do the findings of the second study figure into Triandis's theory? Triandis interpreted them as a warning that conclusions about collectivist and individualistic cultures should not be overly sweeping and must be carefully applied to selective, specific behaviors, situations, and cultures. He stated this idea as follows:

> The data of this study tell us to restrict and sharpen our definition of collectivism . . . that we must consider each domain of social behavior separately, and collectivism, defined as subordination to the ingroup's norms, needs, views, and emotional closeness to ingroups is very specific to ingroup and to domain. . . . Collectivism takes different forms . . . that are specific to each culture. (p. 334)

Study 3

The third study reported attempted to do exactly what Triandis suggested in the above quote: restrict and sharpen the research focus. This study extended previous findings that collectivist societies provide high levels of social support to their members, while those in individualistic cultures tend to experience greater loneliness. Here a 72-item collectivist-individualist questionnaire was completed by 100 subjects, equally divided by sex, at the University of Chicago and at the University of Puerto Rico. Participants also filled out questionnaires measuring their perceived degree of social support and perceived amount of loneliness.

The results of this study clearly indicated that collectivism correlated positively with social support, meaning, as the degree of collectivism increased, the level of social support also increased. Moreover, collectivism was negatively associated with loneliness, implying that as the effect of collectivism increased, participants' perceived level of loneliness diminished. Finally, as further evidence for Triandis's model, the most important factor in this study for the American students (accounting for the most variance) was "self-reliance with competition," while the most influential factor for the Puerto Ricans was "affiliation" (interacting with others). These results are exactly what you would expect from the individualistic-collectivist theory.

DISCUSSION

Overall, Triandis explained, the studies described in this article supported, but also modified his definitions of collectivism and individualism. Looking back at the characteristics of each type of culture in Table 1, the picture that emerges is one of opposition. That is, individualistic and collectivist cultures appear to be nearly exact opposites of each other. This article, however, seems to demonstrate that these cultural descriptions fall at two ends of a continuum, and a particular society will be best described as falling somewhere in between the two but usually clearly closer to one end than the other. In addition, within any single culture will be found specific individuals, groups, subcultures, and situations that may violate that culture's overall placement on the continuum by fitting better toward the opposite end. A graphical, hypothetical representation of this interpretation is shown in Figure 1. "In short," Triandis states, "The empirical studies suggest that we need to consider individualism and collectivism as multidimensional constructs . . . [each of which] depends very much on which ingroup is present, in what context, and what behavior was studied" (p. 336).

SIGNIFICANCE OF THE FINDINGS AND RELATED RESEARCH

Over a relatively short period of historical time, Triandis's work has found its way into the fundamental core of how psychologists view human behavior. You would be hard pressed, for example, to open any recent text in most sub-fields of psychology—introductory psychology, social psychology, developmental psychology, personality psychology, human sexuality, abnormal psychology, cognitive psychology, to name a few—without finding multiple references to this and many other of his individualism-collectivism studies. Arguably, the individualistic-collectivistic cultural dimension, as articulated, clarified, and refined by Triandis, is the most reliable, valid, and influential factor seen in current studies on the role culture plays in determining the personalities and social behaviors of humans. Moreover, the range of research areas to which this dimension has been applied is remarkably broad. Here are just two examples.

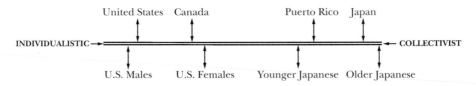

FIGURE 1 Collectivist–individualistic cultural continuum (culture and subculture placements approximate).

In the article that is the subject of this discussion, Triandis offers evidence that the psychosocial concepts of collectivism and individualism may play a significant part in the physical health of the members of a given culture. A case in point relates to coronary heart disease. In general, heart attack rates tend to be lower in collectivist societies than in individualistic ones. Triandis suggests that unpleasant and stressful life events often related to heart disease are more common in individualistic cultures where pressures are intense on solitary individuals to compete and achieve on their own. Along with these negative life events, individualistic social structures inherently offer less social cohesion and social support which have been clearly demonstrated to reduce the effects of stress on health. Of course, there are many factors that might account for cultural differences in heart attack rates or any other disease as discussed at the beginning of this reading. However, numerous studies have shown that members of collectivist cultures who move to countries that are individualistic become increasingly prone to various illnesses including heart disease.

Perhaps, even more convincing, are studies of two different subgroups within the same culture. As Triandis points out (p. 327), one study of 3,000 Japanese Americans compared those who had acculturated, that is, had adapted their lifestyle and attitudes to American norms, to those who still maintained a traditional Japanese way of life *within* the United States. Heart attack rates among the acculturated subjects were *five times greater* than among the nonacculturated participants even when cholesterol levels, exercise, cigarette smoking, and weight were statistically equalized for the two groups.

Of course, you would expect that the collectivism-individualism dimension would affect how children are raised in a particular culture and, indeed, it does. Parents in collectivist societies place a great deal of emphasis on developing the child's "collective self" characterized by conformity to group norms, obedience to those in authority within the group, and reliability or consistency of behavior over time and across situations. Children are rewarded in both overt and subtle ways for behavior patterns and attitudes that support and correspond to the goals of the ingroup (Triandis, 1989). In this context, refusing to do something that the group expects of you, just because you don't enjoy doing it, is unacceptable and rarely seen. Yet in highly individualistic cultures, such as the United States, such refusal is a very common response and is often valued and respected! That is because parenting practices in individualistic cultures emphasize development of the child's "private self." This focus means that children are rewarded for behaviors and attitudes leading to self-reliance, independence, self-knowledge, and reaching their maximum potential as an individual. Another way to look at this distinction is that in individualistic cultures rebellion (within certain socially acceptable limits) and an independent streak are seen as personality *assets*, whereas in collectivist societies they are seen as *liabilities*. The messages from the culture to the children, via the parents, about these assets or liabilities are loud and clear and exert a potent influence upon the kids' development into adulthood.

RECENT APPLICATIONS

Between 2000 and mid-2003, this single article by Triandis was cited in over 140 studies from a wide variety of scientific fields. One article applied Triandis's ideas to a study about the attitudes of college football fans in two cultures (Snibbe et al., 2003). Students at important football games in the United States (Rose Bowl) and in Japan (Flash Bowl) were asked to rate their own and their opponent's universities and students before and after the big game. In both games, the university with the better academic reputation lost the game. However, the reactions of the students in the two cultures were markedly different: "American students from both universities evaluated their in-groups more positively than out-groups on all measures before and after the game. In contrast, Japanese students' ratings offered *no evidence* of in-group bias. . . . Instead, Japanese students' ratings reflected each universities' statuses in the larger society and the students' status in the immediate situation" (p. 581).

Another study employed Triandis's model to examine loneliness across cultures (Rokach et al., 2002). Over 1,000 participants from North America and Spain completed questionnaires about the various causes of their loneliness, including personal inadequacies, developmental difficulties, unfulfilling intimate relationships, relocations and separations, and feeling marginalized by society. "Results indicated that cultural background indeed affects the causes of loneliness. North Americans scored higher on *all five factors*" (p. 70, emphasis added).

Finally, one study highlighted a very important aspect of Triandis's work. When collectivist and individualistic cultures are studied and compared, this is not, by any means, limited to comparisons *between* countries. Many countries contain *within* their borders pockets of widely varying levels of collectivism and individualism. Nowhere on earth is this more true than in the United States. An engaging study by Vandello and Cohen (1999) charted the United States on the basis of Triandis's model. Before you read this, stop and think for a moment about which states you would predict to find the strongest collectivist and individualistic tendencies. The researchers reported that states in the Deep South were most collectivist and Plains and Rocky Mountain states were highest on individualism. However, even within these divergent areas, smaller, subcultural groups of individualistic and collectivist Americans may be found. So, in a sense, Triandis has provided a new lens through which to view a vast country whose richness of diversity may be described less as a "melting pot," and more as an intricate patch-work quilt.

Rokach, A., Orzeck, T., Moya, M., & Exposido, F. (2002). Causes of loneliness in North America and Spain. *European Psychologist, 7,* 70–79.

Snibbe, A., Kitayama, S., Markus, H., & Suzuki, T. (2003). They saw a game: A Japanese and American (football) field study. *Journal of Cross-Cultural Psychology, 34,* 581–595.

Triandis, H. (1989). The self and social behavior in differing cultural contexts. *Psychological Review, 96*(3), 506–520.

Vandello, J., & Cohen, D. (1999). Patterns of individualism and collectivism across the United States. *Journal of Personality and Social Psychology, 77*(2), 279–292.

8 PSYCHOPATHOLOGY

Most people who have never studied psychology, have the impression that the field is primarily concerned with analyzing and treating mental illnesses (the branch of psychology that does study mental illness is called *abnormal psychology*). However, as you may have noticed, nearly all of the research discussed so far in this book has focused on *normal* behavior. Overall, psychologists are more interested in normal behavior than in abnormal behavior because the vast majority of human behavior is normal. Consequently, we would not know very much about human nature if we only studied the small percentage of it that is abnormal. Nevertheless, mental illness is to many people one of the most fascinating areas of study in all of psychology. A variety of studies with crucial historical importance are included here.

First, is a study that has kept the mental health profession talking for over 30 years. In this study, healthy people posing as mental patients entered psychiatric hospitals to see if the doctors and staff could distinguish them from those who were actually mentally ill. Second, no book about the history of psychological research would be complete without reference to Sigmund Freud. Therefore, a discussion of his theory of the *ego defense mechanisms*, through the writings of his daughter, Anna Freud, is included, because it relates to his theories of psychoanalysis. The third study is an experiment with dogs that demonstrated a phenomenon called *learned helplessness*. This condition relates to psychopathology in that it led to a widely held theory explaining depression in humans. And finally, an intriguing and well-known experiment is presented involving overcrowded rats and their resulting deviant behavior, which may have important implications for humans.

WHO'S CRAZY HERE, ANYWAY?
Rosenhan, D. L. (1973). On being sane in insane places. *Science, 179,* 250–258.

The question of how to distinguish between normal and abnormal behavior is fundamental in psychology. The definition of abnormality plays a key role in determining whether someone is diagnosed as mentally ill, and the diagnosis largely determines the treatment received by a patient. The line that divides normal from abnormal is not at all clear. Rather, all behavior can be seen to lie on a continuum with normal, or what might be called *effective psychological functioning*, at one end, and abnormal, indicating mental illness, at the other:

Normal   ⟵——————————————⟶   *Abnormal*

(Effective   (Mental

functioning)   illness)

It is up to mental health professionals to determine where on this continuum a particular person's behavior lies. To make this determination, clinical psychologists, psychiatrists, and other psychotherapists may use one or more of the following criteria.

- *Context of the Behavior.* This is a subjective judgment, but you know that some behaviors are clearly bizarre in a given situation. For example, there is nothing strange about standing outside watering your lawn, unless you are doing it in your pajamas during a pouring rainstorm! So, a judgment about abnormality must carefully consider the context in which a behavior or behavior pattern occurs.

- *Persistence of Behavior.* We all have our "crazy" moments. A person may exhibit abnormal behavior on occasion without necessarily demonstrating the presence of mental illness. For instance, you might have just received some great news and, as you are walking along a busy downtown sidewalk, you dance for half a block or so. This behavior, while somewhat abnormal, would not indicate mental illness, unless you began to dance down that sidewalk on, say, a weekly or daily basis. This criterion for mental illness requires that a bizarre, antisocial, or disruptive behavior pattern persist over time.

- *Social Deviance.* When a person's behavior radically violates expectations and norms, it may meet the criteria for social deviance. When deviant behavior is extreme and persistent, such as auditory or visual hallucinations, it is evidence of mental illness.

- *Subjective Distress.* Frequently, as intelligent beings, we are aware of our own psychological difficulties and the suffering they are causing us. When a person is so afraid of enclosed spaces that he or she cannot ride in an elevator, or when someone finds it impossible to form meaningful relationships with others, they often do not need a professional to tell them they are in psychological pain. This subjective distress is an important sign mental health professionals use in making psychological diagnoses.

- *Psychological Handicap.* When a person has great difficulty being satisfied with life due to psychological problems, this is considered to be a psychological handicap. A person who fears success, for example, and therefore sabotages each new endeavor in life, is suffering from a psychological handicap.

- *Effect on Functioning.* The extent to which the behaviors in question interfere with a person's ability to live the life that he or she desires, and that society will accept, may be the most important factor in diagnosing psychological problems. A behavior could be bizarre and persistent, but if it does not impair your ability to function in life, pathology may not be indicated. For example, suppose you have an uncontrollable need to stand on your bed and sing The National Anthem every night before going to sleep. This is certainly bizarre and persistent, but unless you are waking up the neighbors, disturbing other household members, or feeling terrible about it, your behavior may have little effect on your general functioning and, therefore, may not be a clinical problem.

These symptoms and characteristics of mental illness all involve *judgments* on the part of psychologists, psychiatrists, and other mental health professionals. Therefore, the foregoing guidelines notwithstanding, two questions remain: Are mental health professionals truly able to distinguish between the mentally ill and the mentally healthy? And what are the consequences of mistakes? These are the questions addressed by David Rosenhan in his provocative study of mental hospitals.

THEORETICAL PROPOSITIONS

Rosenhan questioned whether the characteristics that lead to psychological diagnoses reside in the patients themselves or in the situations and contexts in which the observers (those who do the diagnosing) find the patients. He reasoned that if the established criteria and the training mental health professionals have received for diagnosing mental illness are adequate, then those professionals should be able to distinguish between the insane and the sane. (Technically, the words *sane* and *insane* are legal terms and are not usually used in psychological contexts. They are used here because Rosenhan incorporated them into his research.) Rosenhan proposed that one way to test mental health professionals' ability to correctly categorize would be to have normal people seek admittance to psychiatric facilities to see if they would be discovered to be, in reality, psychologically healthy. If these "pseudopatients" behaved in the hospital as they would on the outside, and if they were not discovered to be normal, this would be evidence that diagnoses of the mentally ill are tied more to the situation than to the patient.

METHOD

Rosenhan recruited eight subjects (including himself) to serve as pseudopatients. The eight participants (three women and five men) consisted of one graduate student, three psychologists, one pediatrician, one psychiatrist, one painter, and one homemaker. The subjects' mission was to present themselves for admission to 12 psychological hospitals, in five states on both the east and west coasts of the United States.

All the pseudopatients followed the same instructions. They called the hospital and made an appointment. Upon arrival at the hospital they complained of hearing voices that said "empty," "hollow," and "thud." Other than this single symptom, all subjects acted completely normally and gave totally truthful information to the interviewer (except that they changed their names and occupations). All the subjects were admitted to the various hospitals, and all but one was admitted with a diagnosis of *schizophrenia.*

Once inside the hospital, the pseudopatients displayed no symptoms whatsoever and behaved normally. The participants had no idea when they would be allowed to leave the hospital. It was up to them to gain their release by convincing the hospital staff that they were healthy enough to be discharged. All the subjects took notes of their experiences. At first, they tried to conceal this activity, but soon it was clear to all that this secrecy was unnecessary, because *note-taking behavior* was seen as just another symptom of their illness. They all desired to be released as soon as possible, so they behaved as model patients, cooperating with the staff and accepting all medications (which were not swallowed, but flushed down the toilet).

RESULTS

The length of hospital stay for the pseudopatients ranged from 7 days to 52 days, with an average stay of 19 days. The key finding in this study was that not one of the pseudopatients was detected by anyone on the hospital staff. When they were released, their mental health status was recorded in their files as *schizophrenia in remission.* There were other interesting findings and observations.

While the hospital's staff of doctors, nurses, and attendants failed to detect the subjects, the other patients could not be so easily fooled. In three of the pseudopatients' hospitalizations, 35 out of 118 real patients voiced suspicions that the subjects were not actually mentally ill. They would make comments such as, "You're not crazy! You're a journalist or a reporter. You're checking up on the hospital!"

Contacts between the patients (whether subjects or not) and the staff were minimal and often bizarre. One of the tests made by the pseudopatients in the study was to approach various staff members and attempt to make verbal contact by asking common, normal questions (e.g., When will I be allowed grounds privileges? or When am I likely to be discharged?). Table 1 summarizes the responses they received.

TABLE 1 Responses by Doctors and Staff to Questions Posed by Pseudopatients

RESPONSE	PSYCHIATRISTS (%)	NURSES AND ATTENDANTS (%)
Moves on, head averted	71	88
Makes eye contact	23	10
Pauses and chats	2	2
Stops and talks	4	0.5

(From p. 255.)

When the pseudopatient received a response, it frequently took the following form:

PSEUDOPATIENT: "Pardon me, Dr. _____. Could you tell me when I am eligible for grounds privileges?"

PSYCHIATRIST: "Good morning, Dave. How are you today?"

The doctor then moved on without waiting for a response.

In contrast to the severe lack of personal contact in the hospitals studied, there was no shortage of medication. The eight pseudopatients in this study were given a total of 2,100 pills that, as mentioned, were not swallowed. The subjects noted that many of the real patients also secretly disposed of their pills down the toilet.

Another anecdote from one of the pseudopatients tells of a nurse who unbuttoned her uniform to adjust her bra in front of a dayroom full of male patients. It was not her intention to be provocative, according to the subject's report, but she simply did not consider the patients to be real people.

DISCUSSION

Rosenhan's study demonstrated that normal people often cannot be distinguished from the mentally ill in a hospital setting. According to Rosenhan, this is because of the overwhelming influence of the psychiatric-hospital setting on the staff's judgment of the individual's behavior. Once patients are admitted to such a facility, there is a strong tendency for them to be viewed in ways that ignore their individuality. The attitude created is: "If they are here, they must be crazy." More important, is what Rosenhan refers to as the *stickiness of the diagnostic label.* That is, when a patient is labeled as *schizophrenic,* it becomes his or her central characteristic or personality trait. From the moment the label is given and the staff knows it, they perceive all of the patient's behavior as stemming from the diagnosis, thus, the lack of concern or suspicion over the pseudopatients' note taking, which was perceived as just another behavioral manifestation of the psychological label.

The hospital staff tended to ignore the situational pressures on patients and saw only the behavior relevant to the pathology assigned to the patients. This was demonstrated by the following observation of one of the subjects:

> One psychiatrist pointed to a group of patients who were sitting outside the cafeteria entrance half an hour before lunchtime. To a group of young resident psychiatrists he indicated that such behavior was characteristic of the "oral-acquisitive" nature of the syndrome. It seemed not to occur to him that there were simply very few things to do in a psychiatric hospital besides eating. (p. 253)

Beyond this, the sticky diagnostic label even colored how a pseudopatient's *history* would be interpreted. Remember, all the subjects gave honest accounts of their pasts and families. Here is an example from Rosenhan's research of a pseudopatient's stated history, followed by its interpretation by the staff doctor in a report after the subject was discharged. The subject's true history was as follows:

The pseudopatient had a close relationship with his mother, but was rather remote with his father during his early childhood. During adolescence and beyond, however, his father became a very close friend while his relationship with his mother cooled. His present relationship with his wife was characteristically close and warm. Apart from occasional angry exchanges, friction was minimal. The children had rarely been spanked. (p. 253)

The director's interpretation of this rather normal and innocuous history was as follows:

This white 39-year-old male manifests a long history of considerable ambivalence in close relationships which begins in early childhood. A warm relationship with his mother cools during his adolescence. A distant relationship with his father is described as becoming very intense. Affective stability is absent. His attempts to control emotionality with his wife and children are punctuated by angry outbursts and, in the case of the children, spankings. And while he says he has several good friends, one senses considerable ambivalence embedded in those relationships also. (p. 253)

There was no indication that any of the staff's distortions were done intentionally. They believed in the diagnosis (in this case, schizophrenia) and interpreted a patient's history and behavior in ways that were consistent with that diagnosis.

SIGNIFICANCE OF FINDINGS

Rosenhan's study shook the mental health profession. The results pointed out two crucial factors. First, it appeared that the *sane* could not be distinguished from the *insane* in mental hospital settings. As Rosenhan himself stated in his article, "The hospital itself imposes a special environment in which the meaning of behavior can be easily misunderstood. The consequences to patients hospitalized in such an environment . . . seem undoubtedly countertherapeutic" (p. 257). Second, Rosenhan demonstrated the danger of diagnostic labels. Once a person is labeled as having a certain psychological *condition* (such as schizophrenia, manic-depressive illness, etc.), that label eclipses any and all of his or her other characteristics. All behavior and personality characteristics are seen as stemming from the labeled disorder. The worst part of this sort of treatment is that it can become self-confirming. That is, if a person is treated in a certain way consistently over time, he or she may begin to behave that way.

Out of Rosenhan's work grew greater care in diagnostic procedures and increased awareness of the dangers of applying labels to patients. Additionally, the problems addressed by his study began to decline with the decrease in patients confined to mental hospitals. This decrease in hospital populations was brought about by the discovery and widespread use of antipsychotic medications, which have the power to reduce symptoms in most patients enough for them to live outside a hospital and in many cases lead relatively normal lives. Concurrent to this was the growth of community mental health facilities, crisis intervention centers, and behavior therapies that focus on specific problems and behaviors and tend to avoid labels altogether.

This does not imply by any means that the mental health profession has eliminated labels. However, largely because of Rosenhan's research and other research in the same vein, psychiatric labels are now used carefully and treated with the respect their power demands.

QUESTIONS AND CRITICISMS

One research and teaching hospital whose staff had heard about Rosenhan's findings before they were published doubted that such mistakes in diagnosis could be made in their hospital. To test this, Rosenhan informed the hospital staff that during the next three months one or more pseudopatients would try to be admitted to their psychiatric unit. Each staff member was asked to rate each presenting patient on a 10-point scale as to the likelihood that he or she was a pseudopatient. At the end of three months, 193 patients had been admitted. Of those, 41 were considered with high confidence to be pseudopatients by at least one staff member. Twenty-three were suspected by at least one psychiatrist, and 19 were identified as pseudopatients by one psychiatrist and one other staff member. Rosenhan (the tricky devil) had not sent any pseudopatients to the hospital during the three-month period! "The experiment is instructive," states Rosenhan. "It indicates that the tendency to designate sane people as insane can be reversed when the stakes (in this case prestige and diagnostic ability) are high. But one thing is certain: Any diagnostic process that lends itself so readily to massive errors of this sort cannot be a very reliable one" (p. 252).

Rosenhan replicated this study several times in 12 hospitals between 1973 and 1975. Each time he found similar results (see Greenberg, 1981, and Rosenhan, 1975). However, other researchers dispute the conclusions Rosenhan drew from this research. Spitzer (1976) has argued that while the methods used by Rosenhan appeared to invalidate psychological diagnostic systems, in reality they did not. For example, it should not be difficult for pseudopatients to lie their way into a mental hospital, since many such admissions are based on verbal reports (and who would ever suspect someone of using trickery to get *into* such a place?). The reasoning here is that you could walk into a medical emergency room complaining of severe intestinal pain and you might get yourself admitted to the hospital with a diagnosis of gastritis, appendicitis, or an ulcer. Even though the doctor was tricked, the diagnostic methods were not invalid. Additionally, Spitzer has pointed out that although the pseudopatients behaved normally once admitted to the hospital, such symptom variation in psychiatric disorders is common and does not mean that the staff was incompetent in failing to detect the ruse.

The controversy over the validity of psychological diagnosis that began with Rosenhan's 1973 article continues. Regardless of the eventual outcome, there is little question that Rosenhan's study remains one of the most influential in the history of psychology.

RECENT APPLICATIONS

As an indication of this continuing controversy, we can consider two of many studies that have used Rosenhan's research in challenging the validity of diagnoses made by mental health professionals. One of these is by Thomas Szasz, a psychiatrist who has been a well-known critic of the concept of mental illness since the early 1970s. His contention has been that mental illnesses are not diseases and cannot be properly understood as such, but rather must be seen as *problems in living* that have social and environmental causes. In one article, he makes the case that the *crazy talk* exhibited by some who have been diagnosed with a mental illness "is not a valid reason for concluding that a person is insane" simply because one person (the mental health professional) cannot comprehend the other (the patient) (Szasz, 1993, p. 61).

Another study building on Rosenhan's 1973 article examined how, in some real life situations, people may purposely fabricate symptoms of mental illness (Broughton & Chesterman, 2001). The case study discussed in the article involved a man accused of sexually assaulting a teenage boy. When the perpetrator was evaluated for psychiatric problems, he displayed various psychotic behaviors. Upon further examination, clinicians found that he had faked all of his symptoms. The authors point out that traditionally, mental health professionals have assumed the accuracy of patient statements in diagnosing psychological disorders (as they did with Rosenhan's pseudopatients). However, they suggest that inventing symptoms "is a fundamental issue for all psychiatrists, especially [when] . . . complicated by external socio-legal issues which could possibly serve as motivation for the fabrication of psychopathology" (p. 407). In other words, we have to be careful that criminals are not able to fake mental illness as a "get-out-of-jail free card."

How do the people themselves feel who have been given a psychiatric diagnostic label? In a survey of more than 1300 mental health consumers, Wahl, (1999) asked about their experiences of being discriminated against and stigmatized. The majority of respondents reported feeling the effects of the stigma surrounding mental illness from various sources, including community members in general, family, church members, coworkers, and even mental health professionals. In addition, the author reported, "The majority of respondents tended to try to conceal their disorders and worried a great deal that others would find out about their psychiatric status and treat them unfavorably. They reported discouragement, hurt, anger, and lowered self-esteem as a result of their experiences and urged public education as a means for reducing stigma" (p. 467).

Perhaps psychologists are making some progress on the public education front about mental illness. In a study by Boisvert and Faust (1999), subjects were presented with scenarios about an employee who behaved in a violent manner toward his boss. The scenarios varied in the amount of stress the employee was experiencing, and in some of the scenarios the employee was described as having been previously diagnosed with schizophrenia. The researchers predicted that subjects would be more likely to attribute the violence to the employee's personality when the schizophrenia label was attached, but would lean more toward blaming the environmental stress when there was no evidence of mental illness. Guess what. They found just the opposite. As stress increased, the subjects blamed the personality of the employee *less,* regardless of the presence of the schizophrenia label. Furthermore, the researchers obtained the same results whether the participants were real-life, practicing mental health clinicians or college students.

So, it is hoped we can take some comfort in this evidence that tolerance and understanding of mental illness is increasing. The reality is that, so far, diagnosing mental illnesses continues to be as much art as it is science. Chances are we will never do away with labels; they appear to be a necessary part of effective treatment of psychological disorders, just as names of diseases are part of diagnosing and treating physical illnesses. So, if we are stuck with labels (no pun intended), we must continue to work to take the stigma, embarrassment, and shame out of them.

Boisvert, C., & Faust, D. (1999). Effects of the label "schizophrenia" on causal attributions of violence. *Schizophrenia Bulletin, 25,* 479–491.

Broughton, N., & Chesterman, P. (2001). Malingered psychosis. *Journal of Forensic Psychiatry, 12,* 407–422.

Greenberg, J. (1981, June/July). An interview with David Rosenhan. *APA Monitor,* 4–5.

Rosenhan, D. L. (1975). The contextual nature of psychiatric diagnosis. *Journal of Abnormal Psychology, 84,* 442–452.

Spitzer, R. L. (1976). More on pseudoscience in science and the case of the psychiatric diagnosis: A critique of D. L. Rosenhan's "On being sane in insane places" and "The contextual nature of psychiatric diagnosis." *Archives of General Psychiatry, 33,* 459–470.

Szasz, T. (1993). Crazy talk: Thought disorder or psychiatric arrogance? *British Journal of Medical Psychology, 66,* 61–67.

Wahl, O. (1999). Mental health consumers' experience of stigma. *Schizophrenia Bulletin, 25*(3), 467–478.

YOU'RE GETTING DEFENSIVE AGAIN!
Freud, A. (1946). *The ego and the mechanisms of defense.* New York: International Universities Press.

In a book about the history of research that changed psychology, one imposing figure would be extremely difficult to omit: Sigmund Freud (1856–1939). It is very unlikely that psychology would exist today as it does, in spite of its varied and complex forms, without Freud's contributions. He was largely responsible for elevating our interpretations of human behavior (especially abnormal behavior) from superstitions of demonic possession and evil spirits to the rational ideas of reason and science. Without an examination of his work, this book would be incomplete. Now, you may be asking yourself, if Sigmund Freud is so important, why does this discussion focus on a book written by his daughter, Anna Freud (1895–1982)? The answer to that question requires a bit of explanation.

Although Sigmund Freud was integral to psychology's history and, therefore, is a necessary part of this book, the task of including his research here along with all the other researchers was a difficult one. The reason for this difficulty was that Freud did not reach his discoveries through a clearly defined scientific methodology. It was not possible to choose a single study or series of experiments to represent his work, as has been done for other researchers in this book. Freud's theories grew out of careful observations of his patients over decades of clinical analysis. Consequently, his writings were abundant, to say the least. The English translation of his collected writings, *The Standard Edition of the Complete Psychological Works of Sigmund Freud* (London: Hogarth Press, 1953 to 1974), totals 24 volumes! Obviously, only a very small piece of his work could be discussed here.

In choosing what to include here, consideration was given to the portions of Freud's theories that have stood the test of time relatively unscathed. Over the past century, a great deal of criticism has been focused on Freud's ideas and, in the last 40 years especially, his work has been drawn into serious question from a scientific perspective. Critics have argued that many of his theories either cannot be tested scientifically; or if they are tested, they prove to be generally unreliable. Therefore, while few would doubt the historical importance of Freud, many of his theories about the structure of personality, the development of personality through the psychosexual stages, and the sources of people's psychological problems have been rejected by most psychologists today. However, some aspects of his work have received more positive reviews through the years and now enjoy relatively wide acceptance. One of these is his concept of the *defense mechanisms*. These are weapons that your ego uses to protect you from your own self-created anxiety. This element from his work has been selected to represent Freud in this book.

Sigmund Freud's discovery of defense mechanisms occurred gradually over 30 or more years as his experiences in dealing with psychological problems grew. A cohesive, self-contained discussion of this topic does not appear anywhere in Sigmund Freud's many volumes. In fact, he passed that job on to his daughter, who was an important psychoanalyst in her own right, specializing in children. Freud acknowledged this fact in 1936 just before Anna's book, *The Ego and the Mechanisms of Defense,* was originally published in German: "There are an extremely large number of methods (or mechanisms, as we say) used by the ego in the discharge of its defensive functions. My daughter, the child analyst, is writing a book about them" (S. Freud, 1936). Since it was Anna Freud who synthesized her father's theories regarding the defense mechanisms into a single work, her book has been chosen for our discussion of the work of Sigmund Freud.

THEORETICAL PROPOSITIONS

In order to examine Freud's notion of defense mechanisms, it is necessary to explain briefly his theory of the structure of personality. Freud proposed that personality consists of three components: the id, the ego, and the superego.

The id consists of basic biological urges such as hunger, thirst, and sexual impulses. Whenever these needs are not met, the id generates strong motivation for the person to find a way to satisfy them, and do so immediately! The id operates on what Freud called the *pleasure principle* and demands instantaneous gratification of all desires, regardless of reason, logic, safety, or morality. Freud believed that there are dark, antisocial, and dangerous instinctual urges (especially sexual ones) present in everyone's id that constantly seek expression. You are not usually aware of these because the id operates on the unconscious level. However, if you were lacking the other parts of your personality and only had an id, your behavior would be amoral, shockingly deviant, and even fatal to you and others.

The reason you do not behave in these dangerous and deviant ways is that your ego and superego develop to place limits and controls on the impulses of your id. According to Freud, the ego operates on the *reality principle,* which means it is alert to the real world and the consequences of behavior. The ego is conscious and its job is to satisfy your id's urges, but to do so using means that are rational, socially acceptable, and reasonably safe.

However, the ego also has limits placed upon it by the superego. Your superego, in essence, requires that the solutions the ego finds to the id's needs are moral and ethical, according to your own internalized set of rules about what is good or bad. These rules were instilled in you by your parents, and if you behave in ways that violate them your superego will punish you with its own very effective weapon: guilt. Do you recognize this? It is commonly referred to as your conscience. Freud believed that your superego operates on both conscious and unconscious levels.

So, Freud's conceptualization of your personality was a dynamic one in which the ego is constantly trying to balance the needs and urges of the id with the moral requirements of the superego in determining your behavior. Here is an example of how this might work. Imagine a 16-year-old boy strolling down the street in a small town. It is 10 P.M. and he is on his way home. Suddenly he realizes he is hungry. He passes a grocery store and sees food on the other side of the large windows, but the store is closed. His id might say, "Look! Food! Jump through the glass and get some!" (Remember, the id wants immediate satisfaction, regardless of the consequences.) He would probably not be aware of the id's suggestion because it would be at a level below his consciousness. The ego would "hear" it, though, and since its job is to protect the boy from danger, it might respond, "No, that would be dangerous. Let's go around back, break into the store, and steal some food!" At this, the superego would remark indignantly, "You can't do that! It's immoral, and if you do it I will punish you!" So, his ego reconsiders and makes a new suggestion that is acceptable to both the id and the superego: "You know, there's an all-night fast-food place four blocks over. Let's go there and buy some food." This solution, assuming that the boy is psychologically healthy, is the one that makes it to his consciousness and is reflected in his behavior.

According to Freud, the reason most people do not behave in antisocial or deviant ways is because of this system of checks and balances among the three parts of the personality. But what would happen if the system malfunctioned—if this balance were lost? One way this could happen would be if the demands of the id became too strong to be controlled adequately by the ego. What if the unacceptable urges of the id edged their way into your consciousness (into what Freud called the *preconscious*) and began to overpower the ego? Freud contended that if this happens, you will experience a very unpleasant condition called anxiety. Specifically, he called it *free-floating* anxiety, because although you feel anxious and afraid, the causes are not fully conscious, so you are not sure why you feel this way.

When this state of anxiety exists, it is uncomfortable and we are motivated to change it. To do this the ego will bring on its big guns, called the *defense mechanisms*. The purpose of the defense mechanisms is to prevent the id's forbidden impulse from entering consciousness. If this is successful, the discomfort of the anxiety associated with the impulse is relieved. How do the defense mechanisms ward off anxiety? Well, they do it through self-deception and the distortion of reality so that the id's urges will not have to be acknowledged.

METHOD

Freud discovered the defense mechanisms gradually over many years of clinical interactions with his patients. In the years since Sigmund Freud's death and since the publication of Anna Freud's book, many refinements have been made in the interpretation of the defense mechanisms. The next section summarizes a selection of only those mechanisms identified by Sigmund Freud and elaborated on by his daughter.

RESULTS AND DISCUSSION

Anna Freud identified 10 defense mechanisms that had been described by her father (see p. 44 of her book). Five of the original mechanisms that are commonly used and widely recognized today are discussed here: repression, regression, projection, reaction formation, and sublimation. Keep in mind that the primary function of the defense mechanisms is to alter reality in order to protect against anxiety.

Repression

Repression is the most basic and commonly used mechanism of defense. In his early writings, Freud used the terms repression and defense interchangeably and interpreted repression to be virtually the only defense mechanism. Later, however, he acknowledged that repression was only one of many psychological processes available to protect a person from anxiety (p. 43). Repression does this by forcing disturbing thoughts out of consciousness. If this is accomplished successfully, the anxiety associated with the "forbidden" thoughts is avoided. In Freud's view, repression is often employed to defend against the anxiety that would be produced by unacceptable sexual desires. For example, a woman who has sexual feelings about her father would probably experience intense anxiety if these impulses were to become conscious. To avoid that anxiety, she might repress her unacceptable desires, forcing them fully into her unconscious. This would not mean that her urges are gone, but since they are repressed, they cannot produce anxiety.

You might be wondering how such thoughts are ever discovered if they remain in the unconscious. According to Freud, these hidden conflicts may be revealed through slips of the tongue, through dreams, or by the various techniques used in psychoanalysis, such as free association or hypnosis. Furthermore, repressed desires can create psychological problems that are expressed in the form of neuroses. For instance, consider again the woman who has repressed sexual desires for her father. She might express these impulses by becoming involved in successive failed relationships with men in an unconscious attempt to resolve her conflicts about her father.

Regression

Regression is a defense used by the ego to guard against anxiety by causing the person to retreat to the behavior of an earlier stage of development that was less demanding and safer. Often when a second child is born into a family, the older sibling will regress to using earlier speech patterns, wanting a bottle, and even bed-wetting. Adults can use regression as well. Consider a man experiencing a *midlife crisis* who is afraid of growing old and dying. To avoid the anxiety associated with these unconscious fears, he might regress to an adolescent stage by becoming irresponsible, cruising around in a sports car, trying to date younger women, and even eating the foods associated with his teenage years. Another example of regression is the married adult who *goes home to mother* whenever there is a problem in the marriage.

Projection

Imagine for a moment that your ego is being attacked by your id. You're not sure why, but you are experiencing a lot of anxiety. If your ego uses the defense mechanism of projection to eliminate the anxiety, you will begin to see your unconscious urges in other people's behavior. That is, you will project your impulses onto others. This externalizes the anxiety-provoking feelings and reduces the anxiety. You will not be aware that you're doing this, and the people onto whom you project may not be guilty of your accusations. An example of this offered by Anna Freud involves a husband who is experiencing impulses to be unfaithful to his wife (p. 120). He may not even be conscious of these urges, but they are creeping up from his id and creating anxiety. To ward off the anxiety, he projects his desires onto his wife, becomes intensely jealous, and accuses her of having affairs, even though there is no evidence to support his claims. Another example is the woman who is afraid of aging and begins to point out how old her friends and acquaintances are looking. The individuals in these examples are not acting or lying, but truly believe their projections. If they did not, the defense against anxiety would fail.

Reaction Formation

The defense identified by Freud as a reaction formation is exemplified by a line from Shakespeare's Hamlet, when Hamlet's mother, after watching a scene in a play, remarks to Hamlet, "The lady doth protest too much, me thinks." When a person is experiencing unacceptable, unconscious *evil* impulses, anxiety over them might be avoided by engaging in behaviors that are the exact opposite of the id's real urges. Anna Freud pointed out that these behaviors are usually exaggerated or even obsessive (p. 9). By adopting attitudes and behaviors that demonstrate outwardly a complete rejection of the id's true desires, anxiety is blocked. Reaction formations tend to appear rapidly and usually become a permanent part of an individual's personality unless the id-ego conflict is somehow resolved. As an example of this, reconsider the husband who unconsciously desires other women. If he employs reaction formation rather than projection to prevent his anxiety, he may become obsessively devoted to his wife and shower her with gifts and pronouncements of his unwavering love. Another example comes from many disturbing news reports of the violent crime referred to as *gay bashing*. In a Freudian interpretation, men who have unconscious homosexual tendencies might engage in this extreme opposite behavior of attacking and beating gay men to avoid their true desires and the anxiety associated with them (this concept is discussed further later in this reading).

Sublimation

Both Sigmund and Anna Freud considered most of the defense mechanisms, including the four described above, as indicating problems in psychological adjustment (neuroses). Conversely, the defense of sublimation was seen as not only normal, but desirable (p. 44). When people invoke sublimation, they are finding socially acceptable ways of discharging energy that is the result of unconscious forbidden desires. Freud maintained that since everyone's id contains these desires, sublimation is a necessary part of a productive and healthy life. Furthermore, he believed that most strong desires can be sublimated in various ways. Someone who has intense aggressive impulses might sublimate them by engaging in contact sports or becoming a surgeon. A teenage girl's passion for horseback riding might be interpreted as sublimated unacceptable sexual desires. A man who has an erotic fixation on the human body might sublimate his feelings by becoming a painter or sculptor of nudes.

Freud believed that all of what we call civilization has been possible through the mechanism of sublimation. In his view, humans have been able to sublimate their primitive biological urges and impulses, allowing them to build civilized societies. Sometimes, Freud suggested, our true unconscious forces overpower our *collective ego* and these primitive behaviors burst out in uncivilized expressions such as war. Overall, however, it is only through sublimation that civilization can exist at all (S. Freud, 1936).

IMPLICATIONS AND RECENT APPLICATIONS

Although Anna Freud made it clear in her book that the use of defense mechanisms is often associated with neurotic behavior, it should be pointed out that this is not always the case. Nearly everyone uses various defense mechanisms occasionally in their lives, especially to help them deal with periods of increased stress. They help us reduce our anxiety and maintain a positive self-image. Use of certain defense mechanisms has even been shown to reduce unhealthy physiological activity. For example, use of projection has been found to be associated with lower blood pressure (Cramer, 2003). Nevertheless, defense mechanisms involve self-deception and distortions of reality that can produce negative consequences if they are overused. For example, a person who uses regression every time life's problems become overwhelming might never develop the strategies necessary to deal with the problems and solve them. Consequently, the person's life will not become as effective as it could be. Moreover, Freud and many other psychologists have contended that when anxiety over specific conflicts is repressed, it is sometimes manifested in other ways, such as phobias, anxiety attacks, or obsessive-compulsive disorders.

Freud's theories have always been extremely controversial. Do the defense mechanisms really exist? Do they actually function unconsciously to block the anxiety created by the forbidden impulses of the id trying to enter the conscious? Probably the most often cited criticism of all of Freud's work is that to test it scientifically is difficult at best, impossible at worst. Many studies have tried to demonstrate the existence of various Freudian concepts. The results have been mixed. Some of his ideas have found scientific support (see Cramer, 2000), while others have been disproven, and still others simply cannot be studied (see Fisher & Greenberg, 1977, 1995).

One fascinating study may have found scientific evidence that *homophobia,* an irrational fear, avoidance, and prejudice toward gay and lesbian individuals, may be a *reaction formation* used to ward off the extreme anxiety caused by their own repressed homosexual tendencies (Adams, Wright, & Lohr, 1996). A group of men were given a test to determine their level of homophobia and divided into two groups: homophobic and nonhomophobic. Then, subjects were exposed to videos depicting heterosexual, gay, or lesbian explicit sexual scenes and, while they viewed these videos, monitored for physiological signs of sexual arousal. The only difference found between the groups was when they viewed the videos of gay males. In this condition, "the results indicate that the homophobic men showed a significant increase in [arousal], but that the [nonhomophobic] men did not" (p. 443). In fact,

66% of the nonhomophobic group showed no significant signs of arousal while viewing the homosexual video, but only 20% of the homophobic group showed little or no evidence of arousal. Furthermore, when asked to rate their level of arousal, the homophobic men *underestimated* their degree of arousal in response to the homosexual video. This study's results are clearly consistent with Anna Freud's description of the defense mechanism of reaction formation and lend support for the explanation of violence against gay individuals discussed earlier in this section.

CONCLUSION

As evidenced by studies discussed earlier, scientific interest in the defense mechanisms appears to be on the upswing among psychologists in various subfields, including cognitive, developmental, personality, and social psychology (Cramer, 2000). Through an awareness and understanding of the defense mechanisms, your ability to obtain important insights into the causes of people's actions is clearly enhanced. If you keep a list of the defense mechanisms handy in your "brain's back pocket," you may begin to notice them in others or even in yourself. By the way, if you think someone is using a defense mechanism, remember, he or she is doing so to avoid unpleasant anxiety. Therefore, it is probably not a great idea to bring it to his or her attention. Knowledge of the defense mechanisms can be a powerful tool in your interactions with others, but it must be used carefully and responsibly.

You can easily experience for yourself the continuing influence of Anna Freud's synthesis and analysis of her father's concept of the defense mechanism by picking up virtually any recent academic or scholarly work that discusses psychoanalytic theory in detail. Most of the Freud citations you will encounter will be referring to Sigmund, and rightly so. But, when the discussion turns to the defense mechanisms, it is Anna Freud's 1946 book and its various revisions that serve as the authoritative work on the topic (see Couch, 1995).

Adams, H., Wright, L., & Lohr, B. (1996). Is homophobia associated with homosexual arousal? *Journal of Abnormal Psychology, 105*(3), 440–445.

Couch, A. (1995, February). Anna Freud's adult psychoanalytic technique: A defense of classical analysis. *International Journal of Psychoanalysis, 76,* 153–171.

Cramer, P. (2003). Defense mechanisms and physiological reactivity to stress. *Journal of Personality, 71,* 221–244.

Cramer, P. (2000). Defense mechanisms in psychology today: Further processes for adaptation. *American Psychologist, 55*(6), 637–646.

Fisher, S., & Greenberg, R. (1977). *The scientific credibility of Freud's theories and therapy.* New York: Basic Books.

Fisher, S., & Greenberg, R. (1995). *Freud scientifically reappraised: Testing the theories and therapy.* New York: Wiley.

Freud, S. (1936). *A disturbance of memory on the Acropolis.* London: Hogarth Press.

Freud, S. (1961). *Civilisation and its discontents.* London: Hogarth Press. (Original publication in German, 1930.)

LEARNING TO BE DEPRESSED
Seligman, M. E. P., & Maier, S. F. (1967). Failure to escape traumatic shock.
Journal of Experimental Psychology, 74, 1–9.

If you are like most people, you expect that your actions will produce certain consequences. Your expectations cause you to behave in ways that will produce desirable consequences, *and* to avoid behaviors that will lead to undesirable consequences. In other words, your actions are determined, at least in part, by your belief that they will bring about a certain result; they are contingent upon a certain consequence.

Let's assume for a moment that you are unhappy in your present job, so you begin the process of making a change. You make contacts with others in your field, read publications that advertise positions in which you are interested, begin training in the evening to acquire new skills, and so on. All those actions are motivated by your belief that your effort will eventually lead to the outcome of a better job and a happier life. The same is true of interpersonal relationships. If you are in a relationship that is wrong for you because it is abusive or it otherwise makes you unhappy, you will take the necessary actions to change it or end it because you expect to succeed in making the desired changes.

All these are issues of power and control. Most people believe they are personally powerful and able to control what happens to them, at least part of the time, because they have exerted control in the past and have been successful. They believe they are able to help themselves achieve their goals. If this perception of power and control is lacking, all that is left is helplessness. If you feel you are stuck in an unsatisfying job and you are unable to find another job or learn new skills to improve your professional life, you will be unlikely to make the effort needed to change. If you are too dependent on the person with whom you have a damaging relationship and you feel powerless to fix it or end it, you may simply remain in the relationship and endure the pain.

Perceptions of power and control are crucial for psychological and physical health (refer to the discussion on the research by Langer and Rodin earlier in this book on issues of control for the elderly in nursing homes. Imagine how you would feel if you suddenly found that you no longer had the power or control to make changes in your life, that what happened to you was independent of your actions. You would probably feel helpless and hopeless, and you would give up trying altogether. In other words, you would become depressed.

Martin Seligman, a well-known and influential behavioral psychologist, proposed that our perceptions of power and control are learned from experience. He believes that when a person's efforts at controlling certain life events fail repeatedly, the person may stop attempting to exercise control altogether. If these failures happen often enough, the person may generalize the perception of lack of control to all situations, even when control may actually be possible. This person then begins to feel like a *pawn of fate* and becomes helpless and depressed. Seligman termed this cause of depression, *learned helplessness.* He developed his theory at the University of Pennsylvania, in a series of now classic experiments that used dogs as subjects. The research discussed here that Seligman conducted with Steven Maier is considered to be the definitive original demonstration of his theory.

THEORETICAL PROPOSITIONS

Seligman had found in an earlier experiment on learning that when dogs were exposed to electrical shocks they could neither control nor escape from, they later failed to learn to escape from shocks when such escape was easily available. You have to imagine how odd this looked to a behaviorist. In the laboratory, dogs had experienced shocks that were designed to be punishing, but not harmful. Later, they were placed in a *shuttle box,* which is a large box with two halves divided by a partition. An electrical current could be activated in the floor on either side of the box. When a dog was on one side and felt the electricity, it simply had to jump over the partition to the other side to escape the shock. Normally, dogs and other animals learn this escape behavior very quickly (it's not difficult to see why!). In fact, if a signal (such as a flashing light or a buzzer) warns the dog of the impending electrical current, the animal will learn to jump over the partition before the shock and thus avoid it completely. However, in Seligman's experiment, when the dogs that had already experienced electrical shocks from which they could not escape were placed in the shuttle box, they did not learn this escape-avoidance behavior.

Seligman theorized that there was something in what the animals had learned about their ability to control the unpleasant stimulus that determined the later learning. In other words, these dogs had learned from previous experience with electrical shocks that their actions were ineffective in changing the consequence of the shocks. Then, when they were in a new situation where they did have the power to escape—to exercise control—they just gave up. They had learned to be helpless.

To test this theory, Seligman and Maier proposed to study the effect of controllable versus uncontrollable shock on later ability to learn to avoid shock.

METHOD

This is one of several classic studies in this book that used animals as subjects. However, this one, probably more than any of the others, raises questions about the ethics of animal research. Dogs received electrical shocks that were designed to be painful (though not physically harmful) in order to test a psychological theory. Whether such treatment was (or is) ethically justifiable is an issue that must be faced by every researcher and student of psychology. (This issue is addressed again after a discussion of the results of Seligman's research.)

Subjects for this experiment were 24 "mongrel dogs, 15 to 19 inches high at the shoulder and weighing between 25 and 29 pounds" (p. 2). They were divided into three groups of eight subjects each. One group was the *escape group,* another the *no-escape group,* and the third was the *no-harness control group.*

The dogs in the escape and no-escape groups were placed individually in a harness similar to that developed by Pavlov (see the discussion of Pavlov's methods in chapter 3, Learning and Conditioning); they were restrained, but not completely unable to move. On either side of the dog's head was a panel to keep the head facing forward. A subject could press the panel on either side by moving its head. When an electrical shock was delivered to a dog in the escape group, it could terminate the shock by pressing either panel with its head. For the no-escape group, each dog was paired with a dog in the escape group (this is an experimental procedure called *yoking*). Identical shocks were delivered to each pair of dogs at the same time, but the no-escape group had no control over the shock. No matter what those dogs did, the shock continued until it was terminated by the panel press of the dog in the escape group. This ensured that both groups of dogs received exactly the same duration and intensity of shock, the only difference being that one group had the power to stop it and the other did not. The eight dogs in the no-harness control group received no shocks at this stage of the experiment.

The subjects in the escape and no-escape groups received 64 shocks at about 90-second intervals. The escape group quickly learned to press the side panels and terminate the shocks (for themselves and for the no-escape group). Then, 24 hours later, all the dogs were tested in a shuttle box similar to the one described earlier. There were lights on either side of the box. When the lights were turned off on one side, an electrical current would pass through the floor of the box 10 seconds later. If a dog jumped the barrier within those 10 seconds, it escaped the shock completely. If not, it would continue to feel the shock until it jumped over the barrier or until 60 seconds of shock passed, at which time the shock was discontinued. Each dog was given 10 trials in the shuttle box.

Learning was measured by the following: (1) how much time it took, on average, from the time the light in the box went out until the dog jumped the barrier, and (2) the percentage of dogs in each group that failed entirely to learn to escape the shocks. Also, the dogs in the no-escape group received 10 additional trials in the shuttle box seven days later to assess the lasting effects of the experimental treatment.

RESULTS

In the escape group, the time it took for the dogs to press the panel and stop the shock quickly decreased over the 64 shocks. In the no-escape group, panel pressing completely stopped after 30 trials.

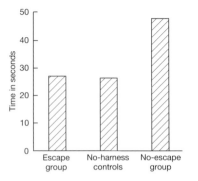

FIGURE 1   Average time to escape in shuttle box. (From p. 3.)

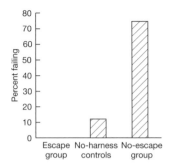

FIGURE 2   Percent of subjects failing to learn to escape shock in shuttle box. (From p. 3.)

Figure 1 shows the average time to escape for the three groups of subjects over all the trials in the shuttle box. Remember, this was the time between when the lights were turned off and when the animal jumped over the barrier. The difference between the no-escape group and the other two groups was statistically significant, but the small difference between the escape group and the no-harness group was insignificant. Figure 2 illustrates the percentage of subjects from each group that failed to jump over the barrier and escape the shock in the shuttle box in at least 9 of the 10 trials. This difference between the escape and no-escape groups was also highly significant. Six of the subjects in the no-escape group failed entirely to escape on either 9 or all 10 of the trials. Those six dogs were tested again in the shuttle box 7 days later. In this delayed test, five of the six failed to escape on every trial.

DISCUSSION

Because the only difference between the escape and the no-escape groups was the dogs' ability to actively terminate the shock, Seligman and Maier concluded that it must have been this control factor that accounted for the clear difference in the two groups' later learning to escape the shock in the shuttle box. In other words, the reason the escape group subjects performed normally in the shuttle box was that they had learned in the harness phase that their behavior was correlated with the termination of the shock. Therefore, they were motivated to jump the barrier and escape from the shock. For the no-escape group, the termination of shock in the harness was independent of their behavior. Thus, since they had no expectation that their behavior in the shuttle box would terminate the shock, they had no incentive to attempt to escape. They had, as Seligman and Maier had predicted, learned to be helpless.

Occasionally, a dog from the no-escape group made a successful escape in the shuttle box. Following this, however, it reverted to helplessness on the next trial. Seligman and Maier interpreted this to mean that the animal's previous ineffective behavior in the harness prevented the formation of a new behavior (jumping the barrier) to terminate shock in a new situation (the shuttle box), *even after a successful experience.*

In their article, Seligman and Maier reported the results of a subsequent experiment that offered some interesting additional findings. In this second study, dogs were first placed in the harness-escape condition where the panel press would terminate the shock. They were then switched to the no-escape harness condition before receiving 10 trials in the shuttle box. These subjects continued to attempt to panel press throughout all the trials in the no-escape harness and did not give up as quickly as did those in the first study. Moreover, they all successfully learned to escape and avoid shock in the shuttle box. This indicated that once the animals had learned that their behavior could be effective later experiences with failure were not adequate to extinguish their motivation to change their fate.

SUBSEQUENT RESEARCH

Of course, Seligman wanted to do what you are probably already doing in your mind: Apply these findings to humans. In later research, he asserted that the development of depression in humans involves processes similar to those of learned helplessness in animals. In both situations there is passivity, giving up and *just sitting there,* lack of aggression, slowness to learn that a certain behavior is successful, weight loss, and social withdrawal. Both the helpless dog and the depressed human have learned from specific past experiences that their actions are useless. The dog was unable to escape the shocks, no matter what it did, while the human had no control over events such as the death of a loved one, an abusive parent, the loss of a job, or a serious illness (Seligman, 1975).

The learned helplessness that leads to depression in humans can have serious consequences beyond the depression itself. Research has demonstrated that the elderly who, for various reasons such as nursing-home living, are forced to relinquish control over their daily activities have poorer health and a greater chance of dying sooner than those who are able to maintain a sense of personal power (for a discussion of related research by Langer and Rodin, see the reading on their nursing home study). In addition, several studies have demonstrated that uncontrollable stressful events can play a role in serious diseases such as cancer. One such study found an increased risk of cancer in individuals who in previous years had suffered the loss of a spouse, the loss of a profession, or the loss of prestige (Horn & Picard, 1979). In hospitals, patients are expected by the doctors and staff to be cooperative, quiet, and willing to place their fates in the hands of the medical authorities. Patients believe that they must follow doctors' and nurses' instructions without question in order to recover as quickly as possible. A prominent health psychologist has suggested that being a *good hospital patient* implies that one must be passive and give up all expectations of control. This actually may create a condition of learned helplessness in the patients whereby they fail to exert control later when control is both possible and desirable for continued recovery (Taylor, 1979).

As further evidence of the learned helplessness effect, consider the following remarkable study by Finkelstein and Ramey (1977). Groups of human infants had rotating mobiles mounted over their cribs. One group of infants had special pressure-sensitive pillows so that by moving their heads, they could control the rotation of the mobile. Another group of infants had the same mobiles, but these were programmed to turn randomly without any control by the infants. After a two-week exposure to the mobiles for 10 minutes each day, the control-pillow group had become very skilled at moving their heads to make the mobiles turn. However, the most important finding came when the no-control group of infants was later given the same control pillows and an even greater amount of learning time than the first group. The infants failed entirely to learn to control the rotation of the mobiles. Their experience in the first situation had taught them that their behavior was ineffective, and this knowledge transferred to the new situation where control was possible. In terms of moving mobiles, the infants had learned to be helpless.

RECENT APPLICATIONS

Seligman's study of learned helplessness continues to influence current research and stimulate debate in many fields. His ideas dovetail with those of other researchers working to increase our understanding of the importance of personal control over events in our lives (such as Langer and Rodin's study on perceived control in nursing homes discussed in chapter 5).

One terribly timely example of this broad influence may be found even in research on the psychology of biological, chemical, and nuclear warfare. Stokes and Banderet (1997) applied Selignam's theory to reactions of military and nonmilitary individuals' experiences during World War I, the Gulf War in 1991, and a chemical terrorist attack in a Tokyo subway in 1995. The researchers found that people's sense of utter helplessness in the face of a biological, chemical, or nuclear warfare attack tends to produce underreactions (such as denial and doing nothing) or overreactions (such as blind panic), both of which are completely ineffective in the face of such dangers. The authors suggest the incorporation of proven psychological principles to enhance effectiveness in the training of military and law enforcement personnel for these potential threats.

Of course, you may now be thinking of how Seligman's theory relates to the aftermath of the terrorist attacks on the World Trade Center and Pentagon on September 11, 2001. Unfortunately, his theory is right on target. The psychological reverberations of that horrific event echoed across the United States and throughout the world. Symptoms included increased anxiety, anger, nervousness, increased alcohol use, feelings of a loss of control over external events, and helplessness (CDC, 2002). Indeed, one of the goals of terrorist attacks is to make people feel vulnerable and helpless. One clinical psychologist summarized the effects of the attack like this:

> The threat of terrorism creates the textbook psychological setup for anxiety and depression to occur. Psychologists call this "anticipatory anxiety"—waiting for the proverbial shoe to drop or, in this case, terrorist bomb to go off. Add the element of "learned helplessness"—the perception that there is nothing or very little you can do to stop the terrorism—and depression, vulnerability, and a profound sense of loss of control will develop. These are precisely the conditions to which we have all been exposed since the September 11 attacks. They define the "New Normalcy" and the "September 11 Syndrome." (Braiker, 2002)

CONCLUSION

We must return now to the issue of experimental ethics. Most of us have difficulty reading about animals, especially dogs, being subjected to painful shocks in a psychology laboratory. Over the years, strict standards have been developed to ensure that laboratory animals are treated humanely (see the discussion of these standards in the preface to this book). However, many, both within and outside the scientific professions, believe these standards to be inadequate. Some advocate the complete elimination of animal research in psychology, medicine, and all the sciences. Whatever your personal stand on this issue, the question you should be asking is this: Do the findings from the research extend our knowledge, reduce human suffering, and improve the quality of life, sufficiently to justify the methods used to carry out the study?

Ask yourself that question about this study by Seligman and Maier. This study found the beginnings of a theory to explain why some people become helpless, hopeless, and depressed. Seligman went on to develop a widely accepted model of the origins of and treatments for depression. Over the years his theory has been refined and detailed so that it applies more accurately to types of depression that occur under well-defined conditions, from the death of a loved one to massive natural and human-made disasters.

Through Seligman's research, for example, we now understand that individuals are most likely to become depressed if they attribute their lack of control to causes that are (1) permanent rather than temporary, (2) related to factors within their own personality (instead of situational factors), and (3) pervasive across many areas of their life (see Abramson, Seligman, & Teasdale, 1978). Through this understanding, therapists and counselors have become better able to diagnose, intervene in, and treat serious depression.

Does this body of knowledge justify the methods used in this early research on learned helplessness? Each person must decide that thorny issue for him- or herself.

Abramson, L., Seligman, M., & Teasdale, J. (1978). Learned helplessness in humans: Critique and reformulation. *Journal of Abnormal Psychology, 87,* 49–74.

Braiker, H. (2002). *The September 11 syndrome: A nation still on edge.* Retrieved September 15, 2003 from http://www.harrietbraiker.com/OpEd.htm.

CDC. (2002). Psychological and emotional effects of the September 11 attacks on the World Trade Center—Connecticut, New Jersey, and New York, 2001. *Centers for Disease Control and Prevention: Morbidity and Mortality Weekly Report, 51,* 784–786.

Finkelstein, N., & Ramey, C. (1977). Learning to control the environment in infancy. *Child Development, 48,* 806–819.

Horn, R., & Picard, R. (1979). Psychosocial risk factors for lung cancer. *Psychosomatic Medicine, 41,* 503–514.

Seligman, M. (1975). *Helplessness: On depression, development, and death.* San Francisco, CA: Freeman.

Stokes, J., & Banderet, L. (1997). Psychological aspects of chemical defense and warfare. *Military Psychology, 9*(4), 395–415.

Taylor, S. (1979). Hospital patient behavior: Reactance, helplessness, or control? *Journal of Social Issues, 35,* 156–184.

CROWDING INTO THE BEHAVIORAL SINK
Calhoun, J. B. (1962). Population density and social pathology. *Scientific American, 206*(3), 139–148.

The effects of crowding on our behavior is something that has interested psychologists for decades. You have probably noticed how your emotions and behavior change when you are in a situation that you perceive as very crowded. You may withdraw into yourself and try to become invisible; you might look for an escape; or you may find yourself becoming irritable and aggressive. How you react to crowding depends on many factors.

You will notice that the title of the article of discussion in this chapter uses the phrase *population density* rather than *crowding.* While these may seem very similar, psychologists draw a clear distinction between them. Density refers to the number of individuals in a given amount of space. If 20 people occupy a 12-by-12-foot room, the room would probably be seen as densely populated. Crowding, however, refers to the subjective psychological experience created by density. That is, if you are trying to concentrate on a difficult task in that room with 20 people, you may experience extreme crowding. Conversely, if you are at a party with 20 friends in that same room, you might not feel crowded at all.

One way behavioral scientists can study the effects of density and crowding on people is to observe places where crowding already exists, such as Manhattan, Mexico City, some housing projects, prisons, and so on. The problem with this method is that all these places contain many factors that can influence behavior. For example, if we find high crime rates in a crowded inner-city neighborhood, there's no way to know for sure that crowding is the cause of the crime. Maybe it's the fact that people there are poor, or that there's a higher rate of drug abuse, or perhaps all these factors combine with crowded conditions to produce the high crime rates.

Another way to study crowding is to put human subjects into high-density conditions for relatively short periods of time and study their reactions. While this method offers more control and allows us to isolate crowding as a cause of behavior, it is not very realistic in terms of real-life crowded environments, since they usually exist over extended periods of time. It should be pointed out, however, that both of these methods have yielded some interesting findings about crowding that will be discussed later in this chapter.

Since it would be ethically impossible (because of the stress and other potential damaging effects) to place humans in crowded conditions over long periods of time simply to do research on them, there is a third way of addressing the effects of density: Do research using animal subjects (see the preface to this book for a discussion of ethics in animal research). One of the earliest and most classic series of studies of this type was conducted by John B. Calhoun (1917–1995) in 1962. Calhoun allowed groups of white rats to increase in population to twice the number that would normally be found in a space the size of a 10-by-14-foot room and observed their "social" behavior for 16 months.

THEORETICAL PROPOSITIONS

Calhoun especially wanted to explore the effects of high density on social behavior. It may seem strange to you to think of rats as social animals, but they do socialize in various ways in their natural environment.

To appreciate what led Calhoun to the study being discussed in this chapter, it is necessary to back up several years to an earlier project he conducted. Calhoun had confined a population of rats to a quarter-acre of enclosed, protected outdoor space. Plenty of food was available; there were ideal protected nesting areas; there were no predators; and all disease was kept to a minimum. In other words, this was a rat's paradise. The point of Calhoun's early study was simply to study the population growth rate of the rats in a setting free from the usual natural controls on overpopulation (predators, disease, etc.). After 27 months, the population consisted of only 150 adult rats. This was very surprising since with the low mortality rate of adult rats in this ideal setting, and considering the usual rate of reproduction, there should have been 5,000 adults in this period of time! The reason for this small population was an extremely high infant mortality rate. Apparently, reproductive and maternal behavior had been severely altered by the stress of social interaction among the 150 rats, and very few young rats survived to reach adulthood. Even though this number of rats (150 in a quarter-acre) does not seem to be particularly dense, it was obviously crowded enough to produce extreme behavioral changes.

These findings prompted Calhoun to design a more controlled and observable situation inside the lab in order to study more closely what sorts of changes occur in the rats when they are faced with high population density. In other words, he had observed what happened, and now he wanted to find out why.

METHOD

In a series of three studies, either 32 or 56 rats were placed in a 10-by-14-foot laboratory room that was divided into four sections or pens (see Figure 1). There were ramps that allowed the rats to cross from pen 1 to pen 2, from pen 2 to pen 3, and from pen 3 to pen 4. It was not possible for the rats to cross directly between pen 1 and pen 4. Therefore, these were end-pens. If a rat wanted to go from 1 to 4, it would have to go through 2 and 3. The partitions dividing the pens were electrified, so the rats quickly learned that they could not climb over them.

These pens consisted of feeders and waterers and enclosures for nests. The rats were supplied with plenty of food, water, and materials for building nests. In order to observe and record the rats' behavior there was a viewing window in the ceiling of the room.

From his years of studying rats, Calhoun was aware that this particular strain normally is found in colonies of 12 adults. Therefore, the observation room was of a size to accommodate 12 rats per pen, or a total of 48. After the groups were placed in the room, they were allowed to multiply until this normal density was nearly doubled to 80. Once the population level of 80 was reached, young rats that survived past weaning were removed so that the number of rats remained constant.

FIGURE 1   Diagram of laboratory room as arranged in Calhoun's study of crowding.

With this arrangement in place, all that was left was to observe these crowded animals for an extended period of time and record their behavior. These observations went on for 16 months.

RESULTS

It is important to keep in mind that the density of the rats was not extreme; in fact, it was quite moderate. If the rats wanted to spread out, there would only have to be 20 or so per pen. But this is not what happened. When the male rats reached maturity, they began to fight with each other for social status as they do naturally. These fights took place in all the pens, but the outcome was not the same for all of them. If you think about the arrangement of the room, the two end-pens only had one way in and out. So when a rat won a battle for dominance in one of these pens, he could hold his position and territory (the whole pen) simply by guarding the entrance and attacking any other male that ventured over the ramp. As it turned out, only one male rat ended up in charge of each of the end-pens. However, he was not alone. The female rats distributed themselves more or less equally over all four pens. Therefore, the masters of pens 1 and 4 each had a harem of 8 to 12 females all to themselves. And they didn't take any chances. In order to prevent infiltration, the males took to sleeping directly at the foot of the ramp and were always on guard.

On occasion, there were a few other male rats in the end-pens, but they were extremely submissive. They spent most of their time in the nesting burrows with the females and only came out to feed. They did not attempt to mate with the females. The females in these pens functioned well as mothers. They built comfortable nests and nurtured and protected their offspring. In other words, life for most of the rats in these end-pens was relatively normal and reproductive behavior was successful. About half of the infant rats in those pens survived to adulthood.

The rest of the 60 or so rats crowded into the middle two pens. Since these two pens each had central feeding and watering devices, there were many opportunities for the rats to come in contact with each other. The kinds of behaviors observed among the rats in pens 2 and 3 demonstrate a phenomenon that Calhoun termed the *behavioral sink*. A behavioral sink is "the outcome of any behavioral process that collects animals together in unusually great numbers. The unhealthy connotations of the term are not accidental: A behavioral sink does act to aggravate all forms of pathology that can be found within a group" (p. 144). Let's examine some of the extreme and pathological behaviors he observed:

1. *Aggression.* Normally in the wild, male rats will fight other male rats for dominant positions in the social hierarchy. These fights were observed among the more aggressive rats in this study as well. The difference was that here, unlike in their natural environments, top-ranking males were required to fight frequently in order to maintain their positions and

often the fights involved several rats in a general brawl. Nevertheless, the strongest males were observed to be the most normal within the center pens. However, even those animals would sometimes exhibit "signs of pathology; going berserk; attacking females, juveniles, and less active males; and showing a particular predilection—which rats do not normally display—for biting other rats on the tail" (p. 146).

2. *Submissiveness.* Contrary to this extreme aggression, other groups of male rats ignored and avoided battles for dominance. One of these groups consisted of the most healthy-looking rats in the pens. They were fat and their fur was full, without the usual bare spots from fighting. However, these rats were complete social misfits. They moved through the pens as if asleep or in some sort of hypnotic trance, ignoring all others, and were, in turn, ignored by the rest. They were completely uninterested in sexual activity and made no advances, even toward females in heat.

   Another group of rats engaged in extreme activity and were always on the prowl for receptive females. Calhoun termed them *probers*. Often, they were attacked by the more dominant males, but were never interested in fighting for status. They were hypersexual and many of them even became cannibalistic!

3. *Sexual deviance.* These probers also refused to participate in the natural rituals of mating. Normally, a male rat will pursue a female in heat until she escapes into her burrow. Then, the male will wait patiently and even perform a courtship dance directly outside her *door.* Finally, she emerges from the burrow and the mating takes place. In Calhoun's study, this ritual was adhered to by most of the sexually active males except the probers. They completely refused to wait and followed the female right into her burrow. Sometimes the nests inside the burrow contained young that had failed to survive, and it was here that late in the study the probers turned cannibalistic.

   Another group of male rats was termed *the pansexuals* because they attempted to mate with any and all other rats indiscriminately. They sexually approached other males, juveniles, and females that were not in heat. This was a submissive group that was often attacked by the more dominant male rats, but did not fight for dominance.

4. *Reproductive abnormalities.* Rats have a natural instinct for nest building. In this study, small strips of paper were provided in unlimited quantities as nest material. The females are normally extremely active in the process of building nests as the time for giving birth approaches. They gather the material and pile it up so that it forms a cushion. Then they arrange the nest so that it has a small indentation in the middle to hold the young. However, the females in the behavioral sink gradually lost their ability (or inclination) to build adequate nests. At first they failed to form the indentation in the middle. Then, as time went on, they

collected fewer and fewer strips of paper so that eventually the infants were born directly on the sawdust that covered the pen's floor.

The mother rats also lost their maternal ability to transport their young from one place to another if they felt the presence of danger. They would move some of the litter and forget the rest, or simply drop them onto the floor as they were moving them. Usually these infants were abandoned and died where they were dropped. They were then eaten by the adults. The infant mortality rate in the middle pens was extremely high, ranging from 80% to 96%.

In addition to these maternal deficits, the female rats in the middle pens, when in heat, were chased by large groups of males until they were finally unable to escape. These females experienced high rates of complications in pregnancy and delivery. By the end of the study, almost half of them had died.

DISCUSSION

You might expect that a logical extension of these findings would be to apply them to humans in high-density environments. However, for reasons to be discussed shortly, Calhoun did not draw any such conclusions. In fact, he discussed his findings very little—probably assuming, and logically so, that his results spoke volumes for themselves. He did comment on one clear result: that the natural social and survival behaviors of the rats were severely altered by the stresses associated with living in a high-population-density environment. In addition, he noted that through additional research, with improved methods and refined interpretation of the findings, his studies and others like them may contribute to our understanding of similar issues facing human beings.

SIGNIFICANCE OF FINDINGS

As with many of the studies in this book, one of the most important aspects of Calhoun's studies was that they sparked a great deal of related research on the effects on humans of high-density living. It would be impossible to examine this large body of research in detail here, but perhaps a few examples should be mentioned.

One environment where the equivalent of a behavioral sink might exist for humans is in extremely overcrowded prisons. A study funded by the National Institute of Justice examined prisons where inmates averaged only 50 square feet each (or an area about 7-by-7 feet), compared with less crowded prisons. It was found that in the crowded prisons there were significantly higher rates of mortality, homicide, suicide, illness, and disciplinary problems (McCain, Cox, & Paulus, 1980). Again, however, remember that other factors besides crowding could be influencing these behaviors.

Another interesting finding has been that crowding produces negative effects on problem-solving abilities. One study placed people in small, extremely crowded rooms (only 3 square feet per person) or in larger, less crowded rooms. The subjects were asked to complete rather complex tasks, such as placing various shapes into various categories while listening to a story on which they were to be tested later. Those in the crowded conditions performed significantly worse than those who were not crowded (Evans, 1979).

Finally, what do you suppose happens to you physiologically in crowded circumstances? Research has determined that your blood pressure and heart rate increase. Along with those effects, you tend to feel that other people are more hostile and that time seems to pass more slowly as density increases (Evans, 1979).

CRITICISMS

Calhoun's results with animals have been supported by later animal research (see Marsden, 1972). However, as has been mentioned before in this book, we must always be careful in applying animal research to humans. Just as substances that may be shown to cause illness in rats may not have the same effect on human physical health, environmental factors influencing rats' social behaviors may not be directly applicable to people. At best, animals can only represent certain aspects of humans. Sometimes animal research can be very useful and revealing and lead the way for more definitive research with people. At other times, it can be a dead end.

In 1975, a study was undertaken in New York City that attempted to replicate with people some of Calhoun's findings (Freedman, Heshka, & Levy, 1975). Data were collected for areas of varying population density on death rates, fertility rates (birth rates), aggressive behavior (court records), psychopathology (admissions to mental hospitals), and so on. When all the data were analyzed, no significant relationships were found between population density and any form of social pathology.

Nevertheless, Calhoun's work in the early 1960s focused a great deal of attention on the psychological and behavioral effects of crowding. This line of research, as it relates to humans, continues today.

RECENT APPLICATIONS

John Calhoun died on September 7, 1995, and left behind a legacy of insightful and historically meaningful research. The kinds of social problems discussed by Calhoun in his 1962 article are increasingly relevant to the human condition. Consequently, when scientists undertake research to better understand and intervene in such problems as aggression, infertility, mental illness, or various forms of social conflict, it is not unusual for them to make reference to Calhoun's research on crowding and behavioral pathology.

An interesting study citing Calhoun's work, examined changes in animal behavior that accompany domestication (Price, 1999). This author contended that species of animals that are domesticated, that is, kept as pets, have undergone genetic and developmental changes over many generations that have altered their behaviors in ways that allow them to share a common living environment with humans. Basically, what Price is suggesting is that as wild animals have become domesticated over centuries, they have had to adapt to human settings that are very different from their original habitats. This usually includes living in peaceful harmony (most of the time, at least) with others of their own species, other animal species, and humans, usually in relatively crowded conditions. This is accomplished, the author contends, through the evolution of increased response thresholds, meaning it takes a lot more provocation for a domesticated animal to become territorial and aggressive. In other words, dogs, cats, and humans are all able to live together in a relatively small space without running away or tearing each other to pieces as would occur among nondomesticated animals in the wild.

In a different direction, an article by Torrey and Yolken (1998) incorporated Calhoun's study in examining the association between growing up in crowded conditions and the development of schizophrenia and bipolar disorder (manic-depression). Many studies have found that people who are raised in high-density urban environments are at increased risk for these psychological disorders later in life. Numerous factors are present in crowded, urban settings that may account for such increased risks. However, the authors of this study hypothesized that it is not the increased density of living conditions in the neighborhood, but rather in the individual homes (more people occupying less space) that may explain the higher rates of mental illness later in life. Why? This study contended that exposure to a larger number of infectious agents may account for this association.

Finally, a related study found a possible key difference in human reactions to population density compared to animals. In animal studies, pathology appears to increase in a linear way as a direct result of increased density: as one increases the other increases. However, a study by Regoeczi (2002) found that for humans, the effect of household population density on social withdrawal and aggression actually *decreased* as the number of people in a single household increased. However, this effect was only observed until the number of people exceeded the total number of rooms; very much beyond that, the antisocial effects begin to appear with increasing density. In other words when living conditions are such that, say, 5 people occupy a 3-room apartment or 7 people are squeezed into a 4-room house, the tendency for people to withdraw and/or display more aggression increases. Two possible causes may be at work here. Either density is causing the pathology, or people who are more withdrawn or more aggressive end up in less crowded living situations, by choice or by ostracism, respectively.

These studies demonstrate how social scientists are continuing to explore and refine the effects of density and crowding. The causes of social pathology are many and complex. The impact of population density, first brought to our attention by Calhoun over 40 years ago, is only one, but a very crucial, piece of the puzzle.

Evans, G. W. (1979). Behavioral and psychological consequences of crowding in humans. *Journal of Applied Social Psychology, 9*, 27–46.

Freedman, J. L., Heshka, S., & Levy, A. (1975). Population density and social pathology: Is there a relationship? *Journal of Experimental Social Psychology, 11*, 539–552.

Marsden, H. M. (1972). Crowding and animal behavior. In J. F. Wohlhill & D. H. Carson (Eds.), *Environment and the social sciences.* Washington, DC: American Psychological Association.

McCain, G., Cox, V. C., & Paulus, P. B. (1980). The relationship between illness, complaints, and degree of crowding in a prison environment. *Environment and Behavior, 8,* 283–290.

Price, E. (1999). Behavioral development in animals undergoing domestication. *Applied Animal Behavior Research, 65*(3), 245–271.

Regoeczi, W. (2002). The impact of density: The importance of nonlinearity and selection on flight and fight responses. *Social Forces, 81,* 505–530.

Torrey, E., & Yolken, R. (1998). At issue: Is household crowding a risk factor for schizophrenia and bipolar disorder? *Schizophrenia Bulletin, 24*(3), 321–324.

9 PSYCHOTHERAPY

Psychotherapy simply means therapy for psychological problems. Therapy involves a close and caring relationship between a therapist and a client. The history of psychotherapy consists primarily of a long series of hundreds of therapeutic techniques, each one considered to be the best by those who developed it. The research demonstrating the effectiveness of all those methods has been generally weak and not very scientific. The subfield of psychology that focuses on treating psychological problems is *clinical psychology*, and much of the research is anecdotal. However, there have been some important and influential treatment breakthroughs.

One question people often raise about psychotherapy is, "Which method is best?" The first study in this section addressed this question using an innovative (at that time) statistical analysis and demonstrated that, in general, various forms of therapy are equally effective. Another line of research discussed in the second study, however, suggested one exception to this. If you have a phobia (an intense and irrational fear of something), a form of behavior therapy called *systematic desensitization* has been shown to be a superior method of treatment. The study included here was conducted by Joseph Wolpe, the psychologist who invented systematic desensitization. Both the third and the fourth studies in this section involved the development of two popular therapeutic and diagnostic, tools: the *Rorschach Inkblot Method* and the *Thematic Apperception Test* (TAT). These tests are commonly used by therapists to try to diagnose mental problems and help their clients discuss sensitive, traumatic, or hidden psychological problems.

CHOOSING YOUR PSYCHOTHERAPIST
Smith, M. L., & Glass, G. V. (1977). Meta-analysis of psychotherapy outcome studies. *American Psychologist, 32*, 752–760.

You *do not* have to be crazy to need psychotherapy. The vast majority of people treated by counselors and psychotherapists are not mentally ill, but are simply having problems in life that they are unable to resolve through their usual coping mechanisms and support network.

Imagine for a moment you are experiencing a difficult emotional time in your life. You consult with your usual group of close friends and family members, but you just cannot seem to work things out. Finally, when you have endured the pain long enough, you decide to seek some professional help. Because you are an informed, intelligent person, you do some reading on psychotherapy and discover that many different approaches are available. You read about various types of therapy such as *behavior therapies,* (including *systematic desensitization* which we discuss in the next reading on Wolpe's work), *humanistic therapy, cognitive therapies, cognitive-behavioral therapy,* and various Freudian-based *psychodynamic therapies.* These assorted styles of psychotherapy, although they stem from different theories and employ different techniques, all share the same basic goal: to help you change your life in ways that make you a happier, more productive, and effective person. (See Grohol, 1995, for a more complete discussion of the various forms of psychotherapy.)

Now you may be really confused. Which one should you choose? What you would really like to know now is (1) Does psychotherapy really work? and (2) If it does, which method works best? Well, it may (or may not) help you to know that over the past 40 years, psychologists have been asking the same questions. While many comparison studies have been done, most of them have tended to support the method used by the psychologists conducting the study. In addition, most of the studies were rather small in terms of both the number of subjects and the research techniques used. And to make matters worse, the studies are spread over a wide range of books and journals, making a fully informed judgment extremely difficult.

To fill this gap in the research literature on psychotherapy techniques, Mary Lee Smith and Gene Glass, at the University of Colorado, undertook in 1977 the task of compiling virtually all of the studies on psychotherapy effectiveness that had been done up to that time and reanalyzing them. By searching through 1,000 various magazines, journals, and books, they selected 375 studies that had tested the effects of counseling and psychotherapy. The researchers then applied a technique developed by Glass called *meta-analysis* to the data from all the studies to determine overall and relative effectiveness. A meta-analysis takes the results of many individual studies and integrates them into a larger statistical analysis so that the evidence is combined into a more meaningful whole.

THEORETICAL PROPOSITIONS

The goals of Smith and Glass's study were the following (p. 752):

1. To identify and collect all studies that tested the effects of counseling and psychotherapy
2. To determine the magnitude of the effect of therapy in each study
3. To compare the effects of different types of therapy

The theoretical proposition implicit in these goals was that when this meta-analysis was done, psychotherapy would be shown to be effective, and differences in effectiveness of the various methods, if any, could be demonstrated.

METHOD

Although the 375 studies analyzed by Smith and Glass varied greatly in terms of the research method used and the type of therapy assessed, each study examined at least one group that received psychotherapy compared with another group that received a different form of therapy or no therapy at all (a control group). The most important finding in all the studies for Smith and Glass to include in their meta-analysis was the magnitude of the *effect of therapy*. This effect size was obtained for any outcome measure of the therapy that the original researcher chose to use. Often, studies provided more than one measurement of effectiveness, or the same measurement may have been taken more than once. Examples of outcomes used to assess effectiveness were increases in self-esteem, reductions in anxiety, improvements in school work, and improvements in general adjustment. Wherever possible, all of the measures used in a particular study were included in the meta-analysis.

A total of 833 effect sizes were computed from the 375 studies. These included approximately 25,000 subjects in each of the combined experimental and control groups. The authors reported that the average age of the subjects in the studies was 22 years. They had received an average of 17 hours of therapy from therapists with an average of 3.5 years of experience.

RESULTS

First, Smith and Glass compared all the treated subjects with all the untreated subjects for all types of therapy and all measures of outcome. They found that "the average client receiving therapy was better off than 75% of the untreated controls. . . . The therapies represented by the available outcome calculations moved the average client from the 50th percentile to the 75th percentile" (pp. 754–755). Percentiles indicate the percentage of individuals whose scores on any measurement fall beneath the specific score of interest. For example, if you score in the 90th percentile on an aptitude test, it means that 90% of those who took the same test scored lower than you. Furthermore, only 99 (or 12%) of the 833 effect sizes were negative (meaning the client was worse off than before therapy). The authors pointed out that if psychotherapy were ineffective, the number of negative effect sizes should equal 50%, or 417.

Second, various measures of psychotherapy effectiveness were compared across all of the studies. These findings are represented in Figure 1, which clearly demonstrates that therapy, in general, was found to be more effective than no treatment.

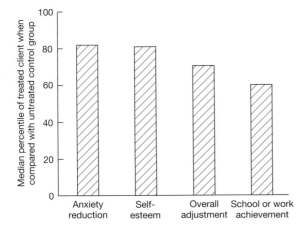

FIGURE 1 Combined effectiveness of all studies analyzed for four outcome measures. If there had been no improvement, the clients would have had scores of 50. If their condition had become worse, their scores would have been below 50. (Adapted from p. 756.)

Third, Smith and Glass compared the various psychotherapy methods found in the studies analyzed using similar statistical procedures. Figure 2 is a summary of the more familiar psychotherapeutic methods.

Finally, Smith and Glass combined all the various methods into two *superclasses* of therapy: a behavioral superclass consisting of systematic desensitization, behavior modification, and implosion, and a nonbehavioral superclass made up of the remaining types of therapy. When they analyzed all the studies in which behavioral and nonbehavioral therapies were compared with no-treatment controls, all differences between the two superclasses disappeared (73rd vs. 75th percentile, relative to controls).

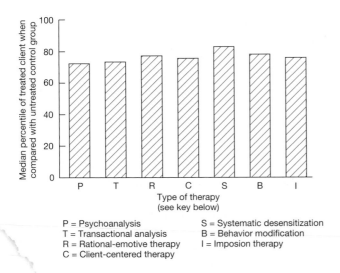

FIGURE 2 Comparison of the effectiveness of seven methods of psychotherapy. As in Figure 1, any score above 50 indicates improvement. (Adapted from p. 756.)

DISCUSSION

Overall, psychotherapy appeared to be successful in treating various kinds of problems (Figure 1). In addition, no matter how the different types of therapy were divided or combined, the differences among them were found to be insignificant (Figure 2 and other percentile findings).

Smith and Glass drew three conclusions from their findings. One is that psychotherapy works. The results of the meta-analysis clearly support the assertion that people who seek therapy are better off with the treatment than they were without it. Second, "despite volumes devoted to the theoretical differences among different schools of psychotherapy, the results of research demonstrate negligible differences in the effects produced by different therapy types. Unconditional judgments of superiority of one type or another of psychotherapy . . . are unjustified" (p. 760). And third, the knowledge and information researchers and therapists have about psychotherapy's effectiveness is lacking because the information has been spread too thinly across multitudes of publications. Therefore, they suggested that this study was a step in the right direction toward solving the problem, and that research using similar techniques deserves further attention.

IMPLICATIONS AND SUBSEQUENT RESEARCH

The findings in Smith and Glass's study made the issue of psychotherapy effectiveness less confusing for consumers, but more confusing for therapists. Those who choose psychotherapy as a career often have an investment in believing that one particular method (theirs) is more effective than others. The conclusions from Smith and Glass's study have been supported by subsequent research (Landman & Dawes, 1982; Smith, Glass, & Miller, 1980). One of the outcomes of this line of research is an increase in therapists who take an eclectic approach to helping their clients, meaning that they draw from several methods. In fact, 40% of all therapists in practice consider themselves to be eclectic. This percentage is by far the largest of all of the other specific approaches. By being eclectic, these therapists do not confine themselves to any one method, but choose among the various techniques and combine them to develop a treatment plan that best fits the client and the problem he or she is facing.

It would be a mistake to conclude from this and similar studies that all psychotherapy is equally effective for all problems and all people. These studies take a very broad and general overview of the effectiveness of therapy. However, depending on your personality and the circumstances of your specific problem, some therapies might be more effective for you than others. For example, it has been demonstrated that behavior therapies are significantly more effective than nonbehavioral approaches in the treatment of phobias.

The most important consideration when choosing a therapist may not be the type of therapy at all, but rather what your expectations of psychotherapy are, and the characteristics of the therapist. If you believe that psychotherapy can help you, and you enter the therapeutic relationship with optimistic expectations, the chances of successful therapy are greatly increased. The connection you feel with the therapist can also make an important difference. If you see your therapist as genuine, caring, warm, and able to achieve empathy with you, you are much more likely to experience effective and rewarding therapy (Hock & Mackler, 2005).

RECENT APPLICATIONS

Smith and Glass's findings and methodology continue to exert a strong influence in research on the efficacy of the many forms of therapeutic intervention for various psychological problems. This influence stems from their conclusions that most forms of psychotherapy are equally effective, as well as from their use of the meta-analytic research technique.

Examples of research that followed the methodological trail of Smith and Glass include a study to assess the effectiveness of the effect of a group therapy approach to treating depression (McDermut, Miller, & Brown, 2001). The authors conducted a meta-analysis of 48 studies on group therapy and depression and found that, on average, those receiving treatment improved significantly more than 85% of an untreated comparison group. The researchers concluded that "group therapy is an efficacious treatment for depressed patients. However . . . little empirical work has investigated what advantages group therapy might have over individual therapy" (p. 98). Based on Smith and Glass's research, you might predict that the effectiveness is likely to be similar for group and individual approaches to therapy, but further research is needed for us to know for sure.

Another study demonstrating the diverse applications of the meta-analysis strategies described in Smith and Glass's article concerned various behavioral (i.e., non-medication) treatments for people who suffer from recurrent migraine and tension headaches (Penzien, Rains, & Andrasik, 2002). Through meta-analytic analyses, the researchers compared relaxation training, biofeedback, and stress-management interventions over 30 years of studies. Overall, they found a 35–50% reduction in these types of headaches with behavioral strategies alone. This is an important finding because, as the authors point out, "the available evidence suggests that the level of headache improvement with behavioral interventions may rival those obtained with widely used pharmacologic therapies" (p. 2002). Based on this finding, the authors suggest that if behavioral therapies for chronic headaches can be made more available and less expensive, more doctors as well as their patients, might opt for nondrug treatment.

Finally, a study exemplifying the broad influence of the Smith and Glass's method and findings examined the effectiveness of psychotherapy for individuals who are mentally retarded (Prout & Nowak-Drabik, 2003). Their meta-analysis examined studies with widely varying research methodologies, styles of psychotherapy, and characteristics of the clients. Results across all the studies revealed a moderate, yet significant degree of benefit to clients with mental retardation. The researchers concluded that "psychotherapeutic interventions should be considered as part of overall treatment plan for persons with mental retardation" (p. 82).

CONCLUSION

Smith and Glass's study was a milestone in the history of psychology because it helped to remove much of the temptation for researchers to try to prove the superiority of a specific method of therapy and encouraged them instead to focus on how best to help those in psychological pain. Future research may now concentrate more directly on exactly which factors promote the fastest, most successful, and especially most healing, therapeutic experience.

Grohol, J. (1995). Types of therapies. Retrieved October 20, 2003 from http://www.grohol.com/therapy.htm.

Hock, R., & Mackler, M. (2005). *Do you need psychotherapy?* Unpublished manuscript, Mendocino College.

Landman, J., & Dawes, R. (1982). Psychotherapy outcome: Smith and Glass's conclusions stand up under scrutiny. *American Psychologist, 37,* 504–516.

McDermut, W., Miller, I., & Brown, R. (2001). The efficacy of group psychotherapy for depression: A meta-analysis and review of the empirical research. *Clinical Psychology: Science and Practice, 8,* 98–116.

Penzien, D., Rains, J., & Andrasik, F. (2002). Behavioral management of recurrent headaches: Three decades of experience and empiricism. *Applied Psychology and Biofeedback, 27,* 163–181.

Prout, H., & Nowak-Drabik, K. (2003). Psychotherapy with persons who have mental retardation: An evaluation of the effectiveness. *American Journal of Mental Retardation, 108,* 82–93.

Smith, M., Glass, G., & Miller, T. (1980). *The benefits of psychotherapy.* Baltimore, MD: Johns Hopkins University Press.

RELAXING YOUR FEARS AWAY
Wolpe, J. (1961). The systematic desensitization treatment of neuroses. *Journal of Nervous and Mental Diseases, 132,* 180–203.

Before discussing the very important technique in psychotherapy called *systematic desensitization* (which means decreasing your level of anxiety or fear very gently and gradually), the concept of *neuroses* should be clarified. *Neuroses* is a somewhat outdated term used to refer to a group of psychological problems for which extreme anxiety was the central characteristic. Today, such problems are usually called *anxiety disorders.* We are all familiar with anxiety, and sometimes experience a high degree of it in situations that make us nervous, such as public speaking, job interviews, exams, and so on. However, when someone suffers from an anxiety *disorder,* the reactions are much more extreme, pervasive, frequent, and debilitating. Often such disorders interfere with a person's life so that normal and desired functioning is impossible.

The most common anxiety-related difficulties are phobias, panic disorder, and obsessive-compulsive disorder. If you have ever suffered from one of them, you know that this kind of anxiety can take control of your life. This chapter's discussion of Joseph Wolpe's (1915–1997) work in treating those disorders will focus primarily on phobias.

The word *phobia* comes from *Phobos*, the name of the Greek god of fear. The ancient Greeks painted images of Phobos on their masks and shields to frighten their enemies. A phobia is an irrational fear. In other words, it is a fear reaction that is out of proportion with the reality of the danger. For example, if you are strolling down a path in the forest and suddenly happen upon a rattlesnake, coiled and ready to strike, you will feel fear (unless you're Indiana Jones or something). This is *not* a phobia, but a normal, rational fear response to a real danger. On the other hand, if you are unable to go to the zoo because you might see a snake in a glass cage, that would probably be considered a phobia. This may sound humorous to you, but to those who suffer from phobias, it's not funny at all. Phobic reactions are extremely uncomfortable events that involve symptoms such as dizziness, heart palpitations, feeling faint, hyperventilation, sweating, trembling, and nausea. A person with a phobia will carefully avoid situations in which the feared stimulus might be encountered. Often, this avoidance can interfere drastically with a person's desired functioning in life.

Phobias are divided into three main types. Simple phobias involve irrational fears of animals (such as rats, dogs, spiders, or snakes) or specific situations such as small spaces (claustrophobia) or heights (acrophobia). Social phobias are characterized by irrational fears about interactions with others, such as public speaking or fear of embarrassment. Finally, agoraphobia is the irrational fear of being in unfamiliar, open, or crowded spaces. While the various types of phobias are quite different, they share at least two common features: they are all irrational, and they all are treated in similar ways.

Early treatment of phobias centered around the Freudian concepts of psychoanalysis. This view maintains that a phobia is the result of unconscious psychological conflicts stemming from childhood traumas. It further contends that the phobia may be substituting for some other, deeper fear or anger that the person is unwilling to face. For example, a man with an irrational fear of heights (acrophobia) may have been cruelly teased as a small boy by his father, who pretended to try to push him off a high cliff. Acknowledging this experience as an adult might force the man to deal with his father's general abusiveness (something he doesn't want to face), so he represses it, and it is expressed instead in the form of a phobia. In accordance with this view of the source of the problem, psychoanalysts historically attempted to treat phobias by helping the person to gain insight into unconscious feelings and release the hidden emotion, thereby freeing themselves of the phobia in the process. However, such techniques, while useful for most other types of psychological problems, have proven relatively ineffective in treating phobias. It appears that even when someone uncovers the underlying unconscious conflicts that may be related to the phobia, the phobia itself persists.

Joseph Wolpe was not the first to suggest the use of a behavioral technique called *systematic desensitization*, but he is generally credited with perfecting it and applying it to the treatment of anxiety disorders. The behavioral approach differs dramatically from psychoanalytic thinking in that it is not concerned with the unconscious sources of the problem or with repressed conflicts. The fundamental idea of behavioral therapy is that you have learned an ineffective behavior (the phobia), and now you must unlearn it. This formed the basis for Wolpe's method for the treatment of phobias.

THEORETICAL PROPOSITIONS

Earlier research by Wolpe and others had discovered that fear reactions in animals could be reduced by a simple conditioning procedure. For example, suppose a rat behaves fearfully when it sees a realistic photograph of a cat. If the rat is given food every time the cat is presented, the rat will become less and less fearful, until finally the fear response disappears entirely. The rat had originally been conditioned to associate the cat photo with fear. However, the rat's response to being fed was incompatible with the fear response. Since the fear response and the feeding response cannot both exist at the same time, the fear was inhibited by the feeding response. This incompatibility of two responses is called *reciprocal inhibition* (when two responses inhibit each other, only one may exist at a given moment). Wolpe proposed the more general proposition that "if a response inhibitory to anxiety can be made to occur in the presence of anxiety-provoking stimuli . . . the bond between these stimuli and the anxiety will be weakened" (p. 180). He also argued that human anxiety reactions are quite similar to those found in the animal lab and that the concept of reciprocal inhibition could be used to treat various human psychological disorders.

In his work with people, the anxiety-inhibiting response was deep relaxation rather than feeding. The idea was based on the theory that you cannot experience deep physical relaxation and fear at the same time. As a behaviorist, Wolpe believed that the reason you have a phobia is that you learned it sometime in your life through the process of classical conditioning, by which some object became associated in your brain with intense fear (see the reading on Pavlov's research). We know from the work of Watson (see the reading on Watson's study with little Albert) and others that such learning is possible even at very young ages. So, in order to treat your phobia, you must experience a response that is inhibitory to fear or anxiety (relaxation) while in the presence of the feared situation. Will this treatment technique work? Wolpe's article reports on 39 cases randomly selected out of 150, where the subjects' phobias were treated by the author using his systematic desensitization technique.

METHOD

Imagine that you suffer from an irrational fear of heights called acrophobia. This problem has become so extreme that you have trouble climbing onto a ladder to trim the trees in your yard or going above the second floor in an office building. Your phobia is interfering so much with your life that you decide to seek out psychotherapy from a behavior therapist such as Joseph Wolpe. Your therapy will consist of several stages.

Relaxation Training

The first several sessions will deal very little with your phobia. Instead, the therapist will focus on teaching you how to relax your body. Wolpe recommended a form of progressive muscle relaxation introduced by Edmund Jacobson in 1938 that is still in common therapeutic use today. The process involves tensing and relaxing various groups of muscles (such as the arms and hands, the face, the back, the stomach, the legs, etc.) throughout the body until a deep state of relaxation is achieved. This relaxation training may take most of your first five or six sessions with the therapist. After the training, you are able to place yourself in this state of relaxation whenever you want. It should be noted that for most of the cases reported in this article, Wolpe also incorporated hypnosis to ensure full relaxation, but this has since been shown to be usually unnecessary for effective therapy because full relaxation can be obtained without the need of hypnosis.

Construction of an Anxiety Hierarchy

The next stage of the process is for you and your therapist to develop a list of anxiety-producing situations or scenes involving your phobia. The list would begin with a situation that is only slightly uncomfortable and proceed through increasingly more frightening scenes until finishing with the most anxiety-producing event. The number of steps in a patient's hierarchy varies from 5 or 6 to 20 or more. Table 1 shows what might appear on your list for your phobia of heights, as well as a hierarchy directly from Wolpe's article about a patient suffering from claustrophobia.

Desensitization

Now comes the actual unlearning. According to Wolpe, no direct contact with the feared situations is necessary to reduce a person's sensitivity to them. The same effect could be accomplished through description and imagination. Remember, you developed your phobia through the process of association, so you will eliminate the phobia the same way. First, you are instructed to place yourself in a state of deep relaxation as you have been taught. Then the therapist begins with the first step in your hierarchy and describes the scene to you: "You are walking down the sidewalk and you come to a large grating. As you continue walking, you can see through the grating to the bottom 10 feet below." Your job is to imagine the scene while remaining completely relaxed. If this is successful, the therapist will proceed to the next step:

TABLE 1 Anxiety Hierarchies

ACROPHOBIA

1. Walking over a grating in the sidewalk.
2. Sitting in a third-floor office near the window (not a floor-to-ceiling window).
3. Riding an elevator to the 45th floor.
4. Watching window washers 10 floors up on a platform.
5. Standing on a chair to change a lightbulb.
6. Sitting on the balcony with a railing of a fifth-floor apartment.
7. Sitting in the front row of the second balcony at the theater.
8. Standing on the third step of a ladder to trim bushes in the yard.
9. Standing at the edge of the roof of a three-story building with no railing.
10. Driving around curves on a mountain road.
11. Riding as a passenger around curves on a mountain road.
12. Standing at the edge of the roof of a 20-story building.

(Adapted from Goldstein, Jamison, & Baker, 1980, p. 371.)

CLAUSTROPHOBIA

1. Reading of miners trapped.
2. Having polish on fingernails without access to remover.
3. Being told of someone in jail.
4. Visiting and unable to leave.
5. Having a tight ring on finger.
6. On a journey by train (the longer the journey, the more the anxiety).
7. Traveling in an elevator with an operator (the longer the ride, the more the anxiety).
8. Traveling alone in an elevator.
9. Passing through a tunnel on a train (the longer the tunnel, the greater the anxiety).
10. Being locked in a room (the smaller the room and the longer the duration, the greater the anxiety).
11. Being stuck in an elevator (the greater the time, the greater the anxiety).

(Adapted from Wolpe, p. 197.)

"You are sitting in an office on the third floor . . . ," and so on. If at any moment during this process you feel the slightest anxiety, you are instructed to raise your index finger. When this happens, the presentation of your hierarchy will stop until you have returned to full relaxation. Then the descriptions will begin again from a point further down the list so that you can maintain your relaxed state. This process continues until you are able to remain relaxed through the entire hierarchy. Once you accomplish this, you might repeat the process several times in subsequent therapy sessions. In Wolpe's work with his clients, the number of sessions for successful treatment varied greatly. Some people claimed to be recovered in as few as six sessions, while one took nearly 100 (this was a patient with a severe phobia of death, plus two additional phobias). The average number of sessions was around 12. This, by the way, was considerably fewer than the number of sessions generally required for formal psychoanalysis, which usually lasted years.

The most important question relating to this treatment method is this: Does it work?

RESULTS

The 39 cases reported in Wolpe's article involved many different phobias. The themes of their hierarchies included, among others, claustrophobia, storms, being watched, crowds, bright light, wounds, agoraphobia, falling, rejection, and snakelike shapes. The success of their therapy was judged by the patients' own reports and by occasional direct observation. Generally, patients who report improvement and gradual recovery describe the process in ways that led Wolpe to accept their reports as credible. The desensitization process was rated as either completely successful (freedom from phobic reactions), partially successful (phobic reactions of 20% or less of original strength), or unsuccessful.

For the 39 cases, there were a total of 68 phobias treated. Sixty-two of these (in a total of 35 patients) were judged to be completely or partially successful. This was a success rate of 91%. The remaining six hierarchies (9%) were unsuccessful. The average number of sessions needed for successful treatment was 12.3. Wolpe explained that most of the unsuccessful cases displayed special problems that did not allow for proper desensitization to take place, such as an inability to imagine the situations presented in the hierarchy.

Critics of Wolpe, mainly from the psychoanalytic camp, claimed that his methods were only treating the symptoms and not the underlying cause of the anxiety. They maintained that other symptoms would appear to replace the ones treated in this way. They likened it to a leaking dike: when one hole is plugged, another appears. Related to this was the question of how lasting this treatment would be. Any form of therapy would be of little value if the symptoms returned soon after the sessions ended. Wolpe responded to criticisms and questions by obtaining follow-up reports from 25 of the 35 patients who had received successful desensitization at various times from six months to four years after treatment. Upon examining the reports he wrote, "There was no reported instance of relapse or new phobias or other neurotic symptoms. I have never observed resurgence of neurotic anxiety when desensitization has been complete or virtually so" (p. 200).

DISCUSSION

The discussion in Wolpe's article focuses on responding to the skepticism of the psychoanalysts at the time his research was done. During the 1950s, psychoanalysis was a very common and popular form of psychotherapy. As behavior therapies began to make their way into the mainstream of clinical psychology, a great deal of controversy was created, much of which continues in various forms today. Wolpe pointed out that the desensitization method offered several advantages over traditional psychoanalysis (see p. 202 of the original study):

1. The goals of psychotherapy can be clearly stated in every case.
2. Sources of anxiety can be clearly defined.
3. Changes in the patient's reactions during descriptions of scenes from the hierarchy can be measured during the sessions.
4. Therapy can be performed with others present (Wolpe found that having others present, such as therapists in training, during the sessions did not interfere with the effectiveness).
5. Therapists can be interchanged if desired or necessary.

SUBSEQUENT RESEARCH AND RECENT APPLICATIONS

Since Wolpe published this article and a book on the use of reciprocal inhibition in psychotherapy (Wolpe, 1958), the use of systematic desensitization has grown to the point that now it is considered the treatment of choice for anxiety disorders, especially phobias. This growth has been due in large part to more recent and more scientific research on its effectiveness.

A study by Paul (1969) treated college students who suffered from extreme phobic anxiety in public-speaking situations. First, all the subjects were asked to give a short, ad-libbed speech to an unfamiliar audience. Their degree of anxiety was measured by observer's ratings physiological measures, and a self-report questionnaire. The students were then randomly assigned to three treatment groups: (1) systematic desensitization, (2) insight therapy (similar to psychoanalysis), or (3) no treatment (control). Experienced therapists carried out the treatment in five sessions. All the subjects were then placed in the same public-speaking situation, and all the same measures of anxiety were taken. Figure 1 summarizes the results. Clearly, systematic desen-

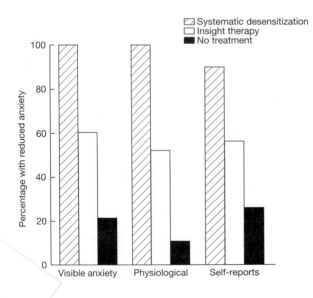

FIGURE 1 Results of treatment for anxiety. (From Paul, 1969.)

sitization was significantly more effective in reducing anxiety on all measures. Even more convincing was that in a *two-year* follow-up, 85% of the desensitization group *still* showed significant improvement, compared with only 50% of the insight group.

Numerous studies on behavior therapy continue to cite Wolpe's early work as part of their theoretical underpinnings. His application of classical conditioning concepts to the treatment of psychological disorders has become part of intervention strategies in a wide range of settings. For example, one study (Fredrickson, 2000) relied in part on Wolpe's concept of reciprocal inhibition in developing a new treatment strategy for difficulties stemming primarily from negative emotions such as anxiety, depression, aggression, and stress-related health problems. Fredrickson proposes assisting and teaching patients with such psychological problems to generate more and stronger positive emotions, such as love, optimism, joy, interest, and contentment, which directly inhibit negative thinking. The author contends that:

> Positive emotions loosen the hold that negative emotions gain on an individual's mind and body by undoing the narrowed psychological and physiological preparation for specific action. . . . Therapies optimize health and well being to the extent that they cultivate positive emotions. Cultivated positive emotions not only counteract negative emotions, but also broaden individuals' habitual modes of thinking, and build their personal resources for coping. (p. 1)

Another article resting on Wolpe's research studied the effectiveness of systematic desensitization for a condition many students know all too well: *math phobia* (Zettle, 2003). In this study Wolpe's treatment techniques were used to help students overcome extreme levels of math anxiety. Participants were given instructions on progressive muscle relaxation and a tape to practice relaxing each day at home. Each student worked with the researcher to develop an 11-item math fear heirarchy containing items such as "being called upon by my math instructor to solve a problem at the blackboard," or "encountering a word problem I don't know how to solve on the final" (p. 205). The hierarchy was then presented to each student as described earlier in this reading. To summarize briefly, it worked! At the end of the treatment, 11 out of 12 students "displayed recovery or improvement in their levels of math anxiety. . . . Furthermore, clinically significant reductions in math anxiety were maintained during the 2 months of follow-up (p. 209)."

CONCLUSION

Wolpe was quick to point out that the idea of overcoming fear and anxiety was not new. "It has long been known that increasing measures of exposure to a feared object may lead to the gradual disappearance of the fear" (p. 200). In fact, you probably already knew this yourself, even if you had never heard of systematic desensitization prior to reading this chapter. For example, imagine a child who is about 13 years old and has a terrible phobia of dogs. This fear is probably the result of a frightening experience with a dog when the child was much younger, such as being jumped on by a big dog, being bitten, or even having a parent who was afraid of dogs. Because of these experiences, the child developed an association between dogs and fear. If you wanted to cure this child of the fear of dogs, how might you break that association? Many people's first response to this question is, "Buy the child a puppy!" If that's what you thought of, you have just recommended a form of systematic desensitization.

Fredrickson, B. (2000). Cultivating positive emotions to optimize health and well-being. *Prevention and Treatment, 3(article 00001a),* 1–22. Retrieved October 10, 2003 from http://www.umich.edu/~psycdept/emotions/preventreat_00.pdf.

Paul, G. L. (1969). Outcome of systematic desensitization: Controlled investigation of individual technique variations and current status. In C. Franks (Ed.), *Behavior Therapy: Appraisal and Status.* New York: McGraw-Hill.

Wolpe, J. (1958). *Psychotherapy through reciprocal inhibition.* Palo Alto, CA: Stanford University Press.

Zettle, R. (2003). Acceptance and commitment therapy (ACT) vs. systematic desensitization in treatment of mathematics anxiety. *Psychological Record,* 53, 197–215.

PROJECTIONS OF WHO YOU ARE

Rorschach, H. (1942). *Psychodiagnostics: A diagnostic test based on perception.* New York: Grune & Stratton.

Picture yourself and a friend relaxing in a grassy meadow on a warm summer's day. The blue sky above is broken only by a few white puffy clouds. Pointing to one of the clouds, you say to your friend, "Look! That cloud looks like a woman in a wedding dress with a long veil." To this your friend replies, "Where? I don't see that. To me, that cloud is shaped like a volcano with a plume of smoke rising from the top." As you try to convince each other of your differing perceptions of the same shape, the air currents change and transform the cloud into something entirely different. But why such a difference in what the two of you saw? You were looking at the same shape, and yet interpreting it as two entirely unrelated objects.

Since everyone's perceptions are often influenced by psychological factors, perhaps the different objects found in the cloud formations revealed something about the personalities of the observers. In other words, you and your friend were projecting something about yourselves onto the shapes in the sky. This is the concept underlying Hermann Rorschach's (1884–1922) development of his "form interpretation test," better known as *the inkblot test.* This was one of the earliest versions of a type of psychological tool known as the *projective technique.*

The two most widely known and used projective tests are the Rorschach inkblot and the *Thematic Apperception Test,* or *TAT* (to be discussed in the next reading). Both of these instruments are pivotal in the history of clinical psychology. Since Rorschach's test, first described in 1922, involves direct comparisons among various groups of mental illnesses and is often associated with the diagnosis of psychological disorders, we will discuss it first.

A *projective test* presents a person with an ambiguous stimulus and assumes that the person will *project* his or her inner or unconscious psychological processes onto it. In the case of Rorschach's test, the stimulus is nothing more than a symmetrical inkblot that can be perceived to be virtually anything. Rorschach suggested that what a person sees in the inkblot often reveals a great deal about his or her true psychological nature. He called this *the interpretation of accidental forms*. An often-told story about Rorschach's inkblots tells of a psychotherapist who is administering the test to a client. With the first inkblot card the therapist asks, "What does this suggest to you?" The client replies, "Sex." The same question is asked of the second card, to which the client again replies, "Sex." When the same one-word answer is given to the first five cards, the therapist remarks, "Well, you certainly seem to be preoccupied with sex!" To this the surprised client responds, "Me? Doctor, you're the one showing all the dirty pictures!" Of course, this story oversimplifies Rorschach's test and, although the inkblots themselves are selected to be vaguely suggestive of objects in order to encourage active interpretation, sexual meanings should, on average, be no more likely than any other.

Rorschach believed that his projective technique could serve two main purposes. One was that it could be used as a research tool to reveal unconscious aspects of personality. The other purpose, claimed somewhat later by Rorschach, was that the test could be used to diagnose various types of psychopathology.

THEORETICAL PROPOSITIONS

The theory underlying Rorschach's technique was that in the course of interpreting a random inkblot, attention would be drawn away from the subject so that the person's usual psychological defenses would be weakened. This, in turn, would allow normally hidden aspects of the psyche to be revealed. When the stimulus being perceived is ambiguous (that is, having few clues as to what it really is), the interpretation of the stimulus has to come from inside the person doing the perceiving (for an expanded discussion of this concept, see the next reading on Murray's *Thematic Apperception Test*). In Rorschach's conceptualization, inkblots were about as ambiguous as you can get and, therefore, would allow for the greatest amount of projection from a person's unconscious.

METHOD

An examination of Rorschach's formulation of his inkblot test can be divided into two broad sections: the process he used to develop the original forms and the methods suggested for interpreting and scoring the responses made by subjects or clients.

Development of the Test

Rorschach's explanation of how the forms are made sounded very much like instructions for a fun children's art project: "The production of such accidental forms is very simple: A few large inkblots are thrown on a piece of paper, the paper folded, and the ink spread between the two halves of the sheet" (p. 15). However, the simplicity stopped there. Rorschach went on to explain that only those designs that met certain conditions could be used effectively. For example, the inkblot should be relatively simple, symmetrical, and moderately suggestive of objects. He also suggested that the forms should be symmetrical, because asymmetrical inkblots are often rejected by subjects as impossible to interpret. After a great deal of testing, Rorschach finally arrived at a set of 10 forms that made up his original test. Of these, 5 were black on white, 2 used black and red, and 3 were multicolored. Figure 1 contains three figures of the type Rorschach used.

FIGURE 1 Examples of accidental forms similar to the type used in Rorschach's Form Interpretation test. (From Archiv Medizinischer Verlag Hans Huber, Bern und Stuttgart.)

Administration and Scoring

Rorschach's form interpretation test is administered simply by handing a subject each figure, one at a time, and asking, "What might this be?" Subjects are free to turn the card in any direction and to hold it as close to or as far from their eyes as they wish. The researcher or therapist administering the test notes down all the responses for each figure without suggestions to the subjects. There is no imposed time limit.

Rorschach pointed out that subjects almost always think the test is designed to study imagination. However, he is very careful to explain that it is not a test of imagination, and the creativity of a person's imagination does not significantly alter the result. It is, Rorschach claimed, a test of perception involving the processes of sensation, memory, and unconscious and conscious associations between the stimulus forms and other psychological forces within the individual.

Rorschach listed the following guidelines for scoring the subjects' responses to the 10 inkblots (p. 19):

1. How many responses were made? What was the reaction time; that is, how long did the subject look at the figure before responding? How often did the subject refuse to interpret a figure?

2. Was the subject's interpretation only determined by the shape of the figure, or were color or movement included in the perception?

3. Was the figure seen as a whole or in separate parts? Which parts were separated, and how were they interpreted?

4. What did the subject see?

Interestingly, Rorschach considered the content of the subject's interpretation the *least* important factor in the responses given to the inkblots. The following section summarizes Rorschach's observations, related to these four guidelines, of numerous subjects with a variety of psychological symptoms.

RESULTS

To discover how various groups of people might perform differently on the inkblot test, Rorschach and his associates administered it to subjects from several psychological groups. These included, but were not limited to, normal individuals with varying amounts of education, schizophrenic patients, and individuals diagnosed as manic-depressive.

Table 1 presents typical responses reported by Rorschach for the 10 inkblot figures. These, of course, vary from person to person and among different psychological groups, but the answers given in the table serve as examples.

Rorschach found that subjects generally gave between 15 and 30 total responses to the 10 figures. Depressed subjects generally gave fewer answers; happy subjects gave more; and among schizophrenics the number of answers varied a great deal from person to person. The entire test usually took between 20 and 30 minutes to complete, with schizophrenics taking much less

TABLE 1 Typical Responses to Rorschach's Inkblot Figures for an Average Normal Subject

FIGURE NUMBER	RESPONSE
I.	Two Santa Clauses with brooms under their arms
II.	A butterfly
III.	Two marionette figures
IV.	An ornament on a piece of furniture
V.	A bat
VI.	A moth or a tree
VII.	Two human heads or two animal heads
VIII.	Two bears
IX.	Two clowns or darting flames
X.	A rabbit's head, two caterpillars, or two spiders

(Adaped from pp. 126–127.)

time on average. Normal subjects almost never failed to respond to all the figures, but schizophrenics would frequently refuse to answer.

Rorschach believed that the portion of the form interpreted by the subject, whether movement was part of the interpretation, and to what degree color entered into the response were all very important in analyzing the subject's performance on the test. His suggestions for scoring those factors were quite complex and required training and experience to analyze a person's responses properly. However, a useful and brief overall summary has been provided by Gleitman (1991):

> Using the entire inkblot is said to indicate integrative, conceptual thinking, whereas the use of a high proportion of small details suggests compulsive rigidity. A relatively frequent use of white space is supposed to be a sign of rebelliousness and negativism. Responses that describe humans in movement are said to indicate imagination and a rich inner life; responses that are dominated by color suggest emotionality and impulsivity. (p. 684)

Finally, Rorschach addressed the final guideline for analyzing responses: what the subject actually sees in the inkblot. The most common category of responses involved animals and insects. The percentage of animal responses ranged from 25% to 50%. Interestingly, depressed subjects were among those giving the greatest percentage of animal answers, while artists were reported as giving the fewest.

Another category proposed by Rorschach was that of *original responses*. These were answers that occurred fewer than once in 100 tests. Original responses were found most often among subjects who were diagnosed as schizophrenic and least often among normal subjects of average intelligence.

DISCUSSION

In his discussion of his form interpretation test, Rorschach pointed out that originally it had been designed to study theoretical questions about the unconscious workings of the human mind and psyche. The discovery that the test had the potential to serve as a diagnostic tool was made accidentally. Rorschach claimed that his test was often able to indicate schizophrenic tendencies, hidden neuroses, potential for depression, characteristics of introversion versus extroversion, and intelligence. He did not, however, propose that the inkblot test should substitute for the usual practices of clinical diagnosis, but rather could aid in this process. Rorschach also warned that while the test can indicate certain unconscious tendencies, it cannot be used to probe the contents of the unconscious in detail. He allowed that the other common practices at the time, such as dream interpretation and free association, were superior methods for such purposes.

CRITICISMS AND SUBSEQUENT RESEARCH

Numerous studies over the decades since Rorschach developed his test have drawn many of his conclusions into question. One of the most important criticisms relates to the validity of the test—whether it actually measures what Rorschach claimed it measured, that is, underlying personality characteristics. Research has demonstrated that many of the response differences attributed by Rorschach to personality factors can be more easily explained by such things as verbal ability, age of the subject, intellectual level, amount of education, and even the characteristics of the person administering the test. (See Anastasi & Urbinai, 1996, for a detailed discussion of these criticisms.)

Taken as a whole, the scientific research on Rorschach's test does not provide an optimistic view of its reliability or validity as a personality test or diagnostic tool. Nevertheless, the test remains in common use among clinical psychologists and psychotherapists. This apparent contradiction may be explained by the fact that in actual use, Rorschach's inkblot technique is used not as a formal test, but rather as a means of increasing a therapist's understanding of individual clients. It is, in essence, an extension of the verbal interaction that normally occurs between a therapist and a client. In this less rigid interpretation of the responses on the test, it appears to offer helpful insights for effective psychotherapy.

One interesting application of the Rorschach test has been to present the figures for interpretation by more than one person, such as couples, families, coworkers, gang members, and so on. Participants are asked to reach a consensus about what the figures represent. This use of the test has shown promise as a method for studying and improving human interaction (Aronow & Reznikoff, 1976).

RECENT APPLICATIONS

A review of recent psychological and related literature shows that the validity of the Rorschach assessment scale continues to be studied and debated. Several hopeful studies from the psychoanalytic front have indicated that newer methods of administration and scoring may increase the scale's interscorer reliability and its ability to diagnose and discriminate between various psychological disturbances. For example, Arenella and Ornduff (2000) employed the Rorschach Inkblot Method to study differences in body image of sexually abused girls compared to nonabused girls from otherwise stressful environments. The researchers found that sexually abused girls responded to the Rorschach Test in ways that indicated a greater concern about their bodies than did their nonabused counterparts. In a similar vein, researchers obtained Rorschach scores for a group of 66 male psychopathic youth criminal offenders between the ages of 14 and 17 (Loving & Russell, 2000). This study found that at least some of the standard Rorschach variables were significantly associated with various levels of psychopathology. The authors suggest that the Rorschach may provide a valuable means of predicting which teens are at highest risk of violently criminal behaviors and enhance intervention strategies.

Another recent application of the Rorschach Inkblot Test was an examination of the potential psychological damage from membership in cults (Aronoff, Lynn, & Malinowski, 2000). This study, using responses to the Rorschach and other measures, found that new cult members did not appear to be suffering from any specific psychological disorders, and current members appeared to be generally well adjusted psychologically. However, the researchers did find evidence of significant post-membership social and psychological adjustment difficulties.

Finally, an intriguing development in the validity debate stems from a study comparing the Rorschach to a commonly used *objective* psychological test called the MMPI (for *Minnesota Multiphasic Personality Inventory*) in evaluating sex offenders (Grossman et al., 2002). A common problem in testing sex offenders for psychological disorders is that they often deny having, or minimize the severity of, any such problems. This study found that sex offenders who were able to "fake good" on the MMPI and score normal psychological profiles, were exposed as psychopaths by the Rorschach. "These findings indicate that the Rorschach is resilient to attempts at faking good and may therefore provide valuable information in forensic settings where intentional distortion is common" (p. 484).

Of course, the validity of this use of the Rorschach is equally open to questions about validity as is the original test on which it is based. However, these studies, along with many others, demonstrate the enduring influence and use of Rorschach's work and the potential for the development and application of projective tests that may have greater validity and therapeutic value.

Anastasi, A., & Urbinai, S. (1996). *Psychological testing,* 7th ed. New York: Macmillan.

Arenella, J., & Ornduff, S. (2000). Manifestations of bodily concern in sexually abused girls. *Bulletin of the Menniger Clinic, 64*(4), 530–542.

Aronoff, J., Lynn, S., & Malinowski, P. (2000). Are cultic environments psychologically harmful? *Clinical Psychology Review, 20*(1), 91–111.

Aronow, E., & Reznikoff, M. (1976). *Rorschach content interpretation.* New York: Grune & Stratton.

Gleitman, H. (1991). *Psychology,* 3rd ed. New York: Norton.

Grossman, L., Wasyliw, O., Benn, A., & Gyoerkoe, K. (2002). Can sex offenders who minimize on the MMPI, conceal psychopathology on the Rorachach? *Journal of Personality Assessment, 78,* 484–501.

Loving, J., & Russell, W. (2000). Selected Rorschach variables of psychopathic juvenile offenders. *Journal of Personality Assessment, 75*(1), 126–142.

PICTURE THIS!

Murray, H. A. (1938). *Explorations in personality* (pp. 531–545). New York: Oxford University Press.

In the previous reading, a method clinical psychologists use to expose under-lying aspects of personality, called the *projective test* was discussed in relation to Rorschach's inkblot technique. The idea behind Rorschach's test was to allow individuals to place or project their own interpretations onto objectively meaningless and unstructured forms. Also, Rorschach examined a subject's focus on particular sections in the inkblot, the various specific features of that section, and perceptions of movement in the figure, to draw conclusions about the subject's personality characteristics. The content of the subject's in-terpretation was also taken into account, but was of secondary importance.

Several years after Rorschach developed his test, Henry A. Murray (1893–1988), at the Harvard Psychological Clinic, and his assistant, Chris-tiana D. Morgan, developed a very different form of a projective test called the *Thematic Apperception Test*, or *TAT*, which focused entirely on the content of the subjects' interpretations. Rather than formless shapes like Rorschach's inkblots, the TAT consists of black-and-white drawings depicting people in various ambiguous situations. The client or subject is asked to make up a story about the drawing. The stories are then analyzed by the therapist or re-searcher to reveal hidden unconscious conflicts (apperception means *conscious* perception).

The theory behind the TAT was that when you observe human behav-ior, either in a picture or in real life, you will interpret that behavior accord-ing to the clues that are available in the situation. When the causes for the observed behavior are clear, your interpretation will not only be correct, it will be in substantial agreement with other observers. However, if the situa-tion is vague and it is difficult to find reasons for the behavior, your interpre-tation will more likely reflect something about yourself—about your own fears, desires, conflicts, and so on. For example, imagine you see the faces of a man and a woman looking up into the sky with different expressions on their faces: He looks terrified, but she is laughing. As you observe the situa-tion further, you see that they are waiting in line for a ride on "Batman," North America's highest mega–roller coaster located at Magic Mountain theme park in California. It is not difficult to interpret the couple's behavior in this situation and your analysis would probably be more or less the same as that of other observers. Now imagine seeing the same expressions in isola-tion, without any situational clues to explain the behavior. If you were asked, "What are these people experiencing?" your answer would depend on your internal interpretation and might reveal more about you than about the peo-ple you are observing. Furthermore, because of the ambiguity of the isolated behavior, different observers' answers would vary greatly (i.e., they're looking at a UFO, a ski run, small children playing on a high climbing toy, or an approaching tornado). This is the idea behind Morgan and Murray's Thematic Apperception Test, which to this day is a very popular tool among psychotherapists for helping their clients.

THEORETICAL PROPOSITIONS

At the most basic level, the theory underlying the TAT, like that of the Rorschach test, is that people's behavior is driven by unconscious forces. Implicit in this notion is an acceptance of the principles of psychodynamic psychology developed originally by Freud (see the discussion of Freud's theories). In this view, unconscious conflicts must be exposed for accurate diagnosis and successful treatment of psychological problems to take place. This was the purpose of Rorschach's inkblot test, discussed in the previous reading, and it was also the goal of Murray's TAT.

Morgan and Murray wrote, "The purpose of this procedure is to stimulate literary creativity and thereby evoke fantasies that reveal covert and unconscious complexes" (p. 530). The way they conceived of this process was that a person would be shown ambiguous drawings of human behavior. In trying to explain the situation, the subject would become less self-conscious and less concerned about being observed by the therapist. This would, in turn, cause the person to become less defensive and reveal inner wishes, fears, and past experiences that might have been repressed. Murray also pointed out that part of the theoretical foundation for this test was that "a great deal of written fiction is the conscious or unconscious expression of the author's experiences or fantasies" (p. 531).

METHOD

In the test's original conceptualization, subjects were asked to guess the events leading up to the scene depicted in the drawing and what they thought the outcome of the scene would be. After testing the method, it was determined that a great deal more about the psychology of subjects could be obtained if they were simply asked to make up a story about the picture, rather than asked to guess the facts surrounding it.

The pictures themselves were developed to stimulate fantasies in the subjects about conflicts and important events in their own experiences. Therefore, it was decided that each picture should involve at least one person with whom the subject could easily identify. Through trial and error with several hundred pictures, a final set of 20 was chosen. Since the TAT is in common use today, many believe that widespread publication of the pictures used might compromise its validity. However, it is difficult to understand the test without being able to see the type of drawings chosen. Therefore, Figure 1 is one of the original drawings that was under consideration, but was not ultimately chosen as one of the final 20.

FIGURE 1 Example of a TAT card. How would *you* interpret this picture? (Reprinted by permission of the publishers from Henry A. Murray, *Thematic Apperception Test,* plate 12F, Cambridge, MA. Harvard University Press. Copyright © 1943 by the President and Fellows of Harvard College. © 1971 by Henry A. Murray.)

An early study of the TAT was conducted by Morgan and Murray and reported in Murray's 1938 book cited at the beginning of this chapter. The subjects for that study were men between the ages of 20 and 30. Each subject was seated in a comfortable chair facing away from the experimenter (as has been commonly practiced by psychotherapists when administering the TAT). These are the exact instructions given to each subject:

> This is a test of your creative imagination. I shall show you a picture and I want you to make up a plot or a story for which it might be used as an illustration. What is the relation of the individuals in the picture? What has happened to them? What are their present thoughts and feelings? What will be the outcome? Do your very best. Since I am asking you to indulge your literary imagination, you may make your story as long and as detailed as you wish. (p. 532)

The experimenter handed the subject each picture in succession and took notes on what the subject said for each one. Each subject was given one hour. Due to the time limitations, most subjects only completed stories for about 15 of the 20 drawings.

A few days later the subjects returned and were interviewed about their stories. In order to disguise the true purpose of the study, subjects were told that the purpose of the research was to compare their creative experiences with those of famous writers. Subjects were reminded of their responses to the pictures and were asked to explain what their sources for the stories were. They were also given a free-association test, in which they were to say the first thing that came to mind in response to words spoken by the experimenter. These exercises were designed to determine to what extent the stories the subjects made up about the drawings reflected their own personal experiences, conflicts, desires, and so on.

RESULTS AND DISCUSSION

Murray and Morgan reported two main findings from this early study of the TAT. The first was the discovery that the stories the subjects made up for the pictures came from four sources: (1) books and movies, (2) real-life events involving a friend or a relative, (3) experiences in the subject's own life, and (4) the subject's conscious or unconscious fantasies (see p. 533 of the original study).

The second and more important finding was that the subjects clearly projected their own personal, emotional, and psychological existence into their stories. One such example reported by the authors was that most of the subjects who were students identified the person in one of the drawings as a student, but none of the nonstudent subjects did so. In another example, the subject's father was a ship's carpenter, and the subject had strong desires to travel and see the world. This fantasy appeared in his interpretations of several of the drawings. For instance, when shown a drawing of two workers in conversation, the subject's story was, "These two fellows are a pair of adventurers. They always manage to meet in out-of-the-way places. They are now in India. They have heard of a new revolution in South America and they are planning how they can get there. . . . In the end they work their way there on a freighter" (p. 534). Murray reports that, without exception, every person who participated in the study injected aspects of their personalities into their stories.

To illustrate further how the TAT reflects personal characteristics, the authors report one subject in detail. "Virt" had emigrated to the United States from Russia after terrible childhood experiences during World War I, including persecution, hunger, and separation from his mother. Picture number 13 of the TAT was given the following written description by Murray and Morgan: "On the floor against the couch is the huddled form of a boy with his head bowed on his right arm. Beside him on the floor is an object which resembles a revolver" (p. 536). Virt's story about this drawing was as follows:

> Some great trouble has occurred. Someone he loved has shot herself. Probably it is his mother. She may have done it out of poverty. He being fairly grown up sees the misery of it all and would like to shoot himself. But he is young and braces up after a while. For some time he lives in misery, the first few months thinking of death. (p. 536)

It is interesting to compare this story with other, more recent stories made up about the same drawing:

1. A 35-year-old junior high school teacher: "I think that this is someone who has been put in prison for something he did not do. He has denied that he committed any crime and has been fighting and fighting his case in the courts. But he has given up. Now he is completely exhausted, depressed, and hopeless. He made a fake gun to try to escape, but he knows this won't work either" (author's files).

2. A 16-year-old high school student: "This girl is playing hide-and-seek, probably with her brothers. She is counting from one to a hundred. She is sad and tired because she is never able to win and always has to be 'it.' It looks like the boys were playing some other game before because there's a toy gun here" (author's files).

You don't have to be a psychotherapist to make some predictions about the inner conflicts, motives, or desires that these three people might be projecting onto that one drawing. These examples also demonstrate the remarkably diverse responses that are possible on the TAT.

CRITICISMS AND RELATED RESEARCH

Although the TAT uses stimuli that are very different from Rorschach's inkblot test, it has been criticized on the same grounds of poor reliability and validity. (See the previous reading on Rorschach's test for additional discussion of these issues.) The most serious reliability problem for the TAT is that different clinicians offer differing interpretations of the same set of TAT responses. Some have suggested that therapists may unknowingly inject their own unconscious characteristics onto the subject's descriptions of the drawings. In other words, the interpretation of the TAT might, in some cases, be a projective test for the clinician who is administering it!

In terms of validity (that is, the extent to which the TAT truly measures what it is designed to measure), several types of criticisms have been cited frequently. If the test measures underlying psychological processes, then it should be able to distinguish between, say, normal people and people who are mentally ill, or between different types of psychological conditions. However, research has shown that it fails to make such distinctions. In a study by Eron (1950), the TAT was administered to two groups of male veterans. Some were students in college and others were patients in a psychiatric hospital. When the results of the TAT were analyzed, there were no significant differences found between the two groups or among psychiatric patients with different illnesses.

Other research has questioned the ability of the TAT to predict behavior. For example, if a person includes a great deal of violence in the stories and plots used to describe the drawings, this does not differentiate between aggression that merely exists in the subject's fantasies and the potential for real violent behavior. For some people, it is possible to fantasize about aggression without ever expressing violent behavior, while for others, aggressive fantasy will predict actual violence. Since TAT responses do not indicate into which category a particular person falls, the test is of little value in predicting aggressive tendencies (see Anastasi & Urbinai, 1996).

Another basic and very important criticism of the TAT (which has been made of the Rorschach inkblot technique as well) relates to whether the projective hypothesis itself is valid. The assumption underlying the TAT is that subjects' stories about the drawings reveal something about their stable, unconscious processes about who they are. There is scientific evidence to suggest, however, that responses to projective tests such as the Rorschach and TAT may depend on temporary and situational factors. What this means is that if you are given the TAT on Monday, just after work, when you've had a big fight with your boss, and then again on Saturday, just after you've returned from a relaxing day at the beach, the stories you make up for the drawings might be completely different on the two occasions. Critics argue that, to the extent that the stories are different, the TAT has only tapped into your temporary state and not your *real* underlying self.

As a demonstration of this criticism, numerous studies have found variations in TAT performance relating to the following list of influences: hunger, lack of sleep, drug use, anxiety level, frustration, verbal ability, characteristics of the person administering the test, the attitude of the subject about the testing situation, and the subject's cognitive abilities. In light of these findings, Anne Anastasi, one of the leading authorities on psychological testing, has written, "Many types of research have tended to cast doubt on the projective hypothesis. There is ample evidence that alternative explanations may account as well or better for the individual's responses to unstructured test stimuli" (Anastasi & Urbinai, 1996).

RECENT APPLICATIONS

Murray's research and the TAT continue to be cited and incorporated in numerous studies of personality characteristics and their measurement. Over 160 such articles appeared in scientific journals between 2000 and the middle of 2003, as the current edition of this book was in preparation.

One study compared TAT responses of patients diagnosed with *dissociative disorders,* such as *traumatic amnesia* and *dissociative identity disorder* (more commonly known as *multiple personality disorder*), with those of other inpatients in a psychiatric facility (Pica et al., 2001). The researchers found that, among dissociative patients, responses to the TAT cards contained virtually no positive emotions, and the "testing behaviors of dissociative participants were characterized by switching, trance states, intra-interview amnesia (blocking out parts of the TAT interview *during* testing), and affectively loaded [highly emotional) card rejections" (p. 847).

Murray's 1938 work has also been incorporated into research on personality disorders, including *antisocial personality* (a disregard for other people's rights; lack of guilt or remorse); *avoidant personality* (chronic and consistent feelings of inadequacy); *borderline personality* (intense anger, very unstable relationships); and *narcissistic personality* (exaggerated sense of self-importance, great need for admiration). Some studies have found that the TAT is successful in differentiating among personality disorders and that TAT scores are consistent with scores on the MMPI (Minnesota Multiphasic Personality Inventory), a widely used and fairly well validated objective personality assessment tool (Ackerman et al., 1999).

Finally, a study by Murray himself that might be of particular interest to many readers of this book, examined the teaching effectiveness of academic psychologists as they age (Renaud & Murray, 1996). The authors found that teaching effectiveness declined with age, and was linked to certain specific personality traits. For example, the trait of *approval-seeking*, which was associated with good teaching, decreased with age, and the characteristic of *independence*, which tended to be associated with poorer teaching, increased with age. It should be kept in mind that the study included only 33 professors from a very small number of institutions and, therefore, may not (and, in the opinion of this author, most likely does *not!*) apply to psychology professors in general.

CONCLUSION

One of the most remarkable aspects of projective tests such as the TAT and the Rorschach inkblot test is that, in spite of a massive body of evidence condemning them as invalid, unreliable, and possibly based on faulty assumptions, they are among the most frequently used psychological tests. The fact that clinicians continue to be enthusiastic about these tools while experimental psychologists grow increasingly wary is a key point of contention between those two groups (see Lilienfeld, Wood, & Garb, 2000, for a review). How can this contradiction be reconciled? The most common answer to this question is that the TAT and the Rorschach tests are usually employed in psychotherapy *not* as formal diagnostic tool, but rather as extensions of the early give-and-take between clinicians and their patients. It follows, then, that many therapists apply these devices in very individual ways to open up channels of communication with clients and enter psychological domains that might have been avoided or hidden without the prompting by the stories on the TAT. As one practicing psychotherapist explains, "I don't score my clients' responses on the TAT or use them for diagnosis, but the drawings are a wonderful and valuable vehicle for bringing to light troubled areas in a client's life. The identification and awareness of these issues that flows from the TAT, allows for more focused and effective therapy" (author's files).

Ackerman, S., Clemence, A., Weatherill, R., & Hilsenroth, M. (1999). Use of the TAT in the assessment of *DSM-IV* Cluster B personality disorders. *Journal of Personality Assessment, 73*(3), 422–442.

Anastasi, A., & Urbinai, S. (1996). *Psychological testing,* 7th ed. New York: Macmillan.

Eron, L. (1950). A normative study of the thematic apperception test. *Psychological Monographs, 64*(Whole No. 315).

Lilienfeld, S., Wood, J., & Garb, H. (2000). The scientific status of projective techniques. *Psychological Science in the Public Interest, 1*, 27–66.

Pica, M., Beere, D., Lovinger, S., & Dush, D. (2001). The responses of dissociative patients on the TAT. *Journal of Clinical Psychology, 57*, 847–864.

Renaud, R., & Murray, H. (1996). Aging, personality, and teaching effectiveness in academic psychologists. *Research in Higher Education, 37*(3), 323–340.

10 SOCIAL PSYCHOLOGY

Social psychology is the branch of psychology that looks at how your behavior is influenced by that of others and how their behavior is influenced by you. It is the study of human interaction. This psychological subfield is vast and covers a wide array of topics, from romantic relationships to group behavior to prejudice, discrimination, and aggression. This is probably the area in psychology many nonpsychologists find the most relevant. We all spend most of our waking hours interacting with others, so we naturally seek to learn more about the psychological processes involved in our social relationships. Social psychology may also be the research domain that contains the greatest number of landmark studies.

The four studies chosen for this section clearly changed psychology by (1) providing new insights into human social behavior; (2) sparking new waves of research to either confirm, refine, or contest the original findings; and (3) creating heated controversy that ultimately enriched the field in general.

First is an early study that surprised behavioral scientists by suggesting that people's *attitudes* about a person or object do not always predict how they will *behave* toward that person or object. Second is a recounting of a crucial study that demonstrated the power of *conformity* in determining behavior. The third study revealed a surprising phenomenon called the *bystander effect*, which says that the more people who witness an emergency, the less likely anyone is to help. And finally we arrive at what may be the most famous (and in some ways, infamous) study in the history of psychology: Stanley Milgram's study of blind *obedience* to authority.

NOT PRACTICING WHAT YOU PREACH
LaPiere, R. T. (1934). Attitudes and actions. *Social Forces, 13,* 230–237.

Stanford psychologist Richard LaPiere's 1934 study may have generated more subsequent research projects in the history of psychology than any other research presented in this book. It was a study about *social attitudes*—the attitudes you hold about other people or groups of people. It is logical to think that a person's attitude about an *attitude object* (either a person or a thing) will influence that person's behavior toward the object. If you tell me your attitude toward brussels sprouts is one of hate and disgust, I would predict that when faced with those little green vegetables, you will very likely refuse to eat them. And I would probably be correct.

In the early years of psychological science, there was an untested assumption that this correspondence between attitude and behavior was generally true, whether the subject of the attitude was vegetable preferences or opinions regarding other people (social attitudes). Consequently, it was quite common for psychologists and sociologists to measure attitudes through the use of questionnaires, and then assume that the measured attitude would be reflected in future behavior when the attitude object is actually encountered.

LaPiere questioned this assumption, particularly as it pertained to social attitudes. To illustrate his criticism, he used the example of a researcher asking American men the question, "Would you get up to give an Armenian woman your seat in a streetcar?" (Remember, this article was published in 1934!) Whatever the answer, LaPiere explained, the response would only be a symbolic (or hypothetical) response to a symbolic situation, and would not necessarily predict what a man would actually do if faced with a real Armenian woman on a real crowded streetcar. Even so, most researchers would, according to LaPiere, be quite willing to suggest that they could predict the respondents' actual behavior from the symbolic attitude as measured by the answer to the hypothetical question. Not only that, but the same researchers might even draw conclusions about the overall relationship between Americans and Armenians based on the same data. LaPiere argued that the assumption researchers were making of a direct correspondence between symbolic behavior (responses on questionnaires) and real behavior was far too simple, unwarranted, and probably wrong.

Throughout the following discussion of LaPiere's famous study, it is important to keep in mind that in the 1930s, there was a great deal of racial and ethnic prejudice and discrimination in American society. This is not to say that such attitudes do not exist today, but 60 years ago discriminatory practices were generally more widespread, blatant, and accepted. For example, it was a common practice for hotels and restaurants to have policies refusing service to members of certain racial or ethnic groups. LaPiere decided to capitalize on such discriminatory policies to test his idea that spoken attitudes are often poor predictors of actual behavior.

THEORETICAL PROPOSITIONS

During 1930 and 1931, LaPiere traveled extensively with a young Chinese student and his wife. "Both were personable, charming, quick to win the admiration and respect of those with whom they had the opportunity to become intimate" (p. 231). There was in the United States then a great deal of prejudice and discrimination toward anyone of Asian descent. Because of this, LaPiere reported feeling quite apprehensive when, early in their trip, the three of them approached the clerk in the best hotel "in a small town noted for its narrow and bigoted attitude toward Orientals" (p. 231). So he was surprised when they all were immediately and politely accommodated. LaPiere went on to explain, "Two months later I passed that way again, phoned the hotel, and asked if they would accommodate 'an important Chinese gentleman.' The reply was an unequivocal 'No.' That aroused my curiosity and led to this study" (p. 232).

The theory implied in LaPiere's study was that, contrary to prevailing beliefs, people's *social actions* track very poorly with their spoken social attitudes. In other words, what people say is often not what they do.

METHOD

This study was conducted in two distinctly separate parts. The first part focused on actual behavior, while the second assessed related symbolic attitudes.

Real Behavior Phase

LaPiere and his Chinese friends traveled by car twice across the United States, as well as up and down the full length of the Pacific Coast. Their journey totaled approximately 10,000 miles. From a careful examination of LaPiere's article, it appears that his research on attitudes was not the purpose of the trip, but rather was coincidental. For one thing, LaPiere did not inform the Chinese couple that he was making careful observations of the treatment they received wherever they went. His justification for this was that had they known, they might have become self-conscious and altered their behavior in some way that would have made the study less valid.

Between 1930 and 1933, the travelers approached 67 hotels, auto camps, and tourist homes (whatever those were) for accommodations. They ate at 184 restaurants and cafés. LaPiere kept detailed records of the responses of hotel clerks, bell boys, elevator operators, and waitresses to the presence of the Chinese couple. So that reactions would not be unduly altered because of his presence, LaPiere often let the Chinese couple secure the room or other accommodations while he took care of the luggage, and whenever possible he allowed them to enter restaurants before him. The treatment the Chinese couple received are discussed in detail shortly.

Symbolic Behavior Phase

In the second part of the study, LaPiere mailed questionnaires to all of the establishments they had visited. He allowed six months to pass between the actual visit and the mailing of the questionnaire. His reason for this delay was to allow the effect of the Chinese couple's visit to fade.

The question of primary interest on the questionnaire was, "Will you accept members of the Chinese race as guests in your establishment?" These questionnaires were returned by 81 of the restaurants and cafés and 47 of the lodging establishments. This was a response rate of 51%.

To ensure that the questionnaire responses were not directly influenced by the Chinese couple's visit, LaPiere also obtained responses to the same questionnaire from 32 hotels and 96 restaurants located in the same regions of the country, but not visited by the travelers.

So, after nearly three years, LaPiere had the data necessary to make a comparison of social attitudes with social behavior.

RESULTS

LaPiere reported that of the 251 hotels and restaurants they patronized on their travels, there was only one instance in which they were denied service because of the ethnicity of his companions. This single rejection, in a small California town, was described by LaPiere as occurring at a *rather inferior auto camp.* The proprietor came toward the car and upon seeing the occupants said, "No. I don't take Japs!" This ugly experience aside, most of their other experiences involved average or even above-average treatment, although at times the treatment was altered due to *curiosity* about the Chinese couple. LaPiere explained that in 1930, outside the Pacific Coast region, Chicago, and New York, most people in the United States had little experience with, and perhaps had never even seen, people of Asian heritage. Table 1 summarizes LaPiere's ratings of the service they received. As you can see, in all but a very few establishments, the service they received was rated by LaPiere to be the same as or better than what he would have expected if he had been traveling alone.

The responses to the questionnaires mailed to the establishments six months later and those mailed to the places not visited are summarized in Table 2. Nearly all (over 90%) of the hotels, campgrounds, tourist homes, restaurants, and cafés visited by LaPiere and the Chinese couple replied that they would not serve Chinese individuals! In addition, the distribution of responses from the establishments not visited were virtually the same, indicating that the findings were not somehow caused by the travelers' recent visit. On the contrary, the one "Yes" response to the questionnaire came from the manager of a small auto camp who enclosed a "chatty letter describing the nice visit she had had with a Chinese gentleman and his sweet wife during the previous summer" (p. 234).

TABLE 1 LaPiere's Ratings of Service Received

QUALITY OF RECEPTION	LODGINGS	RESTAURANTS AND CAFÉS
Very much better than expected if investigator had been alone	25	72
Good, but different because of increased curiosity	25	82
Equal to normal expectations	11	24
Perceptibly hesitant for racial reasons	4	5
Definitely, but temporarily, embarrassing	1	1
Not accepted	1	0
Total	67	184

(Adapted from p. 235.)

TABLE 2 Number of Questionnaire Responses to Question: "Will You Accept Members of the Chinese Race as Guests in Your Establishment?"

ANSWER	LODGINGS VISITED	RESTAURANTS VISITED	LODGINGS NOT VISITED	RESTAURANTS NOT VISITED
No	43	75	30	76
Undecided, depends on circumstances	3	6	2	7
Yes	1	0	0	1

(Adapted from p. 234.)

DISCUSSION

LaPiere's discussion of his findings focused on the lack of validity of questionnaires in determining a person's true attitude. He contended that "it is impossible to make direct comparisons between the reactions secured through questionnaires and from actual experience" (p. 234). He pointed out that if a Chinese person were to consult the findings of the questionnaire prior to setting out on a tour of the United States (in 1930), he would undoubtedly decide to stay home! However, LaPiere's friends enjoyed an almost discrimination-free trip and became increasingly confident about approaching new social situations without fear of rejection or embarrassment.

So was LaPiere suggesting that we eliminate the use of questionnaires altogether? No. He suggested that such data might be useful in determining people's symbolic attitudes about issues that would remain symbolic. For example, he allowed that questionnaires could measure political attitudes, but this information would provide little information about how people will vote or behave if they meet a candidate on the street or at a party. Another example of an acceptable use of questionnaire data was the measurement of religious attitudes. LaPiere pointed out that "an honest answer to the question 'Do you believe in God?' reveals all there is to be measured. 'God' is a symbol; 'belief,' a verbal expression" (p. 235).

His conclusion was that if you want to predict how someone will behave when actually faced with a certain situation or another person, a verbal reaction to a symbolic situation (i.e., an attitude questionnaire) is wholly inadequate. He contended that social attitudes can only be reliably measured by studying human behavior in actual social situations. His article ended with what might be interpreted as a warning to other researchers:

> The questionnaire is cheap, easy, and mechanical. The study of human behavior is time-consuming, intellectually fatiguing, and depends for its success on the ability of the investigator. The former method gives quantitative results, the latter mainly qualitative . . . Yet it would seem far more worthwhile to make a shrewd guess regarding that which is essential than to accurately measure that which is likely to prove quite irrelevant. (p. 237)

CRITICISMS, SUBSEQUENT RESEARCH, AND RECENT APPLICATIONS

Psychologists reacted to LaPiere's findings almost as an athlete would react to being challenged to a competition. A great deal of research was generated, and this response took three directions. First, some leveled several strong criticisms at LaPiere's methods and findings. Second, researchers set about trying to determine why attitude assessments fail to predict actual behavior. And third, behavioral scientists have attempted to determine the conditions under which attitude measurements will *reliably* predict behavior.

LaPiere's methods were criticized on the basis that a simple yes-no answer to a question in a letter is not a valid measurement of a person's attitude regarding a specific group of people. For example, the image of "members of the Chinese race" in the minds of the respondents may have been very different from the Chinese couple they actually encountered. Another criticism has suggested that only half of the places the three travelers visited responded to the questionnaire. The critics contend it is possible that those who took the time to respond may have been the ones with the strongest prejudicial attitudes against Asians. Finally, after six months, the person responding to the letter may not have been the same person who met the travelers face to face.

However, nearly 40 years after LaPiere's findings, a review of the attitude-behavior research that had accumulated over the years concluded that the correlation between measured attitudes and actual behavior was indeed weak and perhaps nonexistent (Wicker, 1971). Some researchers have focused their attention on trying to determine why this inconsistency exists and they have proposed a variety of reasons (see Fishbein & Ajzen, 1975, for a complete discussion). A few of these are discussed here.

First, you have many attitudes and some may compete with each other. Which attitude will exert the most influence on your behavior depends on the specifics of the situation. Second, there are times when you might behave in ways that are contrary to your attitudes because you have no alternative, such as situations in which your job or a friendship depends on a certain action. Third, social pressures and the human desire to avoid embarrassment can exert strong influences that may produce behaviors that are inconsistent with attitudes.

So this question remained: When, if ever, will attitude measurements be successful in predicting behavior? Recently, there has been a major research effort to identify the factors that produce greater consistency between attitudes and behavior. These factors can be summarized into the following five categories (see Taylor, Peplau, & Sears, 2002):

1. *Strength of the attitude.* The stronger you feel toward certain people or situations, the more likely you are to behave accordingly when you encounter them in person. On the other hand, weak or ambivalent attitudes may exert little or no influence on your behavior.

2. *Stability of the attitude.* This factor deals with how your attitudes change over time. Attitudes that are stable, predict behavior better than those that change with time. Ideally, for an accurate attitude-behavior connection researchers should measure both at nearly the same time.

3. *Relevance of attitude to the behavior.* Some early studies asked people if they believed in God, and then tried to use their answers to predict their attendance in church. It didn't work. If you measure someone's attitude about sports, it is likely to be a poor predictor of how often they attend athletic events. This implies that attitudes will predict behavior much better if the attitude measured relates *exactly* to the behavior of interest. To demonstrate this, one study asked a group of college women about their attitudes toward birth control and asked another similar group about their attitudes toward using birth control pills during the next two years. The correlation between the measured attitude and actual use of birth control pills during the following two years was .08 (non-significant) for the first group, but .57 (highly significant) for the specific-attitude group (Davidson & Jaccard, 1979).

4. *Salience of the attitude.* If an attitude you hold toward something or someone is salient, it is conspicuous, important, and readily accessed from your memory. The more salient the attitude, the more likely it will predict your behavior. Suppose you have a positive attitude about the act of donating blood. If a friend or family member has recently had surgery that required a lot of blood, your attitude about giving blood is probably much more salient than usual. Under these circumstances, you are more likely to give blood than at other times, even though the attitude itself did not change.

5. *Situational pressures.* Sometimes the external pressures that exist in a particular situation are so strong that your internal attitude will have little effect on your behavior. For example, imagine a new stop sign has recently been installed at a corner near your home. The street usually has little traffic, and you believe the sign is an unnecessary nuisance, so you usually just roll right through it. This week, however, a police car is parked at that corner every day. Suddenly, your internal attitude toward the sign loses all its power and your behavior falls under the influence of the situation: you come to a full stop. Can you see how this concept could explain LaPiere's findings? When the various proprietors in the study were face-to-face with a nicely dressed couple asking for food or lodging, the situational pressures to accommodate them were very strong and may have prevailed over their internal racist attitudes.

LaPiere's research of more than 70 years ago continues to be cited in studies of attitude-behavior connections and prejudice and discrimination. One ambitious study examined the extent to which the discrimination toward Chinese Americans experienced by the couple in LaPiere's study has changed in the decades years since its publication (Goto, Gee, & Takeuchi, 2002). In interviews with over 1,500 Chinese Americans, participants were asked about unfair treatment thay had received due to race, ethnicity, language, or accent. "Nearly 21% of the participants reported being unfairly treated in their lifetime. . . . Retention of cultural practices, age at immigration, and contact opportunity were associated with racial discrimination" (p. 211). *Contact opportunity,* the amount of contact between those of various races, was inversely related to discrimination; that is, direct contact *reduced* discrimination based on race as well as on language and accent. You can see from these findings that when people have greater opportunity for interaction with people of other racial and ethnic groups, stereotyping and discrimination may be reduced. This has become known as the *contact hypothesis* (Gutek, Cohen, & Konrad, 1990).

A new word related to attitude-behavior research has crept into the American English vocabulary over the past 10 years or so: *NIMBY.* This is an acronym for *not in my backyard.* The context in which the NIMBY concept usually appears is when an event, a project, or an environmental change of some sort is under consideration. Often the issue receives widespread support, and many people agree that the project will serve the public good. However, when it appears that such an undertaking may affect them personally, they become emphatically opposed to it. In other words, "It's a great idea, but *not in my backyard!"* A frequent example of the NIMBY attitude-behavior discrepancy relates to nuclear waste dumps. Most people agree that such radioactive waste should be disposed of safely in sealed underground storage facilities. However, just try to find a place where the local residents will allow such a facility to be built. NIMBY! This concept has broad applications for psychological services and public health initiatives. A study by Zsambok, Hammer, and Rojahn (1999), called "Put Your Money Where Your Mouth Is," cited LaPiere's early work in assessing the attitudes of residents to a proposal to open a group home for mentally retarded individuals in the neighborhood. Some residents responded to a survey in which they expressed agreement with the need for such facilities. Other, however, were asked to sign a petition in favor of opening such a facility nearby. You've already guessed the results, haven't you? The correlation between the two measures was very low, demonstrating that the survey did a very poor job of predicting the petition responses.

CONCLUSION

The research on attitudes and behavior constitutes a huge body of literature, of which only a minuscule sample has been included here. Behavioral scientists may never unravel all the complexities of this relationship, but the research continues. As theories and methods have been refined and perfected over the years, evidence has increased to suggest that our attitudes do play an important role in determining our behavior. It is no longer a question of whether attitudes predict behavior, but exactly how and when they do so.

Most importantly, in the present context, is that the beginning of all this interest in the attitude-behavior connection rests largely on a single study by LaPiere, more than 70 years ago.

Davidson, A., & Jaccard, J. (1979). Variables that modulate the attitude-behavior relation: Results of a longitudinal survey. *Journal of Personality and Social Psychology, 37,* 1364–1376.

Fishbein, M., & Ajzen, I. (1975). *Belief, attitude, intention, and behavior: An introduction to the theory and research.* Reading, MA: Addison-Wesley.

Goto, S., Gee, G., & Takeuchi, D. (2002). Strangers still? The experience of discrimination among Chinese Americans. *Journal of Community Psychology, 30,* 211–224.

Gutek, B. A., Cohen, A. G., & Konrad, A. M. (1990). Predicting social-sexual behavior at work: A contact hypothesis. *Academy of Management Journal, 33,* 560–577.

Taylor, S., Peplau, L., & Sears, D. (2002). Social psychology, 11th ed. Upper Saddle River, NJ: Prentice Hall.

Wicker, A. (1971). Attitudes vs. action: The relationship between verbal and overt behavior responses to attitude objects. *Journal of Social Issues, 25,* 41–78.

Zsambok, J., Hammer, D., & Rojahn, J. (1999). Put your money where your mouth is: Direct and indirect measures of attitude community integration. *American Journal on Mental Health Retardation, 104*(1), 88–92.

THE POWER OF CONFORMITY
Asch, S. E. (1955). Opinions and social pressure. *Scientific American, 193*(5), 31–35.

Do you consider yourself to be a conformist, or are you more of a rebel? Most of us probably like to think that we are conformist enough to not be considered terribly strange or frightening, and nonconformist enough to demonstrate that we are individuals and capable of independent thinking. Psychologists have been interested in the concept of conformity for decades. It is easy to see why when you remember that psychology tries to study the influences on human behavior. The differences in the amount to which people conform can help us a great deal in predicting the behavior for various individuals.

When psychologists talk about conformity, they refer to an individual's behavior that adheres to the behavior patterns of a particular group of which that individual is a member. The usually unspoken rules or guidelines for behavior in a group are called *social norms*. If you think about it, you can probably remember a time in your life when you behaved in ways that were out of sync or in disagreement with your attitudes, beliefs, or morals. Chances are you were in a group in which everyone was behaving that way, so you went along with them. This indicates that sometimes conformity is a powerful force on our behavior and can even at times make us do things that conflict with our attitudes, ethics, and morals. Therefore, conformity is clearly very worthy of interest and study by behavioral scientists. It was not until the early 1950s that someone decided to make a systematic study. That someone was Solomon Asch. His experiments offered us a great deal of new information about conforming behavior and opened many doors for future research.

THEORETICAL PROPOSITIONS

Suppose you are with a group of people that you see often, such as friends or coworkers. The group is discussing some controversial issue or political candidate. It quickly becomes clear to you that everyone in the group shares one view, which is the opposite of your own. At one point the others turn to you and ask for your opinion. What are you going to do? The choices you are faced with are to state your true views and risk the consequences, to agree with the group consensus even though it differs from your opinion, or, if possible, to sidestep the issue entirely.

Asch wanted to find out just how powerful the need to conform is in influencing our behavior. Although conformity often involves general and vague concepts such as attitudes, ethics, morals, and belief systems, Asch chose to focus on a much more obvious form: perceptual conformity. By examining conforming behavior on a simple visual comparison task, he was able to study this phenomenon in a controlled laboratory environment.

If conformity is as powerful a force as Asch and many others believed, then researchers should be able to manipulate a person's behavior by applying group pressure to conform. This is what Asch set about testing in a very elegantly designed series of experiments, all incorporating a similar method.

METHOD

The visual materials consisted simply of pairs of cards with three different lengths of vertical lines (called comparison lines) on one and a single standard line the same length as one of three comparison lines on the other (see Figure 1). Here is how the experimental process worked. Imagine you are a subject who has volunteered to participate in a *visual perception study*. You arrive at the experiment room on time and find seven other subjects already seated in a row. You sit in the empty chair at the end of the row. The experimenter reveals a pair of cards and asks you to determine which of the three comparison lines is the same length as the standard line. You look at the lines and immediately decide on the correct response. Starting at the far end of the row away from you, each subject is asked individually for his or her an-

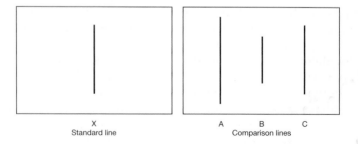

X
Standard line

A   B   C
Comparison lines

FIGURE 1 An example similar to Asch's line judging task cards. (Adapted from p. 32.)

swer. Everyone gives the correct answer, and when your turn comes you give the same obviously correct answer. The card is changed, the same process happens, and—once again, no problem—you give the correct answer along with the rest of the group. On the next trial, however, something odd happens. The card is revealed and you immediately choose in your mind the correct response. (After all, this is not very difficult.) But when the other subjects give their answers, they all choose the wrong line! And they all choose the *same* wrong line. Now, when it is your turn to respond again, you pause. You can't believe what is happening. Are all these other people blind? The correct answer is obvious. Isn't it? Have *you* gone blind? Or crazy? You now must make a decision like the one described above with your friends or coworkers. Do you maintain your opinion (after all, the lines are right in front of your nose), or do you conform and agree with the rest of the group?

As you have probably figured out by now, the other seven "subjects" in the room were not subjects at all, but confederates of the experimenter. They were in on the experiment from the beginning and the answers they gave were, of course, the key to this study of conformity. So, how did the real subjects in the study answer?

RESULTS

Each subject participated in the experimental situation several times. Approximately 75% of them went along with the group's consensus at least once. For all trials combined, subjects agreed with the group on the incorrect responses about one-third of the time. Just to be sure that the line lengths could be judged accurately, each individual in a control group of subjects was asked to individually write down his or her answer to the line comparison questions. Subjects in this group were correct 98% of the time.

DISCUSSION AND RELATED RESEARCH

The powerful effects of group pressures to conform were clearly demonstrated in Asch's study. If individuals are willing to conform to a group of people they hardly know about a clearly incorrect judgment, how strong must this influence be in real life, where groups exert even stronger forces and issues are more ambiguous? Conformity as a major factor in human behavior, the subject of widespread speculation for years, had now been scientifically established.

Asch's results were extremely important to the field of psychology in two crucial ways. First, as discussed above, the real power of the social pressure to conform was demonstrated clearly and scientifically for the first time. Second, and perhaps even more important, this early research sparked a huge wave of additional studies that continue right up to the present. The body of research that has accumulated since Asch's early studies has greatly elaborated our knowledge of the specific factors that determine the effects conformity has on our behavior. Some of these findings follow:

1. *Social support.* Asch conducted his same experiment with a slight variation. He altered the answers of the confederates so that in the test condition one of the seven gave the correct answer. When this occurred,
only 5% of the subjects agreed with the group consensus. Apparently, a
single ally is all you need to "stick to your guns" and resist the pressure
to conform. This finding has been supported by several later studies
(see, e.g., Morris & Miller, 1975).

2. *Attraction and commitment to the group.* Later research has demonstrated
that the more attracted and committed you are to a particular group,
the more likely you are to conform to the behavior and attitudes of that
group (see Forsyth, 1983). If you like the group and feel that you belong with them (they are your *reference group*) your tendency to conform
to that group will be very strong.

3. *Size of the group.* At first, research by Asch and others demonstrated that
the tendency to conform increases as the size of the group increases.
However, upon further examination, it was found that this connection
is not so simple. While it is true that conformity increases as the size of
the group increases, this only holds for groups up to six or seven members. As the group size increases beyond this number, conformity levels
off, and even decreases somewhat. This is shown graphically in Figure 2.
Why is this? Well, Asch has suggested that as the group becomes large,
people may begin to suspect the other members of working together
purposefully to affect their behavior and they become resistant to this
obvious pressure.

4. *Sex.* Do you think there is a difference between men and women in
their tendency or willingness to conform? Early studies that followed
Asch's work indicated that women seemed to be much more willing to
conform than men. This was such a strong and frequently repeated
finding that it entered the psychological literature as an accepted difference between the sexes. However, later research drew this notion into
question. It appears that many of the early studies (conducted by men)
inadvertently created testing conditions that were more familiar and
comfortable for men in those days than for women. Psychologists know

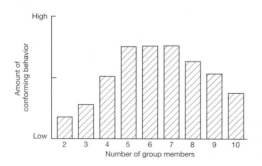

FIGURE 2   The relationship between group size and conformity. (Adapted from p. 35.)

that people will tend to conform more when placed in a situation where the appropriate behavior is unclear. Therefore, the finding of greater conformity among women may have simply been a systematic error caused by subtle (and unintentional) biases in the methods used. More recent research under better controlled conditions has failed to find this sex difference in conformity behavior (see Sistrunk & McDavid, 1971, for a discussion of these gender-related issues).

Numerous additional areas related to the issue of conformity have been studied as well. These include, cultural *influences,* the amount of information available when making decisions about conforming, social norms, personal privacy, and many others.

CRITICISMS

Asch's work on conformity has received widespread support and acceptance. It has been replicated in many studies, under a wide variety of conditions. A line of criticism commonly heard concerns whether Asch's findings can be generalized to situations in the real world. In other words, does a subject's answer in a laboratory about the length of some lines really have very much to do with conforming behavior in life? This is a valid criticism to make for all research about human behavior that is carried out in a controlled laboratory setting. What this criticism says is, "Well, maybe the subjects were willing to go along with the group on something so trivial and unimportant as the length of a line, but in real life, and on important matters, they would not conform so readily." It must be pointed out, however, that although real-life matters of conformity can certainly be more meaningful, it is equally likely that the pressures for conformity from groups in the real world are also proportionately stronger.

RECENT APPLICATIONS

An article examining why young adults continue to engage in unsafe sexual practices demonstrates how Asch's work continues to influence research on important social issues (Cerwonka, Isbell, & Hansen, 2000). The researchers assessed nearly 400 students between the ages of 18 and 29 on various measures of their HIV/AIDS knowledge risk behaviors (such as failure to use condoms, multiple sex partners, alcohol and other drug use, and sexual history). Numerous factors were shown to predict high-risk sexual behaviors, including *conformity to peer group pressures.* You can see how an understanding of how conformity pressures affect people's choice about their sexual behaviors might be a valuable tool in fighting the continuing spread of HIV.

Another fascinating study incorporated Asch's 1955 article to examine why men are less likely than women to seek help, even when they are in dire need of it (Mansfield et al., 2003). This article begins with the following (old) joke: "Why did Moses spend 40 years wandering in the desert? Because he wouldn't ask for directions" (p. 93). This joke is funny because it taps into a stereotype about men and help-seeking. Of course, failure to ask for directions *usually* does not cause serious problems, but men also tend to resist seeking medical and mental health care, and that can be dangerous or even fatal. The authors suggest that one of the primary forces preventing men from seeking help is conformity. "In the context of help seeking, men may be disinclined to seek help if they believe they will be stigmatized for doing so. . . . If a man greatly admires the people in his life who discourage or speak badly of seeking help, he will be less likely to seek help himself (p. 101).

On a final note, culture appears to play an especially important role in conformity (Bond & Smith, 1996). Research in collectivist countries, such as Japan or India, has consistently found higher levels of conformity than in individualistic countries, such as the United States (see Triandis's research on collectivist and individualistic cultures in the *Personality* section of this book). Such findings add to the ever-growing body of evidence that psychological research must never overlook the impact of culture on virtually all human behaviors.

Bond, R., & Smith, P. (1996). Culture and conformity: A meta-analysis of studies using Asch's line-judgement task. *Psychological Bulletin, 119*(1), 111–137.

Cerwonka, E., Isbell, T., & Hansen, C. (2000). Psychosocial factors as predictors of unsafe sexual practices among young adults. *Aids Education and Prevention, 12*(2), 141–153.

Forsyth, D. (1983). *An introduction to group dynamics.* Pacific Grove, CA: Brooks/Cole.

Mansfield, A., Addis, M., & Mahalik, J., (2003). Why won't he go to the doctor? The psychology of men's help-seeking. *International Journal of Men's Health, 2,* 93–109.

Morris, W., & Miller, R. (1975). The effects of consensus-breaking and consensus-preempting partners on reduction in conformity. *Journal of Experimental Social Psychology, 11,* 215–223.

Sistrunk, F., & McDavid, J. (1971). Sex variable in conforming behavior. *Journal of Personality and Social Psychology, 17,* 200–207.

TO HELP OR NOT TO HELP

Darley, J. M., & Latané, B. (1968). Bystander intervention in emergencies: Diffusion of responsibility. *Journal of Personality and Social Psychology, 8, 377–383.*

One of the most influential events in the history of psychology and psychological research was not an experiment or a discovery made by a behavioral scientist, but a news item about a violent and tragic event in New York City that was picked up by most media news services across the United States. In 1964, Kitty Genovese was returning to her apartment in a quiet, middle-class neighborhood in Queens after closing the Manhattan bar that she managed. As she left her car and walked toward her building, she was viciously attacked by a man with a knife. As the man stabbed her several times, she screamed for help. One neighbor yelled out his window for the man to "leave that girl alone," at which time the attacker began to walk away. But then he turned, knocked Genovese to the ground, and began stabbing her again. She continued to scream until finally someone telephoned the police. The police arrived two minutes after they were called, but Genovese was already dead and her attacker had disappeared. The attack had lasted 35 minutes. During police investigations, it was found that 38 people in the surrounding apartments had witnessed the attack, but only one had eventually called the police. One couple (who said they assumed someone else had called the police) had moved two chairs next to their window in order to watch the violence. Genovese's killer, Winston Moseley, now in his late 60s, remains incarcerated at a maximum-security prison in upstate New York.

If someone had acted sooner to help Genovese, she probably would have survived. New York City and the nation were appalled by the seeming lack of caring on the part of so many neighbors who had failed to try to stop this violent act. People attempted to find a reason for this inaction. The alienation caused by living in a large city was blamed; the neighborhood of Queens was blamed; basic human nature was blamed.

The Genovese tragedy sparked the interest of psychologists, who set out to try to understand what psychological forces might have been at work to prevent all those people from helping. There is an area of psychology that studies what behavioral scientists call *prosocial behavior*, or behavior that produces positive social consequences. Topics falling into this research area include altruism, cooperation, resisting temptation, and helping. If you witness an emergency situation in which someone may be in need of help, there are many factors that affect your decision to step in and offer assistance. John Darley at New York University and Bibb Latané at Columbia, both social psychologists, were among those who wanted to examine these factors. They termed the behavior of helping in emergencies, *bystander intervention* (or in this case, nonintervention).

Have you ever been faced with a true emergency? Contrary to what you may think from watching television and reading newspapers, emergencies are not very common. Darley and Latané estimated that the average person will encounter fewer than six emergencies in a lifetime. This is good and bad: good for obvious reasons; bad because if and when you find yourself facing an emergency, you will have to decide what to do, without the benefit of very much experience. Society dictates that we take action to help in emergencies, but often, as in the famous Genovese case, we do not. Why is this? Could it be because we have so little experience that we do not know what to do? Is it because of the alienation caused by urban living? Or are humans, by nature, basically uncaring?

Following the Genovese murder, Darley and Latané analyzed the bystanders' reactions. They theorized that the large number of people who witnessed the violent event decreased the willingness of individuals to step in and help. They decided to test their theory experimentally.

THEORETICAL PROPOSITIONS

Your common sense might tell you that the more bystanders there are in an emergency, the more likely someone will intervene. But Darley and Latané hypothesized just the opposite. They believed that the reason no one took steps to help Kitty Genovese was a phenomenon they called *diffusion of responsibility*.

That is, as the number of bystanders in an emergency increases, the greater is the belief that "someone else will help, so I don't need to." Have you ever witnessed an accident on a busy street or arrived at the scene of one soon after it has happened? Chances are that as you drove by you made the assumption that someone surely has called the police or ambulance by now, and therefore you did not feel the personal responsibility to do so. But imagine discovering the same accident on a deserted country road with no one else around. Would your response be different? Mine probably would be, too.

The concept of diffusion of responsibility formed the theoretical basis for this chapter's study. The trick was to re-create a Genovese-like situation in the laboratory so that it could be manipulated and examined systematically. Darley and Latané were very ingenious in designing an experiment to do this.

METHOD

For obvious reasons, it would not be practical or even possible to reproduce the events of the Kitty Genovese murder for experimental purposes. Therefore, a situation needed to be devised that would approximate or simulate a true emergency so that the intervention of bystanders could be observed. In this experiment, Darley and Latané told students in an introductory psychology class at New York University that they were interested in studying how students adjust to university life in a highly competitive, urban environment and what kinds of personal problems they were experiencing. The students were asked to discuss their problems honestly with other students, but to avoid any discomfort or embarrassment, they would be in separate rooms and would speak with each other over an intercom system. This intercom, they were told, would only allow one student to speak at a time. Each student would be given two minutes, after which the microphone for the next student would be activated for two minutes, and so on.

All of this was a cover story designed to obtain natural behavior from the subjects and to hide the true purpose of the experiment. The most important part of this cover story was the way the students were divided into three different experimental conditions. The subjects in group 1 believed that they would be talking with only one other person; those in group 2 believed there would be two other people on the intercom; and the group 3 subjects were told that there were five other people on the line. In reality, each subject was alone and all the other voices were on tape.

Now that the size of the groups was varied, some sort of emergency had to be created. The researchers decided that a very realistically acted epileptic seizure would be interpreted by most people as an emergency. As the discussions over the intercom system between the subjects and the other "students" began, subjects heard the first student, a male, tell about his difficulties concentrating on his studies and problems adjusting to life in New York City. He then added, with some embarrassment, that he sometimes had severe seizures, especially when under a lot of stress. Then the conversation switched to the next student. In group 1, the actual subject's turn came next, whereas in the other two conditions, the subject heard one or more other students speak before his or her turn. After the subject spoke it was the first student's turn again. This is when the emergency occurred. The first student spoke normally as before, but then began to have a seizure (remember, this was all on tape). Latané and Darley quote the seizure in detail in a later report as follows:

> I-er-um-I think I-I need-er-if-if could-er-er somebody er-er-er-er-er-er give me a little-er-give me a little help here because-er-I-er-I'm-er-h-h-having a-a-a real problem-er right now and I-er-if somebody could help me out it would-it would-er-er s-s-sure be good . . . because-er-there-er-ag cause I er-I-uh-I've got one of the-er-sei—er-er-things coming on and-and-and I could really use some help so if somebody would-er give me a little h-help-uh-er-er-er-er c-ould somebody-er er-help-er-uh-uh-uh [choking sounds] . . . I'm gonna die-er-er . . . help-er-er-seizure [chokes, then quiet]. (pp. 95–96)

To the subjects, this was clearly an emergency. There was no question that the "student" was in trouble and needed help immediately. In order to analyze the responses of the subjects, Darley and Latané measured the percentage of subjects in each condition who helped the student in trouble (helping was defined as leaving the cubicle and notifying the experimenter of the problem). They also measured the amount of time it took subjects to respond to the emergency and try to help. Subjects were given four minutes to respond, after which the experiment was terminated.

RESULTS

The findings from this study offered strong support for the researchers' hypothesis. As subjects believed there were a greater number of others present, the percentage who reported the seizure *quickly*, that is, as the attack was occurring, decreased dramatically (see Figure 1). Among those who *eventually* helped, the amount of delay in helping was greater when more bystanders were present. For group 1, the average delay in responding was less than one

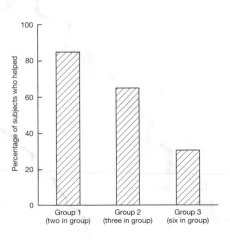

FIGURE 1 Number of subjects in each condition who helped quickly *during* seizure. (Adapted from data on p. 380.)

minute, whereas for group 3 it was over three minutes. Finally, the total number of subjects who reported the seizure at all, either during or after it occurred, varied among the groups in a similar way. *All* of the subjects in group 1 reported the emergency, but only 85% of group 2 and 60% of group 3 did so *at any time* during the four-minute period.

DISCUSSION

As in the real-life case of Kitty Genovese, you might think that the subjects in this study were simply uncaring toward the victim having the seizure. However, Darley and Latané are quick to point out that this was not the reason for the inaction of subjects in groups 2 and 3 (or of Genovese's neighbors). All the subjects reported experiencing a great deal of anxiety and discomfort during the attack and showed physical signs of nervousness (trembling hands, sweaty palms). The researchers concluded, therefore, that the reason for their results must lie in the difference in the number of other people the subjects believed were present. Whenever your behavior is changed because of the presence of others, this is called *social influence*. Obviously, social influence played a significant role in this study. But we are still left wondering why. What was it about the presence of others that was so influential?

Darley and Latané claimed to have demonstrated and supported their theory of diffusion of responsibility. As the number of people in the group increased, the subject felt less personal or individual responsibility to take action. It was easier in groups 2 and 3 for the subjects to assume that someone else would handle the problem. In a related point, it is not only the responsibility for helping that is shared when others are present, but also the potential guilt or blame for not helping. Since helping others is considered to be a positive action in our culture, refusing or failing to help carries shameful connotations. If you are the only person present in an emergency, the negative consequences of not helping will be much greater than if others are there to bear some of the burden for nonintervention.

Another possible explanation for this type of social influence is something that psychologists have termed *evaluation apprehension*. Darley and Latané contended that part of the reason we fail to help when others are present is that we are afraid of being embarrassed or ridiculed. Imagine how foolish you would feel if you were to spring into action to help someone who did not need or want your help. I remember a time when, as a teenager, I was swimming with a large group of friends at a neighbor's pool. As I was about to dive from the board I saw the neighbor's 13-year-old daughter lying facedown on the bottom of the pool. I looked around and no one else seemed to be aware of, or concerned about, this apparent emergency. Was she drowning? Was she joking? I wasn't sure. Just as I was about to yell for help and dive in for the rescue, she swam lazily to the surface. I had hesitated a full 30 seconds out of the fear of being wrong. Many of us have had experiences such as this. The problem is, they teach us the wrong thing: helping behavior carries with it the possibility of looking foolish.

SIGNIFICANCE OF THE FINDINGS

From this and other studies, Darley and Latané became the leading re-searchers in the field of helping behavior and bystander intervention. Much of their early work was included in their book *The Unresponsive Bystander: Why Doesn't He Help?* (Latané & Darley, 1970). In this work, they outlined a model for helping behavior that has become widely accepted in the psychological literature on helping. They proposed five steps you probably would go through before intervening in an emergency:

1. You, the potential helper, must first notice that an event is occurring. In the study this chapter examines, there was no question that such notice would occur, but in the real world, you may be in a hurry or your attention may be focused elsewhere, and you might completely fail to notice the event.

2. You must interpret the situation as one in which help is truly needed. This is a point at which fear of embarrassment exerts its influence. Again, in the present study, the situation was not ambiguous and the need for help was quite clear. In reality, however, most potential emergencies contain some degree of doubt or ambiguity, such as in my swimming pool example. Or, imagine you see a man stagger and pass out on a busy city sidewalk. Is he sick or just drunk? How you interpret the situation will influence your decision to intervene. Many of those who failed to help in the Genovese case claimed that they thought it was a lover's quarrel and did not want to get involved.

3. You have to assume personal responsibility. This will usually happen immediately if you are the only bystander in the emergency. If others are also present, however, you may instead place the responsibility on them. This step was the focus of this chapter's experiment. The more people present in an emergency, the more diffused the responsibility, and the less likely help will occur.

4. If you assume responsibility, you then must decide what action to take. Here, if you do not know what to do or you do not feel capable of taking the appropriate action, you will be less likely to help. In our present study, this issue of competence did not play a part, since all that the subject had to do was report the seizure to the experimenter. But if a crowd were to witness a pedestrian run over by a car, a member of the group who was a doctor, a nurse, or a paramedic would be more likely to intervene because he or she would know what to do.

5. Finally, after you've decided what action to take, you have to take it. Just because you know what to do doesn't guarantee that you will do it. Now you will weigh the costs and benefits of helping. Are you willing to personally intervene in a fight in which one or both of the participants has a knife? What about victims of accidents—can you help them, or will you make things worse by trying to help (the competence issue again)?

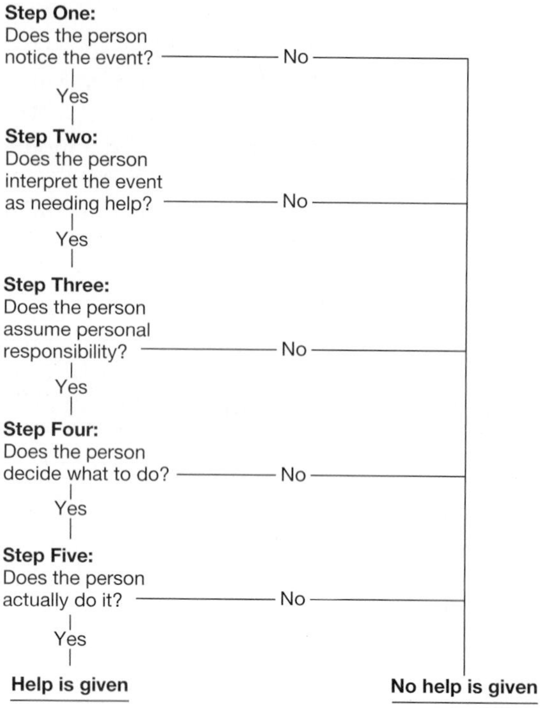

Step One:
Does the person
notice the event? —————— No ——————

|
Yes
|

Step Two:
Does the person
interpret the event
as needing help? —————— No ——————

|
Yes
|

Step Three:
Does the person
assume personal
responsibility? —————— No ——————

|
Yes
|

Step Four:
Does the person
decide what to do? —————— No ——————

|
Yes
|

Step Five:
Does the person
actually do it? —————— No ——————

|
Yes
|

Help is given   **No help is given**

FIGURE 2 Latané and Darley's model of helping.

If you get involved, can you be sued? What if you try to help and end up looking like a fool? Many such questions, depending on the situation, may run through your mind before you actually take action.

Figure 2 illustrates how helping behavior may be short-circuited or prevented at any one of these stages.

SUBSEQUENT FINDINGS AND RECENT APPLICATIONS

Both the Kitty Genovese murder and the experiment we have been discussing here involved groups of onlookers who were cut off from each other. What do you suppose would happen if the bystanders could see and talk to each other? Would they be more likely to intervene when they could be judged by others? Darley and Latané believed that in some cases, even groups in close contact would be less likely than individuals to help. This would be especially true, they theorized, when the emergency is somewhat ambiguous.

For example, imagine you are sitting in a waiting room and smoke begins to stream in through a vent. You become concerned and look around at the others in the room. But everyone else appears quite calm and unconcerned. So, you think your reaction to the smoke must be exaggerated, and you decide against taking any action. Why? Because if you take action and are wrong (maybe it wasn't smoke, just steam or something from the next room), you would feel sheepish and embarrassed. However, you don't realize that everyone in the room is feeling the same as you and hiding it, just as you are, to avoid embarrassment! Meanwhile, no one is doing anything about the smoke. Sound unbelievable? Well, it's not.

Latané and Darley (1968) tested this idea in a slightly later study by creating the situation just described. Psychology students volunteered to participate in interviews to "discuss some of the problems involved in life at an urban university." When they arrived for the interview, they were seated in a room and asked to fill out a preliminary questionnaire. After a few minutes, smoke began to pour into the room through a vent. The smoke was a special mixture of chemicals that would not be dangerous to the subjects. After several minutes, the smoke became so thick that vision in the room was obscured. The researchers timed the subjects to see how long they would wait to report the smoke. Some of the subjects were in the room alone; others were with either two or three confederates, believed by the subject to be other participants, who behaved very passively when the smoke appeared. Once again, Latané and Darley's results supported their theory. Fifty-five percent of the subjects in the alone condition reported the smoke within the first two minutes, while only 12% of the subjects in the other two groups did so. Moreover, after four minutes, 75% of the alone subjects had acted, but no additional subjects in the other groups ever reported the smoke.

Beyond their specific findings, Darley and Latané's groundbreaking research on helping behavior and diffusion of responsibility continues to influence a wide array of studies on very topical issues. For example, an article applied Darley and Latané's findings to issues of child abuse and domestic violence (Hoefnagles & Zwikker, 2001). The goal of the study was to shed light on the characteristics of individuals who witness child abuse. The researchers analyzed nearly 700 records of bystanders (other than human services professionals) who reported incidents of child abuse. Their investigation revealed the bystanders to be a very diverse group of both male and females in various age groups, including many children. Various characteristics of the bystanders, including sex, age, and their perceptions of what they saw and heard were shown to influence their interpretation of the abusive event and their confidence that the event was truly abusive. This knowledge is an important factor in working to intervene in and reduce the incidence of child abuse and domestic violence.

Another study demonstrated the cognitive power of the bystander effect and diffusion of responsibility. In a recent study titled, *Crowded Minds: The Implicit Bystander Effect,* by a team of researchers that included Darley, found that merely *imagining* being in a group changed helping behavior (Garcia, et al., 2002). In this study, subjects were asked either to imagine that they were part of a group of people or alone with one other person. Then, all subjects were asked to donate to a charity. The participants who imagined themselves in the presence of others donated significantly less money, and felt less personal accountability than those who imagined being alone with one other person.

These findings imply that our brains immediately "leap" at the chance to assume less individual responsibility when we are part of a group.

CONCLUSION

The results of this body of research may seem rather pessimistic, but you should recognize that these studies deal with extremely specific situations in which people fail to help. Frequent examples may be found every day of people helping other people, of altruistic behaviors, and heroic acts. Darley and Latané's research is important, however, not only to explain a perplexing human behavior, but to help change it. Perhaps, as more people become aware of the bystander effect, they will make the extra effort to intervene in an emergency, even if others are present. In fact, research has demonstrated that people who have learned about the bystander effect, are more likely to help in emergencies (Beaman et al., 1978). The bottom line is this: Never assume that others have intervened or will intervene in an emergency. *Always act as if you are the only person there.*

Beaman, A., Barnes, P., Klentz, B., & Mcquirk, B. (1978). Increasing helping rates through information dissemination: Teaching pays. *Personality and Social Psychology Bulletin, 4,* 406–411.

Garcia, S., Weaver, K., Darley, J., & Moskowitz, G. (2002). Crowded minds: The implicit bystander effect. *Journal of Personality and Social Psychology, 83,* 843–853.

Hoefnagels, Cees, and Machteld Zwikker. (2001). The Bystander Dilemma and Child Abuse: Extending the Latané and Darley Model to Domestic Violence: *Journal of Applied Social Psychology, 31,* 1158–1183.

Latané, B., & Darley, J. M. (1968). Group inhibition of bystander intervention in emergencies. *Journal of Personality and Social Psychology, 10,* 215–221.

Latané, B., & Darley, J. M. (1970). *The unresponsive bystander: Why doesn't he help?* New York: Appleton-Century-Crofts.

OBEY AT ANY COST?
Milgram, S. (1963). Behavioral study of obedience. *Journal of Abnormal and Social Psychology, 67,* 371–378.

If someone in a position of authority ordered you to deliver an electrical shock of 350 volts to another person, because the other person answered a question incorrectly, would you obey? Neither would I. If you met someone who was willing to do such a thing, you would probably think of him or her as cruel and sadistic. This study by Stanley Milgram of Yale University set out to examine the idea of obedience and produced some shocking and disturbing findings.

Milgram's research on obedience is among the most famous in all of psychology's history. It is included in every general psychology text and every social psychology text. If you talk to students of psychology, more of them are familiar with this study than with any other. Out of this study came a book by Milgram (1974) on the psychology of obedience and a film about the research itself that is widely shown in college and university classes. Not only is this experiment referred to in discussions of obedience, but it has also been highly influential in issues of research methodology and the ethics of using human subjects in psychological research.

Milgram's idea for this project grew out of his desire to investigate scientifically how people could be capable of carrying out great harm to others simply because they were ordered to do so. Milgram was referring specifically to the hideous atrocities committed on command during World War II, and also, more generally, to the inhumanity that has been perpetrated throughout history by people following the orders of others. It appeared to Milgram that in some situations, the tendency to obey is so deeply ingrained and powerful that it cancels out a person's ability to behave morally, ethically, or even sympathetically.

When behavioral scientists decide to study some complex aspect of human behavior, their first step is to gain control over the behavioral situation so that they can approach it scientifically. This can often be the greatest challenge to a researcher, since many events in the real world are difficult to re-create in a laboratory setting. So Milgram's problem was how to cause one person to order another person to physically injure a third person without anyone actually getting injured.

THEORETICAL PROPOSITIONS

Milgram's primary theoretical basis for this study was that humans have a tendency to obey other people who are in a position of authority over them, even if, in obeying, they violate their own codes of moral and ethical behavior. He believed that, for example, many individuals who would never intentionally cause someone physical harm would inflict pain on a victim if ordered to do so by a person perceived to be a powerful authority figure.

METHOD

Probably the most ingenious portion of this study is the technique that was developed to test the power of obedience in the laboratory. Milgram designed a rather scary-looking shock generator: a large electronic device with 30 toggle switches labeled with voltage levels starting at 30 volts and increasing by 15-volt intervals up to 450 volts. These switches were labeled in groups such as *slight shock, moderate shock,* and *danger: severe shock.* The idea was that a subject could be ordered to administer electric shocks at increasing levels to another person. Before you conclude that Milgram was truly sadistic himself, this was a very realistic-looking simulated shock generator, but no one ever actually received any painful shocks.

The subjects for this study were 40 males between the ages of 20 and 50. There were 15 skilled or unskilled workers, 16 white-collar sales- or businessmen, and nine professional men. They were recruited through newspaper ads and direct-mail solicitation asking for subjects to be paid participants in a study about memory and learning at Yale University. Each subject participated in the study individually. In order to obtain an adequate number of subjects, each was paid \$4.50. (Remember, these are 1963 dollars.) All subjects were clearly told that this payment was simply for coming to the laboratory, and it was theirs to keep no matter what happened after they arrived. This was to ensure that subjects did not behave in certain ways because they were fearful of not being paid.

In addition to the subjects, there were two other key participants: a confederate in the experiment (a 47-year-old accountant) posing as another subject, and an *actor* (dressed in a gray lab coat, looking very official) playing the part of the experimenter.

As a participant arrived at the social interaction laboratory at Yale, he was seated next to another *subject* (the confederate). Obviously, the true purpose of the experiment could not be revealed to subjects, since this would completely alter their behavior. Therefore, a *cover story* was given by the experimenter, who explained to the subjects that this was a study on the effect of punishment on learning. The subjects then drew pieces of paper out of a hat to determine who would be the teacher and who would be the learner. This drawing was rigged so that the true subject always became the teacher and the accomplice was always the learner. Keep in mind that the *learner* was a confederate in the experiment, as was the person playing the part of the *experimenter.*

The learner was then taken into the next room and was, with the subject watching, strapped to a chair and wired up with electrodes (complete with electrode paste to *avoid any blisters or burns*) connected to the shock generator in the adjoining room. The learner, although his arms were strapped down, was able to reach four buttons marked *a, b, c,* and *d,* in order to answer questions posed by the teacher from the next room.

The learning task was thoroughly explained to the teacher and the learner. Briefly, it involved the learner memorizing connections between various pairs of words. It was a rather lengthy list and not an easy memory task. The teacher-subject would read the list of word pairs and then test the learner's memory of them. The teacher was instructed by the experimenter to administer an electric shock each time the learner responded incorrectly. Most important, for each incorrect response, the teacher was to move up one level of shock on the generator. All of this was simulated so realistically that no subject suspected that the shocks were not really being delivered.

The learner-confederate's responses were preprogrammed to be correct or incorrect in the same sequence for all the subjects. Furthermore, as the amount of voltage increased with incorrect responses, the learner began to shout his discomfort from the other room (in prearranged, prerecorded phrases, including the fact that his heart was bothering him), and at the 300-volt level, he pounded on the wall and demanded to be let out. After 300 volts he became completely silent and refused to answer any more questions. The teacher was instructed to treat this lack of a response as an incorrect response and to continue the procedure.

Most of the subjects would turn to the experimenter at some point for guidance on whether to continue the shocks. When this happened, the experimenter ordered the subject to continue, in a series of commands increasing in severity as more prodding was necessary:

Command 1: Please continue.

Command 2: The experiment requires that you continue.

Command 3: It is absolutely essential that you continue.

Command 4: You have no other choice, you must go on.

A measure of obedience was obtained simply by recording the level of shock at which each subject refused to continue. Since there were 30 switches on the generator, each subject could receive a score of 0 to 30. Subjects who went all the way to the top of the scale were referred to as *obedient subjects* and those who broke off at any lower point were termed *defiant subjects*.

RESULTS

Would the subjects obey the commands of this experimenter? How high on the voltage scale did they go? What would you predict? Think of yourself, your friends, people in general. What percentage do you think would deliver shocks all the way through the 30 levels; all the way up to 450 volts—danger: severe shock? Before discussing the actual results of the study, Milgram asked a group of Yale University seniors, all psychology majors, as well as various colleagues to make such a prediction. The estimates ranged from 0% to 3%, with an average estimate of 1.2%. That is, no more than 3 people out of 100 were predicted to deliver the maximum shock.

Table 1 summarizes the "shocking" results. Upon command of the experimenter, every subject continued at least to the 300-volt level, which was when the confederate banged on the wall to be let out and stopped answering. But most surprising is the number of subjects who obeyed orders to continue all the way to the top of the scale.

Although 14 subjects defied orders and broke off before reaching the maximum voltage, 26 of the 40 subjects, or 65%, followed the experimenter's orders and proceeded to the top of the shock scale. This is not to say that the subjects were calm or happy about what they were doing. Many exhibited signs of extreme stress and concern for the man receiving the shocks, and even became angry at the experimenter. Yet they obeyed.

The researchers were concerned that some of the subjects might suffer psychological distress from having gone through the ordeal of shocking another person, especially when the learner had ceased to respond for the last third of the experiment. To help alleviate this anxiety, after the subjects finished the experiment, they received a full explanation (called a debriefing) of the true purpose of the study and of all the procedures, including the deception that had been employed. In addition, the subjects were interviewed as to their feelings and thoughts during the procedure and the confederate "learner" was brought in for a friendly reconciliation with each subject.

TABLE 1 Level of Shock Delivered by Subjects

NUMBER OF VOLTS TO BE DELIVERED	NUMBER WHO REFUSED TO CONTINUE AT THIS LEVEL
Slight shock	
15	0
30	0
45	0
60	0
Moderate shock	
75	0
90	0
105	0
120	0
Strong shock	
135	0
150	0
165	0
180	0
Very strong shock	
195	0
210	0
225	0
240	0
Intense shock	
255	0
270	0
285	0
300	5
Extreme intensity shock	
315	4
330	2
345	1
360	1
Danger: severe shock	
375	1
390	0
405	0
420	0
XXX———	
435	0
450	26

(From Milgram, 1963, p. 376.)

DISCUSSION

Milgram's discussion of his findings focused on two main points. The first was the surprising strength of the subjects' tendency to obey. These were average, normal people who agreed to participate in an experiment about learning, not sadistic, cruel individuals in any way. Milgram points out that from childhood these subjects had learned that it is immoral to hurt others against their will. So, why did they do so? The experimenter was a person in a position of authority, but if you think about it, how much authority did he really have? He had no power to enforce his orders, and subjects would lose nothing by refusing to follow orders. Clearly the *situation* carried a force of its own that somehow made obedience significantly greater than was expected.

The second key observation made during the course of this study was the extreme tension and anxiety manifested by the subjects as they obeyed the experimenter's commands. Again, it might be expected that such discomfort could be relieved simply by refusing to go on, and yet this is not what happened. Milgram quotes one observer (who watched a subject through a one-way mirror):

> I observe a mature and initially poised businessman enter the laboratory smiling and confident. Within 20 minutes he was reduced to a twitching, stuttering wreck who was rapidly approaching a point of nervous collapse. . . . At one point he pushed his fist into his forehead and muttered, "Oh, God! Let's stop it." And yet he continued to respond to every word of the experimenter and obeyed to the end. (p. 377)

Milgram listed several points at the end of the article to attempt to explain why this particular situation produced such a high degree of obedience. In summary, from the point of view of the subject, his main points were that (1) if it's being sponsored by Yale, it must be in good hands, and who am I to question such a great institution; (2) the goals of the experiment appear to be important, and therefore, since I volunteered, I'll do my part to assist in the realization of those goals; (3) the learner, after all, also voluntarily came here and he has an obligation to the project too; (4) hey, it was just by chance that I'm the teacher and he's the learner—we drew lots and it could have just as easily been the other way around; (5) they're paying me for this, I'd better do my job; (6) I don't know all that much about the rights of a psychologist and his subjects, so I will yield to his discretion on this; and (7) they told us both that the shocks are painful, but not dangerous.

SIGNIFICANCE OF THE FINDINGS

Milgram's findings have held up quite well in the nearly 30 years since this article was published. Milgram himself repeated the procedure on similar subjects outside of the Yale setting, on unpaid college student volunteers, and on women subjects, and he found similar results each time.

In addition, he expanded further on his findings in this study by conducting a series of related experiments designed to reveal the conditions that promote or limit obedience (see Milgram, 1974). He found that the physical, and therefore emotional, distance of the victim from the teacher altered the amount of obedience. The highest level of obedience (93% going to the top of the voltage scale) occurred when the learner was in another room and could not be seen or heard. When the learner was in the same room with the subject and the subject was required to force the learner's hand onto a shock plate, the rate of obedience dropped to 30%.

Milgram also discovered that the physical distance of the authority figure to the subject also influenced obedience. The closer the experimenter, the greater the obedience. In one condition, the experimenter was out of the room and telephoned his commands to the subject. In this case obedience fell to only 21%.

Finally, on a more positive note, when subjects were allowed to punish the learner by using any level of shock they wished, no one ever pressed any switch higher than No. 2, or 45 volts.

CRITICISMS

While Milgram's research has been extremely influential in our understanding of obedience, it has also had far-reaching effects in the area of the ethical treatment of human subjects. Even though no one ever received any shocks, how do you suppose you would feel, knowing you had been willing to shock someone (possibly to death) simply because a person in a lab coat told you to? Critics of Milgram's methods (e.g., Baumrind, 1964; Miller, 1986) claim that unacceptable levels of stress were created in the subjects during the experiment. Furthermore, it has been argued that the potential for lasting effects existed. When the deception is revealed to subjects at the end of their ordeal, they may feel used, embarrassed, and possibly distrustful of psychologists or legitimate authority figures in their future lives.

Another line of criticism focused on the validity of Milgram's findings. The basis for this criticism was that since the subjects had a trusting and rather dependent relationship with the experimenter, and the laboratory was an unfamiliar setting, obedience found there did not represent obedience in real life. Therefore, critics claim, the results of Milgram's studies were not only invalid, but because of this poor validity the treatment his subjects were exposed to could not be justified.

Milgram responded to criticisms by surveying subjects after they had participated. He found that 84% of his participants were glad to have participated, and only about 1% regretted the experience. In addition, a psychiatrist interviewed 40 of the subjects who were judged to have been the most uncomfortable in the laboratory and concluded that none had suffered any long-term effects. As to the criticism that his laboratory findings did not reflect real life, Milgram said, "A person who comes to the laboratory is an active, choosing adult, capable of accepting or rejecting the prescriptions for action addressed to him" (Milgram, 1964, p. 852).

The Milgram studies reported here have been a focal point in the ongoing debate over experimental ethics involving human subjects. It is, in fact, arguable whether this research has been more influential in the area of social psychology and obedience or in policy formation on the ethical treatment of human subjects in psychological research.

RECENT APPLICATIONS

The breadth of influence that Milgram's obedience project continues to exert on current research can best be appreciated through a brief annotated selection of recent studies that have been primarily motivated by Milgram's early methods and findings. As has been the case in every year since the early 1960s when Milgram carried out his studies, these studies are divided between attempts to refine and elaborate on people's tendency to obey authority figures, and the omnipresent debate about the ethics of using deception in research involving human subjects.

Thomas Blass, a leading authority on the work and career of Stanley Milgram, and author of his biography, *The Man Who Shocked the World* (2004), has reviewed all the research and social implications stemming from Milgram's obedience studies (Blass, 1999; 2002). In general, Blass has found universal support for Milgram's original findings, but, more importantly, he suggests that obedience rates have not changed significantly during the 40 plus years since Milgram first published his findings. This is contrary to many people's intuitive judgments that Americans in general have become less respectful of authority and more willing to rebel and fight back when ordered to perform behaviors with which they disagree. Another question that often arises about Milgram's early studies concerns gender and the fact that all his original subjects were male. Do you think, overall, that men or women would be more likely to obey an authority figure? Blass's review of later studies by Milgram and numerous others found *no difference* in obedience rates for males versus females. For more details about the history and influences of Milgram's work, see Blass's Web site at http://www. stanleymilgram.com.

A very pertinent application of Milgram's findings examined the psychological experience of "execution teams" charged with carrying out the death sentence in Louisiana State prisons (Osofsky & Osofsky, 2002). The researchers interviewed 50 correctional officers who were directly involved with executions. They found that, although exposed far more than most people to trauma and death, the subjects were not found to be clinically depressed. They reported relying on religious beliefs, identification with their peer group, and their ability to diffuse responsibility to deal with painful emotions. "Nevertheless, the officers experience conflicted feelings and frequently report having a hard time carrying out society's 'ultimate punishment' " (p. 358).

On the ethics side, a recent study employs Milgram's study in examining potentially thorny ethical issues for social science research conducted on the Internet (Pittenger, 2003). Today, a great deal of research is conducted via the World Wide Web, and the number of such studies is likely to increase significantly in the future. Pittenger contends that researchers must be alert to potential ethical violations relating to invasion of privacy, obtaining informed consent, using deceptive tactics on line. "The Internet offers unique challenges to researchers," Pittenger writes. "Among these are the need to define the distinction between private and public behavior performed on the Internet, ensure mechanisms for obtaining valid informed consent from participants, and performing debriefing exercises, verify the validity of data collected" (p. 45).

An important question is: What should be done to protect subjects from irresponsible, deceptive practices in psychological research, while at the same time allowing for *some* deception when absolutely necessary for scientific advancement? A study by Wendler (1996) seeks to answer this question by proposing that subjects in studies involving deception be given an increased level of "informed consent." (See the discussion of this concept in the preface to this book.) This enhanced informed consent would inform you of the study's *intention* to use deception before you agree to be a subject in the experiment. "This 'second order consent' approach to acceptable deception," claims Wendler, "represents our best chance for reconciling respect for subjects with the occasional scientific need for deceptive research" (p. 87).

In closing, Milgram historian Thomas Blass remarks in his 2002 biographical review of Milgram's life and work:

> We didn't need Milgram to tell us we have a tendency to obey orders. What we didn't know before Milgram's experiments is just how powerful this tendency is. And having been enlightened about our extreme readiness to obey authorities, we can try to take steps to guard ourselves against unwelcome or reprehensible commands (Blass, 2002, p . 73).

Baumrind, D. (1964). Some thoughts on the ethics of research: After reading Milgram's "Behavioral Study of Obedience." *American Psychologist, 19,* 421–423.

Blass, T. (1999). The Milgram paradigm after 35 years: Some things we now know about obedience to authority. *Journal of Applied Social Psychology, 29*(5), 955–978.

Blass, T. (2002). The man who shocked the world. *Psychology Today, 35,* 68–74.

Blass, T. (2004). *The man who shocked the world.* NY: Basic Books.

Milgram, S. (1964). Issues in the study of obedience: A reply to Baumrind. *American Psychologist, 19,* 448–452.

Milgram, S. (1974). *Obedience to authority.* New York: Harper & Row.

Miller, A. G. (1986). *The obedience studies: A case study of controversy in social science.* New York: Praeger.

Osofsky, M., & Osofsky, H. (2002). The Psychological Experience of Security Officers Who Work with Executions. *Psychiatry: Interpersonal and Biological Processes, 65,* 358–370.

Pittenger, D. (2003). Internet research: An opprotunity to revisit classic ethical problems in behavioral research. *Ethics and Behavior, 13,* 45–60.

Wendler, D. (1996). Deception in medical and behavioral research: Is it ever acceptable? *Milbank Quarterly, 74*(1), 87.

AUTHOR INDEX

317

SUBJECT INDEX